In this series

122. DAVID ADGER, DANIEL HARBOUR and LAUREL J. WATKINS: *Mirrors and Microparameters: Phrase Structure beyond Free Word Order*
123. NIINA NING ZHANG: *Coordination in Syntax*
124. NEIL SMITH: *Acquiring Phonology*
125. NINA TOPINTZI: *Onsets: Suprasegmental and Prosodic Behaviour*
126. CEDRIC BOECKX, NORBERT HORNSTEIN and JAIRO NUNES: *Control as Movement*
127. MICHAEL ISRAEL: *The Grammar of Polarity: Pragmatics, Sensitivity, and the Logic of Scales*
128. M. RITA MANZINI and LEONARDO M. SAVOIA: *Grammatical Categories: Variation in Romance Languages*
129. BARBARA CITKO: *Symmetry in Syntax: Merge, Move and Labels*
130. RACHEL WALKER: *Vowel Patterns in Language*
131. MARY DALRYMPLE and IRINA NIKOLAEVA: *Objects and Information Structure*
132. JERROLD M. SADOCK: *The Modular Architecture of Grammar*
133. DUNSTAN BROWN and ANDREW HIPPISLEY: *Network Morphology: A Defaults-based Theory of Word Structure*
134. BETTELOU LOS, CORRIEN BLOM, GEERTBOOIJ, MARION ELENBAAS and ANS VAN KEMENADE: *Morphosyntactic Change: A Comparative Study of Particles and Prefixes*
135. STEPHEN CRAIN: *The Emergence of Meaning*
136. HUBERT HAIDER: *Symmetry Breaking in Syntax*
137. JOSÉ A. CAMACHO: *Null Subjects*
138. GREGORY STUMP and RAPHAEL A. FINKEL: *Morphological Typology: From Word to Paradigm*
139. BRUCE TESAR: *Output-Driven Phonology: Theory and Learning*
140. ASIER ALCÁZAR and MARIO SALTARELLI: *The Syntax of Imperatives*
141. MISHA BECKER: *The Acquisition of Syntactic Structure: Animacy and Thematic Alignment*
142. MARTINA WILTSCHKO: *The Universal Structure of Categories: Towards a Formal Typology*
143. FAHAD RASHED AL-MUTAIRI: *The Minimalist Program: The Nature and Plausibility of Chomsky's Biolinguistics*
144. CEDRIC BOECKX: *Elementary Syntactic Structures: Prospects of a Feature-Free Syntax*
145. PHOEVOS PANAGIOTIDIS: *Categorial Features: A Generative Theory of Word Class Categories*
146. MARK BAKER: *Case: Its Principles and Its Parameters*
147. WM. G. BENNETT: *The Phonology of Consonants: Dissimilation, Harmony and Correspondence*
148. ANDREA SIMS: *Inflectional Defectiveness*
149. GREGORY STUMP: *Inflectional Paradigms: Content and Form at the Syntax-Morphology Interface*
150. ROCHELLE LIEBER: *English Nouns: The Ecology of Nominalization*
151. JOHN BOWERS: *Deriving Syntactic Relations*
152. ANA TERESA PÉREZ-LEROUX, MIHAELA PIRVULESCU and YVES ROBERGE: *Direct Objects and Language Acquisition*

(*continued after the Index*)

CAMBRIDGE STUDIES IN LINGUISTICS

General Editors: P. AUSTIN, J. BRESNAN, B. COMRIE, S. CRAIN,
W. DRESSLER, C. J. EWEN, R. LASS, D. LIGHTFOOT, K. RICE, I. ROBERTS,
S. ROMAINE, N. V. SMITH

Mixed Categories

MIXED CATEGORIES

THE MORPHOSYNTAX OF NOUN MODIFICATION

IRINA NIKOLAEVA
*School of Oriental and African Studies,
University of London*

ANDREW SPENCER
University of Essex

CAMBRIDGE
UNIVERSITY PRESS

University Printing House, Cambridge CB2 8BS, United Kingdom

One Liberty Plaza, 20th Floor, New York, NY 10006, USA

477 Williamstown Road, Port Melbourne, VIC 3207, Australia

314–321, 3rd Floor, Plot 3, Splendor Forum, Jasola District Centre, New Delhi – 110025, India

79 Anson Road, #06-04/06, Singapore 079906

Cambridge University Press is part of the University of Cambridge.

It furthers the University's mission by disseminating knowledge in the pursuit of education, learning, and research at the highest international levels of excellence.

www.cambridge.org
Information on this title: www.cambridge.org/9781108415514
DOI: 10.1017/9781108233903

© Irina Nikolaeva and Andrew Spencer 2020

This publication is in copyright. Subject to statutory exception and to the provisions of relevant collective licensing agreements, no reproduction of any part may take place without the written permission of Cambridge University Press.

First published 2020

Printed in the United Kingdom by TJ International Ltd, Padstow Cornwall

A catalogue record for this publication is available from the British Library.

ISBN 978-1-108-41551-4 Hardback

Cambridge University Press has no responsibility for the persistence or accuracy of URLs for external or third-party internet websites referred to in this publication and does not guarantee that any content on such websites is, or will remain, accurate or appropriate.

Contents

List of Figures		*page* xi
List of Tables		xiv
Preface		xv
Acknowledgements		xvii
List of Abbreviations		xviii

1	**Introduction: Word Categories and Category Mixing**	**1**
1.1	Introduction	1
1.2	Word Classes	4
	1.2.1 The Functionalist Perspective	4
	1.2.2 Feature Systems	10
	1.2.3 Word Classes as Canonical Categories and Prototypes	16
1.3	Categorial Mixing	22
	1.3.1 Paradigmatic Category Mixing	22
	1.3.2 Syntagmatic Category Mixing	24
1.4	Mixed Categories in Adnominal Modification	28
	1.4.1 Adjective and Noun Properties	28
	1.4.2 Main Parameters of Variation	33
1.5	Structure of the Book	36

2	**Modification Constructions**	**40**
2.1	Introduction	40
2.2	Attributive Modification	40
	2.2.1 Overview of Semantics	40
	2.2.2 Canonical Attributive Modifiers	42
2.3	Possessive Constructions	46
	2.3.1 Canonical Inalienable Possession	46
	2.3.2 Alienable Possession	49
2.4	Modification-by-Noun	53

vii

viii *Contents*

		2.4.1	Analyses of N-N Compounds	53
		2.4.2	Compounds as Modification-by-Noun	56
	2.5	Towards a Typology		58
		2.5.1	Encoding Strategies	59
		2.5.2	Distinct Encodings	61
		2.5.3	Possession vs. Modification	66
		2.5.4	Modification-by-Nominal-Concept vs. Attributive Modification	70
		2.5.5	Single Strategy	73
		2.5.6	Polyfunctionality Patterns	76
		2.5.7	The Role of Juxtaposition	79
	2.6	Conclusions		84

3 Categorial Mixing in the Nominal Phrase — **85**

	3.1	Introduction		85
	3.2	N-N Compounds as Mixed Categories		85
	3.3	Denominal Adjectives		87
		3.3.1	Denominal Adjectives with Added Semantic Predicate	88
		3.3.2	Noun-to-Adjective Transpositions	91
	3.4	Modification by Case and Adpositional Phrases		105
		3.4.1	Constructions with Added Semantic Predicate	105
		3.4.2	Constructions with No Added Semantic Predicate	113
	3.5	Attributivization by a Phrasal Affix		120
	3.6	Conclusions		124

4 Approaches to Mixed Categories — **126**

	4.1	Introduction		126
	4.2	Dual Projection		126
		4.2.1	Overview	127
		4.2.2	Autolexical Syntax	130
		4.2.3	Reasons for Rejecting Syntactic Affixation	136
	4.3	Single Projection		143
		4.3.1	Overview	143
		4.3.2	Malouf (2000a, b)	146
	4.4	Mixed Categories in LFG		151
		4.4.1	Bresnan and Mugane (2006)	151

Contents ix

	4.4.2	Lowe (2016)	163
4.5	Conclusions		169

5 Lexical Representation and Lexical Relatedness 171

5.1	Introduction		171
5.2	Individuating Lexemes		172
	5.2.1	Lexeme Individuation Problem	172
	5.2.2	Lexical Hierarchies	175
	5.2.3	The Lexeme Concept in HPSG/SBCG – A Critique	180
5.3	Lexical Representations		186
	5.3.1	Inflection/Derivation 'Continuum'	186
	5.3.2	Factorizing Lexical Representations	188
5.4	Lexical Relatedness		192
	5.4.1	Dynamic and Static Relatedness	192
	5.4.2	Types of Dynamic Relatedness	194
5.5	Conclusions		202

6 Generalized Paradigm Function Morphology 204

6.1	Introduction		204
6.2	Representing Lexical Relatedness in GPFM		204
6.3	Lexical Categories		213
	6.3.1	FORM/CONTENT Paradigms	214
	6.3.2	MORSIG	221
	6.3.3	Semantic Function Roles	223
	6.3.4	The Default Cascade Principle	226
6.4	Transpositions in GPFM: The Feature [REPRESENTATION]		230
6.5	Excursus: Comparison with Network Morphology		234
6.6	Conclusions		238

7 Attributive Modification in Lexicalist Morphosyntax 239

7.1	Introduction		239
7.2	Nominal Syntax		239
	7.2.1	Approaches to Nominal Phrase Structure	240
	7.2.2	Attributive Modification in HPSG	244
7.3	A Model of Attributive Modification		247
	7.3.1	The A* Semantic Function Role	247

x *Contents*

	7.3.2	Adjectives as Lexical Categories	249
	7.3.3	The Attributive Modifier Rule	255
7.4	The Syntax of the ℛ Relation		258
	7.4.1	The ℛ Relation in Modification-by-Noun	258
	7.4.2	The ℛ Relation in Possessive Constructions	267
	7.4.3	The Possession-Modification Scale Again	278
7.5	Conclusions		282

8 Noun–Adjective Hybrids — 284

8.1	Introduction		284
8.2	Syntagmatic Mixing in Noun–Adjective Hybrids		284
	8.2.1	The Principle of Lexemic Transparency	284
	8.2.2	The Base Noun Modifiability Property	288
8.3	Syntax of Denominal Modifiers		290
	8.3.1	Relational Adjectives as Transpositional Lexemes	290
	8.3.2	Chukchi Relational Adjectives	297
8.4	Representations of Noun-to-Adjective Derivations		301
	8.4.1	Selkup Relational Adjectives	302
	8.4.2	Meaning-Bearing Transpositions: Selkup	320
	8.4.3	Tungusic (and Nenets) Derived Adjectives – with Agreement	322
	8.4.4	Possessive Adjectives in Upper Sorbian	331
	8.4.5	Awngi Agreeing Genitives	333
	8.4.6	Tundra Nenets Compounds	337
8.5	Conclusions		340
	8.5.1	The Chukchi Relational Adjective	341
	8.5.2	The Selkup Similitudinal Adjective	343
	8.5.3	The Evenki Proprietive	344
	8.5.4	The Awngi and Tundra Nenets Agreeing Noun Forms	346
	8.5.5	Excursus on Possessive Adjectives	347

9 Conclusions and Prospects — 348

Bibliography	356
Language Index	380
Author Index	383
Subject Index	387

Figures

4.1	Generic syntactic affixation analysis of POSS-ACC nominalization	*page* 128
4.2	Generic syntactic affixation analysis of synthetic compounds	129
4.3	Lexical sharing representation of the French *du*	130
4.4	Autolexical representation of syntagmatically mixed Upper Sorbian possessive adjectives	133
4.5	Autolexical Syntax representation for Svan example in (10)	140
4.6	Composite node analysis for POSS-ACC nominalizations	144
4.7	Subject nominalization (Booij and van Haften 1988)	145
4.8	Phrase structure of synthetic compound (Booij and van Haften 1988)	146
4.9	Type hierarchy for English gerunds	148
4.10	Type hierarchy for relational adjectives and deadjectival property nominalizations	150
4.11	C-structure for *Siôn saw the dragon*	152
4.12	C-structure for Gĩkũyũ agentive nominalization	154
4.13	Phrase structure for (24)	158
4.14	Phrase structure for (25)	158
4.15	Phrase structure for (26)	159
4.16	Extended head analysis of (26)	161
4.17	C-structure representation of (25)	163
5.1	Parts of speech hierarchy	176
5.2	Lexeme hierarchy	177
5.3	Constant lexeme hierarchy	177
5.4	Sign hierarchy	178
5.5	SN process (for the suffix-*er*) expressed as INPUT/OUTPUT	181
5.6	Representation of the lexeme LAUGH (Sag, 2012, 101)	184

xii *List of Figures*

6.1	Mismatches between m-/s-features (FORM/CONTENT paradigms)	220
7.1	Szabolcsi's analysis of the Hungarian nominal phrase	243
7.2	Modifier-Head Construction in Tundra Nenets (Ackerman and Nikolaeva, 2013, 202)	257
7.3	Tundra Nenets attributive concord (after Ackerman and Nikolaeva, 2013, 205, with slight corrections)	259
7.4	ℜ on head	261
7.5	ℜ on modifier	261
7.6	ℜ on NP	262
7.7	Structure for the N-N compound *reindeer soup*	263
7.8	Lexical representations of SEA, MARINE	264
7.9	Partial lexical representation of MARINE after Ackerman and Nikolaeva (2013)	265
7.10	Structure for the *marine animal*	266
7.11	The compound construction	268
7.12	The Modification-by-Noun Rule	268
7.13	Inalienable possession: *the bird's wing*	269
7.14	Defining the *noun-possessed* subtype	270
7.15	Syntactic structure of *Werah ti* 'Wera's reindeer' (adapted from Ackerman and Nikolaeva, 2013, 175, Figure 10)	271
7.16	Ackerman and Nikolaeva's (2013, 198) structure for Tundra Nenets possessed noun *temⁱi* 'my reindeer'	272
7.17	Revised syntactic structure for *Werah ti* 'Wera's reindeer'	274
7.18	Compound and possessive construction by juxtaposition	275
8.1	Derivation of a relational adjective lexeme from a base noun lexeme in languages such as Russian	294
8.2	Representation of LYŽNYJ 'pertaining to skis' (Russian)	295
8.3	Structure for Russian *lyžnaja maz'* 'ski grease'	296
8.4	Structure for Selkup *tol'cïl' mïtïn* 'ski grease'	309
8.5	Structure for Selkup *pool' tol'cïl'* 'pertaining to wooden (skis)'	312
8.6	Lexical representation of Selkup *tol'cïl'* 'pertaining to skis'	313
8.7	Structure for Selkup possessed noun relational adjective *äsänïl'* 'pertaining to my father'	315

List of Figures   xiii

8.8	Structure for Selkup *äsänïl' määttï* 'to my father's house'	316
8.9	GPF for Selkup similitudinal adjective representation	321
8.10	Agreement dependencies in (61)	336
8.11	GPF for agreeing modifier nouns in Tundra Nenets compounds	339

Tables

1.1	Binary features: [±N, ±V]	*page* 11
1.2	Binary features: [±predicative, ±transitive]	11
1.3	Binary features: [±referentially dependent, ±articulated]	12
1.4	Binary features: [±subj, ±obj]	12
1.5	Summary: binary feature systems for lexical categories	12
1.6	Three theoretical types of feature system	13
1.7	Prototypical semantic properties of denotations (Croft, 2001, 87)	17
1.8	Association of major word classes and syntactic functions in English	18
1.9	Croft's prototypes as canonical properties	20
1.10	Schematic list of noun and adjective properties	30
2.1	Qualia structure in the Generative Lexicon	55
2.2	Modification/possession in Udihe	71
3.1	Common derivational categories of denominal adjectives	88
5.1	Expression types in lexeme hierarchy	177
5.2	Lexical relatedness with SEM and LI attributes identical	195
5.3	Lexical relatedness with SEM attribute changed, LI attribute identical	197
5.4	Lexical relatedness with SEM attribute identical, LI attribute changed	200
5.5	Lexical relatedness with SEM and LI attributes changed	201
6.1	Russian verb CONTENT paradigm for UDARJAT'/UDARIT' 'hit'	216
6.2	Russian verb FORM paradigm for UDARJAT'/UDARIT' 'hit'	216
6.3	Past tense forms of Russian UDARIT' 'hit'	218
6.4	CONTENT/FORM feature arrays for Russian verbs	220
8.1	GPF for Awngi agreeing genitives	336

Preface

This monograph is devoted to the role that attributive modification plays in language. We explore cross-linguistic variation in modification constructions, paying particular attention to constructions in which a noun modifies another noun. We also propose an explicit formal framework that models cross-linguistic and cross-constructional variation and allows us to map word structure to syntactic structure.

A crucial role will be played by a phenomenon we refer to as the noun–adjective hybrid. This is an adjective which has been derived from a noun but which systematically retains certain of its nominal properties, most saliently its ability to take a determiner and/or attributive modifier as though it were still a noun. Such constructions, while not common, are widespread across the world's languages. They constitute a relatively unexplored species of 'mixed category'. Our monograph shows that they raise important questions about a number of issues: the nature of lexemic identity, that is, how we know when two expressions are either forms of one and the same lexeme or forms of two distinct lexemes; the inflection–derivation divide; the question of so-called Lexical Integrity, and more generally, the relationship between word structure (morphological structure) and phrase structure (syntax) and how that interface can best be modelled. Ultimately, however, at the heart of our exploration is a very traditional question: what properties define the grammatical classes to which the words of a language belong?

In the long gestation period of this book we have presented our thoughts on noun-adjective hybrids and related topics at a number of forums: International Conference on Adjectives, Lille, 2007; Association of Linguistic Typology, Paris, 2007; Linguistics Association of Great Britain, Kings College London, September, 2007, and University College London, 2014; Workshop on Semantic Features in Derivational Morphology, University of Stuttgart, 2008; Workshop on Creating an Infrastructure for Canonical Typology, Surrey Morphology Group, University of Surrey, 2009; CoBaLiSE meeting, University of Essex,

xvi *Preface*

2009; Workshop on Constraint-based grammar, Laboratoire de Linguistique Formelle, Université de Paris VII, 2009; Talk delivered to the School of Oriental and African Studies, 2010; Conference on Syntactic Government and Subcategorization, University of Cambridge, 2011; Talk delivered to the 9th Mediterranean Morphology Meeting, Dubrovnik, 2013.

Acknowledgements

We are grateful to various colleagues for their helpful commentary on earlier versions of this work: Doug Arnold, Matthew Baerman, Olivier Bonami, Oliver Bond, Geert Booij, Bob Borsley, Dunstan Brown, Marina Chumakina, Nick Evans, Bernard Fradin, Klaus von Heusinger, István Kenesei, Ferenc Kiefer, Maria Koptjevskaja-Tamm, Christian Lehmann, Bill Palmer, Louisa Sadler, as well as anonymous referees for some of our earlier publications on these topics. We are also grateful to Grev Corbett for his support throughout various phases of this work.

This monograph originally arose out of the one-year AHRC Project 119393 'Possession and attributive modification' (2006–2007), PI Andrew Spencer. We are grateful to the AHRC for their support.

We are especially grateful to Peter Sells for his extremely helpful and astute criticism of the pre-final draft of the book, which was undertaken at very short notice.

We want to thank Cambridge University Press for accepting the work for publication and for making the production of the book a smooth and pleasant experience. Special thanks go to Helen Barton, who has seen the whole process through.

Abbreviations

A	adjective
A*	attributive (SF role)
ABL	ablative
ABS	absolutive
ACC	accusative
act	active
Adj	adjective
AdjDecl	adjective declension
AdjP	Adjective Phrase
ADJT	adjunct
Adv	adverb
AdvP	adverb phrase
AGR	agreement
AgrO	object agreement (Mainstream Generative Grammar)
AgrS	subject agreement (Mainstream Generative Grammar)
AN	adjectival noun
AP	Adjective Phrase
ARG-ST	argument structure
art	articulated
ATTR	attributivizer
AUG	augmentative
AUX	auxiliary (verb)
AVM	Attribute Value Matrix
BNMP	Base Noun Modifiability Property
C	Complementizer (Mainstream Generative Grammar)
CAT	category
CLASS	classifier
COM	comitative
COMP(S)	Complement(s)

List of Abbreviations   xix

conj	conjunction
CONT	CONTENT (HPSG attribute)
COMPL	completive
Corr	Correspondence (function)
D	determiner
DAT	dative
DEF	definite
DEG	degree
DEL	delative
DEM	demonstrative
DESID	desiderative
DET	determiner
DIM	diminutive
DNA	denominal adjective
DP	Determiner Phrase
DTR	DAUGHTER attribute
DU	dual
ERG	ergative
EXCL	exclusive
EZ	ezafe
E	Eventuality (SF role)
F	feminine
FS	feature structure
fut	future
GDP	General Default Principle
GEN	genitive
GER	gerund
GPF	Generalized Paradigm Function
GPFM	Generalized Paradigm Function Morphology
HPSG	Head-Driven Phrase Structure Grammar
ILL	illative
IND	indicative
INDF	indefinite
INSTR	instrumental
ipfv	imperfective
LE	lexemic entry
LF	Logical Form

xx *List of Abbreviations*

LFG	Lexical Functional Grammar
LFT	lexeme-formation template
LI	Lexemic Index
LID	Lexical Identifier (SBCG)
LKR	linker
LOC	locative
L-PTCP/LPTCP	l-participle
lxm	lexeme
M	masculine
MOD	modifier
MORSIG	morpholexical signature (feature)
MTR	MOTHER attribute
N	noun
NEG	negative
NEUT	neuter
NOM	nominative
NP	Noun Phrase
NUM	number
OBJ	object
OBL	oblique
P	preposition
PASS	passive
PERS	person
PF	Paradigm Function
PFM	Paradigm Function Morphology
pfv	perfective
POSS	possessor; possessive (adjective)
PL	plural
pm	property mapping (function)
pos	part-of-speech
PossA	possessive adjective
PP	Preposition Phrase
PRED	PREDICATE (LF attribute)
PREP	preposition
PRI	Principle of Representational Independence
PROL	prolative
PROPR	proprietive
PRS	present
psoa	parametrized state of affairs
PST	past

PTCP	participle
R	reference (SF role)
RCTR	RESTRICTOR (SF role)
ref dep	referentially dependent
REFL	reflexive
REL	relational (adjective)
REPR	REPRESENTATION (feature)
RESTR	RESTRICTION (SF role)
SBCG	Sign-Based Construction Grammar
SEM	SEMANTICS
SFROLE	Semantic Function Role
SF roles	semantic function roles
SG	singular
SIM	similitudinal (adjective)
SN	Subject Nominalization
Spec	Specifier
SPR	Specifier
SUBCAT	subcategory
SUBJ	subject
SUPER	superessive
SYN	SYNTAX
TAM	Tense/Aspect/Mood
TGT	TARGET
TNS	tense
TR	transitive
V	verb
VAL	Valence
VCE	Voice
VP	Verb Phrase
VSO	verb-subject-object
WFR	word formation rule

PTCP	participle
R	reference (SF role)
RCTR	RESTRICTOR (SF role)
RD	referentially dependent
RFL	reflexive
REL	relational (adjective)
REPR	REPRESENTATION (feature)
RESTR	RESTRICTION (SF role)
SBCG	Sign Based Construction Grammar
SEM	SEMANTICS
SFROLE	Semantic Function Role
SFroles	semantic function roles
SG	singular
SM	semifinished (radioactive)
SN	Spatial Modification test
Spec	Specifier
SPCR	Specifier
St.uCAt	subcategory
SUBJ	subject
SUPER	super-.layer
SYN	SYNTAX
TAM	Tense/Aspect/Mood
TGT	TARGET
TNS	tense
TR	transitive
V	verb
VAL	Valence unit
VCE	Voice
VP	Verb Phrase
VSO	verb-subject-object
WPR	Word Formation rule

1 Introduction: Word Categories and Category Mixing

1.1 Introduction

This book is about the way that nouns can serve as attributive modifiers to other nouns. Many languages have productive morphology which turns nouns into adjectives, i.e. words whose canonical grammatical function is to act as an attributive modifier to a nominal head. In some cases the denominal adjective retains a number of nominal properties, so that it may even take noun-oriented modifiers and specifiers, while still itself serving as an attributive modifier. We will call these elements 'noun–adjective hybrids'. Noun–adjective hybrids constitute a type of 'mixed category'. In such cases the adjectival affix seems to attach to an already modified noun, thus giving rise to the appearance of an adjective being formed on a whole syntactic phrase. It is rather difficult to determine what the lexical category of such adjectives is, if syntactic distribution is the only diagnostic criterion, and the literature contains rather little discussion of how syntax of these constructions is to be represented (Spencer, 2013, 4).

The well-known phenomenon of Suffixaufnahme (see Plank (1995b) for an introduction to this notion) is also often an instance of categorial mixing. The prototypical example of Suffixaufnahme is found when a dependent noun inflected for, say, genitive case acquires the case marking of its head, yielding structures of the form *father*-GEN-INSTR *spear*-INSTR 'with father's spear'. In these structures, genitive case-marked nouns agree with the head in case. As case-marked elements such words are nouns, but as agreeing modifiers they are adjectives.

Various other kinds of mismatch can occur in the nominal phrase, and their examination raises a number of general questions about the nature of word classes. The first goal of this book is to bring together cross-linguistic evidence for categorial mixing in adnominal modifiers and to discuss the variety of intermediate types, concentrating specifically on how certain classes of denominal adjective (DNA) and adjective-like forms are related to their base noun, to nouns generally, and to the canonical adjective class.

2   Introduction: Word Categories and Category Mixing

Some of the implications of such category mixing have been discussed in our earlier work (Nikolaeva and Spencer, 2012; Spencer, 2005b, 2013; Spencer and Nikolaeva, 2017). In particular, Spencer (2013) aimed to solve the conceptual problems associated with mixed categories by factorizing the components of a lexical relation and defining lexical relatedness in terms of that enriched model of lexical representations. The central feature of this analysis is the idea that standard major lexical categories – N(oun), V(erb), A(djective) – arise from combining semantic and syntactic properties in a canonical fashion, but that a host of other categories can be defined by exploiting non-canonical combinations.

It is this intuition that we will make further use of. We believe that the framework based on the factorization of lexical categories provides the best tools for tackling the questions we are interested in here in a transparent and principled manner. We will show how this approach to lexical representations predicts that various kinds of mismatch can occur in the nominal phrase,[1] allowing us to include seemingly unrelated phenomena within a single space of possibilities.

However, the typology of lexical relatedness offered in Spencer (2013) is only a beginning. There are a good many complex morphosyntactic issues here which tend to be skirted over even in overtly lexicalist approaches, and the main aim of Spencer (2013) was not to argue for any particular model of syntax which could account for mixed categories (within the nominal phrase or beyond), but rather to propose an adequate characterization of their lexical representations. In contrast, the second goal of this book is to provide a more explicit account of the morphosyntax of the noun–adjective hybrids which participate in various modification constructions.

In traditional pre-theoretical terms, modification within a nominal phrase means the attribution of a property to the head noun by using another syntactic phrase (a modifier). Modifiers of nouns generally include adjectives, numerals, adnominal demonstratives and wh-words, article-like elements, relative clauses, adpositional and oblique case phrases, and some adverbials (Dryer, 2007). We will only be concerned with those modifiers that have a clearly identifiable lexical content: that is, we will exclude obvious determiners and quantifiers.[2] However, we will expand this typology by treating

---

[1]   In this introduction we use 'nominal phrase' as a general cover term to refer to any phrase whose lexical content is nominal, and whose lexical head is (uncontroversially) a noun. The NP/DP distinction is irrelevant for our present purposes; see the discussion in Chapter 7.

[2]   It should be acknowledged from the outset that the relative lack of concern for attributive modification is very apparent from a review of the pedagogically oriented literature, where

modification together with possession. A close typological connection between these two sorts of construction has not been widely explored, except perhaps by Koptjevskaja-Tamm (2000, 2001a, 2002, 2004) and in our own earlier work (Nikolaeva and Spencer, 2012), but we will argue that it is essential for understanding the nature of adnominal modification. We will refer to the whole class of constructions in which a nominal concept modifies another noun – whether in a compound, possessive structure, or denominal adjective – using the general term 'modification-by-nominal-concept'.

For canonical attributive modification of a canonical, entity-denoting noun by a canonical, gradable property-denoting adjective, we will be assuming a very standard model of morphosyntax, implemented in a variety of head-driven phrase structure grammar (HPSG) derived from Ackerman and Nikolaeva (2013), under which the adjective has a syntactic valency requiring it to combine with a head noun. The semantic content of the resulting phrase is the simple combination (by Boolean 'and') of the semantic content of adjective and noun (both taken to be one-place predicates). For the purposes of our study we can safely ignore for the time being the more subtle and often puzzling manifestations of attributive modifiers.

For the generic examples in which a noun or noun phrase modifies a noun – what we have called 'modification-by-nominal-concept' – we will motivate what seems to be the standard assumed analysis, under which the modifying noun denotation and the head noun denotation bear a relation $\mathfrak{R}$ to each other, whose semantics is underspecified, being determined by shared inferences in the context of utterance, world knowledge/assumptions, and other pragmatic factors. We will, however, offer some modest clarification to the nature of the $\mathfrak{R}$ relation, to allow us to deploy it more generally.

The remainder of this chapter will introduce a number of theoretical concepts important for further presentation, and will summarize a variety of problems and approaches to defining word classes in general and for

typically find little or no serious discussion of attributive modification as such can be found, and this reflects the relative paucity of discussion of the morphosyntax of attributive adjectives compared with that of nouns or verbs in formal frameworks. The principal exception is found with relative clauses (especially the type of finite clause found in European languages, but more rarely elsewhere in the world). However, even the relative clause literature concentrates very largely on the internal structure of the relative clause itself, and devotes less attention to the way in which the clause serves as an attributive modifier and how this relates to other types of attributive modification. Moreover, there is far less discussion of the non-finite participial relative clause type than of the typologically much more restricted European type with its relative pronoun derived from a question word. It is the participial relative clause, based on a verb~adjective hybrid, the participle, that poses the really interesting problems for theories of grammatical categories (Spencer, 2015b).

4   *Introduction: Word Categories and Category Mixing*

noun–adjective hybrids in particular. We close by summarizing the structure of the book.

1.2   Word Classes

It is tempting to think that in an ideal morphosyntactic world there would be nouns, verbs, and adjectives, and each class would be clearly delineated from the other in terms of morphology, syntax (for instance, distribution), and morphosyntax (for instance, agreement properties). However, such an ideal world is not our world. In practice it is notoriously difficult to differentiate word classes,[3] either in a particular language or universally (Baker, 2003; Bisang, 2011; Sasse, 1993; Vogel and Comrie, 2000, among many others). This section will briefly survey the main typological and descriptive challenges; for a comprehensive and relatively recent survey of a variety of theoretical approaches, see Rauh (2010) and Baker and Croft (2017).

1.2.1   The Functionalist Perspective

Traditional grammar mostly relied on the so-called 'notional' approach, that is, the classical semantic definition of 'parts of speech'. In this view nouns essentially denote 'things' or 'entities', verbs denote 'events' or 'actions', and adjectives denote 'properties'. Thus, parts of speech have a grammar-external motivation while morphological, and even more so syntactic, behaviours are of secondary importance. However, it is widely known that grammatical systems of word classes exhibit a great deal of cross-linguistic variation. That semantic properties may be at odds with language-specific morphosyntactic properties is a well-established fact: across languages words of any of the semantic classes can be found as nouns, adjectives, or verbs (e.g. Hengeveld, 1992, 49ff; Sasse, 1993; Croft, 2000). Since class membership cannot be predicted from the lexical meaning alone, a more sophisticated elaboration of the notional approach found its place in many versions of linguistic functionalism. The main idea is that matching word classes across languages is possible by reference to the universal conceptual primitives of various degrees of complexity rather than lexical meanings as such (see Jackendoff, 1990 and, with a very different implementation, Wierzbicka, 2000).

---

[3]   We use the terms 'word classes', 'parts of speech', and 'lexical classes' more or less interchangeably throughout this book (for some discussion see Rauh, 2010, 2). The problem of word classes centres around the major lexical categories of noun, verb, adjective, and (perhaps) adposition, but typically excludes functional categories defined in terms of feature content rather than semantic representations.

1.2 Word Classes 5

Givón (1984), for instance, emphasized the uniformity of semantic construals across languages by attributing importance to the role played by the general cognitive processes through which people categorize experience and construe concepts. In order to make the relevant distinctions, he relied on the notion of 'time stability'. Time-stable concepts are those that do not vary appreciably of time. The class of nouns in any language includes the words that express the most time-stable concepts, such as rock or tree; on the other hand, the class of verbs in any language is the grammatical category that includes lexemes which express the least time-stable concepts, e.g. events such as die, run, and break (Givón, 1984, 51). In Cognitive Grammar (Langacker, 1987, and other work) word classes are schematic symbolic structures, pairings of meaning and form, and defined in terms of their conceptual contents ('abstract schemas'), but inherently linked to grammatical properties and the potential to participate in the networks of constructions. Langacker introduced several other basic notions relevant for conceptualization, for instance, the notion of 'relationality'. Roughly speaking, a noun symbolizes a 'thing', i.e. an entity which is conceptualized as being non-relational, whereas other predications are conceptualized as relational and fall into temporal and atemporal relations. The former account for verbs, which are schematically characterized as 'sequentially scanned processes', while the latter are 'summarily scanned' and account for a number of other words classes including adjectives and adverbs. It can of course be argued that 'time stability', 'relationality', and other similar functional notions only help to identify the prototypical (or canonical) members of the major word classes: e.g. the non-time-stable relational noun *arrival* or the relatively time-stable *exist*. Such cases, as well as various interclass derivational processes, signal alternative conceptualizations or construals: thus, nominalizations represent the construal of the action as a static entity.

These approaches postulate a conceptual basis for word classes and treat grammatical behaviours as essentially the other aspect of the same phenomenon. However, the status of all notional criteria is highly debatable. Unless conceptual analysis is supplied with additional argumentation, we may simply not be in the position to motivate the essential difference between words or classes of words in terms of cognitive construals. In some cases it is extremely difficult to make clear conceptual distinctions even within a single language. For example, in Jaminjung, as analysed in Schultze-Berndt (2000), inflecting verbs and uninflecting 'particles' constitute two grammatically distinct word classes that are also distinct from nominals. Uninflecting particles are an open class: they do not have the morphosyntactic properties of the small closed class of inflecting verbs, although they are conventionally glossed

6   Introduction: Word Categories and Category Mixing

using the names for English verbs – and that is what their meaning appears to convey, just as for inflecting verbs. There is no evidence that conceptual structure is construed any differently (see Sasse, 1993; Baker, 2003, 290ff; Rauh, 2010, 257ff; and Bisang, 2011, 282ff for this and other arguments against notionally/semantically/conceptually based characterization of lexical categories). As a result, many functionally oriented linguists (Haspelmath, 2007; Cristofaro, 2009; Croft and van Lier, 2012, among others) regard word classes as language-specific categories rather than linguistic universals. However, the question of cross-linguistic comparability then becomes even more acute.

Some versions of functionalism rely on discourse-related properties rather than semantic/conceptual content per se. Thus, Hopper and Thompson (1984, 1985) proposed 'prototypical discourse functions' of nouns and verbs: the former relate to introducing discourse participants and referring to them, while the latter concern denoting a situation/state-of-affairs and answering the question 'What happened?' or the like. Non-prototypical instances in which nouns and verbs show reduced categoriality also exist, but in general word classes across languages can be described as grammaticalized discourse functions. The idea of prototypical vs. non-prototypical class membership was taken up by Croft (1991, 2000, 2001), although in his theory prototypical word classes are not categories of particular grammars, but rather language universals. We will return to this in Section 1.2.3.

In a roughly similar manner, Bhat (2000) argued that word classes are grammaticalized sentential functions. In this approach, word classes are defined by set grammatical properties but are not theoretical primitives; they are derived from more basic functional categories based on their role in the act of communication. For instance, the properties of adjectives as a distinct class, such as co-occurrence with degree modifiers, are derived from the sentential function of modifying a noun (Croft, 1991; Hengeveld, 1992). In most languages word classes manifest the relevant properties maximally only when they are used in their typical sentential functions, while in other functions they tend to lose some of their categorial characteristics and acquire properties of other classes. Some languages do not make use of all sentential functions and employ alternative strategies; these languages fail to make relevant categorial distinctions. Thus, Muna (van den Berg, 1989), Kolyma Yukaghir (Maslova, 2003), the Dravidian languages Malayalam and Kannada (Amritavalli and Jayaseelan, 2003), and Lai (Enfield, 2004) have been analysed as not possessing categorially distinct adjectives. (This would be consistent with the view that adjectives cannot be identified by a universal positive

1.2 Word Classes 7

property, see Section 1.2.2). When a language has no adjectives or only a small closed class of adjectives, property concepts are encoded either as verbs, as in Chinese and Korean, or nouns, as in Quechua and Hausa (see Stassen, 1997, for an overview). In Japanese the class of property-denoting words is split: some are morphologically like verbs and others bear a resemblance to nouns (although Backhouse (2004) ultimately concludes that they do represent a distinct adjectival category). So cross-linguistic variation results from different directions of grammaticalization.

Unlike many feature-based approaches, Anderson (1997, 2007) proposed a different kind of notional model based on two semantically interpreted macro-features that are single-valued rather than binary, as discussed in the next section. Essentially, these features describe prototypical notional characteristics. The feature 'referentiable' (represented as (N) by Anderson) promotes perception of something as concrete, stable, discrete, and potentially referential, while the feature 'predicative' (represented as (P) by Anderson) characterizes relational, dynamic, potentially predicative objects. The notional features can combine in varying proportions in different languages, resulting in a wider range of types and ensuring gradience in the definition of word classes and the appearance of various intermediate or, in Anderson's terminology, 'second-order' categories. For example, in English auxiliary verbs have the feature {P} and are a prime example of predicators, while the combination {P; N} describes non-auxiliary verbs which are prototypically predicative but also have the nominal feature. In contrast, {N; P} is a word class in which the N (that is, noun) feature predominates over P, whereas {(N; P) & (P; N)} is how adjectives are defined. The presence of both (N; P) and (P; N) in adjectives results in their intermediate status, which is distributionally and notionally more complex and therefore more marked than the status of nouns and verbs. Thus, some languages lack adjectives as a distinct word class and in others this class is very small or derived.

In this model, the distributional properties of syntactic classes are not semantically arbitrary. The defining distribution for a word class is based on the behaviour of core semantically prototypical members which are not themselves internally complex, so syntax appeals to a combination of prototypical semantic properties and the distribution of prototypical instances. The lexical classes established in this way can contain non-prototypical items which are interpreted in accordance with the notional characteristics of their class and which share the same distribution as semantically prototypical members. For instance, the noun *arrival* is not a prototypical nominal because its denotation is relational and non-stable, but its basic syntax "confers on it the status of a perceived

8 Introduction: Word Categories and Category Mixing

entity" (Anderson, 2007, 25). As a result, lexical categories are ultimately identified by a combination of notional and morphosyntactic (distributional and morphological) information which can vary independently, unlike in Cognitive Grammar, for instance, a conclusion which stands somewhat close to what we will maintain throughout this book and which also lies in the centre of the prototypes-based or canonically based perspective outlined in Section 1.2.3.

One acknowledged problem for virtually all approaches to word classes is presented by those languages where it is common for a single word to have the syntax of several parts of speech indiscriminately, so that we can arguably talk of categorial indeterminacy. Some linguists have even claimed that there are languages which lack any categorial distinctions whatsoever, not even noun/verb, such as Salishan (Kinkade, 1983), Iroquoian (Sasse, 1988), Riau Indonesian (Gil, 1994), and Tongan (Broschart, 1997).[4] Broadly speaking, there are two types here. In languages with little or no morphology, a single form can other be interpreted at will as a noun or a verb (and sometimes as another grammatical class too). In Tongan virtually any word may be used as a final predicate, attributive modifier, argument, or verbal modifier, and there is no overt morphology to mark the change of function. This corresponds to Type 1 in Hengeveld's (1992) typology of word classes. Here there is under-differentiation of word categories in the morphology with automatic interpretation of words as object- or event-denoting depending on the syntactic context. In other languages there is rich inflectional morphology which applies indifferently. For example, tense/aspect and subject agreement morphology applies to words denoting objects used as predicates to give meanings such as '(this) is my future canoe'. This is observed in Tuscarora (Iroquoian) where both the words denoting processes and the words that semantically correspond to English nouns have only a predicative use, and bear tense, aspect, and a number of other predicative markers. Therefore, both should be classified as one undifferentiated grammatical class. This situation corresponds to Hengeveld's Type 7.

In Hengeveld's approach, words with indiscriminate morphosyntactic properties form categories of their own. However, it is fair to say that none of the above claims is uncontroversial (see, for instance, Davis et al., 2014, on Salishan; Mithun, 2000, on Iroquoian; as well as Evans and Osada, 2005, on juxtaposition). The volume edited by Rijkhoff and van Lier (2013) provides an

---

[4] More plausibly, linguists have argued that there are languages which lack minor lexical categories such as adpositions and adverbs. Adpositions are especially hard to incorporate into a general account of word categories. Baker (2003) does not regard them as a lexical category, for instance; see also Beard (1995) for detailed discussion of the outlier status of prepositions.

extensive discussion of what they term 'flexible languages', noting that most controversy arises around the presumed lack of a lexical distinction between nouns and verbs in the languages where one and the same lexical item is used for reference and predication without any change in morphosyntactic encoding or other overt marker of recategorization. The main controversy boils down to the question whether, for example, the Mundari item *buru* represents two homophonous but distinct lexemes in (1a) and (1b), cited after Evans and Osada (2005, 373), or one undifferentiated flexible class:

(1)   a. buru=ko   bai-ke-d-a
          mountain=3PL.S make-COMPL-TR-IND
          'They made the mountain.'

      b. saan=ko   buru-ke-d-a
          firewood=3PL.S mountain-COMPL-TR-IND
          'They heaped up the firewood.'

From Evans and Osada's perspective, examples such as (1) do not meet the criterion of explicit semantic compositionality required to make the claim that Mundari lacks the noun/verb distinction: there is no regular and predictable semantic correspondence between the meaning of *buru* in a referential function as shown in (1a) and the meaning of *buru* in a predicative function as shown in (1b). This, among other things, indicates that the semantic difference is not fully attributable to the syntactic function. Therefore *buru* in (1a) and (1b) belong to homophonous but distinct lexemes, arguably a traditional noun and verb that are related through conversion. For an alternative position see Hengeveld and Rijkhoff (2005).

For a number of contributors to Rijkhoff and van Lier (2013), flexible words occur at the intersection of traditional word classes and form categories on their own. However, the majority seem to agree that they can be viewed as precategorial objects underspecified in the lexicon and which only acquire categorical characteristics later; so in flexible languages categorization takes place at the level of syntax, if at all, while lexemes as such are deprived of any categorical information (Farrell, 2001; Arad, 2005). The major disagreements then have to do with the grammatical level at which categorical distinctions are to be made (lexicon, morphology, or syntax), the definition of lexeme, and whether the syntactic environment (a 'discourse function') in which a lexeme appears contributes the meaning component to its basic semantics. This further raises a number of questions regarding the nature of semantic shifts and the status of conversion as either a lexical process that derives a new lexeme or

10 *Introduction: Word Categories and Category Mixing*

a syntactic phenomenon that involves the use of the same lexeme in multiple syntactic contexts.

1.2.2 Feature Systems

In contrast to notionally based approaches, in feature-based analyses words belong to a single category if and only if they share the same set of properties identified on formal grounds. The problem of word classes is then an essentially syntactic question. Most current formal theories of word categorization, including what we can call 'Mainstream Generative Grammar' (following Culicover and Jackendoff, 2005), adopt the distributional approach handed down by American Structuralism (Matthews, 1993, 111–128). In a nutshell, this approach rejects all notionally based definitions on the grounds that they are hard to apply rigorously, and does not recognize the idea of gradient word class membership either. Instead, preference is given to clearly identifiable syntactic criteria. Word classes are discrete and selected from a more or less closed list of well-established categories defined in terms of their typical combinations, distributions, and possibly other behavioural properties. No external motivation for the existence of word classes is in principle necessary in this approach: they are primarily formal categories ('form-classes' or 'syntactic categories'), that is, classes of words that may occur in the same positions in the sentence structures of a given language. Categorial membership determines syntactic distribution and vice versa: establishing whether a given word is, e.g., a noun or an adjective requires us to decide whether it combines with other words to form phrases in the manner of a noun or in the manner of an adjective.

The strongest version of this model affirms that syntactic distributions must be kept apart from other properties and a consistent distinction is to be made between distributionally defined classes as syntactic categories, on the one hand, and traditional parts of speech as morpho-semantic classes, on the other hand (see Rauh, 2010). The latter are basically restricted to highly inflecting languages where parts of speech are associated with inflectional paradigms, but the number of syntactic categories typically exceeds the number of parts of speech, because of the variety of syntactic contexts where parts of speech are allowed to occur and because some traditional parts of speech (e.g. adverbs) can be split into several classes associated with different functional heads. In languages with poor inflection, parts of speech appear to lose their grammatical function altogether. The weaker version recognizes the importance of inflectional morphology for word categorization. For instance, according to Aarts and Haegeman (2006, 117) word classes are "abstractions

1.2 Word Classes   11

Table 1.1 *Binary features: [±N, ±V]*

	N	V
Noun	+	−
Verb	−	+
Adjective	+	+
Adposition	−	−

Table 1.2 *Binary features: [±predicative, ±transitive]*

	Predicative	Transitive
Noun	−	−
Verb	+	+
Adjective	+	−
Adposition	−	+

over sets of words displaying some common property or properties" in terms of their distributional as well as inflectional behaviours.

It is very common in such discussions of word classes to assume that it is possible to classify words using binary predicates or features accessible to syntax. Since the classification of lexemes into word classes is obviously not the same in all languages, the systems of word classes are defined separately for each particular language. However, for each language cross-categorial generalizations are captured by fractionating classes into binary features selected from a universally available feature set.

There are several feature-based approaches in the literature, and we illustrate the principal ones here. In the classical Government and Binding Theory, (Chomsky, 1981) and all its derivatives, including Principles and Parameters and Minimalist Program, there is the feature set [±N, ±V] (Table 1.1), while in Lexical Functional Grammar (LFG) (Bresnan, 2001; see also Jackendoff, 1977) there is the set [±predicative, ±transitive] (Table 1.2). Table 1.3 shows the system based on the contrast 'referentially dependent' vs 'articulated', argued for by Wunderlich (1996), and the fourth system shown in Table 1.4 is the early system of Jackendoff (1977, 31–32). Table 1.5 provides a summary.

Identical or conceptually similar sets of features are also in use by HPSG and a number of other syntactic theories. A survey of feature-based accounts can be found in Baker (2003, 11ff) and Rauh (2010). In each case features interact with syntactic principles and rules (e.g. the licensing of functional categories which

12 *Introduction: Word Categories and Category Mixing*

Table 1.3 *Binary features: [±referentially dependent, ±articulated]*

	Referentially Dependent	Articulated
Noun	−	−
Verb	−	+
Adjective	+	−
Adposition	+	+

Table 1.4 *Binary features: [±subj, ±obj]*

	subj	obj
Noun	+	−
Verb	+	+
Adjective	−	−
Adposition	−	+

Table 1.5 *Summary: binary feature systems for lexical categories*

	N/V		predicate/ transitive		ref. dependent/ articulated		subject/ object	
	N	V	pred	trans	ref dep	art	subj	obj
Noun	+	−	−	−	−	−	+	−
Verb	−	+	+	+	−	+	+	+
Adjective	+	+	+	−	+	−	−	−
Adposition	−	−	−	+	+	+	−	+

can be realized very differently in different languages, the well-formedness of constituent or functional structure, etc.), so that the interaction of feature specification with syntax ensures that the items assume the same positions and possibly take the same inflectional forms.

Although there is agreement among many formal linguists that language-particular classes need to be defined on morphosyntactic grounds for each individual language, various problems remain. Most feature-based approaches, including Anderson's system, do not clearly specify what distributional behaviours are theoretically relevant and rely on a more or less

1.2 Word Classes   13

Table 1.6 *Three theoretical types of feature system*

	F1	F2	G1	G2	H1	H2
Noun	+	+	+	−	−	+
Verb	+	−	+	+	+	+
Adjective	−	−	−	+	−	−
Adposition	+	+	−	−	+	+

random set of distributional properties. This therefore gives rise to the famous 'splitting' or 'subclass' problem recognized at least since the 1960s (Crystal, 1967). The problem was discussed at length by Croft (2000, 72–81) and Baker (2003, 3–10). Since there is no ranking of distributional criteria and they are of more or less equal importance, any syntactic context may turn out to be definitional. If a full variety of contexts is taken into account, very few words will have an identical formal behaviour. The English modals have different distribution from other verbs, but do they form a separate lexical class? Perhaps they do and this class corresponds to a functional category (Mood or some such), but as more and more distributional contexts are taken into account, the number of classes tends to proliferate to the extent that some classes may only comprise one item. In Mohawk, as Baker shows, putative adjectives are in many respects like intransitive verbs and have been traditionally analysed as such. However, they also have some special properties: unlike verbs, they cannot appear in the habitual or punctual aspect and permit a kind of possessor raising with noun incorporation. This obviously raises the question of whether these differences justify positing a separate category of adjectives for Mohawk. The general point is that there is no principled way to decide whether an observed distributional difference between two groups of items should be rated as a ground for assuming two separate lexical classes or as two subclasses of the same category.

What is more, the features defining word classes appear more or less arbitrary. Clearly, we can in principle propose any combination of binary features to define four distinct major categories. Once we collapse alphabetic variants, we have six distinct sets of categorizations. The additional three types are shown in Table 1.6 using arbitrary feature names F1/F2, G1/G2, H1/H2.

There is no serious theory of what these features actually mean, except perhaps for Baker (2003) and, more recently, Panagiotidis (2011, 2014) who invests traditional binary features [$\pm$N, $\pm$V] with extensive content.[5]

---

[5]   See Rauh (2010, 96ff, 144ff) for an overview of other interpretations of the categorial features.

14   *Introduction: Word Categories and Category Mixing*

For Panagiotidis, lexical categories are essentially about interpretation, hence universal. Categorial features encode 'fundamental interpretive perspective' (and are therefore LF-interpretable): [+N] imposes a sortal perspective and ensures that nouns are 'kinds', whereas [+V] encodes an extending-into-time perspective and ensures that verbs are subevents. In Baker's (2003) theory, too, the categories are universal and presumably belong to the innate substantive universals of language but feature specification, and hence categorization, takes place in syntax rather than the lexicon, an assumption shared by the Distributed Morphology framework. Nouns bear a referential index, understood as the syntactic representation of the "criteria of identity", whereby they can serve as standards of "sameness" (Baker, 2003, 95). This makes nouns uniquely suited for referent tracking in discourse. Verbs denote predication and require a specifier (generally equated with a subject NP/DP), while this is not required for nouns. Adjectives are defined by Baker by the negative specification of categorial features: they are [−N] and [−V] because they have no referential index, unlike nouns, and take no subject specifiers, unlike verbs. In this sense they are a default category and normally appear in syntactic environments where neither nouns nor verbs are likely to appear. In essence, then, Baker follows the traditional view that one only needs two binary features to distinguish the major three (or four) lexical categories.

As will become clear later in the book, our understanding of what we call 'canonical' nouns and 'canonical' verbs is broadly similar to these characterizations of [+N] and [+V], but we differ from Baker on the question of adjectives and their canonical functions. The status of adjectives as a natural class is in fact the most controversial, and many authors before Baker have highlighted their 'negative' properties such as vagueness, and inability to stand on their own or to denote events or identify participants (Bhat, 1994; Hale and Keyser, 2002, among others). Fábregas and Marín (2017, 4) conclude that "there is a positive property that defines adjectives, we have not found it yet". Although adjectives can be defined only negatively, for Baker they are universal, and Dixon (1982, 2004) also argued that all languages have a surface category of adjective (and, we must presume, a categorial distinction between nouns and verbs), even though languages with a very small closed adjective class do exist. But Dixon's claim for adjective as a universal category has been questioned (Stassen, 1997; Enfield, 2004; Spencer, 2008, among others), and it is probably fair to say that his (and Baker's) is the minority view.

Baker does not recognize that the primary function of adjectives is attributive modification and that prototypical adjectives are inherently gradable predicates. Obviously, bare adjectives have an option that is unique to them:

1.2 Word Classes 15

they can form a tight syntactic construction with a noun. However, some adjectives cannot be used as attributive modifiers but only as predicates (e.g. English *ready, asleep*), and it is not even clear that the attributive use of adjectives is the most common one statistically. It is therefore wrong, in Baker's view, to build a theory of adjectives around the property of modification: this property is said to be derived rather than definitional. Adjectives are often used as attributive modifiers because, in contrast to verbs, they are free from the need to assign a theta-role and, in contrast to nouns, do not require a referential index to be licensed. As a result, they can appear inside a nominal phrase without entering into linguistic relationships with anything outside that nominal phrase. Baker provides a variety of interesting arguments to support this position, but we will not discuss them here since at least some of them are based on very theory-internal considerations and many typologists adopt a rather different approach to characterizing the prototypical/canonical function of adjectives, which we also share (see Section 1.2.3).

What is perhaps more important for the purpose of this book is that Baker (2003, 198) does not recognize the possibility for nouns to directly modify other nouns. He claims that nouns can only modify other nouns in less direct ways, e.g. by adpositional constructions or derived adjectives, but not through pure attributive noun constructions. The reason for this is that, in Baker's system, being a noun reduces to having a referential index, but syntactic operations are unable to combine two indices into a new index. The non-head noun index cannot be properly licensed, because referential indices are subject to the Noun Licensing Condition, a syntactic condition that crucially refers to relationships of c-command that are defined in terms of phrase structure. However, as will be shown later in the book, the claim that pure nouns do not modify other nouns is empirically wrong: bare nouns regularly function as attributive modifiers, just as though they were adjectives.

This fact ultimately leads us to the problem of 'mixed categories' (the term of Lefebvre and Muysken, 1988) and the kinds of categorial mixture found in world languages in general, in particular in modificational constructions. Speaking very generally, mixed categories pose problems for the approach to word classes which relies on discrete lexical categories defined by binary features, because the identification of word classes can give conflicting results within a language. Under all feature-based analyses lexical classes are defined by distribution, in keeping with the syntactic presupposition underlying them (see Spencer, 2013, 303–310 for discussion of this point). In other words, when we ask whether a given word is, e.g., a noun or an adjective, we are asking whether it combines to form phrases in the manner of a noun or an

16   *Introduction: Word Categories and Category Mixing*

adjective. However, in mixed category cases we cannot take for granted that we know 'the' class of a word; a mixed category then has an unexpected feature content. As we discuss in Chapter 4, in a number of analyses such a mixed category arises by uniting two regular syntactic heads in a single morphological word. Combining two independent syntactic heads in this way can, in principle, be used to create mixed categories even when the categories themselves are, apparently, defined by unary features, i.e. by simple labels 'N', 'A', and so on. This view is compatible with the so-called 'dual projection' syntactic approach, and to a certain extent it serves to motivate that approach. It is also typical of most single projection analyses, but we will argue that neither of them can adequately handle the variety of mixture phenomena.

1.2.3   *Word Classes as Canonical Categories and Prototypes*

An alternative to the approaches discussed in the preceding two subsections is a 'non-discreteness hypothesis' (Sasse, 1993, 2001). It is manifested primarily by the prototype approach to categories followed by a number of typologists. The prototype approach stands in sharp contrast to the classical model in which each object unambiguously belongs to a single category no matter how it is defined. It permits, as a matter of principle, for word classes to be overlapping and have no clear-cut boundaries. A member of a class may be more or less prototypical because there is no reliance on one single definitional criterion; categoriality is gradient and sensitive to different kinds of cross-cutting information which can vary independently, so categorial mixture does not present a conceptual problem. There are various versions of this idea (for an overview see Aarts, 2006; van der Auwera and Gast, 2011; Rauh, 2010, 313ff; Baker and Croft, 2017), but with respect to word classes it has been especially extensively developed by Croft (1991, 2000).

Croft (1991) argued that traditional syntactic categories are prototypical pairings of semantic types and what he calls 'propositional act functions'. Semantic types are defined by several notional parameters and include objects, properties, and actions. These largely correspond to the ontological types of *Thing, Property* and *Event* in Jackendoff's (1990) theory of semantic representation (Lexical Conceptual Structure), but are based on further decomposition along the lines of Givón and Langacker. Croft's semantic categories are shown schematically in Table 1.7.

Propositional act functions roughly correspond to constructions; they are the primitive units of syntactic representation and include predication, reference, and modification (Croft, 2001, 66). Reference is typically defined in the

1.2 Word Classes 17

Table 1.7 *Prototypical semantic properties of denotations (Croft, 2001, 87)*

	Relationality	Stativity	Transitoriness	Gradability
Objects	nonrelational	state	permanent	non-gradable
Properties	relational	state	permanent	gradable
Actions	relational	process	transitory	non-gradable

typological literature as "that operation which enables us to speak about specific objects. It is a deictic act, whereby one points to a particular object by means of an expression which names that object in such a way that it can be conceived as an individual" (Sasse, 1993, 651). Predication is "that operation which allows a proposition to assume a self-contained linguistic form, a sentence. By the act of predication we posit the existence of a state of affairs" (Sasse, 1993, 651). Modification is "that operation by which we can combine concepts into more specifically modified ones" (Sasse, 1993, 651). The act of modification (of referents) functions to enrich a referent's identity by an additional feature of the referent, denoted by the modifier.

A prototypical category is typologically unmarked with respect to the relevant construction. Object words prototypically serve for reference, property words prototypically serve for modification, and action words prototypically serve for predication. Across languages these associations are grammaticalized as unmarked nouns, unmarked adjectives, and unmarked verbs, respectively. Non-prototypical associations of semantic types and propositional act functions also exist, but are structurally and behaviourally marked. This is represented in Table 1.8 (Croft, 2001, 88; Croft, 2003, 185, 187–188). In this table the grey squares represent the proposed prototypical syntactic functions of the semantic classes on the left-hand side. The items that belong to the classes in the grey boxes exhibit equal or less structural coding when in this preferred syntactic function than when the same item is used in a different syntactic function. These classes can be understood as universal categories whose prototypical status is independent of any language-particular requirements; as such, they cannot be categories of individual grammars.

The lexical class membership for each individual item is determined by the structural characteristics of the construction in which it appears: a given lexical item may belong to class A in one construction and class B in another construction. In other words, since the choice of a given type of construal is motivated by the discourse or logico-semantic function of linguistic

18   *Introduction: Word Categories and Category Mixing*

Table 1.8 *Association of major word classes and syntactic functions in English*

	Reference	Modification	Predication
Objects	**Nouns** John likes *cars*	**NPs or PPs within NPs** (e.g. genitive NP) the man *with a car* *the car's* window	**Predicate nominals** (often with copula) This is *a car*
Properties	**Deadjectival nouns** *smallness*	**Adjectives** the *small* car	**Predicate adjectives** (often with copula) The car is *small*
Actions	**Action nominals, gerunds, complements, infinitives** *the crashing of the car* *NP('s) crashing the car* *that NP crashed the car* *to crash the car*	**Participles, relative clauses** the car *that crashed* the *crashed* car	**Verbs** The car *crashed*

elements, an element with the same denotation may have different syntactic (distributional) behaviours. Given this, there may be mismatches between different properties: a word can inherit its categorial information from several classes simultaneously and many different types of categorical mixture can arise. An important consequence of this viewpoint is that, in the final analysis, the question 'what category does word W belong to?' is not a well-formed question. It is not always useful to provide words with immutable category labels. Instead of asking 'Does language L have adjectives?', the question might be rephrased as 'To what extent do property-denoting words in language L have formal features that distinguish them from other sets of lexical items? And if they have these features, in which constructions are they manifested?'

Croft's idea that lexical categories can be viewed in terms of greater or lesser prototypicality and that constructional patterns are of ultimate importance for word categorization was formalized within HPSG by Malouf (2000a, 124ff). We will discuss his approach in Chapter 4. In this book we will essentially adopt Croft's (and Malouf's) insights, but unlike them we find little to recommend the notion of 'prototype' in this context. Rather than following the customary line of speaking in terms of prototypes, we will base our analysis on the concept of canonical categories as conceived by Corbett (2006, 2007), Brown et al. (2012a), and other works. The idea is to identify a set of uncontroversial canonical criteria for a linguistic category, and to measure attested putative instances of that category against those criteria.

Like prototypes, canonical categories are intended for stating cross-linguistic generalizations. However, they differ from prototypical categories because linguists may rely on different prototypes for the same phenomenon and are free to choose one of the existing characterizations or define their own. In contrast, canonical criteria are, at least in principle, indisputable and therefore more easily compatible with a variety of approaches and theoretical frameworks. They are meant to break down complex concepts in a way that clarifies where disagreements may lie. Another crucial difference between a canonical property and a prototype is that a prototype has to exist. For instance, if we wish to claim that humans categorize the animal kingdom by appeal to notions such as 'prototypical bird', then some bird species (robin? sparrow? eagle?) has to be the prototype from which all other species deviate. But it is hard to say what a prototypical noun or verb would be: for the notion 'prototype' to be meaningful, it would have to be some specific noun/verb in some specific language. Canonical objects, on the other hand, are not necessarily frequent, and in fact there is no guarantee that anything like such a category does exist. It seems to us that talking of canonical properties is more appropriate for lexical classes because we do not want to commit ourselves to the existence of, say, some prototypical adjective in a language.

Speaking very generally, we follow the canonical approach by assuming that a word's category must be fractionated into different kinds of information: semantic, syntactic, and morphological (Spencer, 1999, 2005b, 2010a, 2013). Baker (2003, 267ff) also recognizes that these three domains – morphology, syntax, and semantics – have relevance in the definition of word classes, yet for him the category distinctions inhere fundamentally in one domain (namely syntax) and then project into morphology and semantics. For instance, although the referential index typically corresponds to reference in semantics, it is defined as a fundamentally syntactic property that has to be licensed in phrase structure. Morphology is also derived through syntax. In contrast, for us the three domains do not derive from each other and can vary independently, although we do find that properties show canonical correlations and prototypical/frequent associations.

20 Introduction: Word Categories and Category Mixing

Table 1.9 *Croft's prototypes as canonical properties*

Semantics/ontology

- Canonical Nouns denote (countable physical) objects
- Canonical Adjectives denote (physical, directly perceptible) properties[6]
- Canonical Verbs denote actions and situations

Syntax/distribution

- Canonical Nouns head phrases denoting arguments of predicates
- Canonical Adjectives head phrases used as attributive modifiers
- Canonical Verbs head phrases used as predicates

We can take most of Croft's prototypical properties for semantics and syntax and informally redefine them in terms of canonical properties as shown in Table 1.9. The three major categories are canonically associated with appropriate functional categories. For nouns, these functional categories relate to determination of referentiality and individuation, such as definiteness marking, number marking, and marking of the grammatical relation the noun holds to other words and phrases. For adjectives, we expect to see functional categories relating to the degree to which a gradable property holds of an object. For verbs, the functional categories specify time reference and modify event types, but since the verb is the head of the whole predication, we may also see clause level functional categories such as modality and various discourse properties. In languages with inflectional morphology we may see these functional categories expressed as inflections. Relations between nouns, verbs, and adjectives are also expressed by agreement and government, of course.

We can then factorize the components of a lexical entry and say that lexical representations consist of at least three different sets of properties: morphological, semantic, and syntactic (Mel'čuk, 1982, 2006). The more canonical properties a word exhibits, the more likely we are to achieve a consensus in labelling it. In the canonical approach all the properties converge on a single category. When they line up, we have what Spencer (2005b) refers to as a 'Morpholexically Coherent Lexical Entry', the canonical constitutive element of a Morpholexically Coherent Lexicon, as defined in (2).

---

[6] As we explain in Chapter 2, we take the canonical adjective to be a word denoting some gradable property concept.

1.2 Word Classes 21

(2)   Principle of the Morpholexically Coherent Lexicon

- All syntactic classes correspond to uniquely characterized morphological classes and vice versa
- All semantic classes correspond to uniquely characterized morphological classes and vice versa
- All syntactic classes correspond to uniquely characterized semantic classes and vice versa

A word can deviate from canonicity by failing to some degree to be morpholexically coherent. That is precisely what is at issue in the case of the mixed categories. There can be a mixture of properties, for example, when a syntactic noun exhibits adjectival inflection or when it has the denotation and argument structure of a verb. Morpholexical incoherence generally arises from two sources. It may be a stipulated property of the lexical item itself, unrelated to the structure of any other lexical item. There is a tendency to find the greatest variation in the expression of semantics: there are innumerable exceptions to the canonical semantics-to-structure mappings which are thus (mildly) incoherent. This does not invalidate the semantic/notional basis of word categorization; it just means that there are many deviations between semantics and syntax. But it is also abundantly clear that other types of mismatch too are frequently found e.g. between morphological and syntactic representations (Spencer, 2005b, 2007). Thus, the past tense of a Russian verb has the morphology (and agreement properties) of a predicative adjective rather than that of a finite verb. This is not an idiosyncratic property of any individual lexical item but comes from properties of the inflectional morphology: the morpholexical incoherence arises by virtue of the operation of a morphological rule in the inflectional system of Russian.

Recurrent generalizations of the kind sketched in (2) can in principle be handled using default inheritance. Mismatches can be represented by cross-classifying lexical categories in the form of an inheritance hierarchy, similar to that suggested by Malouf (2000a,b) for English gerunds, as discussed in Chapter 4 (see also the analysis proposed by Nikolaeva (2008) for Tungusic adjectives and nouns). However, the use of default logic has to be handled with care since it is incompatible with some formal approaches to inheritance (Bonami and Crysmann, 2016), and the inheritance hierarchy must be made rather sophisticated and explicit regarding lexical representations. To represent lexical relatedness properly, it should be designed to reflect the properties of words and the relations that hold between different attributes of a lexical entry.

22   *Introduction: Word Categories and Category Mixing*

This idea was explored in Spencer (2005b) (pre-dating the Canonical Typology approach) and more recently has been explicitly presented as a species of Canonical Typology in Spencer (2013). We will elaborate on this approach later in the book, but in order to provide a fuller account of mismatches, we first have to be more explicit about what we mean by categorial mixture. This is the topic of the next section.

1.3   Categorial Mixing

Even in languages where reasonably robust criteria for word classes exist, we often encounter constructions in which it is very difficult to pin down exactly what word class we are dealing with. That is, we frequently find a situation in which a word appears to have some of the properties of one class and some of the properties of a distinct class at the same time. Mixed categories, then, are lexical types that have not only some properties of the morphology, syntax, or semantics of one category, but also some properties of the morphology, syntax, or semantics of another category. In this section we will present a broad typology of mixed categories.

1.3.1   Paradigmatic Category Mixing

Precisely which properties mixed categories have and how they are realized are language-specific or even item-specific facts, but, broadly speaking, there are two ways in which a word can show categorial indeterminacy: syntagmatic mixing and paradigmatic mixing (Spencer, 2013). In most cases it is rather difficult to draw a clear dividing line between them, so that this distinction is meant to be purely heuristic and without any special theoretical import. However, we will see that it is a rather useful way of describing some of the phenomena we will be discussing.

Paradigmatic mixing is found when a word has some of the morphological properties of one category and some of the morphological properties of another category. Good examples of paradigmatic mixing are lacking in English because of the paucity of morphology, but in other languages morphological forms of words reflecting paradigmatic mixing are commonly found. For instance, a deverbal participle may inherit the tense or aspect morphology of the verb while also taking agreement inflections as an adjective does, and in many languages nominalizations are formed by taking a verb form and adding a noun case affix to it.

1.3 Categorial Mixing 23

Malchukov (2000, 2004) has surveyed the kinds of morphosyntactic properties associated with deverbal nominalizations cross-linguistically and has described the typological patterns of paradigmatic mixture in such constructions. He makes the interesting point that there are two aspects to the morphosyntax of such forms. First, we must ask what nominal properties are acquired by the verb lexeme and, second, we must ask what verbal properties are lost by this nominalization. In principle, these two processes are independent of each other (and, indeed, Malchukov argues that there are no strong implicational universals to be had by comparing the two). The more nominal in nature a morphosyntactic property is, the less likely it is to be acquired by the nominalization. Thus, case marking is a relatively neutral property in the sense that it is low on the hierarchy of semantic relevance proposed by Bybee (1985). Local cases denote relational semantics which are not necessarily bound to noun denotations, and even syntactic cases such as nominative and accusative are properties of clausal argument positions rather than inherent properties of noun denotations, so it is not uncommon for a language to permit case marking of a deverbal nominalization. On the other hand, plural marking is more intimately related to noun semantics and is therefore highly relevant to nominal denotations, in Bybee's sense; for this reason it is rare for nominalizations to permit plural marking. Conversely, we find that the more a property of the base verb lexeme exhibits Bybeean Relevance to verb denotations, the more likely it is to be preserved under nominalization. Verbal properties such as voice and aspect/Aktionsart might well be preserved, while less relevant, clause-related properties such as tense or modality are less likely to be retained. Agreement properties are the least likely to be retained and, indeed, it would be difficult to speak of a category as a nominalization if it showed verb-like subject agreement.

Russian furnishes another rather clear example of paradigmatic mixing (Spencer, 2013, 122–123). Most Russian nouns fall into well-defined declension classes, whereas while adjectives belong to the same supercategory of nominals that nouns belong to, they take different inflections from nouns. So there is a morphological difference in the inflection of nouns and adjectives. However, there is also a class of nouns (in many, but by no means all, cases etymologically derived from extant Russian adjectives) which inflect exactly like adjectives and belong to the adjectival inflectional class, even though they have the syntactic distribution and meanings typical of nouns. For instance, the noun *bol'noj* '(doctor's) patient' is a noun, but it declines exactly like the adjective *bol'noj* 'sick' from which it is derived. The noun *stolovaja* 'dining room, canteen' has the form of a feminine gender adjective but the syntax of

24   Introduction: Word Categories and Category Mixing

a noun. Its origins lie in the adjective *stolov-yj*, which itself is a relational adjective derived from the noun *stol* 'table', and the reason that *stolovaja* takes the feminine gender agreement forms in its declension is presumably because it originally derives from the phrase *stolovaja komnata* 'room having something to do with tables' headed by the feminine gender noun *komnata* 'room'. In such cases of paradigmatic mixing there is little or no effect on the syntactic behaviour of the morphologically mixed word type. This are nouns in (almost, see Section 8.2.1, Footnote 1) all their syntactic and semantic properties, although they have an adjectival form and are arguably derived by an idiosyncratic process that changes their lexemic status (that is, that changes what we will call the Lexemic Index (LI)).

One area where we seem to find paradigmatic mixing with adjectival bases is with person noun forms meaning 'person who has property P'. In English we can convert certain adjectives into person nouns, though almost always with a generic rather than referential interpretation. In general, that conversion can be applied to any form of the adjective, inflected or modified: *we must consider the needs of the poor/the poorer/the (very) poorest in our society and not those of the obscenely rich.* In this respect English deadjectival person nouns demonstrate paradigmatic mixing similar in nature to what we find in *stolovaja*-type nouns in Russian, that is the syntax and semantics of one class and the morphological properties of another class.

Characteristically, it is precisely such constructions that give rise to controversy in the descriptive literature (e.g. Huddleston and Pullum, 2002, 419–421), and there is virtually no discussion of these types in the theoretical literature. However, as interesting as it is, paradigmatic mixing per se is not central to our topic, so we will leave it aside. In any case, purely paradigmatic mixing without syntagmatic consequences is somewhat rare. In the next subsection we will be considering the more important type of categorial mixing: syntagmatic mixing.

1.3.2   Syntagmatic Category Mixing

Syntagmatic mixing is the ability of the derived form to inherit syntactic (distributional and selectional) properties from two sources. In principle, syntagmatic mixing is independent of morphology (see e.g. Bresnan and Mugane, 2006, 221): it represents a dimension of variability in lexical relatedness, which is often related to paradigmatic mixing but which is in principle orthogonal to it. For example, we could imagine a language with no verbal inflectional morphology but in which arguments of nouns were marked by one preposition and arguments of verbs were marked by a different set of prepositions, and where, in addition, nouns took a special determiner. A language such as this could still display syntagmatic mixing if, say, it had a non-finite dependent construction headed by a nominal determiner in which the subject argument was marked as though it were the argument of a noun while the object argument was marked as though it were the argument of the original verb.[7] But in practice, of course, most of the syntagmatic mixing we observe is linked to morphology.

Syntagmatic mixing arises from a lexical representation which is morpholexically incoherent. Recall that such an entry is one in which there is an inherent mismatch between the value of one lexical attribute and the value of another. Thus, a syntagmatically mixed category may behave as though it were the head of one lexical category to its left (e.g. an NP or DP) and a different lexical category to its right (e.g. a VP). Alternatively, it may behave as though it were c-commanded by functional elements proper to one category (e.g. D elements), while itself c-commanding elements proper to a different category (e.g. complements to a V head). Depending on the approach taken to phrase structure, such phenomena may be more or less troublesome.

A well-known example of syntagmatic mixing is provided by nominalizations, which tend to retain the argument structure of verbs but show other properties of nouns or adjectives, e.g. the agreement morphosyntax or linear ordering. In English we find that the so-called POSS-ING construction, the deverbal nominalization with the suffix *-ing* (a gerund), retains some of its verbal argument structure (itself an indication of category mixing), but it expresses those erstwhile verb arguments in the manner of arguments to a noun, by means of the possessive *'s* marker or by means of an *of*-phrase, as seen in (3):

(3)   a. Tom burnt the letter

        b. Tom's burning of the letter

In other cases we may find that the arguments look rather like those of a verb, as in the ACC-ING construction, also referred to as the gerund:

(4)   (We were surprised at) Tom/him burning the letter

In (4) the subject and object arguments are expressed in essentially the same way that arguments of infinitives are expressed, as seen by comparing (4) with (5).

---

[7] In the domain of noun–adjective mixing something close to this is found when a noun, especially a proper noun, is used like an adjective and takes adjective-oriented modifiers or specifiers: *That remark is more Chomsky than Chomsky; Her dress is so last season.*

26   *Introduction: Word Categories and Category Mixing*

(5)   We arranged for Tom/him to burn the letter

The syntagmatic mixing of categories is observed with the POSS-ACC construction, which begins like the POSS-ING construction but ends like the ACC-ING construction, as seen in (6).

(6)   (We were surprised at) Tom's/his burning the letter

POSS-ACC nominalizations represent the type in which the verb head is turned into a noun, but inherits some of the morphosyntax of the verb base. The word form itself gives little indication of what category it is in, and it is only when we see the construction as a whole that we notice that the *-ing* form has to receive two distinct and incompatible labels, as verb and as noun. It is a straightforward instance of a transposition (Beard, 1995), the process that alters the morphosyntax of the word but generally does not introduce any additional semantic content.[8] Likewise, a deverbal participle is a verb-to-adjective transposition and frequently exhibits syntactic properties of both verb and adjective. Adjectives do not typically have the sorts of arguments associated with verbs and are not typically modified by eventive or agentive adverbials and such like, whereas verbs do not normally appear as adnominal modifiers (for instance in the same prenominal position where adjectives are found). Therefore, typical relative clause-like attributive participial constructions inevitably illustrate syntagmatic category mixing.

Haspelmath (1996) argues that regular and productive asemantic transpositions, such as the German active participle, constitute instances of category-changing inflection. Such a transposition is an inflected word form whose external syntax is different from that of the rest of the lexeme's forms because the form's class is different.[9] On the other hand, the lexeme's word class remains the same and this governs the internal syntax, which remains that of the original verb. We will return to transpositions and the POSS-ACC construction in later chapters.

Another marginal example of this type of mixing which has received rather little attention in the literature is that which is possible when an adjective is nominalized. There is no syntagmatic mixing with property nominalizations in

---

[8]   The term 'transposition' has sometimes been used for other types of relatedness which do involve an added semantic predicate. For example, Beard (1995, 179–87, 191–4) discusses denominal and deadjectival causative verbs of the kind *crystallize* or *thicken* as instances of N → V and A → V transpositions, respectively. However, we would regard such relatedness as straightforward derivational morphology, because it defines a distinct lexeme from the base lexeme.

[9]   For the terms 'external syntax' and 'internal syntax' see Haspelmath (1996, 52).

1.3 Categorial Mixing   27

English (or, indeed, other European languages).[10] Logically, however, given the typology of lexical relatedness proposed in Spencer (2013), we expect to find languages in which property nominalizations give rise to syntagmatic mixing. In that case we might well find the translation equivalents of *slightly oldness*, *very tallness*, *more usefulness*, *most expensiveness* and so on. A case in point is provided by Japanese (Sugioka, 2011; Sugioka and Ito, 2016; see also Martin, 2004, 909–911). The suffix *-sa* combines with adjectives (whether of the 'true' adjective class, A, or the 'adjectival noun' class, AN) to give a nominal with the meaning 'degree/fact of being A/AN', as seen in (7).

(7)   taka-i 'tall' (A)   taka-sa 'height'
       sizuka (no) (AN) 'quiet'   sizuka-sa 'quietness'

It attaches to compound adjectives and to adjectival forms of verbs such as desideratives and adjectival derived forms: see (8), adapted from Sugioka (2011, 148–150).

(8)   a. [$_A$ [$_N$ otoko] -rasi] -sa
           man-like-SA
           'manliness'

       b. [$_A$ [$_N$ oku] -huka] -sa
           end-deep-SA
           'profoundness (profundity)'

       c. [$_A$ [$_V$ mi] -ta] -sa
           see-DESID-SA
           'desire to see'

       d. [$_A$ [$_V$ [$_V$ damas] -are] -yasu] -sa
           deceive-PASS-easy-SA
           'the property of being easy to deceive'

           (lit. 'easy-to-be-deceived-ness')

       e. [$_A$ [$_V$ [$_V$ mukuw] are] -na] -sa
           reward-PASS-NEG-SA
           'unrewardedness'

We see clear instances of syntagmatic mixing with *-sa*. In (9a) the *-sa* suffix attaches to the phrase *motte iki-niku(i)*, headed by an adjectival derived form of *iku* 'go', while in (9b) *-sa* attaches to a verb phrase headed by the desiderative form of the verb *mi(ru)* 'see', which is adjectival in form.

---

[10] This means that they are probably best treated as what Spencer (2013) refers to as 'transpositional lexemes' rather than true transpositions; see Chapter 5.

28   *Introduction: Word Categories and Category Mixing*

(9)   a.   mot-te   iki-[_A niku] -sa
carry-GER go-hard-SA
'the property of being hard to bring'

(lit. 'hard-to-bring-ness')

b.   [_A [_{VP} sikago   o   mi-] -ta] -sa
Chicago ACC see-DESID-SA
'desire to see Chicago'

Not all systematic inter-lexemic relatedness gives rise to syntagmatic mixing, even when this would be theoretically possible. For instance, the German substantivized infinitive (*substantivierter Infinitiv*) derives a nominalization of a verb from its infinitive form. However, in syntactic terms this nominalization behaves exactly like a noun and shows no verb properties (other than preserving its array of arguments). In particular, we see no syntagmatic mixing comparable to that of the English POSS-ACC type. Consequently, we have to assume that mixing is an option that languages can choose when the circumstances permit, but not an obligation. As we will see later in the book, a prerequisite to an adequate description of syntagmatic mixing is a descriptive framework for lexical representations which makes it possible to define such mixing.

1.4   Mixed Categories in Adnominal Modification

In this section we present an overview of the main parameters of variation in adnominal modifiers with mixed properties, which is the main empirical topic of the book. These parameters allow us to distinguish the behaviour of fully canonical nouns and fully canonical adjectives from the behaviour of noun–adjective hybrids.

1.4.1   Adjective and Noun Properties

Spencer (1999) noted that there are several principal ways in which nouns can be used to modify other nouns across languages. On the one hand, we may have a specific morphosyntactic construction which creates a phrase type that functions as an attributive modifier. Examples of such construction types are specific case forms of nouns (notably a genitive case but semantic cases too), construct state, ezafe constructions, relative clause-like structures, adpositional functional words such as English *of*, and possessor agreement strategies under which the head noun agrees with the dependent. On the other hand, a very frequent strategy for achieving modification is simple

1.4 Mixed Categories in Adnominal Modification   29

concatenation or some sort of noun-noun (N-N) compounding. Finally, we may have a morphosyntactically defined type of lexical relatedness which creates an attributive form of a noun, that is, true denominal adjectives and other kinds of adjective-like forms.

When a noun undergoes canonical derivation to an adjective, it loses its nominal properties and gains a set of adjectival properties, becoming a distinct lexeme. However, as argued extensively in Spencer (2013), canonical derivation and inflection represent just two of a great many ways in which words can be related to each other. Processes which define relatedness between a noun base lexeme and a derived attributive modifier form can define word types that fall into one or other of these intermediate types of relatedness, so the noun–adjective hybrids can behave in certain ways as though they were still nouns. They show a variety of mixed effects essentially because the modificational function is non-canonical for 'true' nouns, so they may share properties of either of the two canonical categories (noun or adjective), or they may turn into a fairly uncontroversial adjective, but some aspects of the base noun's lexical representation will still be apparent after the formation of the adjective.

When we compare denominal adjective formation with deverbal nominalizations, we find that there are relatively fewer base lexeme (noun) properties to lose and fewer derived (adjective) properties to gain. The semantic properties of nouns that are most easily lost in a denominal adjective are related to determination and referentiality; consequently the base noun tends to lose its canonical semantic nominal property, namely, the capacity to refer.

There are various respects in which such an adjective can show syntagmatic or paradigmatic mixing, depending on which of the base lexeme's original nominal morphosyntactic properties it retains. It is worthwhile to briefly summarize the logical space of possibilities in terms of morphosyntax. A schematic list is shown in Table 1.10.

Generally speaking, we would expect that the nominal properties most likely to be preserved would be those that instantiate what Booij (1996) calls 'inherent inflection', while the properties most likely to be lost would be those that instantiate 'contextual inflection'. Inherent inflection is obligatory for a given word class, but is in some sense under the control of the speaker in that it serves to realize semantic or grammatical choices. Contextual inflection is a type of inflection which adds no such semantic content and is conditioned entirely by the grammatical context.

It would appear that the most nominal of the noun properties is gender. This is a difficult property to classify, however. On the one hand, where

30   *Introduction: Word Categories and Category Mixing*

Table 1.10 *Schematic list of noun and adjective properties*

Noun properties		
Inflectional:		
	number, definiteness, gender (agreement class), case, possessor agreement, ...	
Syntactic:		
	specifier types:	determiners, possessives, quantifiers, ...
	complement types:	case marking, word order, PP complements
	modification types:	attributive modification

Adjective properties		
Inflectional:		
	gradability, agreement	
Syntactic:		
	specifier types:	degree modifiers
	complement types:	case marking, word order, ...

predicates (adjectives or verbs) agree with a noun, in gender we are dealing with (canonical) contextual inflection. But the gender property of the noun itself is an inherent property, and one which in many cases is not visible from any morphophonological marker. Nonetheless, consider a language which has gender agreement and which has denominal adjectives that show syntagmatic mixing ('noun–adjective hybrids' in our terminology). Then, if that language's noun–adjective hybrids can be modified by an adjective, we expect that adjective to agree in gender with a noun–adjective hybrid. Number is an inherent property too, and we would probably expect that a language with both number and gender would also show gender agreement if it showed number agreement, though not necessarily vice versa.

The next property is one which could be considered either inherent or contextual depending on the syntactic (and sometimes on the lexical) context, namely case marking (Spencer, 2013, 78). As we show later in the book, there are languages in which the genitive case-marked form of a noun takes attributive concord morphology, a form of Suffixaufnahme. These are examples of the inheritance of (structural) case by a denominal adjective. Where semantic case

1.4 Mixed Categories in Adnominal Modification   31

marking is concerned, the one language with noun–adjective hybrids based on case-marked forms that we have studied in detail (Selkup, Uralic) co-opts that case marking for other types of relatedness. In a few languages an arbitrary case-marked form of a noun can be transposed into an adjective, in such a way that the case marking could trigger agreement on a modifier of the base noun lexeme. We would not expect such a situation to occur very often on purely empirical grounds. Even N-N compounds rarely permit the modifying noun to be case-marked (exceptions are found in Finnish and Sanskrit, for instance, but even here the case-marking potential can hardly be called productive).

Definiteness is another category that has some of the properties of inherent inflection and some of the properties of contextual inflection. In general, it serves as an inherent property not of the noun itself but of the entire nominal syntagma (what we can call a 'specifier property'). To a large extent this is also true of number (Spencer, 2013, 219–32), but unlike number, where it is just about possible to imagine cardinality independently of referentiality, it is difficult to begin to ascribe an interpretation to the notion 'definite noun', as opposed to 'definite noun phrase'. The main exception here is proper names, which are inherently definite (though indefinite or non-specific readings can often be coerced). Booij's basic typology does not really distinguish word-based from phrase-based contextual/inherent inflection, so we will here have to arrive at our own typology, on the basis of the discussion in Spencer (2013). In general, definiteness head marking serves to specify the definiteness of the phrase headed by the definite-marked noun. This is typically an instance of inherent inflection, in the sense that it is a matter of choice by the speaker whether or not to present the referent of a noun phrase as definite. However, in some morphosyntactic contexts it might be grammatically conditioned. For instance, in Latvian it is adjectives that inflect for definiteness, but if the noun phrase specifier has a definite determiner such as a demonstrative adjective, then the adjective 'agrees in definiteness', arguably an instance of contextual inflection (Spencer, 2013, 228–29). This situation is similar to that found in a language such as Italian or Hungarian, in which a demonstrative is obligatorily combined with a pleonastic definite article (though that situation is certainly not normally treated as agreement).

Finally, possessor agreement would be an instance of contextual inflection in those cases in which it indicates genuine agreement with an overt possessor. As with subject or object agreement in null subject/object languages, however, the morphology performs a dual role. If there is no overt possessor, then the morphology itself expresses the grammatical properties of the covert possessor. This is the contrast between grammatical agreement on the one hand and

32   *Introduction: Word Categories and Category Mixing*

pronominal incorporation on the other, which is familiar from LFG (Bresnan, 2001; see also Ackerman and Nikolaeva, 2013, 209ff). While possessor agreement with an overt controller is contextual inflection, pronominal incorporation is more like inherent inflection.

It therefore turns out to be quite difficult to make predictions about what nominal properties will be lost in what order on the basis of the contextual/inherent distinction.[11] In Selkup we see remarkable instances of meaning-bearing noun-to-adjective transpositions based (idiosyncratically) on case-marked noun forms and capable of being inflected for possessor properties (at least in their incorporated pronominal guise) (see Chapter 8). Yet such noun bases cannot inflect for any of the four number values which a noun can normally take. The referential/non-referential distinction does not help much either. Semantic cases do not in and of themselves make a case-marked noun referential, yet case marking rarely occurs in noun–adjective hybrids.

We will therefore leave the question of which nominal properties are lost in noun–adjective hybrids for future research and turn to the question of adjectival properties. Here we seem to be on safer ground. In general the properties that a noun can acquire in its adjectival representation are those mandated by grammar, namely word order properties and agreement (sometimes called 'concord'), together with those mandated by lexical semantics, namely the possibility of modification with a degree modifier targeting some kind of scalar property inherent in the adjective's semantics (including polarity in languages with grammaticalized negative forms of adjectives). However, we must also bear in mind that those languages that have a clearly defined adjective class differ considerably in the way that this adjectival class is expressed and how (and whether) it overlaps with the classes of verbs and nouns. Therefore, the question of which adjectival properties are acquired will depend very much on how exactly the adjective class itself is represented. It would take us beyond the scope of this study to investigate that question in detail, though it is one which would merit a systematic typological investigation.

---

[11] Moreover, Kibort and Corbett (2010) and Corbett (2012) argue that it is actually specific pairings of features and feature values that must be classified as contextual or inherent. For instance, within the same language accusative case might be entirely contextual, while locative case might be entirely inherent. Spencer (2013) points out a number of further conceptual issues that need to be clarified. In some constructions an inflected form may realize contextual inflection, as when a verb agrees with an overt subject phrase, while in other constructions it may realize inherent inflection, as when the subject inflection is the sole indicator of the person/number/gender values of a syntactically unexpressed subject.

1.4 Mixed Categories in Adnominal Modification   33

1.4.2   Main Parameters of Variation

We can identify the principal types of category mixing in denominal modifiers on the basis of three main parameters, as summarized in (10).

(10)   Parameters of category mixing

(i)   semantic: whether the formation of a new word adds a semantic predicate

(ii)   syntactic: whether it involves syntagmatic category mixing

(iii)   morphological: whether the morphology is essentially derivational or essentially inflectional

The sense of the semantic parameter is that in some cases the morphology deriving attributive denominal forms adds content, while in other cases it is not possible to discern any additional conceptual input. When a noun is turned into an adjective, in many cases we take a base lexeme and modify it incrementally, by adding a morphological marker of some kind to some basic form of the base lexeme, and by adding a semantic predicate to its lexical meaning. For instance, the English derived adjective *boy-ish* means 'similar to a boy (in some property)' and *child-ish* means 'similar to a child (in some property)'. The resulting denotations make reference both to the notion of 'boy/child' and the predicate which can roughly be represented as 'similar to N' or 'resembling N', where N is the base noun. This is the basic meaning of the *-ish* derivation in English, and it is close to various types of modification by *like*-type PPs and APs in other languages.

On the other hand, when we compare nouns and adjectives even in languages which have well-established examples of these categories, we can see that there is a regular need to modify the denotation of a noun by means of a word that is itself a noun, without the addition of an extra semantic predicate, what we have called (Nikolaeva and Spencer, 2012) 'modification-by-noun'. English has four different ways of doing this. The most direct strategy is N-N : *wood polish, cat food, water level.* Another strategy is to use a postnominal prepositional phrase, that is N P N constructions where P N has a purely attributive, modificational function (*polish for wood, food for cats, level of water*). In other cases, we are allowed to use the Saxon genitive form of the modifying noun: *cats' whiskers, children's story, men's room.* Finally, we can (sometimes) derive a so-called relational adjective from an inanimate noun or a possessive adjective from an animate/human noun: *wooden floor* (cf. *floor of wood*), *prepositional phrase* (cf. *preposition phrase*), *Aristotelean poetics* (cf. *the poetics of Aristotle*), *feline haemoglobin* (cf. *the haemoglobin of cats*). In all these constructions there is

34 *Introduction: Word Categories and Category Mixing*

no construction-specific semantic predicate added to the denotation of the head noun, or perhaps the added predicate is semantically vacuous. The relation between *wood* and *polish* in *wood polish* is not identical to the relation between *cat* and *food* in *cat food*, and is largely determined by the context in which the compound is used, as well as the lexical semantics of its components. The same consideration applies to relational adjectives, in which the base noun serves not as an argument, the function of canonical nouns, but as an attribute, the canonical function of an adjective. Morphology appears not to change the conceptual content of the lexeme at all; the meaning of the structure itself simply consists in expressing some constructionally undetermined relationship between the denotations of two nouns. The fact that the two forms have the same conceptual content is a canonical property of a transposition.

In terms of syntax, the relevant parameter of variation refers to syntagmatic category mixing, i.e. the ability of the derived form to inherit distributional and selectional properties from two categorical sources. We find little evidence of syntactic nounhood in English relational adjectives. The derived adjective *tidal* does not retain any nominal properties in terms of its syntax and therefore does not exhibit syntagmatic mixing. In particular, the base lexeme TIDE is not available for inbound attributive modification, cf. *tidal currents* and the ungrammatical *[[*high tid*]*al*] *currents*. (This contrasts with the grammatically correct form [*high tide*] *currents*.) So the noun-to-adjective derivation creates a completely opaque category. The observation that *tidal* fails to give rise to syntagmatic mixing is a major motivation for claiming that it is not a canonical transposition. In a sense it is a genuine instance of derivational morphology which happens not to introduce any additional semantic content to the derived lexeme and which therefore partially fulfils the function of the true transposition.[12]

On the other hand, when we look at syntax defined at the phrasal level, we can find constructions where the resultant phrase has important properties of an adjectival modifier, but the internal syntax of the phrase remains essentially nominal: adjectives retain aspects of the morphosyntax of the nouns on which they are based, in particular the ability to strand a modifier. Since this property will be of some importance to us, it is worthwhile giving it a specific label. We will refer to it as the Base Noun Modifiability Property (BNMP) (Attributive Transparency in Spencer and Nikolaeva (2017)). It is the BNMP that gives rise to the most important types of syntagmatic mixing in denominal adjectives. For such mixed constructions we will wish to know to what extent the attributive

---

[12] It is therefore an instance of a 'transpositional lexeme': see Chapter 5, Section 5.2.1.

1.4 Mixed Categories in Adnominal Modification 35

modifier of the hybrid's noun base behaves like that language's canonical attributive modifiers.

To some extent the BNMP is even found in the English *ed*-suffixation, e.g. [[*five-point*]*ed*] (*star*) and [[*short-sleev*]*ed*] (*shirt*). Here the modifiers *five* and *short* appear to have access to the internal part of the derived *ed*-adjective. This clearly demonstrates the mixed nature of *ed*-adjectives: on the one hand they function as syntactic modifiers, like other adjectives, and on the other hand they head their own NPs, like nouns. These arguably derivational forms permit syntagmatic mixing because the base noun is transparent to modification in just the same way that, say, the plural of the noun is transparent to modification. In other words, the grammar treats that denominal adjective as a form of the base noun and not as an autonomous adjectival lexeme.

In the case of English *ed*-adjectives the meagre morphology of the language means that we cannot demonstrate conclusively that the adjective is an inflected form of the noun lexeme. However, we will show in later chapters that in other languages the very process which creates a denominal adjective appears to be more of an inflectional one, in the sense that the morphology of the output patterns with the rest of the inflection for that base lexeme. For example, we will see that Selkup relational adjectives are actually part of the inflectional system of the language because the adjectivizing suffix is in a paradigmatic relation to the case suffix series, and because the relational adjectives can be derived from other inflected forms. Since the adjectivizing process fails to add a semantic predicate in this case and serves solely to represent the grammatical relation of attributive modification, it would fall under Booij's definition of contextual inflection, although this is a somewhat counterintuitive result because we are not dealing with some sort of agreement or government dependency. In other cases the process of adjectivization appears to be derivational, but only in the specific sense that it creates a lexical representation that belongs to a different inflectional class from the base lexeme, and which therefore has the character of a new lexical entry (what Spencer (2017b), refers to as a 'lexeme-within-a-lexeme'). This is the case with relational and with some possessive adjectives in a number of Slavic languages, for instance: they are inflected in the manner of regular underived adjectives, not in the manner of nouns.

This suggests that the third parameter of cross-linguistic variation in noun–adjective hybrids by and large concerns morphology: are we dealing with inflection or derivation? The main questions that we will be focussing on when considering this parameter are what inflectional properties, if any, are conserved in the morphology of the noun base of the hybrid itself, and what inflectional properties, if any, can control agreement on an attributive modifier?

36   *Introduction: Word Categories and Category Mixing*

In terms of standard assumptions about morphology and its interfaces, this parameter of variation would not be independent of the other two parameters discussed above. The conventional wisdom on derivation says that if word formation is to be genuinely derivational, then it should always create a new lexeme, which entails the addition of a new semantic predicate to the semantic representation of the base lexeme. Indeed, this property forms part of the definition of canonical derivation in Corbett (2010). What is more, the base lexeme from which a new lexeme is derived should be invisible to syntactic processes such as attributive modification, and to anaphoric reference (outbound anaphora). In other words, derivational morphology should give rise to syntactic and anaphoric islands.

There are of course instances in which the derivational base appears to be targeted by anaphoric relations, as in *Bill is a linguist: he says it's an exciting field.* According to Ward et al. (1991), outbound anaphora is not ruled out by any principles of grammar but instead has to do with pragmatic principles which regulate discourse accessibility of the entity referred to by the base. However, it is still true that what we can see as canonical derivation generally presupposes anaphoric islandhood. So the more the morphology is associated with an added semantic predicate and resembles canonical derivation, the more opaque the construction is, at least in theory. In practice, of course, we will see that inflection and derivation are no more than terms of convenience applied to a particular assemblage of commonly co-occurring properties, and various deviations occur. With this general picture in mind, we will illustrate our typology later in the book.

1.5   Structure of the Book

The rest of the book is structured as follows. Chapter 2 surveys modificational relations within the nominal phrase. Since modification induces a number of the interesting category mixing effects sketched above, it is important for us to be reasonably explicit about the way we understand modifiers, but the discussion in this chapter will be largely informal and a rather general characterization will suffice. Following traditional literature, we treat inalienable and alienable possessives as the two basic semantic types of the possessive relation, and consider the former as more canonical than the latter. In addition we will discuss what we call 'modification-by-noun'. This is a relation between two nouns (or more accurately, two nominal denotations) but a kind of attributive modification, although not a canonical kind. These types of relation will be

1.5 Structure of the Book 37

contrasted with constructions in which a head noun is modified by a canonical attributive modifier such as a qualitative adjective denoting a gradable property.

After introducing the notions of canonical and non-canonical modifiers, we will turn to a more detailed discussion of morphosyntactic strategies employed to express them in the languages of the world. We propose a number of implicational generalizations in this respect and speculate on how they may be motivated. In particular, we will propose the Possession-Modification Scale, which represents typologically common polyfunctionality patterns. Languages can select which segment of this scale to use as their principal strategy for expressing relevant relations. Our conclusion is that there is an inherent connection between possession and modification, and, essentially, the affinity between these distinct, but closely related, types of construction lies in their semantics.

Chapter 3 defines the main empirical domain of the book by providing a descriptive picture of noun–adjective mixing in nominal phrases. We will identify a series of constructions that allow a noun to modify another noun by assuming some aspects of the form of an adjective. Throughout our discussion we will pay particular attention to the ways in which these constructions exhibit categorial mismatch. One of the key phenomena is the BNMP, as seen regularly in N-N compounds but also found in some denominal adjectives. We will cite examples from a number of languages where most or essentially all nouns productively form an adjective, but where this base may itself be modified by a syntactic modifier as though it were still a syntactically represented noun. The categorial mixing is especially evident in languages in which adjectives agree with nouns: an adjective such as *short* in the equivalent of *short-sleeved* would take the same agreement as it would take if it were modifying the noun *sleeve*, even though that noun does not appear as such as a syntactic terminal.

Chapter 4 will survey a number of approaches to the problem of mixed categories, distinguishing broadly between 'single projection' and 'dual projection' approaches, following Bresnan and Mugane (2006). We will demonstrate a number of problems with the accounts on which the derivational affix takes scope over a syntactic phrase because the affix itself is introduced in the syntax. There are cases which cannot be handled in this manner because the affix lacks crucial syntactic properties we would otherwise expect to see, such as taking wide scope over coordinated hosts, and because the syntactic approach cannot account for some of the properties of the derived modifier. For these cases a lexical approach is preferred. We survey a number of previous studies within LFG (Bresnan and Mugane 2006; Lowe 2016) and HPSG (Malouf 2000a, b), and argue that they fail to draw the right distinctions.

38 *Introduction: Word Categories and Category Mixing*

Chapter 5 introduces our assumptions about lexical representations – the form of the dictionary entry of a word. In this model the morphological, syntactic, and semantic dimensions of a lexical representation are in principle independent and can be fractionated. An important question will be how we decide when two word forms are members of one lexeme or members of two distinct lexemes: the Lexeme Individuation problem. We investigate this question against the background of explicit claims made within the HPSG framework, arguing for a conception under which lexemes are linguistic objects, some of whose properties are underspecified. The notion of a highly underspecified lexemic entry, whose properties are specified by default statements, will be central to our analysis of mixed categories of the transpositional type.

In Chapter 6 we outline an approach to lexical relatedness developed in Spencer (2013), Generalized Paradigm Function Morphology (GPFM), and show how this model could be used to describe category mixing. That model makes extensive use of the notion of underspecified entries whose properties are defined by default principles, which are overridden in specific cases. Following Spencer (2017b), we develop an approach to transpositions using the default inheritance machinery in conjunction with a feature REPRESENTATION to solve the problem of a 'paradigm-within-a-paradigm' ('lexeme-within-a-lexeme').

Chapter 7 sketches a model of attributive modification, broadly speaking within an HPSG frame of reference and its constructional variant Sign-Based Construction Grammar (SBCG), relying in particular on the analysis proposed by Ackerman and Nikolaeva (2013), appropriately modified so as to interface with the GPFM model of lexical representation proposed in Chapter 6.

Chapter 8 will make explicit our analysis of the set of noun–adjective mixed categories and illustrate how our model works by applying it to several contrasting types of denominal adjective. The first is the standard type of relational adjective found in English, French, Russian, and most other Indo-European languages. These are not true transpositions, and for this reason they behave like derivational types in respecting Lexical Integrity/Opacity. They are contrasted with three types of noun–adjective hybrid that exhibit syntagmatic mixing:

(i) relational adjectives and meaning-bearing denominal adjectives which can be formed from the base form of a noun or from a form marked for possessor agreement

(ii) genitive case-marked dependent nouns which agree like adjectives

(iii) compound nouns whose dependent noun agrees with the head it modifies (largely) in the manner of an adjective

Members of this class of denominal adjectives allow their noun base to be attributively modified, what we have called the Base Noun Modifiability Property. This property is counter to standard principles of Lexical Integrity, specifically the corollary of lexical opacity: syntactic principles have no access to the inner structure of words. In contrast, the relevant noun–adjective hybrids exhibit transparency effects because at the appropriate level of representation they are still nouns (while also being adjectives at other levels of representation). We conclude Chapter 8 by providing a basic summary of our analysis, before presenting general conclusions in Chapter 9.

2 *Modification Constructions*

2.1 Introduction

This chapter informally introduces the semantics of adnominal modifiers, provides a selective survey of the principal ways in which they can be expressed across the world's languages, and analyses the major typological patterns that emerge. Only unambiguous phrase-internal head-dependent relations are taken into account here, while external possessors, discontinuous modifiers, and so-called non-configurational languages where the notion of NP/DP is problematic altogether are excluded from consideration.

Following Nikolaeva and Spencer (2012) we will be assuming that there are two canonical types of modifiers: attributive property modifiers and possessors (specifically, inalienable possessors). We further show that in addition to canonical attributive modification, which involves a property word, nouns can be modified by an entity with a noun-like denotation, something we refer to as 'modification-by-noun'. This gives us four broadly defined semantic types: inalienable possession, alienable possession, modification-by-noun, and attributive modification proper ('modification-by-adjective').

2.2 Attributive Modification

In this section we summarize the properties of canonical attributive modifiers and the possible semantic restrictions on the head and the modifier.

2.2.1 Overview of Semantics

The standard way in which set theoretic or model theoretic approaches to semantics handle attributive modification is by interpreting both the modifier (i.e. the modifying adjective) and the modified noun as predicates and then combining the meanings of the two: see Siegel (1980), Higginbotham (1985), Larson and Segal (1995), Heim and Kratzer (1998), Morzycki (2016) and many

2.2 Attributive Modification   41

others.[1] Attributive modifiers are usually represented as one-place predicates similar to intransitive verbs, and their only argument is associated with the modified noun. Like nouns, adjectives are of property-denoting type <e,t>, so, for instance, the adjective *big* denotes the set of entities that have the property of being big.

The principal meaning of attributive modification by adjectives is set intersection, at least in their pragmatically neutral usage. The property denoted by the adjective and the property denoted by the noun are combined to yield the property an individual has if and only if it satisfies them both. The type of resulting meaning is just like the unmodified meaning of the head noun, but intersective modification narrows the concept associated with this noun. Distributionally, then, an adjective-noun group is identical to a common noun in isolation.

For example, we can take the intersective adjective *red* and the common noun *ball* to denote sets of individuals. Interpretation can then proceed compositionally, as in (1).

(1)   *the red ball*: the (ball ∩ red) = $\lambda x[\textbf{red}(x) \wedge \textbf{ball}(x)]$

Here the interpretation is conjunctive and ascriptive: the denotation of the adjective identifies a certain subset in the denotation of the head noun by specifying which ball is meant. In other words, the meaning of the phrase *red ball* is essentially the set of all those entities which are both members of the set of red things and also members of the set of balls. Another perspective on this is to look at the entailments of the expression compared with related expressions: *X is a red ball* entails that X is red and X is a ball. But if X is a red ball, then under any other description it remains a red entity. For instance, if X is a red ball and X is also a toy, then it is a red toy.

There are many semantic subtleties associated with intersective modification that are not immediately relevant for our topic, such as the relative order of adjectives, scope properties, ambiguity, degree and comparative constructions, and the stage-level/individual-level contrast (for a recent overview of these issues see Morzycki, 2016). While we can leave aside most of these questions, it is important to note that intersective interpretation of attributive modification is inadequate in a series of well-known cases.

There are adjectives for which less stringent entailments apply, namely subsective adjectives such as *skilful* (*a skilful surgeon*) or *large*. The expression *X is a large mouse* entails that X is an animal but not that X is a large animal. Kennedy (1999) and Kennedy and McNally (2005) show that adjectives such as

---

[1]   For a critique of this position see Truswell (2004) and the literature cited there.

42   *Modification Constructions*

large, small, or *good* are interpreted relative to some relevant standard, that is, a contextually salient property of individuals. In order to interpret the phrase *large mouse*, speakers need to know what sizes are appropriate for mice and then evaluate the size of the individual mouse based on this knowledge. In other instances the relevant property is not determined by the semantics of the modified noun but is established contextually.

Gradable adjectives can in fact be ambiguous in terms of intersectivity or subsectivity, the most well-known example being *Olga is a beautiful dancer,* which can mean (i) 'Olga is beautiful and is a dancer', or (ii) 'Olga dances beautifully', but the choice of both the noun and the adjective is crucial for achieving this kind of ambiguity (see Kennedy, 2007b and Morzycki, 2016, among others).

Other adjectives are not even subsective: *X is an alleged murderer* does not entail that X is a criminal. Of the non-intersective, non-subsective adjectives, some bear a negative entailment: *X is a fake gun* entails that X is not actually a gun. These are sometimes called 'privative adjectives', though that term is also used to denote adjectives that mean 'not having N' and so is better avoided. In any case such adjectives may not even be a separate class (Partee, 2010; Morzycki, 2016) but could be classified together with either subsective adjectives or the so-called 'modal' adjectives, e.g. *a former president.* The common semantic core of modal and 'privative' adjectives is intensionality: the meaning denoted by the modified phrase may hold of an individual even if the unmodified meaning does not. A former president is an individual who used to be a president but the property of being a president no longer holds for this individual; similarly, a fake gun has some properties in common with guns but is not a gun. *Alleged* is inherently modal too: see Morzycki (2016) for an application of intensional semantics to account for its meaning.

This variety of meanings raises the question as to what counts as a prototypical (or indeed canonical) attributive modifier.

2.2.2   *Canonical Attributive Modifiers*

We take intersective modification to be the canonical type of attributive modification and the canonical type of attributive modifier to be a word denoting some gradable property concept. This follows a long typological tradition (e.g. Croft, 1990; Dixon, 1991), as well as Jackendoff's (1990) influential approach to descriptive lexical semantics. Jackendoff assumes a *Property* as one of the universal ontological types. The idea is that the *Property* type is available to all languages, at least to the extent that all languages have ways of expressing the degree to which a *Thing* exhibits a given *Property*, by means of scalar modifiers, comparative/superlative constructions, and so on.

In Jackendoff's model *Property* is instantiated as an adjective in the default case. This is mirrored in prototype and canonical approaches to words classes introduced in Chapter 1. We maintain with others, including Croft (1991), Spencer (1999, 2005b) and Bhat (2000), that it is canonical for an adjective to denote a gradable property and, conversely, it is canonical for a gradable property to be denoted by an adjective.[2] It is of course true that even in English gradability is neither a necessary nor a sufficient condition for being an adjective, that some languages do not express it grammatically (see e.g. Kennedy, 2007a; Bochnak, 2013), and that some adjectives do not denote properties but rather introduce a participant in a situation or act as some kind of operator that shifts the world model. However, if a language has a category of adjective, it lexicalizes gradable property concepts though this category and, even in languages in which the adjective is a minor or peripheral class, its exemplars express prototypically gradable properties (Dixon, 2004). Although adjectives can normally be used for a variety of other functions, i.e. primary or secondary predication, these functions are derived, and therefore often require additional morphosyntactic marking or a collocation with a copular verb. A number of adjectives in English and in numerous other languages are in fact exclusively attributive, and there are languages where adjectives do not appear in the predicative function, e.g. Takelma, Tinrin, the Niger-Congo language Vata (Koopman, 1984), Malayalam, Yoruba, and Hua (see Dixon, 2004, 11).

Some intersective adjectives appear to be more canonical than others. Dixon's (1982) seminal paper, which inspired much subsequent work, offered a list of typical gradable property meanings including dimension (e.g. *big, small, narrow, thick, fat*), physical property (*hard, heavy, rough, smooth, hot, sour*), colour (*black, white, red*), human propensity (*happy, kind, cruel, rude, proud, wicked*), age (*new, young, old*), value (*good, bad*), and speed (*slow, fast*). Dixon's claim is that these meanings must be mapped onto the distinct category of adjective even in the languages which are otherwise short of adjectives such as Chinese or Hausa, and that therefore these meanings

---

[2] There are, of course, languages in which property words are nominal in nature and for which it might be very difficult to motivate an adjective category. In such languages attributive modification by property words is achieved by morphosyntactic strategies reminiscent of modification-by-noun. But that involves a different kind of mismatch from the one we are concerned with here.

44 *Modification Constructions*

can be considered prototypical. For us, prototypical (and canonical) property words are adjectives denoting properties of size, age, value, speed, other physical properties, and possibly some of the adjectives denoting human propensity. We differ, however, from Dixon (1982), Gil (2005), and a number of other typological studies in that we do not take colour terms to represent a prototypical property attribute. The reason is that, first, colour terms are not always gradable and, second, they tend to behave differently from other attributes. They are often grammaticalized from nouns and can sometimes retain nominal properties lacking in true property words. This is even found in English: for instance, in archaic or poetic registers we can say things like *a sky of blue, a coat of green, a wine of deepest red* and so on. These constructions are unavailable to non-colour terms: **a sky of bright, *a coat of warm, *a wine of (sickly) sweet*. On other idiosyncratic properties of colour adjectives see Kennedy and McNally (2010).

As far as syntax is concerned, much work, including Cinque's (1994, 1999, 2010) influential approach, has been devoted to the hierarchies of attributive adjective positions within DPs. For Cinque and his successors adjectives are specifiers of unique functional heads that are essentially semantically driven. In contrast, we take the canonical syntax of attributive modification to be optional adjunction. Where a language has a specifier system, we take it to be canonical for attributive adjuncts to be distinguished from specifiers by iterativity: it is non-canonical to have more than one specifier but canonically it is possible to have an indefinite number of attributive modifiers. This understanding is consistent with grammatical theories such as LFG or HPSG. In LFG attributive modifiers are treated as members of the adjunct set (represented as ADJ) of modifiers of nouns, and their combination with the nouns they modify is defined by a special adjunction rule (Dalrymple, 2001, 255ff). In standard HPSG (Sag et al., 2003) adjuncts are introduced by the Head Modifier Rule which makes reference to the feature MOD in the feature structure of the modifier (for more details see Chapter 7).

An additional point should be mentioned here, one first articulated by Sproat and Shih (1988): there are two ways of achieving attributive modification: 'direct modification' and 'indirect modification'. Direct modification is subject to ordering restrictions, whereas indirect modification has the ability to sidestep such restrictions. In some languages indirect modification involves more structure layered on top of a predicative modifier so it can be used attributively. Sproat and Shih provide the examples in (2) from Mandarin Chinese.

2.2 Attributive Modification   45

(2)   a.   fang-de   xiao-de   zhuo-zi
             square-DE small-DE table
             'small square table'

     b.   * fang   xiao   zhuo-zi
             square small table

The presence of the additional formative *-de* in (2a) is required to approximate the effect of the direct modification attempted in (2b). But reversing the order of the adjectives in (2b) fixes the problem too.

Normally, size adjectives must precede shape adjectives, as in (3).

(3)   xiao   fang   zhuo-zi
      small square table
      'small square table'

This only holds for truly (bare) attributive adjectives; ones augmented with *-de* are not subject to the restriction. What seems to be happening is that indirect modification with *-de* provides a way of sidestepping restrictions on the relative order of attributive adjectives. Indirect modification in Chinese is obviously morphosyntactically more complex than direct modification. The mainstream view is that all indirect modifiers are covertly predicative and sometimes they take the overt form of a relative clause or a structure that could be plausibly analysed as a reduced relative clause, whereas direct modifiers have a simpler internal structure lacking a predicative component and must occur in closer proximity to the head (Baker, 2003; Cinque, 2010). Sproat and Shih's original claim was that direct modification is semantically more versatile in that it can lead to non-intersective readings, whereas indirect modification only permits intersective modifiers. However, there are other positions; for further discussion of these issues across a number of languages see Larson and Takahashi (2007), vander Klok (2009), Cinque (2010), Shimoyama (2011), and Nagano and Shimada (2015), among others. We will think of direct intersective modifiers as canonical.[3]

We can now summarize the canonical syntactic and semantic properties of attributive modifiers adapting them from Nikolaeva and Spencer (2012) as in (4).

---

[3]   If Nagano and Shimada (2015) are right that intersective modifiers must be indirect in Japanese, this means that this language lacks canonical attributive modifiers.

46 *Modification Constructions*

(4)   Semantics:

(i)   Modifiers denote gradable property concepts and hence are one-place predicates
(ii) The modified word denotes a physical object
(iii) Modification is intersective

Syntax:

(iv) Modifiers are adjectives
(v)   The modified word is a noun
(vi) The modified word is the semantic and syntactic lexical head of the construction
(vii) Modifiers are direct adjuncts to noun heads
(viii) Modifiers do not take specifiers and other attributive modifiers

This picture is valid in general terms, but other morphosyntactic properties that may be characteristic of attributive modifiers are heavily language dependent. For example, for languages which have a wealth of adjective-oriented morphosyntactic devices a canonical attributive adjective will agree with the head for typical agreement features such as gender, number, case, and possibly others. We will see many examples throughout the book, but they are not our concern in the present section.

2.3   Possessive Constructions

A number of theories split possessives into two large classes: lexical (or intrinsic) possession and extrinsic possession (see e.g. Barker, 1997; Partee, 1983–1997; and Partee and Borschëv, 2003). The lexical/extrinsic distinction roughly corresponds to the traditional inalienable/alienable distinction, which we will be assuming here. In what follows we will interchangeably use the terms 'possessee' or 'possessed noun' as synonyms for other terms used in the literature such as 'possessum'.

2.3.1   *Canonical Inalienable Possession*

The twofold classification of possessives into lexical/intrinsic/inalienable and non-lexical/extrinsic/alienable raises the question as to which type is semantically 'primary'.

It is sometimes thought that the prototypical possessive relationships include part/whole, kinship, and legal ownership/disposal (Langacker, 1991, 169; Langacker, 1995, 59; Koptjevskaja-Tamm, 2001b, 961). However, while there is no apparent way of grouping these three meanings together in semantic terms, the alienable/inalienable distinction may be expressed in the argument structure as the distinction between relational vs. non-relational head nouns. Moreover, while many languages have unambiguous encoding of the alienable/inalienable distinction (Chappell and McGregor, 1996), the distinction between part/whole, kinship and ownership on the one hand, and other possessive meanings on the other, never seems to be grammaticalized. We therefore prefer to treat alienables and inalienables differently and view the latter as prototypical – and canonical – possession.

This is largely consistent with Taylor's (1989, 1995, 1996) prototype approach, according to which the semantics of possessives is best regarded as a cluster of independent properties. Thus, possession implies an exclusive asymmetric long-term (or permanent) relation and physical proximity between two entities, that for each possessee there is only one possessor who has the right to make use of the possessee, that the possessor is normally an individuated human being, and so on (Heine, 1997, 2001). Inalienable possession is prototypical because it is characterized by essentially all the relevant properties.

As has been known since Chomsky (1970), Jackendoff (1977), and Partee (1983–1997) the semantics (and perhaps the syntax) of possessives is largely determined by the nature of the possessed head nominal. In inalienable possession the head nominal is expected to be a relational noun such as a kin term, a meronym (part-of term, for instance, a body part), a topological noun, or a noun denoting an inherent property. Relational nouns are semantically dependent. Thus, a mother has to be someone's mother, a leg has to be a part of some body, piece of furniture etc., a friend has to be someone's friend, a name has to be the name of something/somebody, and so on. Deverbal relational nominals and gerunds express lexical possessive relations: for example, in the phrase *my purchase* the possessor is restricted to being a 'purchaser'.

The key idea underlying the semantics of inalienability is that certain noun denotations entail the existence of an additional referent bearing a semantic relation to that noun. The nature of this relation is unique and determined by the meaning of the relational head noun, which has some identifiable argument structure in addition to its general meaning. A possessor realizes an argument implicit in the meaning of the possessed noun itself, so the notion of inalienable possession refers to those nouns, or those nouns in certain usages, whose semantics effectively defines them as two-place predicates, say $\lambda x\lambda y.\textbf{head}(x,y)$, where the 'y' variable ranges over possible possessors ('somebody's head'). The representations for *Mary's head/daughter*

48 *Modification Constructions*

will therefore be roughly as in (5) (ignoring irrelevant subtleties, such as implied definiteness).

(5) a. λxλy.**head**(x,y)(**Mary**)

b. λxλy.**daughter**(x,y)(**Mary**)

It is well known that entities classified as inalienable vary from language to language (Chappell and McGregor, 1996, 89; Heine, 1997, among many others), and there does not seem to be any clear semantic basis for the alienable/inalienable opposition in a cross-linguistic sense, nor any universally applicable hierarchy of what counts as inalienable. What is more, while in most languages the alienable/inalienable opposition is binary, there may be different degrees of inalienability: some languages have several possessive classes. In other languages arguably the same nominal can be construed either as relational or non-relational and therefore participate in either inalienable or alienable possessive construction (e.g. see Koptjevskaja-Tamm (2003a, 705–706) on Khinalug, and von Prince (2016) on Daakaka, among others). Even in English some relational nouns are only optionally transitive in the sense that it is not necessary to express the noun's argument overtly (*She will make a good mother*, *A friend in need is a friend indeed*).[4] We will ignore these distinctions for present purposes. The general point is that the meaning of the relational noun provides a unique determinate specification of the nature of the relation between this noun and its possessor and in each language the choice is determined lexically: it has to do with the lexical semantics of the possessed noun rather than style, the speaker's construal of the situation or other similar factors (Nichols, 1992, 120).

The main properties of canonical inalienable possession can be reproduced after Nikolaeva and Spencer (2012) in somewhat modified form as shown in (6):

(6) Semantics:

(i) Possessees are relational nouns and hence are two-place predicates

(ii) Possessors are humans

(iii) The relation between possessor and possessee is permanent
Syntax:

(iv) The possessed entity is a noun

(v) The possessor is a noun

---

[4] More rarely a noun is obligatorily transitive (*sake* can only be used in a possessive construction, for instance).

(vi) The possessed noun is the semantic and syntactic head of the possessive construction

(vii) The possessor expresses the argument of the possessed noun

(viii) (In languages with a specifier system), possessors occupy a specifier position

Criterion (v) captures the intuition that canonical possessors are canonical nouns and therefore have the potential to serve as referential expressions, may show independent number opposition, take attributive modifiers as adjuncts, and take determiners (and other possessors) as specifiers. Canonical possessors are specifiers as per criterion (viii), and therefore are in paradigmatic opposition to other specifiers. However, we will see later in the book that the possessor can be expressed by means of a syntactic (attributive) modifier, even though it is still an argument of the head noun.

2.3.2 Alienable Possession

Canonical inalienable possessives contrast with extrinsic or alienable possessives, which involve non-relational head nouns. Alienable possessives have long been known to convey a wide variety of meanings, of which ownership or possession, in a strict sense, is only one type. Many authors, including Hawkins (1981), Williams (1982, 283), and Sperber and Wilson (1986, 188) have stressed that the list of possible interpretations of the relation between the possessor and the possessee can be extended almost indefinitely, subject to contextual factors. For example, in cultures that have an institution of legal ownership the expression *Mary's book* will often be paraphrasable as something like 'book which Mary owns'. But this is by no means its only possible reading. Although there is often a bias for an ownership interpretation consistent with a paraphrase using the verb *own*, other relations may also be inferable. The phrase can also refer to the book that Mary wrote, the book that she is currently reading, the book she always talks about, the book she wants to buy, and so on.[5] It does not make a great deal of sense semantically to think of these interpretations as possession, despite the fact that this is commonly the type of term used to describe these constructions. The reason for this is that the formal means of expressing them are often the same as those for expressing ownership. Barker (2011) refers to such unspecified association between the possessor and the

---

[5] These widely diverse possessive meanings do not necessarily have the same status. In some situations there are relations that appear to be the only or at least the default interpretation for a specific possessive construction, see e.g. Taylor (1989, 681). Barker (1997) and Storto (2004) provide evidence that (legal) ownership is an unmarked interpretation of extrinsic possessives.

50   *Modification Constructions*

possessed as 'pragmatic', while Partee and Borschëv (2003) and Ackerman and Nikolaeva (2013) call it a 'free reading' and 'associative relation', respectively.

The multiple relations expressed by alienable possessives differ greatly with regard to their relative degree of prototypicality in Taylor's (1996) sense. The more relevant properties characterize the relation, the more it resembles the inalienable prototype. Deviations from the prototype are restricted by contextual conditions and can be described with reference to various parameters, such as control and time (Heine, 1997). Deviations are possible because for non-relational possessed nouns there is no exclusive candidate for possessor, so the interpretation of the intended 'possessive' relation is extrinsic to their lexical semantics. The interpretation of the possessive phrase is determined by the interaction between lexical semantics and the context, allowing for pragmatic/associative/free readings.

Some languages do in fact exhibit several morphosyntactically different alienable constructions which signal different kinds of semantic relation between the possessor and possessed. For instance, in Lonwolwol (Paton, 1971) alienable nouns can occur with one of the six indirect possessive hosts that denote the intended use of the possessum: edible possessive host, liquid possessive host, container possessive host, fire possessive host, vessel possessive host, and the general possessive host used for nouns not belonging to other categories. Which of the six hosts the alienable possessor noun occurs with does not only depend on its own meaning, but rather on the nature of the relation that holds between the possessor and the possessed. As we pointed out in Nikolaeva and Spencer (2012), what this means is that Lonwolwol has grammaticalized the expression of some possible relations within the very general semantically unspecified association which can hold between the alienable possessor and possessed. However, in more familiar cases of alienable possession the relation is open to multiple interpretations and does not involve the addition of a clearly identifiable semantic predicate.

Problems arise in those languages (like English) which usually express inalienable and alienable possession in the same way, for in that case we would expect the two constructions to share the same semantic representation. However, alienable possession expresses a one-place sortal noun denotation, not a two-place relational noun denotation. In other words, while a noun such as *head* or *daughter* implies an (inalienable) possessor and these expressions are really short for *head-of* or *daughter-of*, a non-relational noun such as *book* just denotes an entity.

A helpful summary of the issue is provided by Barker (2011) and Le Bruyn and Schoorlemmer (2016). They observe that the semantics of possessive constructions with relational nouns is relatively easy to account for compared to the one-place or sortal nouns whose argument structure does not contain reference to another entity. The latter must induce type-shifting when in possessive constructions. Barker (2011, 1114) writes:

> there must be some way to take a non-relational nominal and turn it into a relational nominal, perhaps by means of a type-shifting operator such as $\pi = \lambda P \lambda x \lambda y [Py \wedge Rxy]$, where R is a free (pragmatically controlled) variable standing for the possession relation.

In other words, non-relational nouns are generally one-place predicates, like adjectives, but within the alienable possessive construction an ordinary non-relational common noun such as *book* acquires an additional argument creating a relational predicate 'of Y'. Essentially this means that all possessives uniformly represent one type, the one provided by relational head nouns, and that the possessed noun ends up lexically specifying a set of possible readings in all possessive constructions (Partee and Borschëv, 1998; Vikner and Jensen, 2002).

All grammatical models have to have some way of representing the idea that a non-relational noun can undergo a kind of category shift to a two-place predicate to accommodate a possessor. One way of implementing this is to state it directly in the syntactic representation. For example, Szabolcsi (1994) and Laczkó (1997) handle possession in terms of DP-internal predication and analyse all possessive DPs as two-place relations of which the possessor is the subject associated with a specifier position within a maximal projection of a functional category D (Alexiadou and Wilder, 1998; Alexiadou et al., 2007, and references therein). The category D assigns a theta-role to the possessor, but this is arbitrary and largely attributed to a functional component of the construction. It merely serves to satisfy the theta-criterion without having a specified content, so that any semantically unrestricted relation can obtain between the possessor and possessed. What remains invariant is that, whatever the exact interpretation of this relation, the possessor is structurally more prominent than the possessed.[6]

---

[6] This mirrors the fact that the functional relationship between the possessor and the possessee is largely asymmetric: possessors function as pragmatic anchors (Hawkins, 1981; Fraurud, 1990; Koptjevskaja-Tamm, 2000, 2004) or reference points (Langacker, 1993, 1995) for identifying the possessee, but not the other way round.

52 *Modification Constructions*

The LFG model (Bresnan, 2001; Bresnan et al., 2016) deploys a variant of the type-shifting process to account for all types of possessive construction, including syntagmatically mixed nominalizations such as *Mary's writing the letter (so quickly)* (see Chapter 7). Bresnan proposes that the functional structure of a noun can be enriched by the addition of a POSS argument to the PRED value, hence the f-description [PRED: 'book'] becomes [PRED: 'book⟨(↑POSS)⟩'] (Spencer, 2013, 320–321). This approach can be modelled by means of the type-shifting mechanism proposed by Barker (2011).

However, the type-shifting which introduces a possessor argument makes it more difficult to represent the distinction between the two types of possession in those numerous languages that express them with significantly different morphosyntactic constructions. Moreover, it makes it harder to describe the languages among that set in which alienable possession is expressed using the same devices as other modificational constructions, in particular modification-by-noun, which we will introduce in the next section. It would be desirable to develop a more flexible description language which will accommodate all the typologically attested possibilities and patterns of polyfunctionality that we will discuss in Section 2.5.

We will therefore opt for a somewhat different way of handling alienable possession. As discussed above, alienable possession is something of a misnomer. The semantic relationship between the possessor and the possessee can be more or less anything, and legal possession is just one out of many (in those cultures which recognize such a concept). Indeed, one of the hidden difficulties with the type-shifting operation we have just described is that it implies that the possessor of the alienably possessed noun is a semantic argument of the possessee, and not just a syntactic argument. Therefore, we will follow Barker (1997) and others in understanding the alienable possessor and the possessee as co-arguments in a two-place relationship, but we will follow other authors, e.g. Higginbotham (1993), Partee (1983–1997), Partee and Borschëv (1998), Kathol (2002), Nikolaeva and Spencer (2012), and Ackerman and Nikolaeva (2013), in assuming that this relation is actually the underspecified semantically empty predicate. We symbolize it as $\mathfrak{R}$.

The predicate $\mathfrak{R}$ simply denotes a semantically vacuous indeterminate relationship between two entities. In the default case it is interpreted as (legal) ownership, but many languages allow non-ownership readings based on a contextually established association, as shown in (7).

(7) $\mathfrak{R}(\iota x.\mathbf{N}(x), NP)$

e.g. $\mathfrak{R}(\iota x.\mathbf{book}(x), \mathbf{Mary})$

What (7) expresses is the idea that the possessed noun has acquired an argument-like satellite and this is done constructionally. Thus, the overall shape of this semantic representation of alienable possession is very similar to that of inalienable possession, except that it requires the addition of the relation $\mathcal{R}$ in order to introduce the possessor argument, rather than that argument being implicit in the semantics of the head noun itself.

2.4   Modification-by-Noun

While in the canonical attributive construction the modifier is an adjective, we also find very interesting types of a non-canonical modification construction in which the modifier is categorially a noun (at least to some extent). There does not seem to be a standard term for this semantic phenomenon. It was referred to as the 'non-anchoring relation' in Koptjevskaja-Tamm (2000, 2004) and other work, or 'specification' in Heine (1997, 156–157), but the latter term is unfortunate because it is also used in defining phrase structure relations. We will therefore be using the term 'modification-by-noun' following Spencer (1999, 2013) and Nikolaeva and Spencer (2012). Although this notion is not one which has received a great deal of attention in the literature, it will be quite central to our topic. In this section we illustrate modification-by-noun by noun-noun (N-N) compounds of the Germanic type.

2.4.1   Analyses of N-N Compounds

We first look at the claims that the meaning of compounds can be in part determined by the semantics of the modified noun itself. This idea has a long history dating back at least to Lees' (1960) dissertation, and was developed in Levi's (1978) work on N-N compounds and relational adjectives, for instance. Spencer (2011, 49) refers to this mode of analysis as 'Lees' solution'.

One way to implement Lees' solution is to allow for a restricted set of semantic properties. The most well known of these approaches is Pustejovsky's model of the Generative Lexicon (Pustejovsky, 1991, 1995, 2016). Pustejovsky is concerned to explain the phenomenon of systematic polysemy. One simple instance of systematic polysemy is illustrated by the word *book* in English and many (all?) other languages. This word has both an 'abstract' and a 'concrete' interpretation, as in *This book was a bestseller/prescribed text, costs £10 ...* (abstract) vs. *This book has a torn cover, weighs 3 kg, is missing page 23 ...* (concrete). Here we are not dealing with true ambiguity, however, nor even the kind of polysemy illustrated by words such as *head* in *head of the family* vs.

54 *Modification Constructions*

John the Baptist's head. Two closely related meanings of this sort are called 'facets' of meaning by Cruse (1986). Likewise, for Pustejovsky (1993, 1995) a lexeme such as *book* denotes a dot object, that is, an object which consists of more than one constituent type simultaneously. Unlike truly ambiguous senses, the two senses of *book* can be conjoined, for instance: *The book is a bestseller even though it weighs 3kg.* Moreover, any word belonging to the same semantic field as *book* is likely to exhibit the same duality of sense: *newspaper, CD, video,* and so on.

Pustejovsky develops a general theory of the internal semantic structure of nominal and verbal lexemes (in later work the approach was extended to adjectives, see e.g. Bouillon, 1996, 1999; Bouillon and Busa, 2001). There are four 'interpretive levels' of semantic interpretation, called 'qualia' (singular 'quale'), as characterized as in Table 2.1 (Pustejovsky, 1995, 85–86).

The importance of Qualia Structure for our concerns is that it covers a great deal of semantic ground and has been applied to the semantics of N-N compounds and similar patterns. This is evident in Jackendoff's (2009) analysis of English, for instance. He provides a list of the semantic relations that can hold between modifier and head, noting that this list is essentially a summary of similar lists provided by those adopting Lees' solution.

It has also been argued that Romance N-N compounds such as French *homme-grenouille* literally 'man-frog', i.e. 'frogman', or Italian *uomo-pesce* 'man-fish', a cross between a human and a fish, do not involve a pragmatically or contextually defined relationship but rather appeal directly to aspects of the semantic structure of the constituent nouns. Thus, *uomo-pesce* might be a man (*uomo*) sharing certain of the FORMAL qualia of a fish (Delfitto and Melloni, 2009). A version of this idea has been expounded by Scalise and Bisetto (2009) in their typology of N-N compounds. They argue, for example, that we interpret the compound *apple cake* as 'cake made out of apples' because the word 'cake' implies something made out of ingredients and 'apple' is a sensible candidate for one of those ingredients. Thus, Scalise and Bisetto effectively appeal to the CONSTITUTIVE quale of the two components of the compound by identifying the Material of the apple with one of the Parts and Component Elements of the cake.

However, it is not clear that qualia are sufficient to characterize English N-N compounds, not only in ad hoc nonce uses, but even in their lexicalized form, where we tend to see a greater degree of semantic homogeneity. Take a compound with a fairly conventionalized meaning such as *coffee cup*. In addition to denoting a cup designed for drinking coffee from, this could,

Table 2.1 *Qualia structure in the Generative Lexicon*

(i) CONSTITUTIVE: the relation between an object and its constituents, or proper parts

    (a) Material
    (b) Weight
    (c) Parts and component elements

(ii) FORMAL: that which distinguishes the object within a larger domain

    (a) Orientation
    (b) Magnitude
    (c) Shape
    (d) Dimensionality
    (e) Colour
    (f) Position

(iii) TELIC: purpose and function of the object

    (a) Purpose that an agent has in performing an act
    (b) Built-in function or aim that specifies certain activities

(iv) AGENTIVE: factors involved in the origin or 'bringing about' of an object

    (a) Creator
    (b) Artifact
    (c) Natural kind
    (d) Causal chain

in principle, denote, say, the cup in which we keep our change for the coffee machine. Spencer (2011) points out that even some highly lexicalized compounds such as *speed camera* resist all attempts at a simple analysis in terms of a small number of semantic primitives. A speed camera is a camera set up on the roadside in the UK and other countries with the specific purpose (TELIC quale) of taking photographs of vehicles which are exceeding the speed limit or infringing some other traffic regulation. Only knowledge of the world (specifically of local traffic regulations) will allow a speaker to derive this meaning. Without the complete background it is impossible to understand the meaning of the compound, and a list of predicates such as those provided by

56   *Modification Constructions*

Levi (1978) or more recently Jackendoff (2009) will be insufficient to that task, or will be so specific as to be useless as primitives.[7]

The Romance compounds of the *uomo-pesce* type are better candidates for an analysis in terms of a set list of semantic predicates. The point here is that the meaning of *uomo-pesce* is heavily circumscribed compared to a similar-looking endocentric compound in English such as *fish man*. The Italian expression cannot mean 'man with some pragmatically determined relation to the concept "fish"; it can only mean 'man who has some of the formal appearance of a fish; part-man, part-fish'. However, it is just as likely that there is a grammatical reason for this difference. Romance languages do not have Germanic endocentric N-N compounds with canonical modification-by-noun semantics. The *uomo-pesce* examples are closer to appositional compounds of the type seen in English *màn-físh*, with primary stress on the second element. Thus, the Romance N-N compounds have to be interpreted as something like an object which shares some of the form of N1 and N2. This is not an instance of modification-by-noun; rather it is a special type of coordinative construction.

We therefore regard attempts to reduce the semantic interpretation of Germanic N-N compounds to definition in terms of a finite set of semantic primitives as misguided, whether for N-N compounds as such or for other types of grammatical construction in which some form of a noun or noun phrase is used to modify a head noun, such as relational adjectives or any of the other constructions we discuss in Chapter 3 (Newmeyer, 1979). For standard cases of modification-by-noun we will assume what Spencer (2011, 490) calls 'Downing's solution', discussed in the next section.

2.4.2   *Compounds as Modification-by-Noun*

In an important early work, Downing (1977) showed on the basis of an experimental study that it is impossible to catalogue compounding relationships exhaustively. Any list will at most reflect the fact that certain types of relationships are "of greater classificatory values than others" (Downing, 1977, 828). For example, for the newly created non-lexicalized compound *pea princess* the following interpretations were suggested among others by native speakers (Downing, 1977, 820): 'a fairy princess who rules the pea people', 'the fairy-tale princess who felt the pea under her mattresses',

---

[7]   More recently, the term *speed camera* has come to be superseded on roadside signs by a longer variant, which cannot be easily read if travelling at speed: *police enforcement camera*. This, if anything, is even more opaque than *speed camera*.

'the princess of the Pea kingdom', 'the princess shaped like a pea or with the colour of a pea', 'a princess whose family is rich with pea farms', and so on. There is nothing in the meaning of the compounding construction that can explain this and there is no way that we can derive the special meanings of *pea princess* from *pea* and *princess*.

The number of possible compounding relationships is in principle non-finite and the meaning of new coinages is defined pragmatically. If a speaker of English coins a new compound such as, say, *chequebook pen*, and this compound is interpretable in some specific context, then that interpretation can only be construed in terms of the (contextually given) understandings of the relationship between 'chequebook' and 'pen'. If a particular pen is used for signing cheques then it can be called *chequebook pen*, and if a pen came as a free gift when somebody opened a new bank account s/he might also call it *chequebook pen*. So the real function of N-N compounding is to permit this very general semantically unspecified relation to be expressed between two noun denotations (Spencer, 1999, 2013, and other work). The relation seems to be no less free than that between the possessor and possessed in alienable possessive constructions, and we can also symbolize it as $\mathfrak{R}$. Spencer (2013, 351) symbolizes the semantics of modification-by-noun as $\mathfrak{R}(N, N)$.

These considerations suggest that compounding is best thought of as a kind of modification. In the words of Koptjevskaja-Tamm, 'non-anchoring' construction "refers to a subclass of a broader class and often functions as a classificatory label for it, suggesting that the dependent and the head together correspond to one concept" (Koptjevskaja-Tamm, 2004, 156). Similarly, Heine (1997, 157) states that the 'specifying' element "refers to the same general entity as the specified". We agree with these basic characterizations and take modification-by-noun to be a semantic construction that characterizes the head noun by narrowing down the range of its possible referents. It therefore involves set intersection, just like canonical attributive adjectives, so the denotation of the dependent identifies a certain subset in the denotation of the head noun. For example, in the compound expression *chequebook pen* the notion 'pen' is given some kind of relation to the concept 'chequebook', thereby narrowing down its reference. We have an expression whose denotation is a subset of the denotation of *pen*. The subset is conventionally defined as the result of the relation between the denotation of the modifying N and the head N, hence *chequebook pen* means 'pen which bears some relation to the notion of "chequebook"'.

It must be noted that some accounts of N-N compounding are incompatible with the modification analysis. For instance, Ackema and Neeleman (2004, 80ff) claim that the relationship between the head N and the non-head N is

58   *Modification Constructions*

semantically opaque and hence non-compositional. Given that compounding is entirely productive in English, it is difficult to see how it could be analysed as a form of modification if it were completely non-compositional. However, the non-compositionality claim appears to be founded on a misunderstanding. In effect Ackema and Neeleman (2004) think of all compounds as idiomatic, and therefore mistake 'non-compositional' for 'semantically non-determinate'. Compounds do indeed tend to acquire fixed uses and unpredictable lexicalized meanings, especially if they have a high textual frequency, giving rise to the impression that the construction itself expresses some kind of meaning over and above the meaning of its parts. But in non-lexicalized nonce compounds there is no more than a loose relation between the head and its nominal modifier, which can take any conceivable, that is, contextually plausible form. The fact that the relationship between chequebook and pen has to be defined pragmatically rather than in terms of the fixed semantic representation does not make it non-compositional.

What our discussion in this section ultimately shows is that modification-by-noun has an intermediate status as far as its semantics is concerned: it shows some properties of alienable possession and some properties of canonical attributive modification (Nikolaeva and Spencer, 2012). We will see grammatical evidence for this claim in the next section, where we demonstrate that modification-by-noun often grammaticalizes either as a subtype of modification or as a subtype of (alienable) possession.

2.5   Towards a Typology

We have briefly introduced the major semantic types of adnominal modifiers, all of which are ways of establishing some sort of relation between two denotations within a nominal phrase. These are listed in (8).

(8) (A)   canonical attributive modification
     (B)   modification-by-noun
     (C)   alienable possession
     (D)   canonical inalienable possession

In this section we argue that the distinction between these types can be justified typologically. As we have demonstrated in earlier work (Nikolaeva and Spencer, 2012), the same encoding strategy can be used for more than one semantic function, but some polyfunctionality patterns are typologically more common than others.

2.5 Towards a Typology 59

2.5.1 Encoding Strategies

We first explain what we mean by those morphosyntactic encoding strategies that can in principle express adnominal modification in the languages of the world.[8] We will only discuss lexical possessors here. Modification-by-noun as defined above precludes pronominal dependents by definition; therefore, it makes sense to compare it only with lexical possessors. Moreover, pronominal possessors often employ a different strategy, tending to induce more head marking than lexical possessors (Nichols, 1986). In many syntactic frameworks pronominal possession is viewed as part of the functional structure of a nominal.

We will understand the notion of encoding strategy as either an overt morphological device (constructional marker) which expresses a construction-internal syntactic relation between the dependent and head, or the systematic lack of such a device. In the present context the term 'head' will refer to the possessee or a modified noun and the term 'dependent' will refer to possessors and other semantic types of modifiers. The morphological status of the constructional marker can differ, that is, it can be an affix, clitic, or phonologically unbound word, or correspond to a systematic prosodic device. Constructional markers can agree with another component of the construction and/or indicate the features of their own host. As we will see, agreement options work in either direction: head agrees with dependent or dependent agrees with head (or both). As a result agreement does not really define a head/dependent marking dichotomy in modificational constructions, even though this may seem a little perverse against the backdrop of the well-known head/dependent marking typology (Nichols, 1986), in which there is an implied opposition between 'head possessed noun agrees with dependent possessor' and 'dependent possessor noun is marked with genitive case'.

The position of the constructional marker(s) can also differ: they can be syntactically associated with the head or with the dependent, or they can be syntactically independent of either (though in practice such elements tend to be prosodically weak function words and therefore phonologically dependent on the left- or right-adjacent element, i.e. pronounced as enclitics or proclitics). At this stage we ignore possible distinctions in constituent structure. This is not because we do not regard constituency and word order as important (though

[8] Earlier overviews of encoding strategies for non-predicative possessives can be found in Koptjevskaja-Tamm (2001a, 2002, 2003a), Chappell and McGregor (1996), and various other works, whereas for attributive modification a survey of adjectival expressions and other cross-linguistically attested patterns is presented in Wetzer (1996), Bhat (1994), McNally (2016), and Rießler (2016), among others.

60   *Modification Constructions*

there may be languages in which word order never plays a significant role in encoding any of the constructions we discuss). Rather, the justification is practical. The descriptive materials on lesser studied languages are likely to provide us with reasonably secure information about morphology, but it is much rarer to find reliable information about syntactic structure beyond general remarks. At the same time, even for languages which have a long tradition of syntactic description, it is very difficult to know what we would be describing. For instance, a sufficiently careful survey of the literature in generative grammar on the English *'s* construction would reveal analyses which treat it as a genitive case marker, as a marker assigning (abstract) genitive case, as a determiner, as a possessive functional head (with various labels), and so on. For these reasons we ignore the purely syntactic aspects of such constructions until it becomes possible to say something substantive about the issue. It is, of course, quite possible that none of our conclusions will be valid once syntax is properly taken into account, but for the present we see no practicable alternative.

One consequence of this decision is that we will use the neutral term 'juxtaposition' for the patterns with no constructional marker independently of their underlying structure. We thus define this term over the most liberal interpretation of encoding strategy which permits differences in linear order of constituents, but it is important to emphasize that in fact we may be dealing with very different syntactic relations here. For example, we will show in Section 2.5.5 that in Northern Khanty juxtaposition is employed both for modification-by-noun and for regular possession, but Nikolaeva (2002) argues that the possession/modification-by-noun distinction is actually reflected in constituent structure: although the possessor and the modifying noun do not differ in terms of morphology, they occupy different structural positions, the latter being more closely associated with the head. Nonetheless, for the purpose of our typological survey both constructions represent the same encoding strategy in terms of morphological marking (lack of marking = juxtaposition).

The degree of morphosyntactic tightness between the elements of juxtapositional structures is not always clear and the existing descriptions do not always resolve this issue. Even for well-described languages juxtaposition may be difficult to distinguish from other grammatical phenomena which involve more than just linear ordering and adjacency. Frequently juxtaposed elements may receive special prosody (such as English compound stress) or trigger special phrase phonology. In addition, we may have to distinguish between syntactic adjacency and some other, tighter, degree of adjacency. In languages which clearly distinguish a syntactic word level and a phrase level, syntactic

2.5 *Towards a Typology* 61

adjacency is in general defined over phrases. In English, French, and various other languages a noun may be modified by a phrase whose lexical head is an adjective. Yet a prenominal attributive adjective is able to project only very limited types of phrase compared to its postnominal or predicative usage. This prompts Sadler and Arnold (1994) to speak about 'small constructions', mid-way between word level and phrase level, and Kageyama (2001) argues for a similar notion (his 'Word$^+$') on the basis of evidence from Japanese.[9]

Abstracting away from these complications, we can understand simple juxtaposition as the absence of constructional marking and stipulate adjacency between the head and the dependent, usually in a fixed order. Understood this way, juxtaposition is relatively easy to discern. We will have more to say about it in Section 2.5.7.

Before we proceed, it is also important to note the problem of identifying when an encoding strategy should be regarded as the language's principal strategy. Languages often borrow strategies from other languages or develop parallel sets of strategies. Thus, English has innovated a possessive construction with the *'s* clitic in addition to the *of*-phrase strategy, and in Russian the possessive adjectives derived from names and kin terms compete with the default genitive case strategy. This means that care is often required to ensure that the default strategy is identified. In the following the primary strategy for each language will be identified as the strategy which appears to be the most productive and the least lexically restricted.

2.5.2   *Distinct Encodings*

Some languages adopt a four-way split, that is, they employ four different encoding strategies as defined above for expressing the four semantic types A, B, C, and D. We can schematically represent this type as A ≠ B ≠ C ≠ D, where the sign '≠' indicates the non-identity of the main encoding strategy for the relevant semantic construction. Such languages are not that common, but they provide primary motivation for our four-way typology. In addition to Lele cited by Nikolaeva and Spencer (2012) in this context, languages which belong to this type are Tuvaluan (Besnier, 2000) and Hoava (Davis, 2003).

Like many other Austronesian languages, Tuvaluan has two possessive constructions: the so-called O-construction and the A-construction. Languages

---

[9] In the literature on noun incorporation we frequently see reference to N-V constructions in which the incorporated noun does not really form a compound with the verb, but which do not project a phrase either; see, for instance, Miner's (1986) distinction between loose compounding and genuine incorporation, echoed by various subsequent authors, such as Massam (2001) for Niuean, and Megerdoomian (2012) for Persian.

62   *Modification Constructions*

of this family differ as to the conditions under which each are used, but according to Besnier (2000) in Tuvaluan the A/O distinction corresponds to the alienability opposition and is lexically determined. A-possession counts as alienable, while inalienably owned nouns require the O-construction. The latter include parts in part/whole relationships, words denoting inherent properties, emotions, and sensations, inherent objects acquired through inheritance (clothing, canoes, homes, land), as well as things and people that are intimately connected with the possessor (e.g. kinship terms): see (9).

(9) a. te ato o te fale
          the roof O the house
          'the roof of the house'

    b. te tala a Evotia
          the story A Evotia
          'Evotia's story'

Most nouns unambiguously belong to one or the other class, but sometimes the choice of A-class depends on the context. Jackson and Jackson (1999, 27–28) mention that even words that normally belong to the O-class can participate in the A-construction if the relation between the possessor and the possessee is determined contextually rather than lexically. For instance, 'my house' will normally be rendered via O-possession, as in most cases this expression refers to the house which the speaker owns. However, if it means the house which the speaker does not own but is assigned to clean, the A-construction will be used. The point is that the semantic relation between the possessor and possessed noun in the O-construction is established by the meaning of the latter, while in the A-construction it is not predetermined by the argument structure of the head noun.

Modification-by-noun is achieved by what Jackson and Jackson's grammar refers to as 'nominal adjectives'. Nominal adjectives denote non-gradable properties, and they do not participate in comparative constructions or in expressing the degree of a quality. They do not agree with the head in number, as seen in (10).

(10) a. te   tifa   fatu
          DEF   plate   stone
          'the porcelain plate'

     b. tifa   fatu
          plate   stone
          'porcelain plates'

2.5 Towards a Typology 63

On the other hand, canonical attributive modification is expressed by 'verbal adjectives'. These denote gradable property concepts and behave in some ways like verbs. When used as modifiers, they agree in number, as in (11).

(11)   a.   se   tagata   valea
               INDF   man   ignorant
               'an ignorant man'
        b.   ne   taagata   vaallea
               some   man.PL   ignorant.PL
               '(some) ignorant men'

If number agreement is taken to be a constructional marker, we have four different strategies here.

Another Austronesian language, Hoava, has four possessive constructions (Davis, 2003). Three inalienable constructions are as follows: (i) for part/whole, inherent properties, and most family relations possessive agreement is required on the head noun; (ii) so-called 'edible' possession is expressed by an agreeing classifier; (iii) 'exclusive' possession denotes exclusive rights not shared by other people and is expressed by a possessive pronoun preceding the possessed. All other nominals count as alienable. Alienable possessives involve the possessive preposition *ta, te, tana*, which may host agreement.[10] These types are exemplified in (12a) to (12d), respectively:

(12)   a. sa belena sa   boko
           DEF tail.3SG DEF pig
           'pig's tail'
        b. ana   napo sa koburu
           CLASS.3SG drink DEF child
           'child's drink'
        c. nana   siki Jakia
           3SG.POSS dog Jakia
           'Jakia's dog'
        d. sa   hore te Iani
           DEF canoe of Iani
           'Iani's canoe'

As can be seen in (12), all four possessive constructions contain some sort of construction-internal marker, although its nature differs. In contrast,

---

[10] Free-standing possessive and modificational markers will normally be glossed as 'of' throughout the book.

64   *Modification Constructions*

modification-by-noun is expressed by compounds, i.e. juxtaposition, where the dependent follows the head. As in English, compounds are fully productive. Although their meaning may be idiomatic, this is not necessarily the case. Some examples are *nikana vaka* 'European man (literally: ship man)', *kabasa raro* 'kitchen (literally: house of pots)', *kabasa hinigala* 'garden house', and *kaha qato* 'tree bark (literally: tree skin)'. As in Tuvaluan, words expressing gradable properties are verbal in nature. When used as modifiers, they agree in number with the head, as shown in (13).

> (13)   ria   t<in>avete   lavatidi
>   DEF   works<NOM>   be.big.3PL
>   'the major works'

This kind of agreement is also possible on a small closed class of modifiers derived from nouns by reduplication, but the majority of nominal modifiers do not agree.

In a number of other languages an alienability opposition is absent, but modification-by-noun and attributive modification are clearly distinct from possession and from each other, so our four construction types are rendered by three encoding strategies as follows: A ≠ B ≠ C = D.

Kolyma Yukaghir (Uralo-Yukaghir) has a small closed class of basic adjectives which include about half a dozen items such as 'round', 'long', and 'new', but they are mostly used in frozen collocations (Maslova, 2003; Nikolaeva, 2005). The overwhelming majority of property words belong to the class of verbs. They have the full finite paradigm and most non-finite forms, and occur in all or most syntactic environments where non-qualitative verbs can occur. Canonical modification is expressed by attributive verbal forms, i.e. participles. Thus, the attributive construction formally resembles a relative clause, although it is unlikely to have a clausal status as such. The example in (14) shows a 'qualitative' verb *lige-* 'to be old' in the modifying function.[11]

> (14)   lige-jə   terikə
>   old-PTCP woman
>   'old woman'

Modification-by-noun is normally achieved by adding the suffix *-n/-d*, which is called the 'attributive form of nouns' in Maslova (2003). This might be a misnomer given that modification is not its only function: it is also used on objects of postpositions. However, it is true that in modern Kolyma Yukaghir

---

[11]   The transcription from Maslova (2003) has been modified.

2.5 Towards a Typology   65

it is widely used on non-referential nominal modifiers.[12] The relationship between the head and the dependent is one of the typical non-anchoring relationships such as material, species, kind, and the like (Maslova, 2003, 116–118), as seen in (15), but there are virtually no semantic restrictions here.

(15)   a.   ša:-n   qanmuja:jə
             tree-ATTR spoon
             'wooden spoon'
       b.   jaqa-n   pajpə
             Yakut-ATTR woman
             'Yakut woman'
       c.   toukə-n   mi:d'i:
             dog-ATTR sledge
             'dog sledge'
       d.   mure-d   igejə
             shoe-ATTR rope
             'shoe lace'

Alienable and inalienable possession are not formally distinguished. Both types are encoded by juxtaposition of the possessor and possessed, but possessed nouns can optionally host a third person possessive marker (-*gi* in the nominative and -*də*- in oblique cases) conditioned by the discourse prominence of the possessor, as shown in (16).

(16)   a.   mət   terikə   aŋd'ə
             I   woman   eye
             'my wife's eye(s)'
       b.   qa:qa: numö
             bear   house
             'bear's den'
       c.   taŋ   šöjl'bul   iri-də-gə
             that   mouse   belly-POSS.3-LOC
             'in the belly of that mouse'
       d.   qa:qa: numö-gi
             bear   house-POSS.3
             'bear's den'

Turkish shows essentially the same split. Attributive adjectives precede the head and show no agreement. There are two types of izafet

---

[12] Interestingly, in closely related Tundra Yukaghir the -*n*/-*d* marking has spread to possessive and attributive constructions, albeit that it is mostly optional in these functions.

66 *Modification Constructions*

constructions: so-called definite and indefinite izafet. The definite izafet is a double-marking construction, while the indefinite izafet is head marking. The definite izafet expresses both alienable and inalienable possession, while the indefinite izafet typically involves non-referential dependents and renders various kinds of modification-by-noun relations between two nominals (Göksel and Kerslake, 2005). There are other minor strategies for expressing modification-by-noun: the relationship of material and gender, for instance, as well as some nationalities may be expressed by juxtaposition (Boeder and Schroeder, 2000). Ignoring these marginal strategies which are not productive and only apply to a certain subset of lexical items, we can say that, by and large, Turkish and Kolyma Yukaghir employ three distinct strategies to render the four relevant semantic types, due to the fact that the alienability opposition is absent.[13]

2.5.3 *Possession vs. Modification*

The split $A = B \neq C = D$ is perhaps the most natural. It reflects the possession vs. modification distinction and is remarkably widespread. English belongs to this type if N-N compounding introduced in Section 2.4 is taken to represent the juxtapositional strategy in a manner comparable to modification by attributive adjectives (recall that the identity of surface strategies as defined above does not guarantee identity of syntax). Other languages in which juxtaposition is employed for both types of modification and for the head-marked possessives are Hungarian (Uralic) and Malagasy (Austronesian) (Keenan and Polinsky, 1998), whereas Taleshi (Iranian) exhibits two different forms of dependent marking to signal the possession–modification split (Nikolaeva and Spencer, 2012). In Nikolaeva and Spencer (2012) we also described the Tundra Nenets system, where modification-by-noun is expressed by compound-like juxtaposition and modifying nouns agree with the head noun in number, similarly to attributive adjectives but unlike genitive possessors (for an analysis see Chapter 8). A pattern roughly similar to Tundra Nenets obtains in a Numic language, Tümpisa (Panamint) Shoshone, described by Dayley (1989), where genitives do not agree, whereas adjectives and modificational nouns show case agreement.

In Tagalog the principal possessive construction is expressed by marking the possessor with a prenominal marker *ng* (pronounced /naŋ/) for common

---

[13] However, Öztürk and Taylan (2016) argue for an additional alienable-only possessive construction in Turkish. It does not involve any type-shifting operation; instead the possessor is analysed as having modifier syntax.

2.5 Towards a Typology   67

nouns or *ni, nina* for singular/plural proper nouns, glossed 'LKR' for 'linker', as shown in (17).

(17) a. lapis ng bata
          pencil LKR child
          'the/a child's pencil'

      b. bahay nina Maria
          house LKR Maria
          'the house of Maria (and her family/group)'

Attributive adjective modification and modification-by-noun use a different ezafe-type strategy. The modifying adjective or noun is connected to the head noun by means of a linker *na/ng*. The *ng* form is pronounced /ŋ/ and appears as an enclitic or phrasal affix on the rightmost constituent of the attributive phrase, provided the last word ends in a vowel, /h, ʔ, n/, as shown in (18) (Schachter and Otanes, 1972, 118). In all other cases the *na* allomorph is selected, as shown in (19):

(18)   mabuti /mabuːtih/ 'good'
         mayumi /mayuːmi/ 'modest'
         mayaman /mayaːman/ 'rich'

         mabuting tao   'good person'
         mayuming tao   'modest person'
         mayamang tao   'rich person'

(19)   masipag /masiːpag/ 'diligent'
         magalang /magaːlaŋ/ 'courteous'
         matakaw /mataːkaw/ 'greedy'

         masipag na tao   'diligent person'
         magalang na tao   'courteous person'
         matakaw na tao   'greedy person'

In contrast to possessive constructions, the order of head and dependent is not fixed here. This is equally true of attributive adjectives (20a) or modification by phrases, for instance prepositional phrases (20b) (Schachter and Otanes, 1972, 118).

(20) a. bagong libro vs. librong   bago
          new.LKR book   book.LKR new
          'new book'

      b. nasa mesang libro vs. librong   nasa mesa
          on   table.LKR book   book.LKR on   table
          'the book on the table'

68   *Modification Constructions*

The difference in word order is related to information structure, with the new information tending to come after old information. Interestingly, this freedom of word order, or rather the deployment of word order to express information structure, is also found with modification-by-noun. Schachter and Otanes (1972, 118) discuss at some length the distinction between (21a) and (21b), both of which would be translated into English as 'toy stove':[14]

(21)   a.   kalang   laruan
            stove.LKR   toy
       b.   laruang   kalan
            toy.LKR   stove

Given that the *na/ng* linker remains in the same linear position whatever the order of head and dependent, we can conclude that it is not syntactically affiliated with either constituent.

We also find languages with the alienability opposition and homonymy between modification-by-noun and attributive modification. They instantiate the A = B ≠ C ≠ D pattern. Maori is another Austronesian language with O- and A-possession. According to Bauer (1997), the A-construction is used when the possessor exercises some dominance or control over the possessee, and the O-construction is used otherwise, so from this point of view the latter is unmarked. Most items only occur with one type of possession, because of their intrinsic semantic properties. The A-class includes the items which the possessor acquires in his/her lifetime (e.g. spouse, children, uninherited objects) and personal property such as small portable objects and food. The O-class includes clothing, houses, means of transport, furniture, body parts, and emotions, and, for some speakers, water. However, Bauer notes that this distinction is vague in the sense that some nouns may occur in both constructions depending on the construal of the relationship between two nominal denotations by the speaker: see (22a) and (22b)

(22)   a.   te   rongoa   a Pou
            DEF medicine A Pou
            'Pou's medicine (which he made)'

---

[14]   These compounds are syntactic compounds, or productively formed compounds with compositional semantics. Tagalog also has lexical(ized) compounds in which the head noun is always to the right, and which differ morphosyntactically from the productive compounds. In these lexical compounds the *ng* linker appears whenever the phonological conditions for it are met. However, there is no overt linker otherwise, and Schachter and Otanes (1972, 107) regard this as indicating that the *na* linker simply has a zero allomorph in such contexts.

2.5 *Towards a Typology* 69

b. te   rongoa   o Pou
DEF medicine O Pou
'Pou's medicine (for him to take)'

In addition, there seems to be some variation among speakers in the treatment of new items acquired by the Maori culture. The point is that, although the distinction between two types of possessives deviates from standard content of the alienable/inalienable opposition and is described in terms of dominance or control rather than inalienability per se, at its core the possessive classification is still lexically based. There is a default or open class and a specified class of nouns that systematically fall into the closed A-category. For such nouns the possessive relation can only have one interpretation, and presumably this property must be represented in their argument structure.

Modification is postnominal; there is no agreement or any other construction-internal marker. The two main types of modifiers are illustrated below: in (23) we show modification-by-noun and (24) demonstrates a property word equivalent in meaning to a European adjective.

(23)   a. te   huruhuru manu
DEF feather   bird
'the bird feather'

b. te   whakapū ahi
DEF siren   fire
'the fire siren'

(24)   wāhi pai
place good
'good place'

As in other Austronesian languages, property words are actually stative verbs ('state intransitives', in Bauer's terminology) and they exhibit verbal properties in non-attributive use. Some stative intransitives undergo reduplication to realize what Bauer refers to as 'distributiveness', i.e. the attribution of the property to every member of the group. Distributive/plural reduplication does not seem to be obligatory, since some speakers accept non-reduplicated forms modifying plural nouns. In any case, it is only observed in a small subgroup of property words; most of them do not show number agreement, as in Hoava, which was addressed in Section 2.5.2.

The situation in a number of other Austronesian languages, e.g. Samoan (Mosel and Hovdhaugen, 1992) and Tamambo (Jauncey, 2011), is largely the same. In all these languages modification-by-noun patterns together

70   *Modification Constructions*

with canonical attributive modification, but possessive constructions exhibit distinctly different strategies.

2.5.4   *Modification-by-Nominal-Concept vs. Attributive Modification*

Languages which express attributive modification can have a distinct morphosyntactic strategy to do this that is not employed for other kinds of semantic relation. In contrast, modification-by-noun patterns together with possessive constructions. If there is no alienability split, the A $\neq$ B = C = D pattern is produced.

A dependent-double marking strategy is observed in those languages where the genitive contrasts sharply with adjectives in terms of its morphosyntax, but is semantically ambiguous: it is used both for possession and modification-by-noun (see Koptjevskaja-Tamm, 2001a, 2003a,b, 2004 for extensive discussion). We will address such cases at some length in Chapter 3. Head-dependent marking possessive constructions typically involve agreement. According to Nikolaeva and Tolskaya (2001), the possessive construction in Udihe is head-final; the possessor stands in the nominative and must be cross-referenced by person/number agreement on the head. The third person singular possessive affix is *-ni*. The construction conveys the usual range of possessive meanings, both inalienable and alienable, as shown in (25).[15]

(25) a. giuse   ule:-ni
          roe   flesh-3SG
          'roe's flesh'
      b. mama   tege-ni
          grandmother gown-3SG
          'grandmother's gown'

Additionally, what appears to be the possessive construction, at least on the surface, serves to express modification-by-noun, which, in contrast to true possessives, usually contains non-referential dependents. This makes the head-marked construction ambiguous between two readings, as shown in Table 2.2.

Attributive adjectives can be identified by a number of morphological and syntactic criteria (Nikolaeva, 2008). Qualitative adjectives have

---

[15] The additional suffix *-ŋi*, traditionally referred to as 'alienable' in the descriptions of Udihe, can indicate a somewhat looser semantic relation between the possessor and possessed, but this is not equivalent to the alienability distinction.

2.5 Towards a Typology   71

Table 2.2 *Modification/possession in Udihe*

	Modification	Possession
keige sita-ni	'kitten'	'cat's young'
in'ei dili-ni	'dog head'	'dog's head'
xoto skola-ni	'city school'	'the school in/of the city'
niŋka sexi-ni	'Chinese fabric'	'the fabric of a/the Chinese person'

meanings associated with canonical adjectives in other languages, e.g. *sagdi zugdi* 'big house', *imexi mo:* 'new firewood', and *ge: mäna* 'bad flour'. It is also worth mentioning that Udihe has relational adjectives fairly productively derived from nouns. We illustrate them in Chapter 3. This makes it difficult to classify Udihe unambiguously, as it also shows properties of the A ≠ B ≠ C = D type. However, similar splits occur in other languages: modification-by-noun often employs several strategies some of which are more marginal than others, as was noted for Turkish in Section 2.5.2.

We also find languages with an alienability split in which only non-canonical alienable possession (but not canonical inalienable possession) assimilates in some sense to the class of modifiers, that is, A ≠ B = C ≠ D. In this pattern modification-by-noun is formally indistinguishable from alienable possession, but inalienable possession and canonical modification are expressed by other means. In Nikolaeva and Spencer (2012) we discussed Miya (Chadic) and Yamphu (Tibeto-Burman) as belonging to this type. In these languages modification-by-noun and alienable possession exemplify the same encoding strategy: the dependent hosts an attributivizing marker and agrees with the head. This strategy differs from both non-agreeing inalienable genitives and canonical adjectives, but it exhibits canonical modificational morphosyntax (attributive concord).

Another example is Maltese Arabic (Semitic), which has two possessive constructions (Koptjevskaja-Tamm, 1997). Inalienable possession requires the construct state: the possessed noun is followed by the definite form of the possessor and the head noun does not host its own determiner. Alienable possession is expressed by the 'analytical genitive', where the possessor is preceded by the genitive-like preposition and the head noun can host the definite article. These two options are illustrated in (26).

72   *Modification Constructions*

(26)   a.   bin issultān
          son DEF.king
          'the king's son'
       b.   issiġġu   ta'Pietru
          DEF.chair of Peter
          'Peter's chair'

The construct state is mainly used with head nouns referring to kinship relations and body parts, i.e. it instantiates the two most typical inalienable meanings. The meaning of the genitival construction is very broad. It is not limited to alienable possession, as exemplified in (26b), where some kind of ownership relation obtains and the possessor is a referential expression, but is also employed to encode various qualitative meanings studied in Koptjevskaja-Tamm's (1997) paper, for example the relation of material, purpose, quality, time, and so on. In such cases the dependent noun is non-referential and, unlike the construct state possessor, it does not have to host the definite article: see (27).

(27)   a.   gèajnejn ta' serq
          eye.DU   of hawk
          'hawk eyes'

       b.   kittieb ta' talent kbir
          writer of talent big
          'a writer of great talent'

       c.   vjaġġ   ta' sagètejn
          journey of hour.DU
          'a two hour journey'

Simple adjectives are right-adjacent to the head noun and agree with it in definiteness: see (28).

(28)   issiġġu   żzgèir
       DEF.chair DEF.little
       'the little chair'

Definiteness agreement distinguishes the adjectival construction from the construct state, since in the construct state the head noun cannot host the definite article, but importantly, modification-by-noun is homonymous with alienable possession.

2.5.5   Single Strategy

As emphasized in Nikolaeva and Spencer (2012), all four relevant semantic types may be expressed by essentially the same encoding strategy. The close relationship between the expression of possession and modification is particularly clearly revealed by the well-known ezafe family of constructions in Persian and other Iranian languages. The construction-internal relation is signalled here by an invariant marker which is either not attached to either constituent or is encliticized to the right edge of the leftmost member of the construction (this typically means the head). In Persian the ezafe *-(y)e* is an invariable clitic; it signals the dependency between the possessor and the possessed head noun, as well as various attributive relationships (and sometimes other types of phrase, such as prepositional phrases). The examples in (29) are from Mahootian (1997).[16]

(29)   a. ketâb-e an mard
            book-EZ that man
            'that man's book'

        b. angoštar-e almas
            ring-EZ   diamond
            'diamond ring'

        c. almas-e   bozorg
            diamond-EZ big
            'a big diamond'

It is possible to have a sequence of such ezafe-marked modifiers, showing fairly complex dependency structures, as in (30) (Ghomeshi, 1997, 736). Note in particular that the right most ezafe marker (on *shirvuni*) actually serves to link *ali* 'Ali' to *otâq* 'room'.

(30)   [[otâq-e kučik]-e [zir-e   širvuni]]-e ali
        room-EZ small-EZ under-EZ root-EZ   Ali
        'Ali's small room under the roof'

For extensive arguments in favour of the constituent structure implicit in this example see Samvelian (2007). Working within the HPSG model, she proposed that the Persian ezafe is a phrasal affix generated by the morphological component; it attaches to nominal heads and marks them morphologically as expecting a modifier (for alternative analyses see Ghomeshi, 1997 and Bögel

---

16 We normalize transcriptions for the Persian examples here and below.

74 *Modification Constructions*

and Sulger, 2008). This pattern in its core is also characteristic of other Iranian languages related to Persian, e.g. Tajik (Perry, 2005).

Kurmanji Kurdish (Wurzel, 1997; see also Kurdoev, 1978, 70ff) has a construction which is usually referred to as 'ezafe', but which has an important difference from the Standard Persian equivalent. In this language, ezafe signals the gender/number of the possessed noun, though distinguishing gender in the singular only. Thus, in effect the ezafe redundantly signals the number/gender properties of its own host. In other respects the Kurmanji ezafe is much like its Persian congener; in particular, it is used to mark attributive modification as well as possession, and from strings of ezafe constructions it is clear that the ezafe is a kind of edge inflection.

Another language of this type is Hokkien (Sino-Tibetan), where all types of modifiers require the same constructional marker which happens to be an unchangeable free-standing particle (Koptjevskaja-Tamm, 2003a, 698), though it is not known whether it is syntactically associated with the head or dependent. An example of double marking is provided by Aleut (Eskimo-Aleut) (Geoghegan, 1944; Bergsland, 1997; Golovko, 1997). There are two construction-internal markers, one on the head, referred to as 'possessive' by Golovko, and one on the dependent, usually referred to as 'relative'. Both realize the number feature of their host. This essentially possessive strategy expresses attributive modification, possession, and modification-by-noun (the latter only with the singular relative marker).

The neutral juxtapositional strategy is exemplified by Northern Khanty, also known as Northern Ostyak (Uralic) (Nikolaeva, 1999). In this language attributive adjectives are morphologically unmarked and do not agree with the head: see (31).

(31) jăm xot-ət-na
      good house-PL-LOC
      'in the good houses'

The juxtaposition of two nouns renders inalienable (32a) or alienable (32b) possession, but the same construction may have a non-possessive modificational meaning (32c).

(32) a. ewi sem
          girl eye
          'girl's eye(s)'
      b. ewi laraś
          girl box
          'girl's box'

c. ńǎń laraś
bread box
'box for bread, bread box'

Nominal modifiers serve for qualification of the head noun by reference to its various qualia-like properties (material, purpose/function, quality, origin, and the like) or simply express some kind of loose association between the two concepts, e.g. *ur xot* 'forest tent, tent in a forest', *niŋ ńawrem* 'daughter (literally: female child)', and *nǎŋ porɔx* 'larch-tree stump'. Like attributive adjectives, modifying nouns do not agree with the head and do not take determiners, but unlike adjectives they can be modified by an adjective and are recursive: *kǎlaŋ sǎx mǎlśaŋ* 'parka made of reindeer skin (reindeer skin parka)'. We can therefore expect that at least in some instances the juxtapositional construction would be ambiguous between the possessive and non-possessive modificational readings. This prediction turns out to be correct: *kǎlaŋ sem* can mean both 'reindeer's eyes, eyes of the/a reindeer' and 'reindeer eyes'. The meaning of the construction strongly depends, of course, on the meaning of its components. Possessors tend to be animate and often human, while non-possessive modifiers tend to be inanimate and are often mass or abstract nouns. Inanimate concrete nouns are likely to serve in both functions, and this is exactly the area in which ambiguity is the most plausible.

Note also that a possessor optionally triggers third possessive agreement on the head, as illustrated in (33), synonymous with (32b). This is totally impossible for true adjectives (or for modification-by-noun, for that matter).[17]

(33)　ewi laraś-əl
girl box-3SG
'girl's box'

The expressions in (34a) and (34b) are in principle grammatical but only in the meaning 'his/her box for bread' and 'his/her good box', respectively.

(34)　　a.　ńǎń laraś-əl
bread box-3SG
≠ 'box for bread, bread box'

b.　jǎm laraś-əl
good box-3SG
≠ 'good box'

---

[17] Agreement is conditioned by the discourse prominence (topicality) of the possessor, much as in Kolyma Yukaghir.

76   Modification Constructions

On the other hand, nouns and adjectives differ syntactically when used as attributive modifiers. In particular, the modifying noun must be adjacent to the head noun. When it is not, the expression is ungrammatical: see (35).

(35)   * ńăń   jăm   laraś
       bread good box
       [intended: 'good box for bread, good bread box']

Conversely, an attributive adjective can be separated from the head. Thus, (36) is ambiguous because *jăm* 'good' can modify either *ńăń* 'bread' (37a), or *laraś* 'box' (37b).

(36)   jăm   ńăń   laraś
       good bread box
       'good box for bread, box for good bread'

(37)   a.   jăm   [ńăń   laraś]
            good [breadbox]
            'good box for bread'

       b.   [jăm   ńăń]   laraś
            [good bread] box
            'box for good bread'

We can therefore conclude that nouns and adjectives are distinct grammatical classes and that the modifying noun in (32c) does not turn into a fully-fledged adjective.

Some Austronesian languages, e.g. Standard Indonesian (Sneddon, 1996) and Minangkabau (Gil, 2005), provide further examples of polyfunctional neutral marking in the nominal phrase, except that the word order is the mirror image of Northern Khanty: the phrase is head-initial. Finally, a number of languages employ an essentially adjectival strategy to render all relevant types of semantic relation between the two denotations; this will be addressed at length in Chapter 3.

2.5.6   Polyfunctionality Patterns

We have demonstrated in the previous sections that, while in some languages each relevant semantic type corresponds to a dedicated morphosyntactic construction as its default or principal mode of expression, in most cases we find that some of the four types are expressed using the same morphosyntactic device. This conclusion is partly similar to that of Gil (2005), where languages are shown to vary in the degree to which they make grammatical distinctions between different types of modification.[18] However, unlike in Gil's data, the patterns of polyfunctionality we have encountered are not entirely random and seem to suggest an implicational relation.

Languages show a tendency towards a certain kind of uniformity with respect to encoding strategies. In (38) we see the frequent polyfunctionality patterns that have been illustrated in Sections 2.5.2 to 2.5.5.

(38)　　　$A \neq B \neq C \neq D$

　　　　　$A \neq B \neq C = D$

　　　　　$A = B \neq C = D$

　　　　　$A = B \neq C \neq D$

　　　　　$A \neq B = C = D$

　　　　　$A \neq B = C \neq D$

　　　　　$A = B = C = D$

These patterns reflect what we earlier called 'the Possession-Modification Scale' (Nikolaeva and Spencer, 2012) (39).

(39)　Possession-Modification Scale: $A < B < C < D$

The strongest claim we can advance is that encoding strategies tend to respect a monotonicity requirement along the Possession-Modification Scale, according to which, wherever we have overlapping encoding, each strategy covers some continuous segment of the scale. In other words, if a language opts to treat adjectival modifiers using a nominal strategy, then it will tend to use this strategy for the other constructions, and if it tends to use an adjectival strategy

---

[18] Gil's paper concentrates on possessors, adjectives, and relative clauses but does not address modification-by-noun. It is not always clear what the basis of his classification is. Gil describes Albanian as being 'highly differentiated' in that genitive possessors, adjectives, and relative clauses all receive different encodings. Yet in Albanian the standard morphosyntax of both adjectives and genitives involves a proclitic (or prefix) agreeing in gender, number, case, and definiteness with the noun head, and this possessive strategy is also the productive way in which a noun may modify another noun generally. Thus, Albanian represents for us a clear case in which all four of our primary modification functions are expressed in the same way – the exact opposite of Gil's classification. Similarly, Chukchi is said to be highly differentiated, yet the possessive and modification-by-noun encodings are essentially a species of attributive adjective: see Chapter 3. Likewise, Japanese is said to collapse adjectives and genitives. However, the genitive construction is expressed by the postposition ('case marker') *no*, while the prototypical adjective (including basic colour adjectives) is to a large extent a kind of verb (though there is a large class of adjectives marked by a postposition *na* as well as a much smaller number marked with *no*, a homophone of the genitive marker).

78   *Modification Constructions*

for the possessor construction, it will tend to use this strategy throughout. If a language elects to express alienable possession systematically by means of an essentially adjectival strategy, it will be under great pressure to express modification-by-noun using a similar adjectival strategy, and so on.[19]

This observation offers an interesting test case for the benefits of the canonical approach to typology (Nikolaeva and Spencer, 2012). When we describe a category or construction type in the canonical approach, we establish a small number of uncontroversial central properties for that category or construction, thus defining a logical ideal from which real exemplars deviate to varying degrees. On this perspective, we can treat inalienable possession as a canonical type of possessive relationship (one driven by the semantics of the possessed noun) and we can treat modification by gradable property-denoting predicate as canonical attributive modification (driven by the semantics of the adjective). Modification-by-noun and alienable possession both turn out to be non-canonical varieties of modification and possession, which violate (some of) the canonical criteria in one way or another. Being non-canonical by definition, these types often pattern together with other types. All languages will have to make compromises in order to express these relations.

In particular, modification-by-noun is non-canonical as intersective modification because in canonical attributive modification by semantically simple property words there is no relation between two nominal entities; there is only one such entity, of course. In modification-by-noun the semantic structure of the modifier is more complex since it involves another noun-like entity (Beck, 2002, 88). In this sense it falls under our broad notion of 'modification-by-nominal-concept', which also covers possessive constructions.[20] When different strategies are used for different construction types, modification-by-noun occupies a pivotal point in the typology of the possession-modification family of constructions: languages often co-opt either the adjectival strategy or the possessive strategy to express it. Alienable possession differs somewhat minimally from canonical possession in terms of the semantics of the possessed noun, and so it is often expressed by the same encoding strategy, but it is still a distinct construction type, as reflected in languages with an alienability opposition, because it lacks a number of the canonical possessive properties surveyed in Section 2.2.

---

[19] We would also expect to see the $A = B = C \neq D$ pattern but have yet to find clear examples of it. It is difficult to see why this pattern does not often occur.

[20] Nouns can also be modified by complex constructions involving referential DPs, such as adpositional phrases or some kind of relative clause. These are non-canonical cases, which we will address in the next chapter.

2.5 Towards a Typology 79

Thus, the canonical approach can help resolve much of the controversy that surrounds the relevant constructions while at the same time providing us with useful analytical tools for investigating implicational scales of the kind proposed here. But what might motivate such an implicational scale? We will argue in Chapter 7, Section 7.4.3 that it is heavily grounded in semantics: adjacent points exhibit a great deal of semantic affinity.

2.5.7 The Role of Juxtaposition

Although we do believe that our scale represents real tendencies in grammatical and semantic organization, we are well aware that the cross-linguistic patterns are the outcome of complex grammaticalization processes and therefore allow a certain degree of variation. The historical processes being what they are, one might expect a variety of counter-examples to arise. We have so far encountered (rather limited) instances of violations of the Possession-Modification Scale; they are summarized in (40).

(40) $A = B = D \neq C$

$A \neq B = D \neq C$

$A = C \neq B = D$

$A = C = D \neq B$

Languages exist in which modification-by-noun receives identical expression with inalienable possession, while alienable possession differs. This type is in fact quite frequent but, to our knowledge, only if modification-by-noun and inalienable possession (and possibly also attributive modification) are rendered by juxtaposition, while alienable possession is indicated by some kind of genitive-like marking.[21] A number of West African languages exhibit this type (Creissels, 2000, 249). For instance, in Ewe inalienable possession is rendered by simple juxtaposition with the element order dependent-head (41a). Attributive modification is also by juxtaposition (41b), though apparently with

[21] We can imagine a grammaticalization scenario in which a split develops between alienable and inalienable possession, with alienable possession being marked by an innovating genitive case and inalienable possession being minimally marked by juxtaposition. We can equally imagine that the new genitive would then take over the role of coding modification-by-noun. This is what Haspelmath (2008, 208) calls "inhibition of expansion". A novel construction can make an existing meaning more transparent by including an additional exponent and expand to new contexts, but it will not spread to the contexts in which the relevant meaning occurs most often (inalienable possession). At the same time, however, we might find that adjectives modify by pure juxtaposition. This is probably what happened in Miya, but we leave this speculation to future research.

80 *Modification Constructions*

the opposite element order of head-dependent (recall that we have abstracted away from word order and from syntactic structure generally in our typological mini-survey).

(41) a. fia   dada
           chief mother
           'the chief's mother'
     b. xɔ   nyuí
           house good
           'a good house'

Modification-by-noun is dependent-head juxtaposition, though sometimes with tone sandhi (Westermann, 1930, 173): see (42).

(42) a. eʋe   tɔ́
           Ewe   man
           'an Ewe man'
     b. agble tɔ́
           farm   owner
           'a farm owner'

However, alienable possession is expressed by the adposition *ɸé* (Westermann, 1930, 49), as shown in (43). This is presumably a postposition, though this is not clear from Westermann's account.

(43) fia   ɸé xɔ
      chief of house
      'the chief's house'

Another case in point would be Kabba (Nilo-Saharan), as described in Moser (2004). These languages instantiate the A = B = D ≠ C pattern.

A somewhat similar situation is found in the Mande languages. In Jeli, as described in Tröbs (1998), there is a split between alienable and inalienable possession: only the former requires an overt constructional marker. Modification-by-noun is also expressed by some kind of compounding. However, attributive modification requires a special attributive form of a qualitative verb, derived with the suffix *-ra/-rɛ* and referred to as the 'resultative participle' by Tröbs (1998). Unlike other modifiers, such participles follow the head; thus, in the case of Jeli we are dealing with the A ≠ B = D ≠ C subtype.

Noonan (1992) describes Lango (Western Nilotic) inalienable possession expressed by juxtaposition. The inalienably possessed nouns denote parts in

2.5 Towards a Typology 81

'part-of' relations, including body parts, pictures, character features, and other notions relating to the individual's self, blood relatives, locational notions, and the like: see (44).

(44) a. wí   rwòt
          head   king
          'the king's head'
      b. cál   lòcə̀
          picture   man
          'the man's picture'

Both alienable possession and attributive modification employ the so-called associative construction, which consists of the head noun followed by the attributive particle *à*: see (45). (The final consonant is geminated before *à*.)

(45) a. gwôkk   à   lócə̀
          dog   of   man
          'the man's dog'
      b. gwôkk   à   bə̀r
          dog   of   good
          'the good dog'

Unlike possessors, attributive adjectives show number agreement with the head, so on our definitions they follow a different strategy. However, nominal modifiers do not take the attributive *à*, or at least this is not mentioned in the grammar. Instead modification-by-noun is achieved by what Noonan calls "fully productive compounding", which expresses "any contextually reasonable association between the compound elements" (Noonan, 1992, 115): see (46).

(46) a. gwók   ˈrɔmɔ̂
          dog   sheep
          'sheep dog'
      b. dɔ́g   dêl
          mouth   skin
          'lips'

As Noonan (1992, 115) explicitly notes, compounded nouns "are simply juxtaposed in a syntactic configuration like that of inalienable associative constructions". So we seem to have the following, otherwise unattested, pattern in Lango: A = C ≠ B = D.

Mandarin Chinese (Sino-Tibetan) provides an example of a language where modification-by-noun is typically realized by compounding (Liu, 2003,

82 *Modification Constructions*

62ff), while other relevant construction types deploy a highly polyfunctional free-standing marker *de*. Its function is essentially to signal the very general head-dependent relation in the nominal phrase with the result that it is equally employed in possessive constructions, attributive modifiers, and relative clauses. Chinese then exemplifies the A = C = D ≠ B type, but in some situations *de* can be omitted (see Section 2.2.2 and Li and Thompson, 1981, 119–123), which brings it closer to languages with a single juxtapositional strategy such as Northern Khanty or Indonesian. Another Sino-Tibetan language which probably belongs to this type is Lahu (Matisoff, 1973).

When certain data appear to violate a scale motivated by a well-founded directionality hypothesis, one can look for a non-semantic explanation. A relevant consideration here is that all known violations involve juxtaposition. Juxtaposition seems to be involved in all the patterns listed in (40), which suggests that there may be something special about this strategy as opposed to other types of constructional encodings.

In typology there has been much discussion of languages where simple juxtaposition signals inalienable constructions, while alienable possession is indicated by overt morphological marking (Haiman, 1985, 130; Croft, 1990, 174–176; Nichols, 1992, 117; Chappell and McGregor, 1996, 45; Heine, 1997, 172; Haspelmath, 2008). This pattern is observed e.g. in Jarawara (Arawá) (Dixon, 2000), Dogon (Niger-Congo) (Plungian, 1995), Kayardild (Tangic) (Evans, 1995), Chatino (Zapotecan) (Carleton and Waksler, 2000), and a large number of other languages of Africa, Australia, and South America. A popular type of explanation for the rests on the notion of iconicity. It has been argued in various places that inalienable possession involves a conceptually closer relationship between the possessor and the possessed than alienable possession, and this tends to be iconically reflected in the 'linguistic distance' between them. When the alienable/inalienable distinction is formally expressed, the major tendency which seems to be at work is to morphologically mark alienable possession, while inalienable possession is based on juxtaposition. This reasoning goes back to Haiman (1983) and is favoured by Chappell and McGregor (1989), Croft (1990, 175–176), Koptjevskaja-Tamm (1997), and Lazard (2005). It is also reflected in some syntactic accounts, where inalienable possessors are analysed as forming some sort of complex predicate with the possessed noun and are therefore structurally closer to the possessed noun than an alienable possessor would be (Vergnaud and Zubizarreta, 1992; Alexiadou, 2003).[22]

---

[22] Some recent studies on (in)alienability within Mainstream Generative Grammar maintain that inalienable possessors are merged lower than alienable possessors, due to a closer semantic relationship to the head noun (Fábregas, 2011; Lin, 2011, among others).

The iconicity explanation has been challenged by Haspelmath (2008). One of his counter-arguments is this. Iconicity predicts that the constructional marker in alienable constructions should occur between the possessor and the possessee, but this is not always the case, as demonstrated by Dogon, Puluwat, Koyukon, and Achagua, among other languages. Haspelmath suggested instead that the markedness pattern in inalienable possession is based on economy considerations. Coding asymmetries in possessive constructions are due to their differential predictability, something which can be measured by relative frequency. Frequent predictable patterns that can be easily inferred are known to need less formal markedness. Relational nouns normally, or at least very frequently, occur as possessees in possessive constructions, while this is much less frequent for non-relational nouns. This implies that for the former the possessive relation can be inferred and so its overt marking is relatively redundant, while for the latter the possessive relation is not expected and therefore has to be formally marked.

While we basically agree with the essence of the frequency explanation when it comes to the inalienability split in possessives, our question is more general in nature and follows from the fact that we looked at a wider range of constructions, including not only possession but also modification.

Crucially, juxtaposition is commonly used to express all relevant semantic functions. It is very frequent in modification-by-noun and embraces numerous compound-like structures in many languages. In fact, a number of compounds (possibly lexicalized to various degrees) typically exist even in the languages which require a constructional marker as the primary modification-by-noun strategy. Non-agreeing non-derived attributive modifiers (canonical adjectives) found in many languages are also juxtaposed to the head by our liberal definition of juxtaposition. In addition, there are languages where all possessives are morphologically unmarked and languages where juxtaposition serves to express alienable possession alone. This is by far a less frequent situation, but it does occur. One example is provided by Dizi, as cited in Nichols (1992, 119).[23] In this language inalienable possession requires a possessive genitive (47a), and alienable possession is expressed by mere juxtaposition accompanied by tonal alternations (47b).

---

[23] Nichols (1992, 117) argues for the generalization that inalienable possession is commonly head-marked while alienable possession tends to be dependent-marked or has no morphological marking. In other words, inalienable possession is less dependent-marked. However, this generalization may need further investigation: examples of inalienable possession cited in descriptive grammars usually involve pronominal possessors, and pronominal possessors are independently more likely to be marked on the head via pronominal incorporation than lexical possessors.

84　*Modification Constructions*

(47)　a.　dadakn gelì
　　　　　boy.GEN head
　　　　　'boy's head'
　　　b.　dadàkì anù
　　　　　boy　dog
　　　　　'boy's dog'

The varying roles that simple juxtaposition can play, and, the construction-defining adjacency of syntactic terminal elements (syntactic words) more generally, represent an important aspect of syntactic organization. We discuss juxtaposition further in Chapter 7.

2.6　Conclusions

This chapter has introduced four semantic types of adnominal dependents by drawing an informal distinction between canonical attributive modification (modification-by-adjective) and three types of modification-by-nominal-concept: modification-by-noun and two sorts of possessive construction, alienable and inalienable possession. We then surveyed the morphosyntactic strategies languages deploy to express these semantic types, and have proposed a Possession-Modification Scale with respect to which languages tend to observe a monotonicity requirement. We noted that the scale reflects strong tendencies rather than an absolute universal and discussed some counter-examples.

In addition to its potential significance for typology generally, a deeper understanding of the scale and what kinds of lexical categories can instantiate it could illuminate these murky questions of word classes. A detailed study of the various ways in which modification-by-nominal-concept is expressed cross-linguistically is essential for understanding not only the category of noun, but also the category of adjective. The ensembles of constructions we illustrated here can throw important light on the question of how exactly we represent their syntax and semantics and what constitutes a lexical category. A preliminary analysis of the adjective–noun distinction along these lines was offered by Spencer (2013), who argued, inter alia, that it allows us to factor out the various components of non-canonical encodings often found in the intermediate constructions modification-by-noun and alienable possession. In the next chapter we will describe the categorial mixing involved in some of the patterns we have identified.

3 Categorial Mixing in the Nominal Phrase

3.1 Introduction

In this chapter we enlarge the empirical database on which we will be founding our analysis by surveying the principal types of constructions in which a noun modifies another noun and exhibits various types of paradigmatic and syntagmatic mixing. We begin with juxtapositional compounds, then discuss lexically specified adjective formation, and then turn to more complex syntactic constructions.

3.2 N-N Compounds as Mixed Categories

One obvious kind of mismatch is found in modification-by-noun. As we saw in Chapter 2, modification-by-noun is a form of attributive modification: the noun relinquishes its canonical role as referring expression and takes on the role of attributive modifier normally reserved for adjectives, but retains its original denotation. A typical instance of this is Germanic-style headed (endocentric) N-N compounding. As we saw in Chapter 2, compounding does not involve adding an identifiable semantic predicate. Instead the relation between N_1 and N_2 is mediated by the pragmatically determined predicate $\mathcal{R}$.

In typical cases of English N-N compounds the modifying noun is non-referential and hence cannot take determiners or specifiers. This is not to say that such modifying nouns can never be referential, however. In the example *I can't find the garage key*, the speaker would likely be referring to a specific identifiable garage. This is not because the definite article is the specifier of *garage*: in *Someone's left a bedroom window open*, the expression *a bedroom window* is synonymous with *one of the windows of the bedroom*. Indeed, there are instances in which the modifier is a proper name (*a Mozart sonata, the Palme murder*; see Koptjevskaja-Tamm, 2013). This would appear to suggest that the modifier expression must be allowed to be a DP, but proper name modifiers express a wider range of semantic relations than regular

86   *Categorial Mixing in the Nominal Phrase*

genitives and may have variable morphosyntactic statuses. Breban (2017) shows that whereas some proper name modifiers have a complement function (*a Putin supporter*), others (e.g. *a Yorkshire terrier, a Mona Lisa smile*) have the 'typifying' or 'classifying' function and denote a subtype of a type. Yet others can be analysed as 'epithets', a function usually associated with adjectival modifiers, such as *the Kennedy administration* with the meaning 'the administration headed by President Kennedy'. The contribution of the proper name is here not to add a second referent to which the head noun can be anchored, but to add a qualifying description and act as a prompt to the addressee to mentally reconstruct it. This is not a canonical property modification because it is more semantically complex and non-gradable, but it is still a property. A similar distinction is involved in interpreting the different meanings of ethnic adjectives (Alexiadou and Stavrou, 2011). For instance, *Swiss cheese* can be understood as 'cheese that was made in Switzerland' (provenance meaning) or as 'varieties of cheese which can be produced anywhere and which are in the style of traditional cheeses made in Switzerland' (classifying meaning). So at least for non-complement modifying nouns, even proper names tend to have a (non-referential) property interpretation.

Compounding is typically recursive, in the sense that the modifying noun can itself be a compound: [$_N$[$_N$ *coffee table*] *book*]. If we think of the compound as a kind of word, then recursion in the compound induces a weak form of syntagmatic mixing, in that a modifier (*table*) is itself visible to modification (*coffee table*). What is more, in English the modifying noun can itself take attributive modifiers. This induces a slightly stronger notion of syntagmatic mixing, as in [[*low temperature*] *physics*], [[*bad hair*] *day*] and other celebrated examples such as *American history teacher*. In this example, on the reading which is synonymous with *teacher of American history* we have the structure [[*American history*]$_{Mod}$ [*teacher*]$_{Head}$]. This gives rise to interesting questions about the nature of N-N compounds in English: the modifying element appears to be a phrase. The existence of compounds such as *American history teacher*, which apparently have phrasal modifiers, is puzzling. One answer would be to regard *American history* as less than a full phrase, perhaps a 'small construction' in the sense of Sadler and Arnold (1994), and then define compounding over small constructions.

The compounding process does not normally involve extra morphology, although in some Germanic languages the N_1 and N_2 may be joined by an 'intermorpheme', or various compound-specific sandhi processes may apply. In productive syntactic N-N compounds, as opposed to morphological compounds,[1] we do in essence have a relational adjective which retains the morphology of the input noun, except that in the case of compounds the mapping is a result of the construction itself and is not projected from any lexical representation as such. This suggests that the correct morphosyntactic analysis of compounding should be able to take the noun which is used attributively and give it the kind of representation which is proper for an attribute. Spencer (1999, 2003) argues that the morphosyntax of modification-by-noun in endocentric compounding can be represented by essentially the same procedure as the one for relational adjective transpositions, which we will discuss in Section 3.3. In fact, we often find synonymous pairs in which a compound alternates with a relational adjective, e.g. *Paris/Parisian lifestyle*. One might say that *Paris* here is no longer a noun but that it has been converted into an adjective without changing its morphology. However, the only sense in which modifiers such as *coffee* in *coffee table* or *Paris* in *Paris lifestyle* have been claimed to be adjectives is in terms of their syntactic function and environment, not in terms of their morphological category.

In English, of course, it is especially difficult to determine whether *coffee* in *coffee table* is categorially a noun or an adjective because there is little relevant morphology which distinguishes the two categories. However, in some languages such nouns partially acquire the morphosyntax of obvious modifiers (adjectives). For instance, we will see in Chapter 8 that in Tundra Nenets the modifying noun in compound-like structures agrees with the head in the manner of an adjective. That is, it assumes certain morphosyntactic properties of adjectives without completely changing its categorial status.

3.3 Denominal Adjectives

In addition to simple underived attributive modifiers, we find denominal adjectives (DNAs) derived by means of a dedicated morphological process. We would normally regard them as canonical derivational categories, but in some sense they are still based on nouns. The semantic relations between denominal adjectives and their modifiands are somewhat different from any of the relations that hold between the standard semantic types of adjectives and the noun they modify.

---

[1] See Huddleston and Pullum (2002, 448ff) for justification of this distinction and Bell and Plag (2012) for a dissenting view.

88   *Categorial Mixing in the Nominal Phrase*

Table 3.1 *Common derivational categories of denominal adjectives*

Similitudinal	English *god-like, ellipsoid, boyish*; Chagatay *masa-msı* 'table-like' < *masa* 'table'
Temporal	English *dai-ly*; Yakut *sajïŋ-ŋï* '(in) summer' (adjective) < *sajïn* 'summer' (noun)
Locative	English *subterranean*; Tundra Nenets *war°-xi°* 'on the shore' < *war°* 'shore'
Material	English *woollen*; German *eis-ern* 'made of iron' < *Eis* 'iron'

3.3.1   Denominal Adjectives with Added Semantic Predicate

We first survey a variety of denominal adjectives that are semantically enriched: these involve the addition of a predicate that adds lexical-semantic content to the base noun.

In Table 3.1 we provide a list of some of the more common types of denominal adjective categories with clearly identifiable semantic content. Adjectives of this type require definitions such as 'resembling/similar to N (along some dimension)', 'located at/in N', 'occurring at/during N', and 'made of N', where N stands for the semantic representation of the base noun. Other less frequently occurring semantic types can have meanings such as 'tending towards N, inclined to N' (Uyghur *eve* 'house' > *ev-cil* 'domesticated'; Kazakh *su* 'water' > *su-šïl* 'capable of swimming in water'), 'originating from N' (Georgian *sopl-ur-* 'from the village' < *sopl* 'village'), 'smelling or tasting of N' (Nganasan *kiriba-ńəəgə* 'tasting of bread' < *kiriba* 'bread'; see Szeverényi, 2014), 'required by N' (German *schul-mässig* 'didactic' < *Schule* 'school'), and 'until N' (Georgian *om-amdel-* 'until the war' < *om* 'war').

Any approach to lexical semantics will have to account for the fact that such adjectives systematically require a paraphrase with an additional contentful predicate that takes the base noun as its argument. For instance, similitudinal adjectives add the semantic predicate RESEMBLING(N) or SIMILAR_TO(N). The added content is in part nominal, since it contains a noun denotation (N), and in part adjectival, since it includes a property-like predicate RESEMBLING. We have termed it a participle so as to give it the flavour of a modifier. The adjectival affix cumulatively signals the semantic nature of the added predicate and attributivization, that is, the change of the distributional class, N → A.

3.3 Denominal Adjectives　89

Similitudinal adjectives in English such as *boy-ish* or *boy-like* are lexically restricted, but let us assume for the sake of argument that similitudinal adjective formation is fully productive and regular. The rationale for this decision is that, in many cases at least, there is a transparent semantic relation between the derived adjective and the noun base. This is the behaviour we expect from a language which respects the categorial identity of its words. In such cases we see canonical category-changing derivation, in that a new lexeme/lexical entry is defined, adding semantic content to that of the base (nominal) entry as well as changing morphosyntactic class. In canonical meaning-bearing derivation the base noun lexeme can no longer be treated as a noun, either by inflectional morphology or by syntax. The derived adjective's root form is some phonological modification of the base noun's root form, but the inflectional paradigm of the adjective is defined over the derived category, not over the base noun. Similarly, the adjective's semantic representation is derived by enrichment of the base noun's semantics, but the noun's semantics itself plays no further role in determining the meaning of the derived adjective. The properties of the base noun lexeme are preserved only in an opaque form. Canonical derived adjectives therefore show neither paradigmatic nor syntagmatic category mixing, and have the same morphology and syntactic role in modification as simplex adjectives.[2]

If we take similitudinal adjectives in English to be a straightforward example of standard derivational morphology, then they will not inherit syntactic information from their base lexeme. In particular, the base nouns will not be able to serve as independent phrasal heads and will not be accessible for attributive modification. With one possible exception we have not found syntagmatic mixing with such adjectives in English. They fail to license the base noun's specifiers or attributive prenominal modifiers, as well as postnominal modifiers such as relative clauses (see (1), (2) and (3)).

(1)　a.　*[this boy]-ish/like

　　b.　*[your child]-ish/like

　　c.　*[three boys]-ish/like

(2)　a.　*[small boy]-ish

　　b.　*[small child]-ish

---

[2]　Denominal adjectives may pattern differently from (non-derived) qualitative adjectives in other respects not relevant for the present discussion. They are typically incompatible with degree adverbs, often resist the predicative usage, and have a different derivational potential.

90   *Categorial Mixing in the Nominal Phrase*

(3)   a.   i.   *cat-like that you saw
           ii.   *[cat that you saw]-like
       b.   i.   *[cat-like in the garden]
           ii.   *[cat in the garden]-like

We should hardly be surprised by the patterns in (1), (2), (3). After all, nouns which appear in the modifier position in N-N compounds equally fail to license specifiers or postnominal modifiers, though they do permit modification by prenominal adjectives. The exception is found with N-like adjectives modified by adjectives, as in (4), which seem (to one of us) to be moderately acceptable.

(4)   a.   ?[small boy]-like
       b.   ?[black cat]-like
       c.   ?[big cat]-like

It is notable, though, that -*like* is often considered a 'semi-affix' (Marchand, 1969), or even a partially grammaticalized compounding form of the adjective LIKE (see Bauer et al., 2013, 289 for discussion and further references). Bauer et al. (2013) point out that *N-like* constructions fall under their definition of compound, but for 'practical reasons' they treat -*like* as a suffix.

In many other languages denominal adjectives pattern with other derivational categories in the language and we find little syntactic evidence of nounhood. However, there are more complicated cases in which the base noun exhibits the Base Noun Modifiability Property (BNMP). This property ensures that what appear to look like denominal adjectives allow inbound attributive modification, although they behave like canonical adjectives in other respects. In a number of languages the base noun may be modified by attributive adjectives, and sometimes can even head its own possessor. One example is provided by Tundra Nenets similitudinal adjectives in -*rəxa/-r°xa*. Adjectives in Nenets form a well-defined class with distinct syntactic and morphological behaviours (see Nikolaeva, 2003, 2014b), and (optionally) agree with the noun head for PL number and case. Similitudinal adjectives have the typical word order privileges of adjectives and agree with the head noun in the appropriate fashion, as illustrated by the similitudinal adjective *sarm′ik°rəxa* 'wolf-like' in (5).

(5)   pər′id′en′a-q sarm′ik°-rəxa-x°h wen′ako-x°h
       black-PL   wolf-SIM.A-DU   dog-DU
       '(two) dogs (looking) like black wolves'

3.3 Denominal Adjectives   91

The similitudinal form cannot be analysed as an oblique case because oblique nouns never function as prenominal modifiers in Tundra Nenets and because it has other distributional properties of an adjective. Agreement in (5) shows that the constructions have the expected external syntax of an adjective, and in this sense the derived word is categorially an adjective, not a noun. Yet the similitudinal adjective retains (some of) the properties of a noun: the base noun from which the adjective is derived controls number agreement on its modifier (5), and it can serve as the head of a possessive genitive (6).

(6)   numki°-q   tu-r°xa
      star.GEN-PL fire-SIM.A
      'like the light of the stars'

If possessors are specifiers that encode referentiality, the possessed noun *tu* 'fire' in (6) must be referential.

Similar facts are observed in Georgian, where the base noun of the agreeing adjective which indicates origin can take a genitive possessor and antecedent anaphora (Boeder and Schroeder, 2000, 184, 186).

(7)   a. erti mamačem-is   sopl-el-i   ḳac-i
          one father.1SG-GEN village-A-NOM man-NOM
          'a man from the village of my father'

      b. im   sopl-el-i   k'ac-i   iq'o, sadac davibade
          that.OBL village-A-NOM man-NOM was where was.born.1SG
          'It was a man from the village where I was born'

As can be seen in (7b), the base noun *sopl* 'village' controls the relative pronoun 'where', so it retains its potential to be a discourse referent. These examples are typical instances of what we have called 'syntagmatic category mixing'.

3.3.2   Noun-to-Adjective Transpositions

In addition to semantically enriched denominal adjectives, we also frequently find non-meaning-bearing noun-to-adjective transpositions. These are words which have the meaning of a noun but which appear in a morphosyntactic form that permits the noun to serve as a true attributive modifier of the head. Noun-to-adjective transpositions fall into a number of semantic groups, although these are not always defined in a clear-cut manner.

Relational Adjectives

In many languages N-N compounding is not the preferred or even a possible strategy for modification-by-noun. A common alternative strategy is to turn

92   *Categorial Mixing in the Nominal Phrase*

the noun into a word which has all the grammatical properties of an adjective. If they are derived without altering the cognitive content of the word, that is, without the addition of semantic predicate, such adjectives are usually termed 'relational' (see Giorgi and Longobardi, 1991; McNally and Boleda, 2004; and Demonte, 2008, among others).[3] Another term – possibly a more transparent one – for this general class is 'classificatory adjectives' (Lin, 2008; Cinque, 2010) and yet other terms which seem to denote the same concept include 'associative adjective' (Giegerich, 2005, 2015) and 'pseudo-adjective' (Alexiadou and Stavrou, 2011). The view that relational adjectives in their 'pure' form do not introduce any additional predicate to the semantic representation and that they have exactly the same range of denotations as the original (undetermined) noun has been fairly standard since at least the work of Bally (1944) for French[4] and Levi (1978) for English.

Relational adjectives display unique properties among and fit rather poorly into the standard semantic typologies of attributive modification. It is clear that they are not intersective. Consider the English expression *X is a prepositional phrase*. This entails that X is a phrase. Does it also entail that X is prepositional (whatever that would mean)? If X is also a palindrome, we cannot say that X is a prepositional palindrome; therefore, the relational adjective *prepositional* is not intersective. This appears to be generally true of relational adjectives and marks out relational adjectives as semantically anomalous compared with canonical adjectives. In this connection, McNally and Boleda (2004) observe that relational adjectives do not ascribe properties to ordinary individuals; rather, they ascribe properties to kinds, i.e. abstract sorts of individual that, in English, are named by bare plurals (Carlson, 1977). It is certainly true that an object with the description 'technical architect' is not itself technical, but the kind of architect that it instantiates is.

Are relational adjectives then subsective? A prepositional phrase is a phrase, so that at least this type of relational adjective is subsective. We have to be a little careful, however. If we consider English N-N compounds, then we notice that a toy gun is not presumably a gun, so modification-by-noun does not necessarily give rise to subsective readings. The notion 'toy' is not expressed by a relational adjective in English, but the Russian translation equivalent is,

---

[3]   The reader should be warned that the term 'relational' is sometimes used in other senses: some authors reserve it for a particular subclass of relational adjectives (Bosque and Picallo, 1996; Arsenijevic et al., 2014), whereas in the French, Russian, and Polish grammatical traditions the term 'relational' or 'relative' applies to all denominal adjectives, following Bally (1944).

[4]   For a different analysis of French relational adjectives see Fradin (2017) and the literature cited there.

3.3 Denominal Adjectives 93

so Russian *igrušečnyj pistolet* 'toy gun' is an example of a non-subsective relational adjective (*igrušečnyj* derived from the noun *igruška* 'toy'). The challenge, then, is to provide these adjectives with a property denotation while capturing the fact that they lack the basic intersective entailment.

When relational adjectives modify a head noun, N_1, they define a vague all-purpose relation between the denotation of N_1 and the abstract concept denoted by the base noun lexeme N_2.[5] In this respect, they fulfil very much the same function as endocentric N-N compounds, but sometimes also the POSS-*s* construction or modification by *of*-phrase (see Spencer, 1999, 2013; Giegerich, 2005; Bisetto, 2010; ten Hacken, 2013; Rainer, 2013; Nagano and Shimada, 2015). In some cases only one or the other competing strategy for expressing modification-by-noun can be applied. Thus, in linguistic terminology we talk about *verb phrase* but not *#verbal phrase* (or *#verb's phrase*, *#phrase of the verb*). On the other hand, we speak of *morphological operations* not *#morphology operations*, and occasionally we get free variation as in *preposition/prepositional phrase*. These are examples of a pure relational usage.[6]

In such examples an adjective effectively serves as the adjectival form of a noun. Indeed, Fábregas (2007), Alexiadou and Stavrou (2011), Cetnarowska et al. (2011), and Cetnarowska (2015) have emphasized the noun-like syntactic properties of relational adjectives in Spanish, Greek, and Polish, respectively, and analysed them as 'covert nouns'. They provided various syntactic arguments for this claim, including the fact that a subset of relational adjectives

---

[5] According to Rainer (2013), the only relation which seems to be systematically absent from relational adjectives is the privative relation, which, he suggests, is the reason why some languages have a separate class of privative adjectives. We introduce this class in the section on Proprietive and Privative Adjectives below.

[6] Relational adjectives in English do not always have a purely relational semantics: they often acquire additional nuances of meaning or restrictions on meaning. It can sometimes be difficult to distinguish those cases in which there is no difference in meaning from cases in which there semantic shift has occurred. For instance, when it refers literally to 'wood', the adjective *wooden* almost always means 'made out of wood'. In the framework of Giegerich (2005, 2015) this means that *wooden* has an ascriptive function rather than the 'associative' function we see with other relational adjectives and N-N compounds, and this makes *wooden* more similar to a genuine adjective. This restriction is lacking in N-N compounds with *wood* as the first member. The adjective *wooden* can also be used in a metaphorical sense as in *wooden acting*. While *experimental results/methods/procedures* can mean 'the results/methods/procedures of the experiment' (a purely relational meaning), *experimental* more often means 'not yet fully tried and tested, possibly unreliable' or similar, as in *an experimental approach to staff recruitment*. A number of authors therefore conclude that there may be no strict dichotomy between qualifying and relational adjectives; see Mezhevich (2002), Fradin (2008), Bisetto (2010), among others.

94   *Categorial Mixing in the Nominal Phrase*

is argument-like and synonymous with genitive phrases, cf. *presidential visit to China* and *the president's visit to China*. Other authors proposed that relational adjectives contain an interpretable number feature associated with the base noun and can be treated on a par with (genitive) case marking (Bosque and Picallo, 1996; Fábregas and Marín, 2017, 17). However, relational adjectives have canonical adjectival morphosyntax; in particular, in languages with attributive agreement they show agreement with the head. The reason for this is that relational adjective formation is essentially a way of bringing a noun into line with the grammar of the language so that it can serve as a syntactic modifier. For our topic this entails that the basic function of the noun category is at variance with its expected syntactic/distributional property.

In English, occurrences of relational adjectives are somewhat restricted, partly because the standard way of modifying a noun by a noun is by compounding. The relational adjective is essentially a borrowing from Romance languages (mainly Latin and Norman French) and Greek. We analyse English relational adjectives in Chapter 8. In other languages, essentially all nouns productively form a relational adjective. In Udihe, for instance, relational adjectives are derived by means of the suffix *-mA* (where A stands for a harmonizing non-high vowel). They have the same syntactic properties as non-derived adjectives (see Nikolaeva, 2012) and express a virtually infinite range of semantic relationships, often material – especially if the lexical semantics supports this interpretation, e.g. *mo:-mo* 'wooden' (< *mo:* 'wood'), *aisi-me* 'gold(en)' (< *aisi* 'gold'), but also 'resembling N, looking like N' (8), 'being N' (9), as well as temporal relations (10) and some kind of loose association between two concepts which is difficult to characterize in precise terms (11).

(8) a. miki-me   kuliga
         adder-REL.A snake
         'a snake resembling an adder'

     b. mäna-ma   zaka
         flour-REL.A new.snow
         'new snow looking like flour'

     c. zuge-me sata
         ice-REL.A sugar
         'lump sugar (sugar looking like ice)'

(9) a. g'ai-ma   anda
         crow-REL.A friend
         'crow for a friend'

b. kuliga-ma   sita
snake-REL.A child
'snake for a son'

c. lusa-ma   anda
Russian-REL.A friend
'Russian friend'

(10)   teuze-me   zugdi
winter-REL.A house
'winter house (house used in winter)'

(11)   a. sakä:-ma   pusilakta
blood-REL.A callosity
'bleeding callosity'

b. bo:boj-me   olondo
miracle-REL.A ginseng
'miraculous ginseng'

c. sama-ma   tege
shaman-REL.A gown
'gown made with the shaman cut (fashion)'

In contrast to English, Udihe relational adjectives exhibit syntagmatic mixing, so that the base noun is modified even though it is a proper subpart of an adjective, e.g. [*niŋka seule*]-*me tege* (Chinese silk-REL.A gown) 'a gown made of Chinese silk', [*gaŋa sele*]-*me tada* (hard iron-REL.A arrow) 'an arrow made of hard iron'. In other words, they retain some of their nominal morphosyntax; in particular, they exhibit the BNMP. Just as with the Georgian and Tundra Nenets derived adjectives discussed in Section 3.3.1, we can observe a morphosyntactic mismatch here: the word boundaries do not appear to coincide with syntactic boundaries. In a certain sense such adjectives remain nouns, both syntactically and morphologically, and it is this property which permits them to be attributively transparent. They therefore differ crucially from the opaque relational adjectives of more familiar European languages. In Chapter 8 we will also examine relational adjectives in Selkup, which function as forms of the base noun lexeme and give rise to paradigmatically and syntagmatically mixed categories.

Possessive Adjectives

A derivational process can give rise to an adjective that essentially realizes the semantic function of possession. Similar to relational adjectives, possessive adjectives do not require the addition of a semantically non-empty predicate but

96   *Categorial Mixing in the Nominal Phrase*

denote a vague relation ℜ between the head noun and the base noun. Although they appear to be representatives of a derivational category, the meaning they express brings them closer to a functional or inflectional category, corresponding to (all but meaningless) function words such as *of* or to the (all but meaningless) genitive case of a noun. However, possessive adjectives occur even in languages which have the genitive strategy.

A possessive adjective in its pure form is derived from a base noun which has a 'rigid' denotation. In many European languages only pronominal possessors take the form of adjectives, e.g. Italian *il mio libro* and German *mein Buch* 'my book'. English has some possessive adjectives, as in *Galilean revolution* ('revolution instigated by Galileo') or *Jovian moon* ('moon of Jupiter'), but such constructions are difficult to illustrate unambiguously because they are all but impossible to distinguish from relational adjectives. Another group of possessive/relational adjectives may be what is sometimes called 'ethnic adjectives' (Alexiadou and Stavrou, 2011), as in *the American invasion of Vietnam* (cf. *America's invasion, the invasion by America*) or *the Newtonian conception of gravity* (see also Koshiishi, 2011, 128). However, it is not obvious whether this type really exists.[7]

In other languages there are special attributive forms of nouns to indicate canonical possessive relations. Slavic languages have possessive adjectives that are formed with various degrees of productivity. They are usually derived from nouns denoting entities that are prototypically able to (inalienably) own things. Since it is usually sentient beings that are thought of as possessing things, possessive adjectives are most commonly formed from nouns denoting people or animals, giving translation equivalents of expressions such as *Mary's hand/sister/book, the girl's hand/sister/book, the dog's leg/pups/bone* etc. In Russian, for example, they can be derived from kin terms, some nouns denoting professions, and a handful of animal terms, e.g. *papa* 'dad' → *papin* 'dad's', *pastux* 'shepherd' → *pastuxov* 'shepherd's', *koška* → *koškin* 'cat's'. Unlike standard derivation they may also be formed from personal names, e.g. *Marina* 'Marina' → *Marin-in* 'Marina's'. Such possessive adjectives in Russian are characterized by a unique pattern of declension.

Russian possessive adjectives are attributively opaque, as shown in (12), where the base noun cannot be modified by a possessive form of a pronoun.

---

[7]   Alexiadou and Stavrou (2011) motivate the distinction principally with data from Greek, but corresponding constructions in English and Russian do not support their claims (see Arsenijevic et al., 2014). They couch their description in terms of the Distributed Morphology model. For more discussion of how Distributed Morphology can be applied to the problem of possessive and relational adjectives, see Fábregas (2007).

3.3 Denominal Adjectives   97

(12) a. mam-in   dom
          mother-POSS.A.SG.M house[SG.M]
          'mother's house'

  b. * našej mam-in   dom
        our   mother-POSS.A.SG.M house[SG.M]
        'our mother's house'

However, in Upper Sorbian possessive adjectives show the BNMP: the base noun may be modified by an attributive modifier, or a relative or personal pronoun, so the wide-scope adjectival exponent appears externally to the whole phrase. To illustrate this, we reproduce Corbett's celebrated examples in (13) (Corbett, 1987, 300; 1995, 275).

(13) a. mojeho   bratr-ow-e   dźěći
          my.M.GEN.SG brother[M]-POSS.A-NOM.PL child.NOM.PL
          'my brother's children'

  b. našeho   wučerj-ow-a   zahrodka
      our.M.GEN.SG teacher[M]-POSS.A-F.NOM.SG garden[F].NOM.SG
      'our teacher's garden'

In (13) a head noun, 'children' or 'garden', is modified by a possessive adjective form of the noun 'brother/teacher' respectively. The possessive adjective *bratrowe*, 'brother's', agrees in plural number and nominative case with 'children' (there is no gender distinction in the plural) and the possessive adjective *wučerjowa*, 'teacher's', agrees in singular number, nominative case, and feminine gender with the head noun 'garden'. This type of construction is not unique to Upper Sorbian, in that there are other Slavic languages which have, or have had during their history, similar constructions (though of a rather more restricted kind than Upper Sorbian). The range of person-denoting nouns which regularly and idiomatically take possessive adjective morphology differs from one Slavic language to another (see Corbett, 1987 for a detailed survey). This, of course, only strengthens the claim that the affixed noun base retains noun properties, but it also introduces interesting complications which go beyond the scope of our discussion.

Corbett (1995) discussed two alternative analyses of constructions such as (13). On the first analysis, possessive adjectives are derived by an inflectional process. This would then be an instance of Suffixaufnahme (see Section 3.4.1): the base noun is marked for case first to show its attributive function and for the second time to show agreement with the head. Apart from the modification data illustrated in (13), this analysis is supported by the fact that the base noun is able to control a relative pronoun in Upper Sorbian, as shown in (14).

98   *Categorial Mixing in the Nominal Phrase*

(14)   Wićaz-ow-y   hłos   kotryž   je
    Wichaz-POSS.A-M.NOM.SG voice.M.NOM.SG which.M.NOM.SG is
    zastupił
    gone.in.M.NOM.SG
    'Wichaz's voice who has gone in' (Corbett 1995, 273)

This shows that the base noun is relevant to syntax and therefore points towards an inflectional analysis.

On the second analysis, possessive adjectives are derived by a derivational process and therefore are true adjectives. This analysis follows from their distribution as prenominal modifiers, agreement possibilities, and the fact that they take agreement endings identical with those of other adjectives. It is indeed difficult to see the resulting forms as being noun forms, since in Slavic they may also have a declension pattern which is closer to the standard adjectival pattern than the noun declension. This analysis is also supported by the consideration that Slavic generally only allows one inflectional marker per word and that derivational morphology is known to allow idiosyncratic gaps, and this is what is observed in possessive adjectives. Moreover, possessive adjectives in Slavic do not overtly inflect for inherent number: the base noun must be in the singular. This, in a sense, makes them less 'nouny' and more 'adjectival' than agreeing genitives in Romani, addressed in Section 3.4.2. When the inherent plural reference of the possessor is intended, the genitive strategy is chosen.

Corbett (1995, 27) concludes that possessive adjectives show features of both inflectional and derivational behaviour, to varying degrees in different languages across the family. Their status is somewhere 'in-between' inflection and derivation. Like a number of denominal adjectives demonstrated in Section 3.3.1 they have the external syntax and agreement patterns of a regular adjective. On the other hand, they are still based on nouns, whose properties may be in part visible to syntax.

This discussion also raises the question of how (or indeed if) we can distinguish possessive adjectives from relational adjectives. As mentioned above, we assume that relational adjectives denote the unspecified relation $\mathcal{R}$. Similarly, possessive adjectives express a contextually determined relation between the head and the modifier noun, very roughly $\lambda \mathcal{R} \lambda N_{poss} \lambda N_h$ $[\exists y N_{poss}(y) \wedge \exists x N_h(x) \wedge \mathcal{R}(y,x)]$.[8] However, we can argue that the key contrast between possessive and relational adjectives, at least in standard cases,

---

[8]   In fact, the possessor is expressed by a NP/DP, not a bare noun, though in practice many possessors take the form of a noun, for instance, a proper name. We discuss this distinction in more detail in Chapter 7.

lies in the semantics of typical base nouns themselves, which also seems to account for a good deal of the morphosyntactic differences between the two types.

The relation expressed by canonical possessive adjectives holds between the denotation of a head noun and a possessor, and we mentioned in Chapter 2 that a possessor typically corresponds to a referential phrase. On the other hand, canonical relational adjectives express modification-by-noun, that is, they merely establish some pragmatically characterized association between two noun denotations.

As we saw above, the true relational adjective is derived from a 'generic', non-referential reading of the base lexeme (much as in standard derivational morphology). The difference can be illustrated by means of a contrast found in the Russian lexicon. In (15) we see two denominal adjectives derived from the noun *koška* 'cat'.

(15) a. košk-in   korm
cat-POSS.A.M.NOM.SG food[M].NOM.SG
'the cat's food (of a particular cat)'

  b. koš-ačij   korm
cat-REL.A.M.NOM.SG food[M].NOM.SG
'cat food'

The possessive adjective *koškin* in (15a) establishes a relationship between the concept of 'food' and a particular cat, so that the base lexeme *koška* is effectively interpreted referentially here. However, in (15b) we find what we can call a 'zooic adjective', a subtype of relational adjective in Russian. These are most typically derived from names of animals, though they can also be found with ethnic terms, names of professions, and some kin terms, e.g. *kazačij* 'pertaining to Cossack(s)', *oxotničij* 'pertaining to hunter(s)', *vdovij* 'pertaining to widower(s)'. Zooic adjectives are distinct from pure possessive adjectives in that they follow the standard adjectival declension pattern. They are based on non-referential ('generic') terms, like true relational adjectives. So *košačij* establishes a relationship between the concept of 'food' and the concept of 'cat(s)' without referring to any particular cat, hence a minimal pair is possible with *koškin*. We can perhaps say that a possessive adjective differs from a relational adjective in that it functions as though it were a Spec[NP] and not an attribute proper. It is therefore an adjective that fulfils the syntactic role of a determiner (and by default is associated with the definiteness property, at least semantically).

100   *Categorial Mixing in the Nominal Phrase*

Slavic languages are not unique in distinguishing possessive and relational adjectives. Chukchi (Chukotko-Kamchatkan) illustrates a language type in which possession is regularly expressed by possessive adjectives based on essentially the same encoding strategy as attributive modification. Chukchi has distinct morphology for deriving both relational and possessive adjectives and both types of adjective are fully productive (Skorik, 1961). It also has N-N compounds, but relational adjective formation is very productive and in a sense is the standard way to achieve modification-by-noun. In a similar manner, the possessive adjective is the principal way of expressing a possessor–possessed relation because Chukchi lacks a genitive case or an *of*-adposition.

Chukchi possessive and relational adjectives have the external morphosyntax of other members of the adjective class. In particular, they can show attributive agreement with the head, as demonstrated in (16).

(16)   a.   ŋelwəlʔə-kine-k ʔaacekə-k
            herd-REL.A-LOC youth-LOC
            'at the youth from the herd' (i.e. 'belonging to')

    b.   mirg-ine-t   kupre-t
            grandfather-POSS.A-PL net-PL
            'grandfather's nets'

Koptjevskaja-Tamm (1995) argues that both possessive and relational adjectives in Chukchi are actually a type of genitive, though one which itself takes the morphosyntax of an attributive modifier, i.e. shows Suffixaufnahme. This goes against other analyses of the Chukchi case system from the earliest descriptions of Bogoraz (1900) to Dunn's (1999) descriptive grammar. Dunn (1999, 97ff) argues for a reanalysis of two other nominal suffixes as spatial case markers, using the morphological criterion that the marker itself must be in complementary distribution with the core case markers, absolutive and ergative, and the syntactic criterion that the case-marked nominal must be able to function as an independent core argument or adjunct of a predication. The possessive/relational suffixes fail both tests, and Dunn (1999, 149) explicitly contradicts Koptjevskaja-Tamm's claim that the possessive/relational suffixes are cases.

There is one respect, however, in which Chukchi denominal adjectives do indeed behave a little like case-marked forms of the base noun lexeme. Both possessive and relational adjectives allow their base nouns to be modified in specific circumstances, that is, they show the BNMP. In the examples in (17) from Skorik (1961, 394) we see the base noun modified by numerals which have even been incorporated into the head noun they modify.

(17) a. ŋəran-waam-ken ənneen
four-river-REL.A fish
'fish from four rivers'

b. ŋiren-ʔəttʔ-en renreŋ
three-dog-POSS.A fodder
'fodder for three dogs'

This behaviour is precisely what we expect of denominal adjectives which are true transpositions, since a transposition is effectively still a form of the base noun lexeme. In fact, as we show in later chapters, our model predicts that such adjectives should permit modification by adjectives too. Unfortunately, our sources do not provide enough evidence to discuss such cases in Chukchi, so it is unclear whether that prediction is met. None of the sources rule it out, but this is a question that can only be resolved by further field work.

Proprietive and Privative Adjectives

Like possessive and relational adjectives, proprietive (or comitative) adjectives express some kind of loose association between the denotation of the base noun and the head noun. Cross-linguistically they fall within a very large semantic range. Most generally, they can be characterized as denoting possession, if the latter is understood fairly loosely as a certain (pragmatically/contextually and/or lexically defined) association between two entities, as we discussed in Chapter 2. Typical English examples are *milk-y* (*drink*), *rain-y autumn* (= *autumn with rain*), *hungr-y dog* (= *dog with hunger*), *beard-ed man* (= *man with beard*), *wheel-ed transport*. Komi Zyrian (Uralic) proprietive adjectives in *-(j)a* indicate the relationships of (temporary) ownership or disposal (*ružje-a* 'with a gun, armed'), inalienable possession (*śur-a* 'with horns'), content or material (*jöl-a* 'milky, made of milk'), size or measurement (*verda-a* 'bucket-sized'), and shape (*tupös-ja* 'flat-shaped'), but there may be many other semantic relations that are difficult to generalize (Lytkin, 1955, 170–171). We can say that such adjectives involve an added semantic predicate WITH(N) or HAVING(N) and therefore create a special subtype of adjective related specifically to an individual base noun, though this can be misleading because of the vague meaning associated with WITH or HAVE.

We saw above that relational adjectives typically take common noun denotations as their base, essentially denoting (non-referential) concepts, while possessive adjectives typically take referential denotations (proper names, kin terms). Proprietive adjectives can pattern either way depending on the semantics of the noun. Typically, the relation between a head noun

102   *Categorial Mixing in the Nominal Phrase*

and the noun concept denoted by the base of the proprietive adjective will be one of superordinate–subordinate, for instance, whole–part or ground–figure. What is important is that in a sense proprietives show the opposite semantic 'headedness' to possessive adjectives: the head noun is the 'possessor', while the dependent proprietive adjective corresponds to the 'possessed'. In some cases we can actually reverse the headedness relation, to get a possessive construction, a relational adjective or a simple N-N compound: *tattooed arm* vs. *arm tattoo* 'the type of tattoo typically put on an arm'. We might find a case in which *campsite-PROPR.A riverbank* means 'a riverbank which has (many) campsites along it', while *riverbank-PROPR.A campsite* means 'a campsite which is by a riverbank (as opposed to in the forest)'. Given the typical meronymic relation of 'oar = part-of canoe', the interpretation of *canoe-REL.A oar* (= 'oar bearing some relation $\Re$ to the concept canoe') will typically cash out as 'oar which is used for propelling a canoe'. Conversely, *oar-PROPR.A canoe* will be interpreted as 'canoe bearing some relation $\Re$ to the concept oar'. This will typically be cashed out as something like 'canoe which has an oar', so that the proprietive adjective *oar-PROPR.A* is naturally interpreted as something like 'having/containing/with an oar'. In these cases the meanings of the two nouns are such that each can be considered superordinate to the other in differing circumstances. Intrinsic semantic relations generally play a considerable role in determining standard interpretations for such expressions. In other cases, such a reversal is less plausible, generally because of real-world conditions: *wheeled transport* vs. *?transport wheel* (= 'wheel for transport vehicles').

Proprietives are very widespread in Altaic (Turkic, Tungusic, and Mongolic) languages (see Nikolaeva, 2008, 2014a for an overview). In these languages they clearly have the external syntax of attributive modifiers, and at least some of them participate in comparative and superlative constructions and take attributive agreement with the head noun (in some languages). Whereas in some proprietive adjectives the base noun cannot head a syntactic phrase of its own similar to the English proprietives in *-y*, which fail to exhibit syntagmatic mixing, other Altaic proprietives demonstrate the BNMP. In Turkic and Mongolic the modifiers of the base noun can be numerals or qualitative adjectives and they are generally restricted to those proprietives that denote part–whole relations, rather similar to English *ed*-adjectives. In Tungusic, on the other hand, there are no such restrictions, as shown by Udihe *aja mä:usa-xi* (good gun-PROPR.A) 'with a good gun' and Evenki *ńamapču aaw-laan* (warm hat-PROPR.A) 'with a warm hat'. The base noun can head a quantifier, a reciprocal adjective, a nominal modifier, an oblique phrase, or an

3.3 Denominal Adjectives 103

apposition-like noun.[9] The only types of adnominal dependents that seem to be impossible for the base noun are possessors and determiners, so we may say that proprietive derivation involves attributivization of NPs but not DPs.

In addition, at least in Northern Tungusic, proprietives show traces of paradigmatic mixing, since the base noun retains some morphological properties of nouns; in particular, it can be inflected for such nominal property as number. In Evenki, which has attributive agreement, the base noun controls optional number agreement on a stranded adjective. In (45a) the proprietive agrees in case (the dative) with the noun it modifies, as is typical of other attributive adjectives. The base noun is in the plural, as indicated by the plural affix preceding the proprietive exponent. This noun triggers plural agreement on its adjectival modifier *ajal*.

(18) aja-l   oro-l-či-du   asi:-du
     good-PL reindeer-PL-PROPR.A-DAT woman-DAT
     'to the woman with good reindeer (PL)'

Obviously, this property of the underlying noun lexeme is syntactically relevant, so we can conclude that in spite of being embedded by the proprietive exponent, it remains active in syntax. Thus, Tungusic proprietives represent transpositions with paradigmatic and syntagmatic mixing in our typology. We discuss the way they fit into our model in Chapter 8, Section 8.4.3.

A similar situation is observed in a number of Uralic languages. In Tundra Nenets true proprietive adjectives are derived by the suffix -*l'aŋk°*, e.g. *sar'o* 'rain' > *sar'o-l'aŋk°* 'rainy', *n'arco* 'moss' > *n'arco-l'aŋk°* 'mossy'. This pattern is quite productive, but such proprietives do not retain any nominal properties, either in terms of their morphology or in terms of syntax. In addition we find what Nikolaeva (2014a) refers to as proprietive 'adjectival forms of nouns'. These are productively derived from countable inanimate nouns by the suffix -*sawey°*, and the referentiality of the base noun is preserved as shown by the following contrast: *ŋod'a-sawey° xid'a* 'the cup with (the) berries (berry-PROPR.A cup)' vs. *ŋod'a xid'a* 'berry cup, cup for berries'. The base noun of such proprietives can take regular attributive modifiers, e.g. *səwa pad°-sawey° n'enec'°h* (good bag-PROPR.A person) 'the man with a good bag'. We can also observe that it can trigger optional plural concord on its modifier, as shown in (19).

(19) n'ud'a-q xal'a-sawey° to
     small-PL fish-PROPR.A lake
     'lake with small fish (PL)'

---

[9] See Chapter 8, Section 8.4.3 for examples of these types.

104   *Categorial Mixing in the Nominal Phrase*

Since the base noun is typically referential, it is also compatible with determiners, e.g. *t'uku° pad°-sawey°* 'with this bag', but it appears that the proprietive cannot head its own possessor and cannot be cross-referenced by outbound anaphora.

It is worth mentioning that in some Uralic and Altaic languages proprietive forms assume clause-level status. Nikolaeva (2014a) mentions that there is a historical connection between proprietive adjectives and the comitative case in Altaic. The direction of development (from adjectival suffix to the comitative case or the other way round) is not entirely clear, but the diachronic connection between the two suggests that various intermediate stages and forms with mixed properties are likely to arise.

An interesting example of this is Evenki. This language exhibits the proprietive/comitative marker *-nun-* which renders roughly the same semantic relations as proprietive adjectives in other languages. Nedjalkov (1997, 159) refers to it as the 'comitative case'. It can also serve for coordination, while remaining NP-internal. While attributive adjectives are invariably preverbal, the NP-internal comitative may be postnominal. In this it does not differ from other oblique case forms that may be located NP-internally and serve to modify the base noun through various types of semantic relations. However, unlike other oblique cases the NP-internal comitative shows attributive concord with non-nominative cases, as regular attributive adjectives do in this language. The example in (20) illustrates the comitative agreeing in the accusative. The resulting form bears double case, that is, the comitative, which signals the NP-internal relation between 'old woman' and 'old man', and the accusative, which signals concord with the head noun.

(20) bu   iče-re-v   [atirkan-me   etirken-nun-me]
      we.EXCL see-PST-1PL.EXCL old.woman-ACC old.man-COM-ACC
      'We saw the old woman with the old man.'

We can then say that proprietives/comitatives exhibit certain properties of adjectives without being fully adjectival. In this sense they are related to the phenomenon of Suffixaufnahme discussed in Section 3.4.2, although, unlike in the prototypical Suffixaufnahme where the relation between the head and the agreeing dependent is that of 'possession' and expressed by the genitive case, in (20) this relation can be described as involving the semantic head-dependency reversal.

3.4 Modification by Case and Adpositional Phrases 105

Finally, proprietives often have a negative counterpart called 'privative' or 'caritive' adjectives.[10] These can be paraphrased as 'lacking-N', 'without N'. Privative adjectives can be very productive. In Hungarian, they can be derived from virtually every noun by means of the suffix *-t(A)lAn* (where A is a harmonizing vowel), e.g. *csillag-talan éjszaka* 'starless night', *csillag* 'star'; *boldog-talan ember* 'unhappy person', *boldog* 'joy, happiness'; *rende-tlen gyerek* 'disorderly child', *rend* 'order'. Nevertheless, the base noun in such adjectives is no more accessible to attributive modification than the noun base of denominal privative adjectives in English, cf. the ungrammatical **nagy ház-talan* (*nagy* 'big', *ház* 'house') with the intended meaning 'without a big house' and the ungrammatical English [**comfortable home*]-*less* (*person*). It is in fact quite difficult to find good examples of syntagmatic mixing in privative adjectives, even in the languages which allow them.

3.4 Modification by Case and Adpositional Phrases

In languages of very diverse types we find that one and the same grammatical case or prepositional (or postpositional) construction can serve as a modifier of words of a different category, normally either nouns or verbs. In this section we look at case and prepositional constructions that modify nouns and the semantic relations they express. At a very basic level of analysis we can say that such constructions exhibit the same semantic opposition as denominal adjectives: they either lexically specify the kind of relation that exists between the head and dependent (Section 3.4.1) or render a general semantically undetermined association between two nominals (Section 3.4.2).

3.4.1 Constructions with Added Semantic Predicate

We will first look at the classes of constructions which involve oblique (non-nominative, non-genitive) case-marked nominals and phrases headed by prepositions other than *of*-type prepositions. These function as indirect intersective modifiers to a head noun.

Oblique Modifiers
One formal issue requires initial consideration: if a language permits a noun to be modified by an oblique case-marked nominal, do we regard this as

---

[10] As mentioned in Chapter 2, the term 'privative adjective' is often used in a different sense, in which it denotes the class of adjectives that appear to negate the meaning of a noun itself such as *fake*.

106 *Categorial Mixing in the Nominal Phrase*

a species of modification-by-(inflected)-noun or do we regard it as a case of modification-by-postpositional phrase? The issue is not in fact specific to modificational constructions but concerns the very definition of 'adposition', and the characterization of the structure of phrases headed by adpositions.

There is a close diachronic relationship between oblique case-marked nouns and adpositional phrases. We often find that an adposition is derived from a noun (sometimes inflected in a locative case form) and it may retain certain morphosyntactic properties that reflect its historical origins. Uralic languages rarely employ case or adpositional constructions as adnominal modifiers, as we show in the examples below, but they provide a very clear set of examples of how complex the grammaticalization picture can get. The main source of postpositions and oblique cases in virtually all these languages is relational nouns with locational semantics. In some cases the grammaticalization process is still active and can be observed in various intermediate stages. For instance, the Komi Permyak postposition *vyl-* 'on' present in the standard literary variety of the language has agglutinated as a bound case suffix in the southern Komi Permyak dialects, whereas the etymologically related word *vǝl* 'top, surface' in the closely related language Besyermyan Udmurt still functions as a relational noun in some uses, but in other uses it shows properties of postpositions (Usačeva, 2012, 156–157).

In Hungarian, there are two sorts of category that are typically labelled 'postposition'. One type of postposition takes a case-marked nominal complement, whose case form is selected by that postposition (Kenesei et al., 1998, 338). Examples are *kívül* 'beside' and *fogva* 'from/since', e.g. *a ház-on kívül* 'beside the house' (the house-SUPER beside), *e perc-től fogva* 'from/since this minute' (this minute-ABL from/since). These expressions (which Spencer and Stump (2013) refer to as 'pseudo-postpositions') collocate with pronominal complements in the expected way: that is, when the pseudo-postposition selects a pronoun, that pronoun appears in the appropriate case, e.g. *rajtam kívül* 'beside me' where *rajtam* is the superessive form of the 1SG personal pronoun. This type of postposition is very similar to so-called 'compound prepositions' in English, such as *in front of*. In Huddleston and Pullum (2002, 620–623) such constructions are almost always treated as syntactically analysable phrases, either with the right-branching structure [P *in* [N *front* [PP *of the house*]]] or with the 'layered' structure [PP[PP *in* [N *front*]][NP *of* [NP *the house*]]]. In both these analyses we are dealing with a special type of noun construction. The same analysis is valid for Hungarian pseudo-postpositions (see Creissels, 2006). In contrast, what we can call 'true postpositions' following Spencer and Stump (2013) take a nominal complement in the nominative (or bare, uninflected) case form, and

3.4 Modification by Case and Adpositional Phrases 107

are marked for number (singular/plural) and possibly for possessor agreement: see (21).

(21) a ház-a-i-m   mögött
      DEF house-POSS-PL-1SG behind
      'behind our houses'

However, when the postpositions take pronominal complements, they retain the trace of their historical origin from relational nouns and inflect for possessor agreement: *mögött-em* 'behind me (behind-1SG)'.

Similar examples are rife in almost all languages with a postpositional category. Given complex paths of partial grammaticalization such as this, it should not be surprising to find that a good many case marking constructions shade into postpositional constructions in their morphosyntax. So in languages which have rich and relatively systematic case marking we often find that a case-marked nominal has exactly the same function as an adpositional phrase either within the same language or in languages with a less rich case system. For these reasons alone it is advisable to treat adpositional phrases and case-marked nominals as at least very closely related construction types, which we can call 'oblique modifiers'.

It is common for oblique modifiers to express the nature of the relation between two nominals by means of the case or adposition itself. This is the reminiscent of semantically enriched denominal adjectives discussed in Section 3.3.1, where we saw that the relation between the head noun and the dependent expression has a clearly identified semantic content encoded by the constructional marker itself. In such adjectives the constructional marker is the adjectival affix: the Georgian suffix *-el* in (7a) indicates both attributivization and the relation of 'origin', and the Tundra Nenets *-rəxa/-r°xa* in (5) indicates both attributivization and the relation of 'resemblance'. Similarly, in *the tree behind the house* the preposition *behind* denotes the specific locational relation between the tree and the house, while in the Hungarian *könyv a szerelem-ről* 'a book about love' (book DEF love-DEL) the delative case in *-ről* 'denotes', so to speak, the relation of 'aboutness'. However, there is no additional marker of attributivization and the oblique phrase is not lexically transposed into an adjective.

In other languages the attributivization of oblique phrases is expressed using a separate morphological device. Derivational morphology can create attributive adjectives from adpositional phrases. For instance, Slavic languages such as Russian have a wealth of adjectives formed by means of the relational adjectival suffix *-n-* attached to nouns prefixed by prepositions: *za* 'beyond',

108   *Categorial Mixing in the Nominal Phrase*

rubež 'boundary, frontier' > *za-rubež-n-yj* 'foreign, overseas'; *bez* 'without', *dom* 'house' > *bez-dom-n-yj* 'homeless'. In English we see a covert version of the same type of construction formed mainly from neo-classical (Latin, Greek) vocabulary and predominantly found in technical language. Thus, expressions such as *epidermal* or *subcutaneous* mean 'on the skin' and 'under the skin' respectively. Exactly the same pattern is found, however, with less restricted vocabulary: *international* 'between nations', *subterranean* 'under the earth', *supersonic* 'above (the speed of) sound' and many others.

While in English and Russian the formation of such adjectives is lexically restricted, in other languages the attributivization of (some types of) oblique phrases is fully productive. In (22) we see the Turkish locative case-marked noun *sokak-ta* 'on the street' (street-LOC), which has been turned into an attribute by means of the attributivizer -*ki*.

(22)   sokak-ta-ki   araba
        street-LOC-ATTR car
        'the car on the street'

The locative specifies the type of the semantic relation between the head 'car' and dependent noun 'street', while the phrasal affix -*ki* is semantically empty in the sense that it only adds a modificational meaning. In essence, then, the Turkish example is parallel to what we have in (5) and other examples in Section 3.3.1, except that attributivization is expressed by a separate exponent. In Turkish we can form locative and temporal attributive modifiers from nominal phrases by means of -*ki* (Erschen-Rasch, 2007, 121). Unlike the base noun of the English derived adjectives but similar to the Nenets and Georgian examples in (5) and (7), the base noun of such form is fully accessible to syntax. The examples in (23) are from Schroeder (2000).

(23)   a. cam-ın   kenar-ın-da-ki   yatak
            glass-GEN side-POSS.3-LOC-ATTR bed
            'the bed at the side of the window'

        b. bu fotoğraf-ta-ki   hanım kim?
            this photograph-LOC-ATTR woman who
            'Who is the woman in this photograph?'

        c. saat on-da-ki   tren
            hour ten-LOC-ATTR train
            'the 10 o'clock train'

For instance, in (23a) the base noun of the attributive form 'side' heads a genitive possessor and, what is more, bears the third person singular

3.4 Modification by Case and Adpositional Phrases   109

possessive affix that cross-references this possessor. It appears, then, that the function of *-ki* is the attributivization of the fully formed possessive phrase *cam-ın kenar-ın-da*. Lewis (1967, 251) provides an even more elaborate example in (24).

(24) sakallı ihtiyar-ın   [bilhassa bahşiş alır-ken]-ki
      bearded old.man-GEN especially tip   accept-GER-ATTR
      durum-u
      attitude-POSS.3SG
      'the bearded old man's attitude, especially when accepting a tip'

Here the affix *-ki* has turned the entire gerundial phrase *bilhassa bahşiş alır-ken* into an attributive modifier of *durumu* 'his attitude'.

Although in Turkish the locative is the only inflectional case that can be attributivized in this manner, a number of Daghestanian languages have special attributivizers that are compatible with several (although not necessarily all) case forms of nouns. The resulting forms function as modifiers, but their exact meaning largely depends on the respective case. In (25) we present examples from Akhvakh, cited here after Boguslavskaja (1989).

(25) a. žijali-La-sẹ   łẹni
        cow.PL-DAT-ATTR water
        'water for cows'

     b. wacō-k'ena-sẹ   waša
        brother-COM-ATTR boy
        'the boy with the brother'

     c. q̄ēda-Ḻi-sẹ   qot'o
        wall-LOC-ATTR plate
        'the plate on the wall'

It should be noted that this language draws a morphosyntactic distinction between restrictive attributes (that is, those that involve contrast with other possible delimitations) and attributes that are neutral with respect to re-strictivity (Boguslavskaja, 1995, 236). Only restrictive adjectives agree with the head noun in grammatical class, and exactly the same behaviour is observed in the attributivized forms of grammatical cases when they have a restrictive/contrastive interpretation: cf. (25a) and (26).

(26) žijali-La-sẹ-be   łẹni
      cow.PL-DAT-ATTR-III water[III]
      'the water which is for cows (not for humans)'

110 *Categorial Mixing in the Nominal Phrase*

Unlike the non-restrictive attributive form in (25a), the restrictive one in (26) exhibits obligatory concord in class III with the head noun in the manner of restrictive adjectives.

In these examples we have a clearly identifiable semantic predicate, e.g. 'meant for N' in (25a), 'having N, with N' in (25b), 'located on N' in (25c), and so on. These are semantically equivalent to some of the derived adjectives presented in Section 3.3.1. However, in Turkish and Daghestanian the nature of this predicate is indicated by a case marker, which precedes the attributivizing exponent. On the other hand, we can note an intriguing connection between the modifiers, which have the morphosyntax of adjectives and oblique case-marked noun types previously discussed: the Turkish and Daghestanian construction is reminiscent of the way that case-marked nouns realize the role of adnominal modifier in many European languages, as already outlined. Where a language permits attributive formation by means of a specialized attributivizer, this is not typically restricted to case-marked nouns. The Turkish *-ki* suffix attaches to postpositional phrases and temporal and locative adverbs, and is even able to turn whole clauses into attributive modifiers (Schroeder, 2000; Göksel and Kerslake, 2005, 71–72). This is also observed in other Daghestanian languages such as Tsakhur and Chamalal although not in Akhvakh (Boguslavskaja, 1989). This fact demonstrates again that there is a close connection between oblique case-marked nouns and adpositional phrases in the modificational function.

Reduced Relative Clauses

We now turn to another aspect of modification-by-oblique. A general property of Uralic languages is that oblique case-marked nouns and PPs are rarely able to function as attributive modifiers. Modification by PPs typically requires a special attributivizing device, either an adjective-like derivation as in Selkup (see Chapter 8) or a relative clause-like structure in which the syntactic relationship between the modifying oblique phrase and the head noun is mediated by a kind of participial form. Such constructions provide a particularly clear instance in which an oblique case-marked noun or an oblique PP are effectively treated morphosyntactically as though they were adjectives, and the head noun is treated as the target of attributive modification as though the dependent were a property-denoting phrase. They also clearly demonstrate the inherently predicative nature of indirect modification.

The early literature has emphasized that in English and a number of other languages PPs and oblique cases cannot precede the noun they modify, e.g. *a*

3.4 Modification by Case and Adpositional Phrases 111

tunnel under the city vs. **an under the city tunnel* (Williams, 1982).[11] This is also true of Hungarian, but in Hungarian it turns out to be rather difficult to postmodify even a noun with another case-marked noun pure and simple (see Kenesei et al., 1998, 97–98). In general it is necessary to put the case-marked modifying noun in a construction with a particle *való*, etymologically a present participle of the verb 'to be'. The contrasting examples in (27) are from Hegedűs (2016).[12]

(27)   a. a   Péter-rel   való találkozás
            DEF Peter-INSTR ATTR meeting
            'meeting with Peter'

        b. találkozás Péter-rel
            meeting   Peter-INSTR
            'meeting with Peter'

The particle *való* was analysed as an attributivizing exponent by Laczkó (1995). In Laczkó's analysis it is simply a category-changing device, while the nature of the semantic relation between the denotation of the head noun and the denotation of the object of postposition is indicated by the postposition itself. In essence, then, the whole phrase is attributivized, so *való* is a function word with the same role as the Turkish phrasal affix *-ki*. Under this analysis the semantic representation of the attributive construction in (27a) will be essentially identical to that of the instrumental case in (27b). The main difference between the two forms seems to be syntactic: the *való* construction is a specific form for expressing attributive modification, while the instrumental case form of the noun is first and foremost an adverbial form.

Tundra Nenets employs several imperfective participles to perform essentially the same function (Nikolaeva, 2014b).[13] The most common one is *ŋēda* 'being', which typically attributivizes postpositional phrases, as shown in, (28).

(28)   a. mərəd°-h n'ah ŋǣda-q s'ixeri°-q
           city-GEN to   ATTR-PL road-PL
           'roads to the city'

---

[11] There are, of course, compounds with this kind of structure: *out-of-the-box thinking, behind the scenes inquiries, under the table payments*, but these preferentially involve fixed expressions.

[12] Hegedűs (2016) notes that oblique postnominal modifiers have became more widespread; this tendency is to be expected given the changes from OV to VO and less strict head-finality.

[13] In Hungarian too, a number of other semantically empty participles are possible in such constructions, but they do not appear to show the same degree of grammaticalization as *való*. Both languages also have derived attributive forms of postpositions, but what determines the choice between the two constructions is unclear.

112   *Categorial Mixing in the Nominal Phrase*

    b. tol°-h   n'in'a ŋæda xal'a
        table-GEN on   ATTR fish
        'fish on the table'

    c. wen'ako-h n'amna ŋæda kniga
        dog-GEN about ATTR book
        'a book about a dog'

The PPs in (28) are fully regular. The object of the postposition stands in the genitive, as is typical of Tundra Nenets. Unlike in Hungarian, omitting the attributivizing participle appears impossible in most cases and the participle agrees with the head in number, as shown in (28a). The construction is meaning-bearing in the sense that the modifying oblique phrase renders various semantic relations. They are comparable to the relations expressed by the meaning-bearing-derived adjectives addressed in Section 3.3.1 or the attributivized inflectional cases in Daghestanian.

When Nenets nouns in oblique cases are attributivized, a different participle is required, the imperfective participle *meta* derived from the semantically light verb *meq-* 'to keep, to have, to use'. It is totally desemanticized and functions as a sort of attributivizer for a case-marked oblique phrase: the prolative in (29a), locative in (29b), and accusative in (29c).

(29)   a. xəlcoqli°h   syí-w°nya meta yinya
          shaft.bow.GEN hole-PROL ATTR strap
          'strap (going) through a hole in the shaft-bow'

      b. yesy°r-kəna meta ŋəno
          sail-LOC   ATTR boat
          'sailing boat; boat in which one sails'

      c. motor°-m meta ŋəno
          motor-ACC ATTR boat
          'motor boat; boat which uses a motor'

The constructions illustrated in this section and in the previous two sections are realizations of PP-based indirect modifiers with an additional level of structure. Indirect modifiers are obviously syntactically non-canonical. However, in their standard phrasal form they provide little evidence for categorial mixing, except perhaps for their attributive role, which is non-canonical for true nouns. The reason for this is that the more the morphology moves away from head marking and approaches the marking of a phrase by a function word, the more transparent the construction is. It is only a general tendency and we may encounter other combinations of properties, but generally speaking a lexeme

3.4 Modification by Case and Adpositional Phrases   113

which bears inherent and especially contextual inflections is expected to show transparency.

3.4.2   Constructions with No Added Semantic Predicate

As explained in the previous chapter, modification constructions which do not appear to describe any specific semantic relation between the head and the modifier noun are possession and modification-by-noun. They are often expressed by genitives or by *of*-type PPs.

Agreeing Genitives

Genitives are clearly part of the case paradigm, but there are languages where they show certain morphosyntactic properties of adjectives, in particular the patterns of agreement (concord). So a noun marked by the genitive case functions as a kind of attributive modifier and shares agreement properties. The phenomenon of agreeing genitives is rather well known since it constitutes the core case of Suffixaufnahme (Plank, 1995b, 50), in which a case-marked noun assumes a second case marker. The prototypical instances of Suffixaufnahme are found when

> there is a nominal consisting of …a noun or a personal pronoun in a relationship of … attribution to another nominal, in … the basic form that attributive constructions take in the language concerned, with the head nominal morphologically marked by a case suffix for its external syntactic relation, with the … attributive carrying … the inflectional marking of genitive case, and — crucially — with the attributive itself in addition separately marked for the same case, plus perhaps further categories expressed by suffixes, as the head. (Plank, 1995b, 50)

In other words, the dependent noun in the genitive additionally acquires the case (and perhaps other categories) of its head noun, which looks like an instance of attributive concord. It has indeed been analysed as a kind of concord, for instance in Richards' (2013) account of Lardil, while Plank (1995b) points out similarities between Suffixaufnahme and agreeing linkers found in languages like Hindi or Albanian (see Section 3.5) or the agreeing ezafe in Kurmanji Kurdish (Chapter 2).

From our perspective, the phenomenon of Suffixaufnahme can best be generalized to situations in which a genitive-marked noun is treated morphosyntactically as an adjectival modifier. In those constructions, the noun is inflected for case, but that case form then behaves like an attributive adjective

114   *Categorial Mixing in the Nominal Phrase*

and thus appears to shift its syntactic category. Here we would normally expect such a genitive attributive form to be modified in the manner of the base noun, not in the manner of an adjective. Yet when this occurs, inflectional morphology shows paradigmatic category mixing and we obtain a kind of syntagmatic mixing too: 'to the left' the word behaves like a noun, while 'to the right' it behaves like an adjective.

Plank's (1995a) collection contains many examples of agreement by Suffixaufnahme, including examples of the equivalent of agreement expressed by more or less agglutinative combination of exponents. One typical example from Old Georgian (Kartvelian) as shown in (30).[14]

(30)   perx-n-i   ... ḳac-isa-n-i
       foot-PL-NOM   man-GEN-PL-NOM
       'the feet of the man'

In (30) the postnominal genitive has the canonical possessive semantics but also demonstrates case (nominative) and number (plural) concord with the possessed head noun. In a sense, then, the genitive creates the attributive form but additionally indicates the possessive relation. A similar situation is observed in Daghestanian languages, mainly those of the Tzesic subgroup spoken in the area adjacent to Georgian, in which the inflecting genitive marks the gender and/or number of the possessed noun (Boguslavskaja, 1995; Kibrik, 1995; Koptjevskaja-Tamm, 2003a). We can also see agreeing genitives in Central Cushitic languages: see the data reported in Hetzron's 1995, 326 discussion of Awngi and further discussion of the Awngi data in Spencer (2013, 355–356). The Awngi case will be analysed in Chapter 8.

Agreeing genitives are found in Romani, where the genitive marker follows the marker of the oblique stem. This makes the genitive look like any other oblique case in the language (Koptjevskaja-Tamm, 2000, 2003a). However, the genitive also takes gender/number/case concord with the head noun and this makes the genitive form look like a Romani attributive adjective: see (31). None of the other grammatical cases show anything of this kind. In both adjectives and genitives concord is partial, in the sense that it is only sensitive to the opposition nominative vs. oblique rather than to every single case.

(31)   a. i   kraj-es-k-i   rakli
          INDF king-OBL-GEN-F.SG.NOM daughter[F]
          'king's daughter'

---

[14]   In modern Georgian Suffixaufnahme is less widespread and usually considered archaic (Koptjevskaja-Tamm, 2003a, 633).

3.4 Modification by Case and Adpositional Phrases   115

b. o   rom   e   šukar-e
   DEF.M.SG.NOM husband[SG.NOM] DEF.OBL beautiful-OBL
   romn-á-k-o
   woman-OBL-GEN-M.SG.NOM
   'the husband of the beautiful woman'

Koptjevskaja-Tamm argues that genitives are fully regular and productive, and that they conform to the nominal inflectional paradigm. Their base noun shows many properties of regular nouns, e.g. an inherent number opposition, referentiality, and the ability to head its own modifier or possessor as in (31b). In this sense Romani exhibits the phenomenon of Suffixaufnahme; however, this is not a canonical case of Suffixaufnahme.

First, we have already seen that the so-called possessive adjectives have essentially the same semantics as traditional genitives, but agree with the head noun and display other adjectival properties. It makes sense, then, to analyse agreeing genitives along the same lines, that is, as derived adjectives rather than part of the inflectional paradigm. Second, in Romani agreeing genitives of the kind discussed here can also be used for purposes of modification-by-noun. They appear to have a double function: some of them express non-anchoring relations, e.g. *for-os-k-o gras* (town-OBL-GEN-M.SG.NOM horse.M.NOM) 'a town horse'. Thus, a single attributive strategy is employed for essentially all types of modificational relation, which brings Romani closer to the languages we discuss in Section 3.5.[15]

In conclusion, like possessive adjectives, agreeing genitives demonstrate a deep link between the possessive relation and what we have termed 'attributive modification'. They represent essentially the same morphosyntactic strategy for expressing both semantic functions. In other words, possessor nouns exhibit properties of syntactic modifiers.

Genitives in Modification-by-Noun

The well-known function of the genitive case is to mark a nominal whose referent (possessor) is connected by a possessive relation to the entity expressed by the phrase within which the genitive phrase is embedded (possessed noun). However, as a primarily adnominal case, the genitive has a very special role in adnominal modification and exhibits a number of other, less canonical

---

[15] There are indications that Romani non-anchoring genitives differ from regular possessive adjectives in their behaviour; for instance, unlike the latter, they do not head their own possessors due to non-referential semantics.

116   *Categorial Mixing in the Nominal Phrase*

functions including, crucially, modification-by-noun.[16] Such genitives are sometimes called 'type genitives' (Kolliakou, 1999) or 'property-denoting genitives', since they have been shown to exhibit kind or property denotations, e.g. in Russian (Trugman, 2004) and Polish (Cetnarowska et al., 2011). Languages with property-denoting adjectives typically demonstrate homonymy between (alienable) possession and modification-by-noun. The rationale behind such frequent ambiguity of the genitive was discussed in Chapter 2; essentially it has to do with the deep semantic affinity between the two functions, both of which express a semantically undetermined relation $\Re$.[17]

Property-denoting genitives form a rather productive pattern in a number of European languages and languages spoken just outside Europe, such as Germanic, Slavic, Greek, Scottish Gaelic, Lithuanian, Finnish, Georgian, Daghestanian languages, Hebrew, and Armenian (Koptjevskaja-Tamm, 2004). In English, a distinction is usually made between 'specifying/determiner genitives' and 'attributive/descriptive/classifying genitives', the main semantic difference being attributed to the referentiality of the genitive. Another relevant Germanic language is Swedish (it also has Germanic-style compounding as a minor strategy). Koptjevskaja-Tamm (2003a) argues at great length that, in addition to prototypical possessive relations, the genitive in Swedish expresses a range of other, non-anchoring, semantic functions. Possessive genitives function as determiners and are incompatible with articles, while non-anchoring genitives co-occur with articles. Such genitives have a modificational interpretation, as seen in (32) (Koptjevskaja-Tamm 2003c, 522, 527).

(32)   a.   ett   [sex veck-or-s]   barn
              INDF six   week-PL-GEN child
              'a six-week-old baby'

        b.   ett   vinter-väg-at-na-s   land
              INDF winter-road-PL-DEF-GEN country
              'a country of winter roads'

---

[16]   Other cross-linguistically common 'non-possessive' functions of adnominal genitives are constructions "involving several nominals characterizing the same referent" (Lander, 2009, 589) and various kinds of partitives (see Selkirk, 1977; Chisarik and Payne, 2001; Koptjevskaja-Tamm, 2001b, among others). Partitive genitives indicate the whole of which the head nominal is a part. Since they are primarily quantificational, they are not directly relevant here given our pretheoretical understanding of attributive modification.

[17]   Modification-by-noun can be expressed by other possessive strategies such as head marking agreement in Udihe (Chapter 2, Section 2.5.4), although this appears to be cross-linguistically less frequent.

Koptjevskaja-Tamm lists several semantic subtypes of non-anchoring genitives, including 'qualitative' genitives which provide qualitative characteristics of the object referred to by the head nominal (e.g. *a man of duty, a period of cynicism, a land of corruption*). What she terms 'classifying' genitives provide means for a categorization of the entity referred to by the head, e.g. *a masterpiece of children's literature* etc. In her analysis there are more semantic subtypes, but non-anchoring genitives can hardly be classified into well-defined semantic groups. Koptjevskaja-Tamm (2003c, 539) herself notices that the link between the two entities is very loose, so that "there is no general paraphrase which could cover all these cases". A safer option would be to say that the relation which is expressed by non-anchoring genitives is semantically vacuous (that is, our ℜ-relation).

The effects of the modification-by-noun construction are systematically realized by a construction normally associated with possessives in Latvian and Lithuanian, where compounds are frequently formed on the genitive (plural) form of the modifier noun rather than the base/stem form (Mathiassen, 1996, 1997). Property-denoting genitives in Slavic are used less frequently and only for some relations. In Russian, for instance, they are primarily modifiers that require an obligatory modifier of their own (33a) or type genitives (33b) (Koptjevskaja-Tamm, 2004, 163). The example in (33a) is actually a proprietive-like construction.

(33)   a. pisatel' bol'š-ogo   talent-a
             writer big-GEN.M.SG talent-GEN[M.SG]
             'a writer of a great talent'

        b. slovo džentel'men-a
             word gentleman-GEN
             'a gentleman's word'

In Finnish the genitive expresses alienable and inalienable possession, but is also the principal productive strategy for modification-by-noun and as such is extremely ambiguous (see e.g. Mahieu, 2013).[18] However, the latter differs in its position from possessive genitives. To illustrate this point, Christen (2001, 513) shows that Finnish non-referential genitives which typically encode modification-by-noun must be adjacent to the head, while for truly possessive genitives this requirement does not hold: cf. (34a) and (34b).

---

[18] Finnish additionally has non-genitive N-N compounds but their productivity is not as great as in Germanic, and they are mostly used to denote material (Christen, 2001).

118   *Categorial Mixing in the Nominal Phrase*

(34)   a.   kaupungin aktiiviset asukkaat
             town.GEN active.PL people.PL
             'the active people in/of the town'

        b.   aktiiviset kaupungin asukkaat
             active.PL town.GEN people.PL
             '(the) active town people'

This comports well with Koptjevskaja-Tamm's (2004, 164) observation that the non-anchoring genitive "always appears closer to the head than the anchoring one" and sometimes may even show "symptoms of no longer being an autonomous noun". Indeed, in Finnish a large number of such genitives have been lexicalized as non-syntactic compounds (Jokinen, 1991).

Outside Europe this is also true of Japanese, where the genitive particle/clitic *-no* is employed in standard possessive constructions, but also forms prenominal modifiers functionally equivalent to relational adjectives or Germanic N-N compounds. Some examples of non-possessive genitives are: *komugi-no pan* 'wheat bread (wheat-GEN bread)', *chuugoku-no kabin* 'Chinese vase (China-GEN vase)', *sankaku-no heya* 'triangular room (triangle-GEN room)', *jimoto-no wain* 'local wine (home-GEN wine)'. Nagano and Shimada (2015) proposed that non-possessive *no*-forms in Japanese and standard relational adjectives in other languages are morphophonological variations of the 'common functional structure' of non-intersective direct modifiers, and therefore must be immediately prenominal. True relational adjectives are absent in Japanese, but since different languages use different morphological realizations for common grammatical functions, direct modifiers in Japanese are formed not by an adjectival suffix but by a nominal case. Such modifiers instantiate a weaker kind of mismatch than agreeing genitives addressed in the previous section because they fail to display canonical attributive morphosyntax. However they are non-canonical in the same way that N-N compounds are.

Of-Type PPs

Of-type prepositional constructions are cross-linguistically frequent. In European languages they are often ambiguous between possessive and modification-by-noun readings, similar to the inflectional genitives we have just surveyed. This is observed in Germanic (with the exception of Icelandic, Standard Swedish, and Danish), Maltese, and Aramaic, as well as some Celtic, Romance, and Slavic languages (Koptjevskaja-Tamm, 2003a,b, 2004). Maltese was exemplified in Chapter 2; see also the following Italian examples: *la casa di un/il professore* 'the house of a/the teacher' vs. *la casa di pietra* 'the house of stone', *la casa di moda* 'the house of fashion', and *la casa di campagna* 'the country house'. In English, too, the *of*-PPs can be semantically interpreted either as possessors or as modifiers, in which instance they overlap considerably with N-N compounds, e.g. *the song of love* (= love song).[19]

Furthermore, we often find that a specific *of*-type PP functions sometimes as a modifier and sometimes as a complement to the head. In this respect, PPs behave like adjectival words in languages that do not distinguish a category of adjective from a category of (deadjectival) adverb. The crucial role here belongs to the lexical head of the phrase, that is, the noun. To illustrate, consider the English examples in (35) to (39).

(35) a. a teacher of physics
      b. a teacher with red hair

(36) a. a student of physics
      b. a student with red hair

(37) a. a girl (*of physics)
      b. a girl with red hair

(38) a. a map of London
      b. a map with a blue border

(39) a. a page (*of London)
      b. a page with a blue border

In (35) we see that a PP can either serve as an optional adjunct adding inessential information about the denotation of the head noun (*with red hair*) or it can realize an argument, in this case an argument inherited from the argument structure of the verb TEACH. In (36) we see exactly the same pattern, but in (37) we see that the phrase *of physics* is no longer felicitous. This is because it is difficult to interpret it as a genuine adjunct rather than an argument. It might be thought that the contrast arises because STUDENT is like TEACHER in being a deverbal nominalization (from STUDY). However, (38) and (39) show that this is not the case. In (38) the PP *of London* realizes a semantic argument implied by the meaning of MAP. In a sense, MAP is a relational noun, like DAUGHTER or CORNER, but for different reasons. The lexeme MAP is an artefact term, and in terms of Pustejovsky's Generative Lexicon will therefore entail a Qualia Structure including the AGENTIVE and TELIC qualia (see the discussion in Section 2.4.1). The TELIC quale will include a specification of the fact

---

[19] It is not fully clear to what extent the *of*-PPs that participate in 'dependency reversal' constructions of the kind *that idiot of a doctor* (Malchukov, 2000) are modifiers.

120 *Categorial Mixing in the Nominal Phrase*

that a map has to be a representation of some place. It is that quale that is accessed by the PP *of London*. The lexeme PAGE is also an artefact term and it presumably also has a TELIC quale, but one which lacks an indication of being a representation of something or some place. On the other hand, PAGE includes in its Qualia Structure the TELIC quale of being associated with a linguistic, pictorial, etc. representation, as well as the CONSTITUTIVE quale that implies that a PAGE can be a meronym of BOOK, LETTER, and so on. Thus, we can have *a page of writing/pictures/poetry/* or *a page of the book/letter*. Contrast these examples with **a map of writing/pictures/poetry/*, which is very hard to interpret, or *a map of the book/letter*, which, if interpretable, lacks the meronymic reading.

A comparable problem arises with other modification-by-noun constructions and is clearly noticeable in the literature on the interpretation of genitives, relational adjectives, and endocentric N-N compounds in language groups such as Germanic (see Sections 3.2 and 3.3.2). This highlights the close affinity between different types of modification-by-noun constructions, made evident in the structural account of Nagano and Shimada (2015), for instance. The competition between these constructions ensures that their distribution is subject to considerable variation across languages and individual expression types. The principles governing their use and the subtleties of their meaning are complex and elusive, and the reasons for preferring one pattern over the other in each particular language are difficult to pin down. Some specific relations may be blocked due to the paradigmatic interference of a rival pattern (Rainer, 2013), or it may be the case that some preferences simply result from fairly random conventionalizations that arbitrarily favour one particular type. It is not our aim to throw any light on these patterns here; we present them simply to illustrate the general problem.

3.5   Attributivization by a Phrasal Affix

In this section we discuss the languages in which the constructional marker relating the head and the dependent is not obviously an affix or a free-standing preposition. It does not belong to the case paradigm either, even if the language happens to have grammatical cases, and therefore cannot be termed a 'genitive' in its pure form. Rather, the element indicating syntactic dependency is a clitic or phrasal affix bearing agreement with the head, but still syntactically in construction with the dependent. The entire nominal phrase is then turned into an attributive modifier by some kind of a constructional marker. This strategy is employed to render various kinds of relationships between the denotation

3.5 Attributivization by a Phrasal Affix   121

of the head and the dependent. In addition to the expression of possession, it may serve for the purposes of modification-by-noun and canonical attributive modification. In all these cases no clearly identifiable semantic predicate is involved.

One example is the Hindi-Urdu postposition *kaa* (McGregor, 1995; Kachru, 2006), representing a construction which is also present in a number of other Indo-Aryan languages such as Punjabi and Nepalese (Payne, 1995, 286). The postposition *kaa* cliticizes to the right edge of a nominal phrase to establish that phrase as the possessor. It inflects exactly like an adjective, agreeing in number, gender, and case (direct, oblique, and vocative) with the possessed noun head, but it is not a derivational affix that creates an adjectival lexeme from a noun. Albanian has a very similar device, but in the form of a cliticized preposition or inflecting 'article'. Hindi and Albanian are discussed at length in Spencer (2005a) and Nikolaeva and Spencer (2012). Both constructions have traditionally been mislabelled as a 'genitive case' (despite the clearly enunciated warnings to the contrary in Newmark (1957)). However, they have nothing to do with case. We are here dealing with a general marker of syntactic dependency which demonstrates the inherent link between possession and attributive modification: see Koptjevskaja-Tamm (2003a, 660–665), Spencer (2005a), Spencer and Otoguro (2005), and Otoguro (2006) for more detailed exemplification of this point.

In that connection it is worth noting that this construction as a whole is broadly similar to the so-called 'a-of-association' in Bantu languages, which lack a case system altogether. This is a construction, widespread in Bantu, in which a possessor is marked by a preposed *a*-formative agreeing in noun class with the possessed noun. The associative marker *a* also links the head noun with various types of property words.[20] We illustrate this type of dependent marking by Tswana, in which the a-of-association construction has become morphologized, with the *a* element becoming a prefix to the possessor. According to Cole (1979, 159ff), possessives are formed by prefixing possessive affixes to the dependent noun. The affixes indicate agreement with the head in class and sometimes also number. The class of the head may also be shown by a prefix; in (40a) the head noun 'dog' is class 5 and in (40b) the head noun 'wife' is class 1.

---

[20]   In Swahili the possessor is expressed by the pronominal set of agreements found with various pronouns, determiners, and verbs, and not with the agreement set reserved for the rather restricted class of adjectives. The parallel between the possessive construction and attributive modification is therefore not necessarily exact, at least in terms of exponents. See Koptjevskaja-Tamm (2003a, 660–665) for further discussion.

122   *Categorial Mixing in the Nominal Phrase*

(40)   a. mo-sadi wa-motšomi
           5-dog   5-hunter
           'hunter's dog'

        b. n-tša   ya-motšomi
           1-wife 1-hunter
           'hunter's wife'

The same strategy serves in what Cole calls 'descriptive possessives', which "denote some quality, function, feature of other characteristic of the antecedent" (Cole, 1979, 167). The examples in (41) show that descriptive possessives correspond to what we have referred to as 'modification-by-noun'.

(41)   a. n-tlo   ya-ditene
           5-house 5-brick
           'brick house'

        b. n-kgô ya-bojalwa
           5-pot 5-beer
           'a pot of beer'

        c. n-tlo   ya-thapêlô
           5-house 5-prayer
           'a house for prayer, church'

        d. di-tlhako tsa-senna
           PL-shoe   4.PL-man
           'men's shoes'

Property words also agree in class and number, but employ a different set of concord affixes. For example, in class 5 the singular prefix is *ya* for possessors and *êŋ* for property words, as in 'hunter's dog' in (40b) and in (42).

(42)   n-tša êm-pe
        5-dog 5-ugly
        'ugly dog'

These distinctions can be treated in terms of declension classes, which are partly semantically based: under this analysis, we are dealing with semantic grouping of nominals that requires the presence of a particular exponent. Still, we can reasonably claim that this is the same encoding strategy. Roughly the same pattern is observed in Zulu (Poulos and Msimang, 1998). The a-of-association construction, then, is a device for turning any type of phrase into a phrase with the same agreement morphosyntax as an adjective. In this sense we are dealing with a single, across-the-board, modification encoding strategy.

3.5 Attributivization by a Phrasal Affix 123

An intriguing instance of essentially the same type is seen in Hausa, where we also find that a constructional marker redundantly registers the number and gender features of its own host. This is in part reminiscent of the agreeing ezafe in Kurmanji Kurdish (Chapter 2, Section 2.5.5). In the original Hausa pattern, possession and modification-by-noun are indicated by means of a linking element which is in syntactic construction with the dependent but agrees with the head for gender (*na* masculine, *ta* feminine) in the element order head–linker–dependent (Kraft and Kirk-Greene, 1973, 41–42; Newman, 2000): see (43).

(43) a. gidā   na   Audù
          house[M] LKR.M Audu[F]
          'Audu's house'

      b. rĩgā   ta   Audù
          gown[F] LKR.F Audu[F]
          'Audu's gown'

This pattern is constructionally identical to the Hindi-Urdu or Albanian 'genitive' and the Bantu a-of-association. However, the linker can, under certain circumstances, become an enclitic, essentially suffixing to the word on the immediate left, and hence effectively dependent-marking the possessed head noun, as seen in (44).

(44) a. gidā-n   Audù
          house[M]-LKR.M Audu[F]
          'Audu's house'

      b. rĩgā-r̃   Audù
          gown[F]-LKR.F Audu[F]
          'Audu's gown'

The -*r̃* allomorph in (44b) represents a coronal tap/roll as opposed to -*r*, which is a retroflex tap. It is only found after feminine singular nouns ending in *a*; otherwise, the -*n* allomorph is employed. This construction is now no longer an instance of the Albanian/Bantu dependent-marking agreeing type, but rather represents a head marking non-agreeing pattern, where the constructional marker indicates the gender of the head itself. There are rather complex conditions on when the linker appears as an enclitic and when as an adposition. For instance, the pattern seen in (44) is not found when the head noun is otherwise modified, as in (45).

124   *Categorial Mixing in the Nominal Phrase*

(45) dôkìn   nân na   Bellò
      horse[M] this of.M Bello
      'this horse of Bello's'

Crucially, exactly the same marker, with the same allomorphy *-n/-r̃*, is used to signal attributive modification by an adjective. Attributes are normally prenominal in Hausa and yet the linker still marks the leftmost element(s) in the construction, namely the adjective(s). As a result, it is the dependent, not the head, that is marked by the suffixed linker, though the linker still agrees with the head, just as in the case of possession and modification-by-noun. In some respects, therefore, this construction represents the single strategy, but this is obscured by the fact that (i) the linker is effectively a second position enclitic/suffix, and (ii) it is the attributive adjective, not the head noun, that has to appear in the leftmost position.

We have only touched the surface of the complications that can arise from partial grammaticalization of possessive prepositions, possessive pronouns, and such like; it is possible that there are other relevant construction types that we have not encountered. Typological study of these patterns is difficult because we are often dealing with incompletely morphologized clitic-like function words which are prone to be misdescribed and misanalysed, particularly if the grammarian has used misleading terminology for such constructions such as, e.g., 'genitive case'. The main point for us is that in the languages discussed in this section the basic semantic relationship between head and dependent may be essentially that of the possessive construction, but the morphosyntactic realization of the construction makes it into a type of attributive modification. Such languages represent another strategy for turning a nominal phrase into an attributive modifier with the same morphosyntax (agreement) as an adjective. They further demonstrate that there is a very close typological connection between possession and attributive modification. In some sense they also illustrate a particularly clear case of categorial mixing, in that the dependent is semantically a noun, clearly heads a nominal syntagma, and so clearly has nominal syntax, but the phrase as a whole operates as an adjectival attributive modifier with respect to the wider syntax.

3.6   Conclusions

This chapter has provided a basic description of several construction types in which adnominal dependents show a mixture of nominal and adjectival properties. It therefore serves as an introduction to the theoretical discussion

3.6 Conclusions   125

of the following chapters. At this stage we can safely conclude, together with Plank (1995b, 76), that

> it is in attributive function that nouns (or NPs) are most likely to shade into adjectives ..., presupposing that they are distinguished otherwise ...When words that are basically referent-establishing are being put to referent-modifying uses, it may well prove expedient for them to retain or reacquire some of their original properties ...Depending on the extent of this retention or reacquisition, attributes may non-circularly be characterized as more or less nouny.

To put it differently, the transition from nouns to adjectives is gradient, depending on the exact combination of nouny and adjectival properties.

This chapter has also illustrated some of the analytical problems raised by mixed constructions in the nominal phrase. Variation was observed largely along three main parameters: semantics (the addition of a clearly identifiable semantic predicate), morphology (paradigmatic mixing), and syntax (the BNMP, i.e. syntagmatic mixing). The latter is an especially important parameter, and we will see that this type of constructional mismatch will be a leitmotiv throughout the rest of the book. In Chapter 4 we summarize two conceptually distinct ways of tackling some of the syntactic issues at hand, the 'syntactic' class of approaches and the 'lexical' class of approaches to syntagmatically mixed categories. We also summarize a number of phenomena problematical for the syntactic approach, which assumes that the derivational affix is introduced in the syntax and takes scope over a phrase. We will argue that there are cases which cannot be handled in this manner, because the affix lacks crucial properties we would otherwise expect to see and because the syntactic approach cannot account for some of the syntactic properties of the derived modifier.

4 *Approaches to Mixed Categories*

4.1 Introduction

At a purely descriptive level we have identified two principal senses in which we can speak of categorial mixture: on the one hand, a word can have the morphological properties of two different categories (paradigmatic categorial mixing), and on the other hand, it can behave as one category with respect to one part of its syntactic environment and as a different category with respect to another part of the syntax (syntagmatic categorial mixing). The purpose of this chapter is to identify the key conceptual issues surrounding syntagmatic category mixing. While doing so, we will survey a number of approaches to such issues, with particular focus on lexicalist theories.

The two dimensions of categorial mixing are reflected in the two main conceptual approaches to mixed categories, though not necessarily in a way that follows automatically from our pre-theoretical description. Bresnan and Mugane (2006) distinguish these two types of approach under the headings 'single projection' and 'dual projection'. We will summarize them below and then address a number of LFG proposals. Clearly, this does not exhaust the richness of the literature, but it provides what we take to be an overview of the dominant trends.

4.2 Dual Projection

In this section we first discuss the dual projection approach in general terms. We will then take Sadock's (1991) model of Autolexical Syntax as a kind of proxy for other dual projection analyses. We will summarize Sadock's model and show how he deploys it to analyse a well-known instance of syntagmatic category mixing in Slavic possessive adjectives. We will then identify a number of features which we believe are a design fault of such approaches.

4.2.1 Overview

In essence, in the dual projection approach category mixing is represented by associating a single word (syntactic leaf) with two syntactic terminals at some level of description; it arises because the word inherits properties from each of those two syntactic terminals. However, in principle each of the syntactic terminals dominating that word can represent pure, unmixed categories when they are uniquely associated with a word. For instance, we might associate a single deverbal nominal with an ordinary verb node and an ordinary noun node in syntactic representation. The only way in which the verb and noun nodes would differ from those of unmixed structures would be in permitting the sharing of a lexical terminal. Alexiadou et al. (2007), Alexiadou (2010a,b) and Kornfilt and Whitman (2011) provide overviews of the analyses of action nominals and subject nominalizations (of the type *truck driver* ~ *a driver of trucks*) along these lines.

One influential version of the dual projection analysis, in which the mixed category is simultaneously associated with two distinct syntactic nodes, is based on an idea often referred to as 'syntactic affixation' (Fabb, 1984) or 'morphological derivation in the syntax' (Bresnan, 1997). Depending on the precise model of syntax (and morphology), syntactic affixation is instantiated in a variety of ways. In a 'transformational' model of syntax we can set up a syntactic node (usually a functional element) dominating an affix. When an element of a different category is merged with that node, the newly introduced element combines with the affix and acquires some of its properties. It may, for instance, acquire more or less the same categorial properties of the affix, as when a verb adjoins to a nominalizer.

An influential version of the syntactic affixation approach is the incorporation-based analysis of morphologically complex words, pioneered by the work of Baker (1988a), which has become the standard head-raising approach to morphology.[1] In this class of model, syntactic principles account for dependencies such as predicate-argument structure, some aspects of element order, and so on. For instance, in the case of a deverbal nominalization a verb will raise to a c-commanding (functional) nominal head. The morphological aspects are usually handled by the principles of Distributed Morphology (Halle and Marantz, 1993). Baker (1988b) provides explicit

---

[1] Baker (1985) actually proposed an analysis of English gerunds in which the *-ing* suffix is treated as a nominal head lowering into the VP. Such lowering is not generally considered admissible in current models of Mainstream Generative Grammar, however.

128 *Approaches to Mixed Categories*

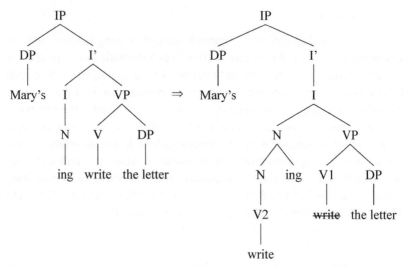

Figure 4.1 *Generic syntactic affixation analysis of POSS-ACC nominalization*

discussion of where morphology might fit into the original incorporation model.

A schematic example of this mode of analysis is presented in Figure 4.1 for a typical POSS-ACC nominalization. In this type of analysis the verb root *write* is associated, by virtue of movement, with two distinct syntactic nodes: V1, V2, and (ultimately) I.

In principle, such analyses should cover the major types of transposition outlined in Spencer (2005b), but it turns out that little systematic work has been conducted in the transformational model of syntax on any kind of transposition other than certain types of deverbal nominalization, many of which are no doubt better treated as transpositional lexemes and not genuine transpositions. Perhaps the most relevant recent work on other types is the discussion of noun-headed compounds, especially English synthetic compounds, presented within the Distributed Morphology framework by Harley (2009), itself almost a unique essay on compounding in that framework (but see also van Hout and Roeper (1988) and Lieber (1992) for pre-Distributed Morphology treatments along similar lines). The synthetic compound *letter writer* is analysed by assuming that the compounded object noun originates as the object of the base verb. That object then moves to the left of the derived agent nominal when the base VP is suffixed with *-er*. A schematic, generic, illustration of this mode of analysis is shown in Figure 4.2. In this kind of analysis the verb's object is

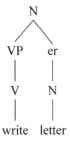

Figure 4.2 *Generic syntactic affixation analysis of synthetic compounds*

simultaneously associated with the direct object position of the base verb and the modifier position of the N-N compound. See Spencer (2011) for a number of problems with Harley's proposals.

One type of dual projection analysis ought to be distinguished from the syntactic affixation type of the dual projection model, as illustrated in Figure 4.3, which shows a representation of the French fused adposition-determiner *du* 'of.M.SG' (from *de le* 'of the.M.SG'). A number of Romance languages have adpositions which show this type of behaviour, as does German. An analysis of the kind shown in Figure 4.3 was proposed by Wescoat (2002), for instance, under the rubric of 'lexical sharing' (see also the discussion in Spencer and Luís, 2012, 286–287). The mixed element *du* is defined as an adposition by virtue of being a daughter of the P node, but it is also defined as a form of the masculine singular definite article by virtue of being dominated by an appropriately annotated determiner node, D. Note that where the definite article is feminine singular, two separate words (syntactic terminals) are used (*de la*), and there is no category mixing. However, the fused adposition-determiners of Romance languages and German are somewhat different from the category mixing we are dealing with in this book. They arise from the proximity in surface form of the adposition and the function word (the determiner): that is, the mixing is an essentially morphophonological phenomenon. The lexical sharing type of analysis developed by Wescoat (2002) is designed specifically for such phenomena and not for the kind of category mixing that we see with noun–adjective hybrids.

As far as we can tell, very little attention has been devoted in the incorporation/head-movement model to the specific class of attributive modification phenomena that we are investigating in this book, in particular the Base Noun Modifiability Property (BNMP). The detailed survey of the Principles

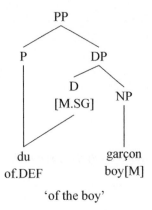

Figure 4.3 *Lexical sharing representation of the French* du

and Parameters literature on DP-internal adjectives provided in Alexiadou et al. (2007, 283–394) contains only a few paragraphs of general discussion on this topic, for instance. Given the lack of relevant literature, we will not attempt to speculate on how our data might be interpreted in the Distributed Morphology/head-movement approach, but in the next subsection we will see that similar effects to those shown in Figures 4.1 and 4.2 can be obtained in a declarative model of syntax.

4.2.2   Autolexical Syntax

Sadock's (1991) model of Autolexical Syntax is concerned with morphosyntactic mismatches in which the implied constituent structure of word forms is at odds with the constituent structure required by the syntax, or in which the linear order of morphosyntactic units (phrases, words, and affixes) is at odds with the linearization required by the syntax. The first type of mismatch is seen with various types of clitic construction. In a typical Wackernagel (second position) clitic system, the clitic or clitic cluster is placed to the right of the first word or phrase in the domain. For instance, in Bulgarian the definite article is placed after the first word of the nominal phrase, whether that word is an adjective (including possessive adjectives) or the head noun. The second type of mismatch is seen with certain instances of noun incorporation. In these cases the noun which corresponds to the direct object of a verb typically forms a compound with the (finite) verb. Frequently, the element order of the noun incorporation structure is different from that found when the object remains unincorporated, yet the grammatical relation between the incorporated noun base and the verb is the same as when the noun heads a direct object nominal phrase.

4.2 *Dual Projection*   131

Sadock (1991, 60ff) argues that the nature of such mismatches is restricted. He proposes the two constraints shown in (1) which govern the way morphology and syntax match up. The Linearity Constraint requires elements to have the same linear order in both representations, while the Constructional Integrity Constraint requires the constituent structure to be the same in both representations.

(1) Mapping between syntactic (Level 1) and morphological (Level 2) structures

Linearity Constraints

(i) Strong: The associated elements of Level 1 and Level 2 representations must occur in the same linear order

(ii) Weak: The associated elements of Level 1 and Level 2 representations must occur as close as possible in the same linear order except where the Level 2 requirements of lexemes make this impossible

Constructional Integrity Constraints

(i) Strong: If a lexeme combines with a phrase P at Level 1 and with a host at Level 2, then the Level 2 host must be associated with the head of the Level 1 phrase P

(ii) Weak: If a lexeme combines with an expression P at Level 1 and with a host at Level 2, then the morphological host must be associated with some element of the Level 1 expression P

The Weak Linearity Constraint permits morphological principles to override syntactic principles. For instance, a language may place determiners initially in a noun phrase (as in English), but an enclitic determiner will be placed after its host and therefore cannot appear initially in the phrase. The Strong Constructional Integrity Constraint requires inflection-like marking to be head marking, but the Weak Constructional Integrity Constraint effectively permits phrasal affixation. The permitted cross-linguistic variation in clitic placement is then said to be the result of the Cliticization Principle, as defined by Sadock (1991, 105) in (2).

(2) **Cliticization Principle**

If a lexeme combines with an inflected word in the morphology and with a phrase in the syntax, its morphosyntactic association will conform to at least the Weak Linearity Constraint.

132 *Approaches to Mixed Categories*

Noun incorporation is a paradigm example of a violation of the Linearity Constraint which still respects Constructional Integrity (the incorporated noun combines in the morphology with the morphological exponent of the verb head with which the noun is in syntactic construction). English auxiliary clitics are paradigm examples of violation of Constructional Integrity without violation of Linearity: the auxiliary clitic forms a morphological unit with the previous phrase (usually the subject NP) even though it is part of the verbal complex, possibly even the head of the VP, as in *Tom's a linguist*. What is not possible, it is claimed, is to have full-blown violations of both constraints by the same pair of representations (Sadock, 1991, 163ff).

We will illustrate the operation of the Autolexical Syntax principles by considering Corbett's examples of possessive adjectives from Upper Sorbian (Corbett, 1987) introduced in Chapter 3. The phrase in (3) is exactly parallel with Corbett's example *mojeho bratrowe dźěći*, except that the modifier of the possessive adjective is itself an adjective and not a possessive determiner.

(3) star-eje   žon-in-a   drasta
     old-F.GEN.SG woman[F]-POSS.A-F.NOM.SG dress[F].NOM.SG
     'the old woman's dress'

As discussed in Chapter 3, possessive adjectives are clearly morphological adjectives, and not nouns, because they belong to a specific adjectival inflectional class. However, possessive adjective forms exhibit attributive transparency. In (3) the adjective 'old' shows adjectival agreement in number and gender with the noun 'woman' from which the possessive adjective is derived, even though that noun is a part of the possessive adjective which in all other respects has the morphological form and syntactic behaviour of adjectives. (It also takes the genitive singular case, a fact which is difficult to explain on any current account.)

Sadock (1991, 159ff) provides an explicit analysis of the Upper Sorbian facts, attempting to combine the benefits of both syntactic and morphological approaches. In Figure 4.4 we reproduce Sadock's diagram for the phrase in (3). In this figure the syntactic representation is the upper tree and the morphological representation is the lower tree. 'Inf' in the morphological representation stands for 'inflectional affix'. A form of X-bar syntax is assumed and this is taken to apply to word structure as well as phrase structure (as in Selkirk (1982)). Inflected words are thus assumed to have a constituent structure, with the inflectional stem being a zero-level category (lacking bar level features in these representations) and the inflected word being of bar level [−1]. In the syntactic representation inflection is indicated, if at all, by features

4.2 Dual Projection 133

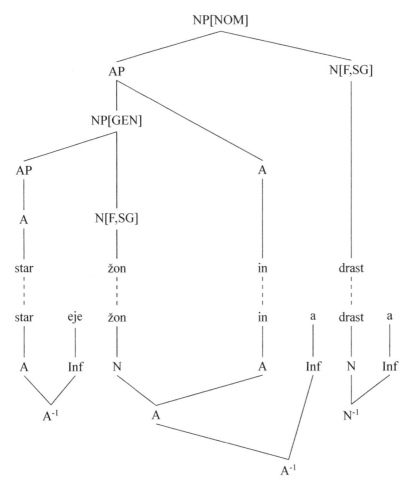

Figure 4.4 *Autolexical representation of syntagmatically mixed Upper Sorbian possessive adjectives*

on syntactic nodes. The morphological inflections themselves have no syntactic representation. In this respect Sadock's model differs from a number of models of syntax, but not in ways that are relevant to possessive adjective structure.

The crucial point to note about Figure 4.4 is that the possessive adjective suffix -*in* is represented both in the syntax and the morphology. In the morphological representation it is the morphological 'head' which creates the adjective from the noun. In the syntactic representation it is a zero-bar level head of the AP which includes the NP consisting of the concatenation

134　*Approaches to Mixed Categories*

of the adjective *star-* 'old' and the noun *žon-* 'woman'. In effect, then, the Autolexical Syntax approach posits a syntactic affixation analysis for Upper Sorbian possessive adjectives, as represented schematically in (4).

(4)　[star-eje　　　žon]=in-a　　　　　　drasta
　　　old-F.GEN.SG woman[F]-POSS.A-F.NOM.SG dress[F].NOM.SG
　　　'the old woman's dress'

Independently of any other way in which the structure figures in the syntax, the representation sketched in (4) analyses the possessive affix as a syntactically active object taking a phrase as its complement. This mode of analysis is comparable with a popular analysis of the English possessive phrasal affix (clitic) = *'s*: [*old woman*]=*'s dress*.

The representation in (4) has the advantage that it immediately accounts for the scope properties of the construction by deploying well-known principles of constituent structure: that is, the morphosyntactic representation mirrors the assumed semantic representation: [[OLD WOMAN] POSS]. The disadvantage is that, for some cases and some languages at least, it brings with it unwelcome assumptions about morphology: in Upper Sorbian, *žonin(a)* is a single morphophonological word and *-in(a)* does not behave in any other respects like a phrasal affix (much less an independent syntactic terminal). For some syntactic models, of course, notably Minimalism, this is irrelevant. In such models even common-or-garden inflection, of the kind that induces no morphosyntactic mismatch, is treated as some sort of syntactic affixation in which each inflection is an autonomous syntactic head and inflected words are constructed in the syntax by head movement (compounding) or merger of heads. However, for syntactic models that maintain a distinction between words and affixes such mismatches are potentially problematical.

Another class of instances in which a modifier appears to modify a noun within a more complex word occurs with noun incorporation and kindred constructions. A well-known example is that of West Greenlandic, in which a noun serving as a direct object can be 'incorporated' into one of about four hundred verbal affixes, creating a complex verb form. Sadock (1980, 1991) discusses cases such as that shown in (5), where the verbal affix means 'have'.

(5)　Hansi　　ataatsi-nik　qamute-qar-poq
　　　Hans.ABS one-INSTR.PL sled-HAVE-3SG.IND
　　　'Hans has one sled'

This example is telling because the noun *qamutit* 'sled' is a plurale tantum noun when not incorporated, and the numeral 'one' agrees with it not only in the case

4.2 Dual Projection 135

it would assume if it were overtly realized in the syntax (the instrumental), but also for its lexically stipulated plural number. Sadock argues that such cases show that even though it is part of a word, the noun is syntactically realized, along with the head inflectional features it would bear if it were an autonomous syntactic terminal. The modifier, so to speak, can 'see into' the complex verb form and gain access to the noun base. In Sadock's model this can be represented by allowing the modification relation to take place over syntactic representations in which the noun is not incorporated into a verbal head.

The Upper Sorbian and West Greenlandic examples illustrate a clear mismatch between morphological form and the syntactic structure expected from such form. We should suppose, therefore, that Upper Sorbian possessive adjective construction would provide strong evidence in favour of an approach such as that of Autolexical Syntax. In point of fact, however, it is rather unclear how the Upper Sorbian construction fits into Sadock's typology of mismatches. The representation in Figure 4.4 respects the strongest version of the Linearity Constraint because the order of syntactic and morphological elements is identical. At the same time it respects the strongest form of Constructional Integrity because the adjectivizing suffix -*in* combines in the morphology with a noun stem corresponding to the head of the NP with which the syntactic correspondent of -*in* combines. Thus, there appears to be no mismatch at all. But in fact the mismatch arises precisely because the suffix -*in* creates forms which have all the hallmarks of traditional words and yet, as seen in (4), the suffix seems to attach to an entire phrase. In effect, such mismatches are too subtle to be detected under Sadock's typology.

It remains possible that some variant of the syntactic affixation approach would be appropriate for this language, though we very much doubt this (for criticism of syntactic approaches generally and a defence of a lexical, or 'derivational', approach to Upper Sorbian, see Corbett, 1987, 1995). However, we will show in the next subsection that there exist cases of adjectival wide scope affixation to which syntactic affixation cannot easily apply. A key feature of this discussion will be the observation we have made about Sadock's Autolexical Syntax analysis of Upper Sorbian possessive adjectives: the Linearity and Constructional Integrity constraints are not sufficient to define the mismatches we will see. In the Autolexical Syntax model, which is specifically designed to deal with morphosyntactic mismatches, a morphologically complex word generally has a morphological structure which maps to a syntactic terminal. For instances of syntactic affixation we exceptionally permit a part of a word to project a syntactic head of its own, which can then

136   *Approaches to Mixed Categories*

take syntactic (and hence semantic) scope over an NP. Although this solution provides a convenient way of describing the wide scope effects and has the additional benefit that it permits us to state simultaneously that the possessive adjective is itself a word and not a (genuine) phrase, it brings with it the assumption that in the syntax the affix will show all the properties of a regular syntactic head. However, this leads to difficulties with the constructions and example types discussed in this subsection. The main problem is that it is only in very selective respects that the morphologically complex word behaves as though it were also syntactically complex.

4.2.3   *Reasons for Rejecting Syntactic Affixation*

In this subsection we show that syntactic affixation is insufficient to capture the full empirical richness of noun–adjective hybrids. We outline several reasons why we cannot assume that an adjective head scopes syntactically over the inner NP/DP and identify several types of construction that pose problems for (obvious interpretations of) a syntactic affixation analysis of wide scope affixes within the nominal phrase.

Coordination

If a possessive element is introduced into the syntax with wide scope, then we expect it to take scope over coordinated nouns and NPs/DPs. For instance, this is borne out by Hindi-Urdu possessive postpositions. Recall from Chapter 3 that they effectively serve to turn the possessor phrase into an attributive modifier. Coordination in such structures is illustrated in (6).

(6)   [Raam aur Raanii] k-e   bhaaiyõ
       Ram   and Rani   of-OBL.PL brother.OBL.PL
       'Ram and Rani's brothers'

This can be compared to a popular representation of the English translation of (6): [*Ram and Rani*]*'s brothers*. In such constructions, the phrasal affix or the postposition take scope over the regular coordinate structure.

In contrast, truly adjectival affixes do not generally scope over coordinate structures. The Russian comitative construction provides an interesting exception which proves this rule. The Russian examples in (7) are cited from Koptjevskaja-Tamm and Šmelev (1994):

(7)   a.   Alëša s   Maš-ej
             Alyosha with Masha-INSTR
             'Alyosha and Masha'

4.2 Dual Projection   137

b.   Alëš-in-y   s   Maš-ej   deti
     Alyosha-POSS.A-PL with Masha-INSTR children
     'Alyosha and Masha's (joint) children'

c.   Alëš-in-y   i   Maš-in-y   deti
     Alyosha-POSS.A-PL and Masha-POSS.A-PL children
     'Alyosha and Masha's (separate or joint) children'

d.   * [Alëša i   Maš]-in-y   deti
     Alyosha and Masha-POSS.A-PL children
     'Alyosha and Masha's (separate or joint) children'

In (7a) we see the comitative coordination construction found with human referents, which is characteristic of Russian. The coordinated phrase is headed by the first noun which takes a 'with' phrase as a dependent (the complement of the preposition *s* 'with' is in the instrumental case). This comitative construction serves as the basis for (7b), but it is only the head noun of the comitative phrase that can take the possessive adjective suffix. Although examples such as (7b) illustrate an interesting problem for the relationship between syntactic structure and semantic structure, they do not represent instances of phrasal affixation proper, because it would be impossible for the possessive suffix to take as its input a case-inflected noun form. Further, in (7c) we see the straightforward coordination of two denominal possessive adjectives by means of the coordinating conjunction *i* 'and'. As shown in (7d), the possessive suffix *-in* is unable to scope over the coordinated phrase *Alëša i Maša* 'Alyosha and Masha'. This demonstrates that the Russian structure differs from phrasal affixation as represented in Hindi-Urdu and English.

Crucially, when we consider Upper Sorbian, in which the possessive adjective suffix seems to take wide scope, we find that it does not permit scoping over coordinate constructions either. Thus, we could not construct phrases such as *[Hilža i Jan]-owe dźěći* 'Hilža and Jan's children' or (using nouns which would take the same adjectival suffix) *[Hilža i Mar]-in bratr* 'Hilža and Maria's brother' parallel to the Hindi-Urdu example in (6). Other languages with syntagmatic mixing that we discussed in Chapter 3 do not allow coordination of base nouns either. For instance, the example in (8), with a similitudinal adjective, is ungrammatical in Tundra Nenets, although coordination of two nouns by juxtaposition is normally allowed.

(8)   * [wen'ako sarm'ik°]-rəxa t'on'a
      dog   wolf-SIM.A   fox
      'the fox (looking) like a wolf and a dog'

138 *Approaches to Mixed Categories*

The failure of adjectival morphology to scope over coordinate structures is extremely puzzling on any syntactically based account of syntagmatic category mixing, including the hybrid model of Sadock. If there is an adjective head, A, in the syntax and this head takes a full NP as its complement, why can it not take a coordinated NP? Although Sadock's analysis may well be appropriate for Hindi-Urdu examples such as (6), it is seriously compromised by other examples, including his own Upper Sorbian example.

Morphotactics

The next argument is similar to the one made by Malouf (2000a, 99ff) for deverbal nominalizations. With some denominal adjectives we find that the linear ordering of the wide scope adjective affix with respect to its host NP does not necessarily mirror syntactic order and hence is not what would be predicted on syntactic grounds. In these constructions we see the semantic scope effects, but they cannot be sensibly modelled in terms of syntactic constituency.

Recall from Chapter 3 that in many languages throughout the world we see a particular semantic type of denominal adjective, the proprietive adjective, traditionally glossed as 'HAVING(N)'. In Georgian and Svan, two closely related Kartvelian languages, proprietives have the surface morphosyntax of adjectives, for example, showing case agreement.

In Georgian the adjectivizing element is a suffix *-ian*. The noun base of the *ian*-suffixed adjectives can be modified as though the adjective were still a noun, giving rise to syntagmatic category mixing. The examples in (9) are from Boeder (2005, 44–45), and Boeder and Schroeder (2000, 183).

(9) a. or   ucnob-ian-i   gant'oleba
         two unknown-PROPR.A-NOM equation[NOM]
         'an equation with two unknowns'

     b. tormeț abaz-ian-ma   cxvar-ma
         twelve abazi-PROPR.A-ERG sheep-ERG
         'a sheep worth twelve abazi [coins]'

     c. tetr   tm-ian-i   ḳac-i
         white hair-PROPR.A-NOM man-NOM
         'white-haired man'

In Svan a similar construction exists, except that the adjectivizing formative is a prefix, yet the modifiers of the denominal adjective still appear to its left, as shown in (10).

(10) a. tvetne lu-patv   mare
          white PROPR.A-hair[NOM] man[NOM]
          'white-haired man'

b. püri   ü(v)i   lə-ṭar   gäc
cow.GEN horn.GEN PROPR.A-handle[NOM] knife[NOM]
'a knife with a handle made of a cow's horn'

The Georgian examples present no obvious difficulty for a syntactic affixation approach. An analysis of (9c) would posit a structure [[[*tetr tm*]-*ian*]-*i*] *k̲ac-i*. However, for the examples in (10) it is not possible to find a corresponding structure which would allow the prefix *lu-/lə-* to scope over the whole of each of the phrases *tvetne patv* and *püri ü(v)i ṭar*. These examples could, of course, be derived from an underlying structure in which the affix was placed externally to the whole phrase and was then moved by some syntactic or morphological process into the right place. However, a transformation of this sort would remove all motivation for the syntactic analysis in the first place.

We can sketch the kind of analysis for Svan we might expect on Sadock's Autolexical Syntax model. The structure is just like the Upper Sorbian case except that we do not have the troubling fact of an adjective agreeing with a possessor-marked noun as though it were in the genitive case. The crossing lines in Figure 4.5 illustrate a violation of the Linearity Constraint. This is still comparatively minor in that the structure still respects the Constructional Integrity Constraint: the adjective suffix is associated with the head of the phrase to which it attaches in the syntax. Although Sadock does not present any examples of precisely this structure, his model contains sufficient apparatus to handle them.

However, another linear order effect related to the linearization of adjectival formatives is seen in the Tungusic language Evenki. Proprietive adjectives in Evenki are productively derived from nouns with the suffix -*či*, for example *saŋari* 'hole' > *saŋari-či* 'with a hole'. Interestingly, the adjectival suffix is not the most peripheral element in the word, let alone the phrase, because it may be followed by diminutive and augmentative affixes that semantically modify the base noun (Nikolaeva, 2008, 979). This is shown in the examples in (11).

(11)   a. saŋari-či-ka:r
          hole-PROPR.A-DIM
          'with little holes'

       b. xegdi dere-či-ke:ku:n
          big   face-PROPR.A-AUG
          'with a big face'

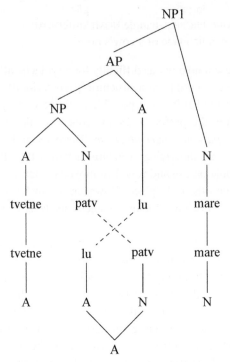

Figure 4.5 *Autolexical Syntax representation for Svan example in (10)*

These constructions violate both relevant constraints in Sadock's Autolexical Syntax model and will be very difficult to account for in other syntactic affixation analyses, in that it is very hard to see how they could be derived syntactically without appeal to a totally arbitrary series of otherwise unmotivated reordering transformations.

The Form of the Modifier

The next argument is based on cases when there is no non-vacuous way in which the adjectival affix can be thought of as syntactic, because the denominal adjective shows category mixing even within its own phrase. The modifier it takes does not behave like a regular modifier of a noun.

In another Tungusic language, Udihe, we find syntagmatic category mixing when a proprietive adjective derived with the suffix *-xi* is modified by an adjective which bears a semantic relationship to its base. As seen in (12), this is similar to regular modification.

4.2 Dual Projection   141

(12) a. ic'a sita
          small child
          'a small child'

     b. ic'a sita-xi
         small child-PROPR.A
         'with a small child, having a small child'

The problem is illustrated in (13) from Nikolaeva (2008, 979). Here, the affix *-xi* is suffixed to the noun *igi* 'tail' to produce a proprietive adjective meaning 'having a tail, with a tail'. The base noun can be modified, for instance, by the numeral *ila* 'three'. As we might now expect, the affix *-xi* has semantic scope over the whole phrase *ila igi* 'three tails', but in such a construction the numeral *ila* can optionally appear in the instrumental case. It is the same as if English were to allow structures such as **thrice-headed* (*dog*) or **quintuply-pointed* (*star*) instead of *three-headed* and *five-pointed.*

(13) ila/ila-zi   igi-xi
      three/three-INSTR tail-PROPR.A
      'with three tails'

This instrumental case form of the numeral is used exclusively to modify adjectival words: it cannot be used to modify an unaffixed (non-adjectival) noun, as shown in (14b).

(14) a. ila igi
          three tail
          'three tails'

     b. * ila-zi   igi
          three-INSTR tail

This means that we cannot assume that (13) derives from some underlying structure of the form [*ila igi*]*xi*, in which the *-xi* suffix takes syntactic scope over the numeral as well as the noun, because then there would be no well-formed source for the instrumental case-marked alternative. In effect, this is the mirror image of the problem presented by West Greenlandic modifier stranding cases, such as (5) discussed above.

The second problem is this. Proprietive adjectives in Udihe can be modified by adverbs of various kinds. This is seen in (15a), in which the adverb *piam* 'through' modifies a proprietive adjective *siexi* 'having a wound, wounded'. However, it is absolutely impossible for an adverb to modify a regular noun. A relative clause of some kind would be needed to render the meaning in (15b).

142 *Approaches to Mixed Categories*

(15) a. piam   sie-xi
           through wound-PROPR.A
           'with an exit wound'

      b. * piam   sie
           through wound
           [intended]'exit wound'

Here, then, there is another mismatch between syntactic form and semantic scope which goes against the assumption that the proprietive marker is a phrasal suffix.

Conclusions

To conclude this section, we have argued against models based on dual projection or syntactic affixation. We have seen that a number of instances of syntagmatic category mixing do not lend themselves to the syntactic affixation type of approach. First, we noted that in some languages the morphology which derives the adjective is bound to the noun and cannot take wide scope in coordinated constructions. Syntactic affixation is unable to account for the failure of the relevant affixes to scope over coordinate structures. Second, we noted that the order of affixation does not always match the implied semantico-syntactic ordering. The syntactic affixation account fails with cases in which the adjectival affixes are internal to other affixes, because the morphological structure does not mirror the putative syntactic structure. Finally, we pointed to occasional instances of 'mixed' denominal adjectives which show properties that are not found with ordinary modification: the adjective could be modified either as though it were still the base noun or as a genuine adjective. If a construction shows any of these properties, this indicates that we should regard the derived form as a word exhibiting Lexical Integrity. These constructions cannot be treated as instances of phrasal affixation and hence cannot be handled efficiently as purely syntactic constructions. Instead, we need to accept that languages permit the formation of lexical categories which have properties that are between those of canonical nouns and canonical adjectives.

It is important to emphasize at this point that we are not arguing that the data discussed in this section disconfirm any syntactic approaches whatever to the relevant phenomena. In some languages there may well be reasons for treating a denominal adjective as a syntactically represented object taking scope over a nominal phrase. Arguably, the Hindi-Urdu 'genitive' postposition discussed above is just such an instance. Yet not all cases can be handled in this fashion. We are advancing a somewhat weaker, but true, claim in denying that those data provide adequate prima facie evidence in favour of a syntactic affixation analysis over their theoretical rivals.

4.3 Single Projection

The single projection approach is based on the idea of lexical affixation. This approach does not generally fall foul of the empirical problems outlined in the previous section, and in this sense is easier to maintain.

4.3.1 Overview

Speaking very generally, in a single projection approach the word/syntactic leaf is associated with a single terminal in syntactic representation, as in the case of unmixed categories. The morphologically derived word is not broken up or analysed by purely syntactic processes or representational devices. But one or more of the syntactic nodes dominating that word is associated with a set of properties which reflect the categorial mixing. Those properties (morphosyntactic features) will then be different from the kinds of properties we see in unmixed categories. However, the overall constituent structure associated with the construction is essentially no different from that of an unmixed construction, in contrast to the representations proposed on a dual projection account.

On the single projection account, the Upper Sorbian possessive adjectives such as *žonin-* would be treated as single words in the syntax, projecting a standard constituent structure, as in (16):

(16) [star-eje   [žon-in-a]]   drasta
       old-F.GEN.SG woman[F]-POSS.A-F.NOM.SG dress[F].NOM.SG
       'the old woman's dress'

Lexical affixation commits us to no additional (and possibly undesirable) assumptions about word structure, but the syntactic structure in (16) raises the fundamental question of how we can obtain the syntagmatic category mixing effects. In other words, how can we ensure that a word such as *žonina* is treated as an adjective by some syntactic principles and as a noun by other syntactic principles? The same question applies to English POSS-ACC gerunds, which are 'externally' nouns and 'internally' verbs, and other instances of syntagmatic mixing.

There are essentially two types of answer to this question. In the first case, the mixed category is dually specified, so that a single syntactic node is provided with categorial features of both categories. We can call this type

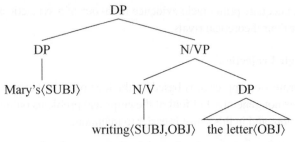

Figure 4.6 *Composite node analysis for POSS-ACC nominalizations*

of analysis the 'composite node' approach.[2] Existing node labels are combined in such a way as to create a composite node, from which the mixed category inherits its properties. The composite node approach can reflect the fact that the new node has properties of its two source nodes. In Figure 4.6 we present a schematic version of the composite node type of analysis representing *Mary's writing the letter*.

In Figure 4.6 the derived nominal *writing* has a complex argument structure, inherited from the base verb. The arguments represented here schematically as ⟨SUBJ, OBJ⟩ are realized in this type of example in the manner of dependents to a noun. The category of the word *writing* is a hybrid category N/V. In a model of this sort the syntax has to be modified in such a way that such a hybrid category is treated as a subtype of N in the context of the syntax of the DP (and not, say, as a subtype of a finite verb).

The main challenge is to define exactly which properties are acquired by the new node. Solutions for this problem are proposed by several authors, including Lefebvre and Muysken (1988), Lapointe (1980), and Spencer (1999). For instance, an action nominal is both a noun and a verb simultaneously and is dominated by a node with a label such as 'N/V', as in Lapointe's (1980) dual head account. The dual category is verbal 'inside' but its top layer projects as a noun, thus ensuring that the gerund has the distribution of a nominal. The gerund suffix *-ing* morphologically derives the dual category N/V from the regular verbal category. Lefebvre and Muysken (1988) present a similar analysis for Quechua nominalizations. Since Quechua, arguably, has no adjective category, these authors propose to label nominalizations as [+N, +V], a combination otherwise reserved for adjectives in languages such as English. Nominalizations head both the N″ projection (as can be seen from the case of the specifier) and the V″ projection (with the internal structure of

---

[2] This is what Bresnan (1997) calls the 'indeterminate category projection theory'.

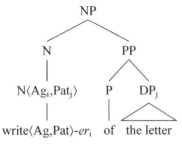

Figure 4.7 *Subject nominalization (Booij and van Haften 1988)*

sentences), and a specific extension of the X-bar convention is introduced in order to account for their features in terms of categorial neutralization.

Another simple example of this type of approach is found in Booij and van Haften's (1988) analysis of agentive nominalizations such as *writer*. Categorially, such nominalizations are (mildly) mixed because they retain certain aspects of the base verb's argument structure. The verb's object argument can be expressed, though only in the manner of a noun complement: *the writer of the letter, a writer of letters, a letter writer*. Booij and ten Haften propose that the nominalization acquires the verb's argument structure by a process known as 'percolation', after Lieber (1980). This is a feature-passing operation under which some of the morphosyntactic properties associated with a lower syntactic node are copied onto higher nodes in the constituent structure representation. It is shown in Figure 4.7, in which the argument structure of the verb *write*, represented by Booij and van Haften as $\langle Ag_i, Pat_j \rangle$, percolates from the base of the derived nominal writer to the noun node. Normally, of course, we do not expect to see a noun with such an argument structure representation.

The percolation operation permits the lexical representation of the noun *writer* to share some of the properties of the base verb, yet the noun itself is not (necessarily) associated with any unusual syntactic structure. Thus, in Figure 4.7 the noun takes a prepositional phrase complement *of the letter*, just as a non-derived noun such as *size, contents, purpose*, and so on. It cannot, however, take a complement in the form of, say, the direct object of the base verb: **the writer the letter*. Notice that on this account, the synthetic compound *letter writer* (Figure 4.8), in which *letter* realizes the Patient (or Theme) argument of the base verb, could be analysed as an ordinary N-N compound, like *coffee table*.

In Figures 4.7 and 4.8 the agent nominal inherits the argument structure of a transitive verb ⟨Agent, Patient⟩. The Agent role is identified with the noun itself (shown schematically as coindexation with the *-er* suffix, though this is just for

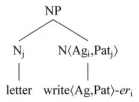

Figure 4.8 *Phrase structure of synthetic compound (Booij and van Haften 1988)*

illustration here). The Patient role is expressed either by the complement of the PP complement to the nominal (Figure 4.7) or by the compounded noun (Figure 4.8). The argument structure inheritance approach entails perhaps the least modification to the content of syntactic nodes.

In the second type of analysis, the mixed category is left underspecified in terms of the categorial features [±V] and [±N]. For instance, an action nominal will be neither a noun nor a verb, but rather will be some distinct third type of category, and Upper Sorbian *žonina* will be a member of some nominal supercategory subsuming nouns and adjectives but identical to neither. A deverbal nominalization then might be associated with a special syntactic node type which directly reflects the nominal and verb properties of the category, effectively creating a new class of word. We therefore increase the inventory of syntactic node labels, including, say, a mixed category of 'verbal noun'. We can call such approaches 'novel node approaches'. Category-neutralizing analyses along these lines can be found as early as Aoun (1981), van Riemsdijk (1983), and Grimshaw (1991). Essentially this is also the analysis of Malouf (2000b,a) described in more detail in the next subsection.[3] The main challenge of that approach is to find a principled way to relate the mixed verbal noun category to its two sources, verb and noun.

4.3.2 Malouf (2000a, b)

As mentioned previously, Malouf (2000a,b) embeds the notional parts of speech approach into an HPSG inheritance hierarchy using the principle of default inheritance. The notion of 'default' he deploys is that of 'default

---

[3] Very closely related to Malouf's model is that of Hudson (2003). Hudson is working within Word Grammar, a type of dependency grammar that describes all syntactic relations in terms of head-dependent relations and has no notion of constituent or phrase structure. On this model it is only possible to define mixed categories such as the English deverbal nominalizations as properties of single nodes because the notion of dual projection is incoherent in a model which lacks phrase structure.

4.3 *Single Projection* 147

unification' (Lascarides and Copestake, 1999), a particular formalization of default inheritance which allows default logic to be deployed alongside unification. The idea is very simple: prototypical categories are represented as default constraints on types, but these constraints can be overridden by individual constraints on more specific types.

In the default case, verbs and adjectives denote objects, events/states-of-affairs, and properties, respectively (recall the prototypical/canonical semantic properties of word classes discussed in Chapter 1). Malouf then sets up HEAD values *verb* and *c-noun* (common noun), essentially corresponding to Croft's (1991) notions of 'predication' and 'reference'. The HEAD value indicates constructions in which the word can occur (the external distribution of the word), whereas the CONT(ent) attribute denotes the semantic type, for instance objects (*nom-obj*) or 'parameterized-state-of-affairs' (*psoa*). Certain specifications are never overridden and thus emerge as 'hard constraints'. The constraints in (17), for instance, state that all HEADs which are of the type *verb* must also be of the type *relational/verb*, while all HEADs of the type *c-noun* must also be of the type *noun*.

(17) a. v → $\begin{bmatrix} \text{HEAD } relational/verb \\ \text{CONT } psoa \end{bmatrix}$

     b. n → $\begin{bmatrix} \text{HEAD } noun/c\text{-}noun \\ \text{CONT } nom\text{-}obj \end{bmatrix}$

The lexical entry for a noun involves a pairing of the HEAD value *c-noun* and the content type *nom-obj*, whereas the lexical entry for a verb involves a pairing of the value *verb* and the *content* type *psoa*.

(18) a. v → $\begin{bmatrix} \text{HEAD/verb} \\ \text{CONT } psoa \end{bmatrix}$

     b. n → $\begin{bmatrix} \text{HEAD/}c\text{-}noun \\ \text{CONT } nom\text{-}obj \end{bmatrix}$

The symbol '/x' is interpreted to mean 'has the value x except where overridden' (Malouf, 2000a, 125). This makes the constraints in (18) violable.

This approach ensures that some members of the class have more prototypical properties than others and opens up the possibility for various types of categorial mixture. Mixed categories are represented by their lexically determined feature structures. In particular, Malouf (2000a,b) treats gerunds (that is, a family of constructions headed by the *ing*-form of a verb) as mixed

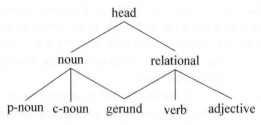

Figure 4.9 *Type hierarchy for English gerunds*

categories which inherit properties from two other categories: nouns and verbs. In the POSS-ING gerunds such as those in (19) the word form *prescribing* is clearly a form of the verb *prescribe*, taking a direct object and being modified by an adverb.

(19) His prescribing the tablets so readily surprised us

However, it also has a 'genitive' subject argument, as though it were a noun. A genuine noun derived from *prescribe*, namely *prescription*, cannot be used in this kind of construction because it lacks the argument structure properties of the verb: **His prescription (of) the tablets so readily*. As we have shown, a word form such as *prescribing* in (19) is therefore a noun for elements to its left and a verb for elements to its right.

In order to capture the dual properties of *ing*-forms of this kind, Malouf (2000a, 65) proposed the type hierarchy shown in Figure 4.9, in which *p-noun/c-noun* means 'proper noun/common noun' and a novel node of type *gerund* is introduced. Gerunds will have the syntactic distribution of nouns because they are a subtype of *noun*, but the only properties of verbs they will inherit are selectional properties. This is because they are not subtypes of *verb*; rather, they are a subtype of the supertype *relational*, which includes verbs, adjectives, and gerunds. This represents a type of composite node, in the sense that the word which shows the category mixing effects is in essence given two labels, one for each of the categories *noun* and *relational*.

While this hierarchy seems to capture the intermediate status of gerunds adequately, it is not entirely clear how it can be reformulated in such a way as to accommodate other types of transposition discussed in Spencer (2005b, 2013). Action nominals (gerunds) do not have a privileged status among transpositions, yet Malouf's hierarchy will make that mixed category unique. This has undesirable consequences when we consider the broader picture. The only way such a hierarchy can describe the full set of transpositions is by introducing an additional novel node for each transposition. However, in that

4.3 Single Projection 149

case we would lose the crucial relationship between the base category and the transposed category. For instance, given the hierarchy in Figure 4.9 it is difficult to see how a deverbal participle will be represented except as a novel node representing a joint subtype of the types *verb* and *adjective*. By Malouf's interpretation of the hierarchy this should mean that participles universally have the syntactic distribution of both verbs and adjectives. This is because the types *adjective*, *verb*, and so on are essentially defined by distributional properties. And yet participles behave just like action nominals in this regard: they have the external distribution of an adjective and the selectional properties of a verb.

What is worse, this kind of novel node solution would fail to capture the asymmetry or directionality implicit in the notion of transposition, because there would be no representational way of distinguishing a V $\Rightarrow$ A transposition (participle) from an A $\Rightarrow$ V transposition (predicate adjective). Both types are found, for instance, in Chukchi. As we have seen in Chapter 3, Section 3.3.2, in that language an adjective used attributively will agree at most in number and occasionally in case with its head noun, while a predicate adjective agrees in number/person with the subject, just as an intransitive verb does, and is an instance of an A $\Rightarrow$ V transposition (see Chapter 8 for more detailed discussion of Chukchi constructions). A type hierarchy such as that shown in Figure 4.9 cannot reflect such distinctions (Spencer, 2013, 307–310).

From the perspective of our study of noun–adjective hybrids, Malouf's hierarchy would force us to posit a schema such as that shown in Figure 4.10. This hierarchy would only be able to define an intermediate subtype which inherited different pieces of information from each of the supertypes. While, a relational adjective is externally an adjective (and hence serves as a typical attributive modifier), it can also remain to varying degrees a noun, whereas a deadjectival property nominalization is externally a noun which may retain certain of the properties of the base adjective. The unrefined type hierarchy would not distinguish property nominalizations from relational adjectives and would falsely imply that relational adjectives have the same syntactic distribution as nouns. The crucial directionality of the relation would therefore be lost, and the crucial fact that transpositions and other sorts of mixed categories imply a type of antisymmetry will be obscured.

It is equally unclear how the hierarchy in Figure 4.10 could account for different types of noun–adjective hybrids within the same language. For instance, we will show in Chapter 8 that Selkup has both denominal adjectives and what we refer to as 'adjectival representations of nouns' (see Spencer, 2013, and other work). Both types have the external distribution of an adjective

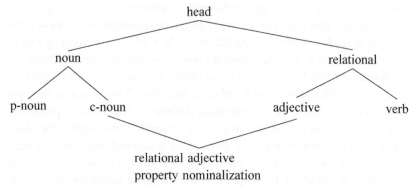

Figure 4.10 *Type hierarchy for relational adjectives and deadjectival property nominalizations*

and inherit certain properties of nouns, but they differ in terms of co-occurrence with possessors.

One can of course account for this difference in syntax, and Malouf (2000b) does introduce a refinement to his analysis which goes some way towards alleviating the problem. He handles the differences between the ACC-ACC and the POSS-ACC gerunds (*Brown painting his daughter* and *Brown's painting his daughter* respectively) by additional lexical rules specifying the way in which the gerund combines with its subject. However, the point is that this information cannot be expressed in the type hierarchy.

To account for syntagmatic category mixing, Malouf (1999) presents an alternative to Sadock's analysis of noun incorporation in West Greenlandic, in which the denominal verb like the one exemplified in (5) is effectively treated as a kind of mixed category. The mixing takes place at the level of argument structure in the HPSG representations of the denominal verb. Malouf analyses the external modification of the incorporated noun as the result of inheritance by a verb of the ARG-ST attributes of both the verbal affix and the noun. Modification is taken to be an ARG-ST operation: the modifier is a non-thematic oblique complement whose lexical representation is added to the (presumably unbounded) list of modifiers included in the COMPS list of the noun. At the same time, the semantic content of that modifier takes the semantic representation of the head noun as its value (Malouf, 1999, 57, Figure 2).

The noun in West Greenlandic takes an optional ergative case-marked specifier denoting a possessor and that property is also inherited by the verb base. The verb affix has a VALENCE|SPR attribute which is normally empty, but which can unify with the noun's optional value VALENCE|SPR⟨NP[erg]⟩.

By treating modification as a kind of argument structure operation and by permitting inheritance of argument structure (and specifiers), Malouf is able to place all the relevant information, including case and number properties, in the representation of the denominal verb form. He argues that such an account is superior in various respects to the Autolexical Syntax account offered by Sadock.

We may ask whether such a manoeuvre would in general suffice to analyse all the syntagmatically mixed adjectives we have described, given that the most salient difference between the West Greenlandic examples and our noun–adjective hybrids is simply that in our examples the resulting denominal word is an adjective, not a verb. For instance, we could say that the lexical representation for the adjective affix in a language such as Upper Sorbian would have to be permitted to inherit the same array of COMP and SPR values from the noun as the West Greenlandic verb affixes. It is certainly possible that an approach along these lines might work, though we would need to be clear that the analysis was able to account for adjective-specific phrasal syntax in all those languages that demonstrate it.

4.4 Mixed Categories in LFG

There are two crucial aspects of LFG architecture that we must consider before we turn to LFG treatments of mixed categories. First, LFG has a finite number of lexical categories and does not recognize intermediate or underspecified category membership, so every lexical word must belong to one (unmixed) category. The second important aspect is the partitioning of the syntactic representation of a phrase into its c-structure (constituent/phrase structure) and its f-structure (functional structure, in the sense of grammatical functions). Lexical specification on syntactic terminals and annotations on phrase structure rules provide instructions on how to construct f-structures for phrases. This means that information about the grammatical function structure of a phrase or clause can come from several places in the c-structure tree. In general, c-structures are built out of standard, X-bar theoretic, endocentric phrases. However, there are occasions when it is appropriate to posit heads which are not in the expected structural relation to their projections.

4.4.1 Bresnan and Mugane (2006)

Following their discussion of single projection and dual projection approaches, Bresnan (1997) and Bresnan and Mugane (2006) argue for a third type of approach in terms of the LFG notion of 'extended head'.[4]

---

[4] For other versions of the extended head analysis see, e.g., Bresnan et al. (2016) and Nikitina and Haug (2016).

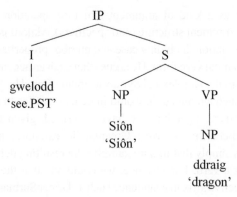

Figure 4.11 *C-structure for* Siôn saw the dragon

Overview

In simple terms the extended head is "the closest element higher up in the tree that functions like the f-structure head of Y" (Bresnan, 2001, 132). The parade example is Kroeger's (1993) analysis of Welsh verb fronting, as described by Bresnan (2001, 126ff). Normally the PRED value of the verb would be provided by a V node heading the VP. In Figure 4.11, 'Siôn saw the dragon', we see that the VP lacks a V head. However, the 'I' head is the next best thing and so serves as the extended head of the VP. All the crucial properties of V, including its lexical meaning, are associated with the element in the position of the 'I' head, *gwelodd*. Those properties provide the verbal meaning (and its inflections) to the f-structure of the sentence as a whole, because the 'I' element is the head of that sentence. The VP node is required in the LFG analysis shown in Figure 4.11 because it is required elsewhere in the grammar of the language, and because the c-structure would wrongly project *ddraig* 'dragon' as a predicate nominal if the VP node were not there.

The simplified f-structure for Figure 4.11 is shown in (20).

(20) F-structure for the c-structure shown in 4.11
$$\begin{bmatrix} \text{PRED} & \text{'see}\langle\text{SUBJ, OBJ}\rangle\text{' (from [}_\text{I}\text{ gwelodd])} \\ \text{SUBJ} & \text{'SIÔN'} \\ \text{OBJ} & \text{'DRAGON'} \end{bmatrix}$$

The crucial point to observe about the diagram in Figure 4.11 is that there is no V node as such, and therefore there is no sense in which two syntactic nodes are linked to a single terminal element. As Dalrymple (2001, 79) points out, this corresponds to the situation of apparent 'head movement'

4.4 Mixed Categories in LFG   153

in models which permit such transformations, but because of the way that c-structures/lexical structures are mapped to f-structures the required analysis falls out automatically (granted certain X-bar theoretic assumptions about c-structure).

Given this brief background we can now see how the notion of extended head can be applied to a particular type of syntagmatically mixed category, the agentive nominal category found in a number of Bantu languages including Gĩkũyũ (also known as Kikuyu), which is analysed in Bresnan and Mugane (2006). The Gĩkũyũ agentive nominals behave much like *-er* nominals in English and take complements in the manner of nouns so as to express the complement grammatical functions of the base verb (i.e. constructions akin to *this bad slaughterer of goats* from the nominal *slaughterer*). However, it is also possible to express the base verb's complements and adjuncts as though they were still part of the verb phrase to obtain construction types which are not possible in English, as seen in (21):

(21) ũyũ mũ-thĩĩnj-i   mbũri ũũru
      1.DEM 1-slaughter-NOM 10.goat badly
      'this bad goat slaughterer'

In (21), *mbũri* 'goat' is a direct object, not a complement to a noun, and *ũũru* 'badly' is a verb modifier, not an adjective.

Bresnan (1997) and Bresnan and Mugane (2006) (following Mugane, 1996) analyse the agentive nominalization construction by positing a special type of argument structure operation as part of the derivation of the nominal. Normally, when a derivational process applies to a lexeme, say, deriving a noun from a verb, the verbal argument structure properties are either inaccessible or are only indirectly accessible as complements to the noun (having been 'inherited' by that noun; see Booij, 1988, for detailed discussion). However, in order to account for phrases such as that in (21), Bresnan and Mugane argue that the verbal quality of the underlying base lexeme is retained.

LFG certainly lacks a well-defined model of derivational morphology. It is therefore not obvious how the theory represents the syntactic category of a morphologically derived word. Bresnan and Mugane propose a notation under which the argument structure representation of a word includes a diacritic mark permitting the grammar to stipulate the derived lexeme's syntactic category. Thus, the argument structure of a verb is furnished with a diacritic 'v' while that of a noun is furnished with a diacritic 'n'. These diacritics are then associated with an inside-out function which specifies that the c-structure label of the phrasal node headed by the lexeme in question is VP, respectively

154 Approaches to Mixed Categories

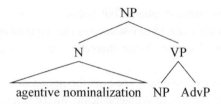

Figure 4.12 C-structure for Gĩkũyũ agentive nominalization

NP. They provide the representations for the English lexemes SLAUGHTER and SLAUGHTERER shown in (22) (Bresnan and Mugane, 2006, 227):

(22) a. slaughter: V: (↑PRED) = 'slaughter⟨(↑SUBJ)(↑OBJ)⟩$_v$'
  v: VP ∈ CAT(PRED↑)
 b. slaughterer: N: (↑PRED) = 'slaughterer⟨(↑OBL$_\theta$)⟩$_n$'
  n: NP ∈ CAT(PRED↑)

The notation (↑OBL$_\theta$) means that the derived nominal takes a subcategorized oblique complement; the *of*-phrase. That phrase corresponds to the verb lexeme's OBJ argument, of course, though it is not entirely clear how this is captured.

Bresnan and Mugane then extend this notation so as to represent the c-structure lexical category of the Gĩkũyũ agentive nominalization using both diacritics, with the diacritic 'v' attached to the argument structure representation of the derived nominal's base verb representation, as in (23a), corresponding to the lexical entry in (23b).

(23) a. mũthĩĩnji: 'agent-of⟨x, slaughter⟨x,y⟩$_v$⟩$_n$'
 b. mũthĩĩnji: N: (↑PRED) = 'slaughterer⟨⟨(↑OBJ)⟩$_v$⟩$_n$'

The inside-out functions associated with the subscripts define an inverse function from f-structure representations to c-structures constraining the categorial labels of nodes serving as c-structure correspondents of portions of f-structures. This means that the c-structure for the agentive nominalization will exhibit categorial mixing in the c-structure, in that two differently labelled nodes will be constrained to map to the f-structure corresponding to the agentive nominal. The kind of tree envisaged is seen in Figure 4.12.

The N-projection of Figure 4.12 will contribute the PRED value of the derived nominal and will also constrain the f-structure to contain an OBJ attribute. The VP node, however, will inherit the information that it contains an NP object and an AdvP adjunct. The f-structure correspondent of the lower NP

4.4 Mixed Categories in LFG   155

will define the OBJ attribute of the f-structure of the whole nominal, while the f-structure correspondent of the AdvP node will add an ADJUNCT attribute, just as in the representation of a complete clause.

At this point it is worth clarifying something which might otherwise confuse the reader who consults Bresnan and Mugane's work. Earlier in their presentation Bresnan and Mugane (2006, 215) provide a version of this tree where the VP is headed by a V which, together with the N head, dominates the agentive nominal. This is reminiscent of a lexical sharing analysis proposed for such phenomena as portmanteau adpositions in Romance languages in Wescoat (2002), but it is important to appreciate that such a syntactic representation is emphatically not what Bresnan and Mugane intend. The agentive nominal does not have two lexical heads; it has one extended noun head which maps to an f-structure that is also associated with a VP node, in much the same way that the f-structure correspondent of *gwelodd* in Figure 4.11 maps to an f-structure which corresponds to a VP node. The difference is that the VP node in Welsh is required by general principles of Welsh syntax, whereas the VP node in Figure 4.12 is required by virtue of the special diacritic 'v' marking in the derived argument structure of the agentive nominal. The diagram with two distinct heads is labelled 'informal' by Bresnan and Mugane, and would appear to serve more as a visualization of the idea that the mixed category has properties both of a noun and a verb at some level of representation. However, the appropriate levels of representation are lexical structure (where the derived nominal is furnished with v, n diacritics) and f-structure, not c-structure.

We can now ask whether the extended head analysis Bresnan and Mugane (2006) have proposed is really a syntactic affixation analysis (that is, dual projection in their terms) or a lexical affixation analysis (single projection). The answer appears to be 'both and neither'. It is a dual projection analysis in so far as the diacritic marking of the argument structure representations licenses a VP node which can house verb-oriented complements and adjuncts. It is a single projection analysis in the sense that the mixed lexical category itself is dominated by a single (albeit extended) head in c-structure. The category mixing arises by virtue of the additional diacritic mark on the argument structure representation. It is the presence of the 'v/n' diacritics in argument structure that distinguishes Gĩkũyũ, which permits structures with the form 'a slaughterer goats badly', from English, which does not. But the status of the diacritics is not entirely clear and there are a number of other aspects of this analysis which are not fully specified. In Chapter 8 we present a reinterpretation of them in broadly the terms sketched at the end of Bresnan (1997), and extend this analysis to the problem of denominal adjectives (following Spencer, 2013).

156 *Approaches to Mixed Categories*

For the present, the crucial point is that it is the enriched lexical representation (with the diacritics) which plays the central role in accounting for the category mixing effects.

Phrasal Coherence

There is another dimension to the structural properties of the deverbal nominalization mixed category, namely the property of 'Phrasal Coherence' (after Malouf, 2000a, 97). This property introduces a further syntactic dimension to category mixing. The idea is that there is a hierarchical phrase structure representation, such that some words and phrases occupy a higher position than other words and phrases; that is, some nodes c-command other nodes. (These assumptions are not shared by proponents of dependency models of grammar such as Word Grammar.) Moreover, this hierarchical structure is defined in terms of the notion of the syntactic head/dependent. (That assumption is also shared by dependency grammar approaches.) Phrasal Coherence is a global property of hierarchical syntactic structures: the category of the base head word can be mismatched at a certain level with those of its dependents, but at a higher level it is impossible for the head-dependent relations of the base word to be restored. Despite the fact that it is not universal, Phrasal Coherence is a pervasive feature of categorial mixing.

Bresnan and Mugane (2006) argue that the phenomenon of Phrasal Coherence poses problems for a single projection approach to nominalizations, although it is a recurrent cross-linguistic feature of mixed categories of this sort, as is amply demonstrated, for instance, in the cross-linguistic survey of action nominalizations in Koptjevskaja-Tamm (2003a) (see also Malouf, 2000a, 96ff). In their analysis the Gĩkũyũ construction introduced above in (21) does respect Phrasal Coherence:

> all and only the post-head immediate constituents of VPs are possible post-head constituents of the mixed agentive nominalization phrase, and all and only the possible orderings of these VP constituents are possible orderings of the same constituents in the mixed agentive phrase. (Bresnan and Mugane, 2006, 211)

Intuitively, what this means is that the construction can remain verbal up to a certain point, and then can switch to being nominal, but it cannot switch back to being verbal once it has been transposed into a noun. In the analysis of Bresnan (1997) and Bresnan and Mugane (2006), Phrasal Coherence results from two things: first, the nominalization reflects category mixing in that it includes reference to verbal as well as to nominal properties; second, the framework permits different properties of the lexical representation to map to different syntactic nodes in c-structure. The Phrasal Coherence property emerges automatically as a consequence of treating the c-structure of the mixed category as an extended head construction. The N node dominating the nominalization itself is the extended head of the VP, which lacks a head otherwise. The extended head device thus captures relations in phrase structure which would be captured by means of head movement of a V into an N head in a transformational approach.

However, Malouf (2000a) argues that Bresnan's (1997) treatment of the Phrasal Coherence phenomenon, and by implication the later treatment of Bresnan and Mugane (2006), is empirically flawed. While, it is somewhat unclear exactly how Bresnan and Mugane's later analysis is supposed to work, as we have seen, it appears that they intend it to respect the Phrasal Coherence hypothesis as formulated by Malouf. We will therefore assume that that is indeed the case and summarize Malouf's arguments against that hypothesis.

The principal problem is seen with languages which have a verb-subject-object (VSO) canonical word order in clauses and nominalizations. Malouf (2000a) discusses two cases, Boumaa Fijian and Modern Standard Arabic (the literary koine of the Arab-speaking world). We will illustrate his analysis of Arabic nominalizations.

Malouf (2000a, 100), following Fassi Fehri (1993), argues that nominalizations in Arabic have essentially the same c-structure as ordinary (possessed) noun phrases. The structure of a possessive construction is given in (24).

(24)   daar-a   r-rajul-i   l-waasiat-a
        house-ACC the-man-GEN the-large-ACC
        'the large house (ACC) of the man'

Malouf follows Borsley (1995) in taking possessors to be the first complement of nouns in Arabic rather than being specifiers. As a result, the structure of the phrase in (25) will be all but identical to that of a non-derived NP.

(25)   ntiqaad-u   Zayd-in   amr-an
        criticizing-NOM Zayd-GEN Amr-ACC
        'Zayd's criticising Amr'

Malouf argues that a structure such as that in (25) violates Phrasal Coherence. It is specifically problematical for the Phrasal Coherence hypothesis because the base verb's direct object is expressed as a noun phrase marked in the accusative, just like the object of a verb, but the base verb has already been converted, so to speak, to a noun by this point, and therefore realizes its subject argument

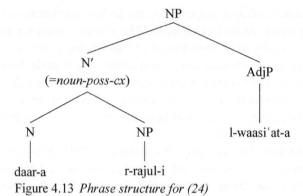

Figure 4.13 *Phrase structure for (24)*

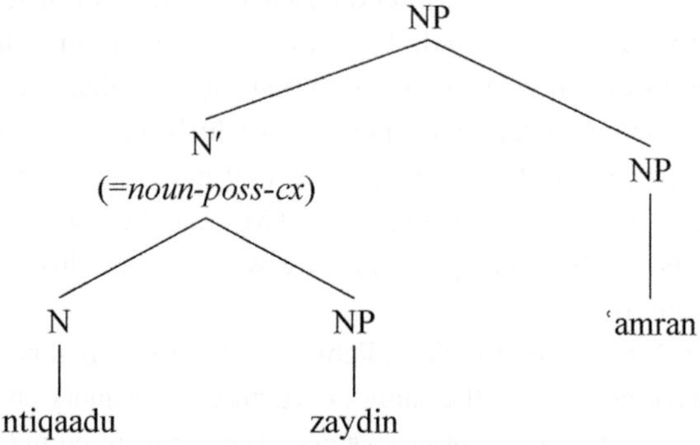

Figure 4.14 *Phrase structure for (25)*

in the manner of a possessor phrase with a genitive marked noun phrase. The problem for Phrasal Coherence analysis is further seen in examples such as that in (26) (Malouf, 2000a, 104).[5] In (26) the complement of the nominalization corresponding to the verb's subject is separated from the object argument by an adverbial. Since adverbials modify verbs and not nouns, it would appear that we have a phrasally incoherent structure in which the verb is first nominalized, takes a possessor complement in the manner of a noun head, and then reverts to being a verb in order to take an adverbial modifier and an accusative marked direct object.

---

[5] Hebrew presents similar counter-examples to Phrasal Coherence: see Borer (2013, Ch 2) for a detailed review of the relevant cases.

4.4 Mixed Categories in LFG

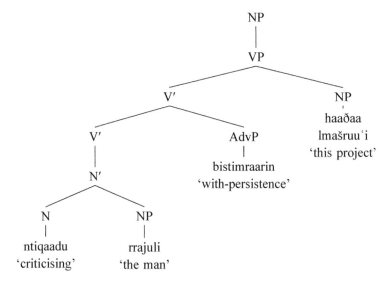

Figure 4.15 *Phrase structure for (26)*

(26) ntiqaad-u   r-rajul-i   bi-stimraar-in   haaðaa
     criticizing-NOM the-man-GEN with-persistence-GEN this
     l-mašruu-i
     the-project-ACC
     'the man's persistent criticizing of this project'

Because a structure such as Figure 4.17 violates Phrasal Coherence, Malouf proposes to replace this principle with a different notion of 'Lexical Coherence'. Malouf (2000a, Ch 3) is a detailed defence of this generalization. By this he means that the patterns are defined in terms of constraints stated over the lexical representations of the nominalizations themselves. In concert with constraints on the mappings between lexical representations and c-structure representations, these lexical constraints will account for the commonalities found cross-linguistically without ruling out patterns which are rare, but nonetheless attested. The Phrasal Coherence effects are then the results of lexical rules which specify the default relations that subtend between, say, a verb and an action nominal. In (27) we see the general form of such a lexical constraint set.

160   *Approaches to Mixed Categories*

(27)   a. $\begin{bmatrix} word \\ \text{VFORM } fin \end{bmatrix}$ ⊃   [SUBJ ⟨synsem⟩]

   b. $\begin{bmatrix} word \\ \text{SUBJ } \langle synsem \rangle \end{bmatrix}$ ⊃   *predicator*

These rules state that (a) a finite verb licenses a subject, and (b) a word which takes a subject is a predicator, by which Malouf means a lexical item with the argument structure and linking patterns of a verb (Malouf, 2000a, 98–99). The Arabic masdar lexical rule is given in (28).

(28) $\begin{bmatrix} \text{HEAD } verb \\ \text{VAL} \begin{bmatrix} \text{SUBJ} & \langle \boxed{1}\,\text{NP}\rangle \\ \text{COMPS} & \boxed{2} \\ \text{SPR} & \langle\,\rangle \end{bmatrix} \end{bmatrix}$ ⇒ $\begin{bmatrix} \text{HEAD } ma\d{s}dar \\ \text{VAL} \begin{bmatrix} \text{SUBJ} & \langle\,\rangle \\ \text{COMPS} & \langle\,\boxed{1}\mid\boxed{2}\,\rangle \\ \text{SPR} & \langle\,\rangle \end{bmatrix} \end{bmatrix}$

(Malouf, 2000a, 104)

The masdar selects a possessor as its first complement.

   Thus, Malouf takes the Arabic construction to be a counter-example to the kind of analysis proposed by Bresnan (1997) and (by implication) Bresnan and Mugane (2006), because those analyses entail the Phrasal Coherence hypothesis. However, it is not immediately obvious that Malouf's objections actually do carry over to the type of model presupposed in Bresnan and Mugane's analysis of Gĩkũyũ. To test this, we will consider an extended head analysis of the Arabic masdar construction parallel to that of the Gĩkũyũ agentive nominalizations.

   The argument structure representations and the lexical representation for the base verb *criticize* would be along the lines of (29) (we label Arabic words with their English translation equivalents for simplicity of exposition).

(29)   a.   criticize: V: (↑PRED) = 'criticize⟨(↑SUBJ)(↑OBJ)⟩'
   b.   criticize-ing: N: (↑PRED) = 'criticizing⟨ ((↑OBJ))(↑OBL$_\theta$)⟩'

The lexical mapping theory principles which relate argument structure representations to lexical representations with grammatical function specifications will presumably define the (↑OBL$_\theta$) grammatical function for *criticizing* as the correspondent of the (↑SUBJ) grammatical function of the base verb. The task is now to ensure that the original object phrase is realized as though it were

4.4 Mixed Categories in LFG   161

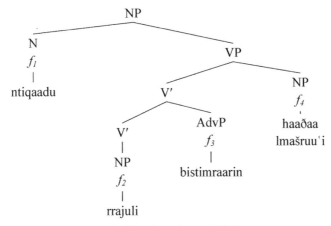

Figure 4.16 *Extended head analysis of (26)*

the object of a verb predicate, while the original subject phrase is realized as though it were the possessor of a noun. The extended head structure shown in Figure 4.16 would accommodate this deployment of grammatical functions.

The annotations f_1 to f_4 on the nodes provide the following information about the f-structure of the construction as a whole, as shown in (30).

(30) f_1: PRED = 'criticizing⟨(↑OBJ)(↑OBL$_\theta$)⟩'
      f_2: OBL$_\theta$ = 'MAN'
      f_3: ADJT = 'CONTINUALLY'
      f_4: OBJ = 'THIS PROJECT'

The shorthand f-descriptions in (30) will serve to define an appropriate f-structure for the masdar. General principles will realize the OBJ expression as an accusative case-marked NP (or, equivalently for our purposes, DP), while the OBL$_\theta$ expression will be realized as a genitive case-marked NP. Finally, in order to guarantee that the c-structure in Figure 4.16 realizes the lexical structure of the masdar, we can assume annotations on the argument structure representation along the lines sketched in (31), where 'nom-of' is a shorthand representation of whatever representational device expresses the notion of action nominal transposition in LFG derivational morphology.

(31) a. criticize-ing: 'nom-of⟨criticize⟨x$_n$,y⟩$_v$⟩$_n$'
     b. criticize-ing: N: (↑PRED) =
        'criticizing ⟨⟨⟨(↑OBJ)⟩$_v$ ⟨(↑OBL$_\theta$)⟩$_n$⟩$_n$'.

162 *Approaches to Mixed Categories*

The diacritic subscripts require there to be corresponding VP and NP nodes in the c-structure representation. The fact that the 'n' subscript appears external to the 'v' subscript in (31a) (by analogy with Bresnan and Mugane's representations for the Gĩkũyũ nominal) suggests that we expect the dominating category for the construction to be nominal. However, the first, subject, argument of the verb is also marked with the 'n' subscript, indicating that its c-structure correspondent has nominal morphosyntax. Note that we have to deploy the 'v/n' subscripts in a somewhat unexpected way, in the sense that each of the two arguments of the masdar is annotated differently, but this simply reflects the typological peculiarity of the construction itself.

Such an analysis seems to get the right word forms in the right order, but it is far from clear that this is a satisfactory analysis. First, it makes *rrajuli bistimraarin* a constituent, but not *ntiqaadu rrajuli bistimraarin*. This has the strange implication that Arabic permits conjunction of the possessor/subject NP with an adjunct but does not permit conjunction of the masdar itself with the possessor/subject NP. In other words, it implies that it would be grammatical to say *the criticizing*[[*continually by the man*] *and* [*persistently by the woman*]] *of the project*, but not [[*the criticizing by the man*] *and* [*the praising by the woman*]] *of the project*. Second, we would lose entirely the parallel between the masdar construction and the standard possessive construction, which is very clearly brought out in Malouf's analysis.

Our conclusion is that an analysis which takes the lexical representations in (31) as its starting point could be made to work, but only at the cost of counter-intuitive (and possibly downright wrong) c-structures. This conclusion seems to be independent of our choice of lexical representation. Suppose we attempt to match the parallelism with possessive constructions by getting the mapping rules to define the base verb's SUBJ role as a POSS role, effectively as proposed by Bresnan (2001, 194) for English gerundive nominalizations.

(32) criticizing: $\langle(\uparrow POSS), (\uparrow OBJ)\rangle$

This would allow us to propose Figure 4.17 as a c-structure for the masdar shown in (25). However, this representation is inadequate because an NP with OBJ function needs to be the sister of a verb, not N'. Again, we would need to propose the extended head structure of Figure 4.16, which we have already rejected.

To conclude, we have updated Malouf's (2000a) empirical critique of the LFG approach to deverbal nominal mixed categories by showing that it applies with equal force to the revised proposals of Bresnan and Mugane (2006) in terms of constituent structure syntax. The property of Phrasal Coherence is

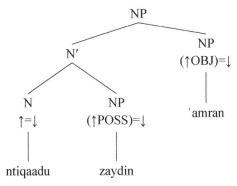

Figure 4.17 *C-structure representation of (25)*

very real, of course, as witnessed by the ingenuity which Malouf required in order to find counter-examples to it, but it is, in effect, only a (very strong) typological tendency and not an architectural property of language or universal grammar. An adequate model of mixed categories for deverbal nominalizations will therefore have to embed some property which makes Phrasal Coherence a default option, but at the same time will have to include sufficient flexibility to permit that option to be overridden in (rather special) circumstances.

4.4.2 Lowe (2016)

A somewhat different approach to certain types of category mixing is taken by Lowe (2016), following from his analysis of Sanskrit participles (Lowe, 2015).[6] He argues that a mixed category analysis of participles in Sanskrit (and Indo-European generally by extension of reasoning) is inappropriate for LFG: the participles in their function as true verb-to-adjective transpositions are verbs at all levels of phrase/constituent structure (c-structure) and this means that they belong to the lexical category of verb at all levels. However, the participles are forms of the verb that receive adjectival features permitting them to inflect like adjectives and therefore permitting them to modify nouns in the manner of attributive adjectives, while retaining (some of) their verb properties. By parity of reasoning, this analysis would have to carry over to the cases of (true) relational adjective that we discuss in the book. These would have to be

---

[6] To appreciate the proposals made by Lowe and our objections to them, it is necessary to have some familiarity with the LFG architecture, the 'PFM2' model of Paradigm Function Morphology (Bonami and Stump, 2016; Stump, 2016), and the model of Generalized Paradigm Function Morphology (Spencer, 2013). Discussion of (Generalized) Paradigm Function Morphology is deferred until Chapter 6.

164   *Approaches to Mixed Categories*

analysed as nouns at all levels of representation, but be provided with adjectival (agreement/concord) features.

The key to Lowe's analysis is the model of the morphology-syntax interface proposed by Dalrymple (2015). For ease of comparison, we follow the exposition of Lowe (2016) on the key points in the Dalrymple proposals, but for ease of comparison with our own approach, we transfer Lowe's discussion of Sanskrit participles to the Russian examples discussed in Spencer (2017b) and summarized in Chapter 6, Section 6.4.

Dalrymple (2015) defines inflected word forms – 'lexical entries'[7] – on the basis of a representation akin to a traditional dictionary entry, the lexemic entry (LE). This is a three-place relation between a stipulated root form (and other stem forms where appropriate), the set of those f-descriptions shared by all the word forms of the lexeme, and a Lexemic Index (LI), as shown in (33) for the Russian adjective vysokij 'tall':

(33)   LE⟨{ROOT:vysok}, {(↑PRED)= 'tall', TALL}⟩

Recall that the term 'f-description' refers to those properties of the lexical representation that contribute the f-structure, a level of representation for grammatical relations (SUBJECT, OBJECT, modifier/ADJUNCT, and so on), AGREEMENT, and semantic interpretable properties such as NUMBER, TENSE, etc. For a Russian adjective the only set of f-structure properties shared by inflected forms is the PRED value, which is virtually identical in its functioning to LI (Spencer, 2015a).

Morphology in Dalrymple (2015) is defined by a realization relation, R, corresponding in large part to Stump's (2001) Paradigm Function (though note that R is a relation, not a function). The relation R is defined by a set of representations called m-entries, which are representations of the form (morphosyntactic and phonological) and morphological feature content of individual inflected word forms, as shown in (34) for the F.ACC.SG form of the Russian adjective vysokij 'tall'.

(34)   R⟨TALL, /visokuju/, [visokuju], {M-CAT:ADJ, M-CASE:ACC, M-NUM:SG, M-GEND: F}⟩

This can be simplified using the shorthand notation of the template, as shown in (35).

(35)   R⟨TALL, /visokuju/, [visokuju], {@MADJ(ACC, SG, F)}⟩

---

[7]   Lexical entries are not to be confused with dictionary entries/lexemic entries; see Chapter 5 for discussion.

4.4 Mixed Categories in LFG   165

In lexicalist studies of the morphology-syntax interface it is widely assumed that it is necessary to distinguish purely morphological (morphomic) grammatical properties or features from property sets that are visible to syntax and/or semantics (e.g. the 'm-/s-feature' distinction in Sadler and Spencer (2001), and the 'FORM/CONTENT paradigm' distinction in Stump (2002, 2006, 2016)). In Dalrymple (2015) the m-feature ~ s-feature relation is coded by means of the description function D, a kind of inverse *Corr* mapping (Stump, 2016, Chapter 6, Section 6.3.1). This function maps m-features to the two core levels of syntactic representation in LFG, c-structure and f-structure (in principle the mapping can be extended to argument structure and information structure, where these are morphologically mediated). The description function for the Russian word form *vysokuju* is shown in (36).

(36)   D⟨TALL, M-CAT:ADJ, M-CASE:ACC, M-NUM:SG, M-GEND: F, Adj, ($\uparrow$CASE) = ACC, ($\uparrow$NUM) = SG, ($\uparrow$GEND) = F⟩

The application of the D function in (36) tells us that the m-feature characterization defines a lexical entry (syntactically visible word form/syntactic terminal) with the f-structure agreement properties indicated, belonging to the c-structure category 'Adj'. The c-structure category labelling can be defined independently of the f-structure properties through the function D_{cat}. Thus, following Lowe's (2015) example in (35) for Sanskrit adjectives, we can assume an application of D_{cat} for Russian adjectives of the form (37).

(37) D_{cat} ⟨LI_{adj}, M, Adj⟩ iff M-CAT:ADJ $\in$ M

Given this way of representing adjectives, Lowe proposes to represent participles by combining a set of adjectival m-features with the m-features of the verb proper. Consider the PRS.ACT.PTCP form *udarjajuščuju* 'hitting (ACC.SG.F)'. The Lexemic Entry is shown in simplified form in (38).

(38)   LE⟨ROOT:udar', ($\uparrow$PRED)= 'hit', HIT⟩

The R relation will specify the form's m-features, as in (39).

(39)   R⟨HIT,   /udarjajuščuju/,   [udarjajuščuju],   M-ASP:IPFV, M-VOICE:ACT, @MADJ(ACC, SG, F)⟩

Lowe (2015, 422) then claims that "morphological 'adjectivehood' now has a unified and coherent contribution in the lexicon".

The crucial step is now the determination of the c-structure category from the participle's m-description. Vanilla morphological adjectives are mapped to

166 *Approaches to Mixed Categories*

c-structure members of the category 'Adj' in the expected way. For participles, what is needed is a somewhat different mapping; Lowe's (36), as instantiated in (40).

(40) $D_{cat}\langle LI_{vb}, \text{m-features}, V_{[ptc]}\rangle$ iff M-CAT:ADJ $\in$ M

Here, 'LI_{vb}' picks out those indexed lexemes which are verbs. Lowe assumes the existence of a complex c-structure category, $V_{[ptc]}$, a subset of the V category, which defines the c-structure category/labelling of those word forms which correspond to participial forms.

Lowe's exposition makes it look as though the set LI_{vb} is defined by lexical listing, but that can hardly be what is intended. The question arises as to how LI_{vb} can be defined in a non-circular fashion, however. The LE of a verb itself provides no clue, so we must examine the R relation associated with each word form of each verb lexeme. Assuming that verb templates are specified in abbreviated form as @M-CAT:VERB(TENSE, aspect, @SUBJAGR, VOICE, ...) then LI_{vb} could be specified as any LI, £, such that for $\langle£,\sigma,\pi,M\rangle$, M-CAT:VERB $\in$ M. Then any set of representations which additionally bears m-features M-CAT:ADJ will be mapped to the $V_{[ptc]}$ subcategory of the V category by the system shown in (40).[8]

What remains unclear in Lowe's account is the relationship between his example in (35), corresponding to our example in (37), and his example (36), our example (40). A specification such as that in (37) defines a lexeme, £, belonging to the 'LI_{adj}' class as having the labelling S-CAT:ADJ iff £ is morphologically an adjective. The 'LI_{adj}' subset of LIs is defined, presumably, as those LIs which are mapped to an m-feature set, M, containing M-CAT:ADJ. Thus, the content of Lowe's examples in (35/37) is:

> Given an LI, £, such that for all values σ in Σ and all values π in Π, where $R\langle£,\Sigma,\Pi,M\rangle$, and M-CAT:ADJ $\in$ M, then
> $D_{cat}\langle£,M',Adj\rangle$ iff M' $\ni$ M-CAT:ADJ

In other words, where we have a word form of a lexeme £ whose image under the R relation contains the M-CAT:ADJ specification, the D_{cat} description function for £, applied to an m-feature set containing M-CAT:ADJ, will deliver an S-CAT:ADJ specification. What is the set M' here, and how does it relate

---

[8] Lowe introduces the $V_{[ptc]}$ subcategory as an alternative to a suggestion made in Spencer (2015b), in which the participle is assigned to an alternative c-structure category, mnemonically labelled 'V2A', and introduced for purely expositional reasons. However, it is difficult for us to distinguish the notational proposals in Lowe's account from those in Spencer's.

4.4 Mixed Categories in LFG   167

to the set M? In fact, for D_{cat} to be applicable, M′ can be very simple. We do not expect all forms of a lexeme to show inflection for all possible features. Indeed, feature contrasts and specifications are frequently lost in different parts of a lexeme's paradigm. Thus, a German adjective shows no agreement in its predicative use, a Russian adjective shows no agreement in the predicative comparative form, infinitive forms of a verb may show no inflection at all for other verbal properties, and so on. The only feature specification that M′ is obliged to share with M for all members of the lexeme £, it seems, is M-CAT:ADJ. This is not, as far as we can tell, explicitly stated in Dalrymple (2015), but it is clearly a requirement if Lowe's characterization of LI_{adj}, the set of adjectival lexemes, is to be coherent.

The content of Lowe's examples in (36/40) is more complex. Here, the set M of m-features must include the specification M-CAT:VERB, because the function is defined over the LI_{vb} subset of lexemes, and these are obliged to be characterized as M-CAT:VERB. However, to qualify as a participial form, a word form of a verbal lexeme, £$_{vb}$, has to be assigned the feature specification M-CAT:ADJ, by the system shown in (40). This raises the question of why (35/37) fail to apply to a category labelled $V_{[ptc]}$. The function in Lowe's (35/37) is so written as to map all morphological adjectives to the S-CAT:ADJ category. But this means that it is in competition with Lowe's (36/40). It is therefore is difficult to see how (37) and (40) can yield a coherent output. The only way to do this, it seems, would be by stipulating that (40) takes precedence over (37). However, that would render void Lowe's claims to have provided an analysis of participles as verbs, because, in effect, their verbal syntactic category is being stipulated.[9]

Whatever the merits of Lowe's account of Indo-European-type participles, it is difficult to see how it can be generalized to languages with richer sets of transpositions, such as predicative adjectives, in addition to participles (as in some of the Samoyedic languages, a number of Altaic languages, and other groups). Here we must distinguish between forms such as (schematically) *hunted-PL* (simplex verb, past tense, plural subject), *tall-PL* (simplex adjective, plural concord) on the one hand, and *hunting-PL* (participle, plural concord) and *were-tall* (predicative adjective, past tense, plural subject) on the other

---

[9] In an inferential-realizational model based on defaults and overrides ('Pāṇinian Determinism') we could say that a representation including the specifications {M-CAT:VERB, M-CAT:ADJ} was more specific than one including just one of those specifications and that the mapping to the c-structure subcategory '$V_{[ptc]}$' therefore overrides the mapping to the 'Adj' category or the more general 'V' category. However, LFG does not operate with default inheritance logic, so this solution is not available.

168   *Approaches to Mixed Categories*

hand. The problem is that both the participle and the predicative adjective will bear the features M-CAT:ADJ, M-CAT:VERB, so both will be simultaneously eligible for categorization as S-CAT:VERB and S-CAT:ADJ. This problem will not, of course, be solved by inventing another complex category for predicative adjectives, say A[pred]. Lowe's proposals thus contain the same flaw that afflicts Malouf's analysis of mixed categories in terms of multiple inheritance.

If we were to adopt a stipulation for predicative adjectives – or predicative nouns for that matter – guaranteeing that they preserve the base lexeme's category, then we will end up with a very curious set of c-structures. Recall that the main aim of Lowe's analysis is to defend the claim that participial relatives are clauses headed by a lexical head of category V. Then by the same logic a predicative adjective (noun) will remain a member of category A (N) when it heads the clause. This means that all such predications will be verbless, because there will be no lexeme of category V anywhere in the clause. This conclusion is somewhat counter-intuitive, but more crucially it contributes to a complication in the definition of phrase structures. As Lowe himself stresses,[10] c-structure categories do not serve the purpose of defining the distribution of words and phrases. In English, for instance, a subject phrase can be not only nominal, of category NP/DP, but can also be a VP ([*Swimming*] *is good for you*, [*To err*] *is human*), an AP ([*The poor*] *are always with us*), a PP ([*Under the bed*] *is a good place to hide*), or a whole clause ([*That you should say such a thing*] *surprises us*). In addition, under Lowe's analysis a clause can be headed by V, A, or N (or, indeed, P in the case of predicative PPs).[11] As a result, the familiar phrase structure rules of LFG, such as the first expansion of S, have to take the general form ZP → XP YP, for (more or less) any X, Y, Z.[12,13]

---

[10]   Along with many others, as we have seen in Chapter 1. Note especially Croft (2001) in a Cognitive/Construction Grammar framework, Van Valin (2008) in the Role and Reference Grammar framework, and Chaves (2014) in the Sign-Based Construction Grammar variant of HPSG; see also Spencer (1998).

[11]   In Russian, in present tense contexts, even a finite clause can serve as the predicate of a main clause without the need for support by a copular verb:

(i)   [Glavaja problema]SUBJ [čto my ne možem skoordinirovat'sja]PREDICATE
      main   problem   that we not can   coordinate.REFL
      'The main problem is that we can't coordinate ourselves'.

[12]   Lowe's proposals also seem to encounter insurmountable problems when confronted by the numerous cases of non-standard lexical relatedness enumerated in Spencer (2013), including instances such as the Russian past tense morphology, *stolovaja*-nouns, *Angestellte(r)*-nouns, just to mention those involving adjectival features.

[13]   A somewhat radical conclusion from this line of reasoning is that it renders all c-structure categories entirely superfluous. See Chaves (2014) and Spencer (1998) for discussion.

In Chapter 6, Section 6.4 we present an analysis of participles that addresses the problems raised here and which also permits us to integrate our morphosyntactic analysis of mixed categories into a lexicalist syntax and an inferential-realizational model of morphology.

4.5   Conclusions

The literature that addresses categorial mixing generally takes one of two approaches. In the first, the dual projection approach, the mixing occurs 'in the syntax', where two syntactic nodes correspond to one lexical item. Movement analyses within transformational models of grammar are prime examples of this. In the second, the single projection approach, the mixing occurs 'in the lexicon/morphology', where a single syntactic node inherits properties corresponding to both types of category from the lexical representation. The LFG extended head approach shares properties of both the single and the single projection analyses. It is like a dual projection approach in the sense that functional (f-structure) information about a word is associated with more than one c-structure node. It is like a single projection approach in that the crucial argument structure information which defines the mixed category construction is specified at the level of the lexeme itself. The elements which give rise to the mixing are not independent elements introduced separately into the syntactic representation (by means of some type of syntactic affixation).

Having contrasted these approaches to mixed constructions, we can conclude that the syntactically motivated dual projection analyses were overall less successful than lexicalist single projection analyses. But in order for a lexicalist account to succeed, it must necessary be explicit about the nature of lexical representations and how they are deployed in the syntax. In many cases the answer lies in the nature of lexical representations themselves: what kind of information they provide and how that information is accessible to other words. This means that we must fractionate constructions into their crucial components: how the morphology of the construction relates to the rest of the morphological system, what properties the construction appeals to in the syntax, what aspects of other syntactic constructions it inherits, what semantic contribution the construction makes, and so forth. Once we have such a defining checklist of properties, not much else needs to be said, since this constitutes the explicit characterization of the construction required of any generative grammatical description. This is one of the reasons for using default inheritance to characterize word categories and for taking lexical representations seriously. Then there remains the onus of demonstrating exactly how such an approach

170   *Approaches to Mixed Categories*

based on lexical factorization actually works in an explicit syntactic model. While it may eventually prove straightforward to reach agreement on the basic canonical properties of categories, there is a great deal to do in mapping out the different kinds of lexical typing that languages permit, and hence showing how the mixed categories relate to the 'pure' categories.

5   *Lexical Representation and Lexical Relatedness*

5.1   Introduction

When we come to study the noun–adjective hybrid type of mixed category, we can see that members of a class of denominal adjectives behave in some respects as though they were nouns. We will claim that this is because, at a certain level of representation, they actually are still nouns. In fact, these adjectives are effectively 'forms' (better, 'representations' – see Chapter 6) of the base noun lexeme, in almost the same way that plural or case-inflected words are forms of a base noun lexeme. We will see how this idea can be implemented throughout the rest of this book. However, before we can turn to the details of the analysis, it is necessary to clarify a number of conceptual issues surrounding the notions of lexeme itself, lexical representation, lexical/lexemic/dictionary entry, and lexical relatedness. Any model of grammar which espouses lexicalism needs to be able to characterize these notions and, in particular, needs to have ways of distinguishing one lexical unit (of whatever type) from another. Yet there is a certain amount of confusion over these issues even within highly articulated lexicalist syntactic models such as HPSG/SBCG, in particular when deciding when two lexical forms are forms of the same lexeme as opposed to being forms of distinct lexemes.

A specific instance is the problem of distinguishing the individual entries in the lexicon, i.e. lexemes (Spencer, 2015a). This is the Lexeme Individuation Problem. It is one of the perennial problems in lexicology and in practical lexicography, and is clearly central to our final goal of accounting for the behaviour of noun–adjective hybrids by taking them to be forms, in effect, of the base noun lexeme. The Lexeme Individuation Problem is difficult for a variety of reasons, not least because of a lack of consensus over how to characterize the notion of lexeme in the first place. This is explored in Section 5.2.

In Section 5.3 we clarify important issues concerning the way words are represented and present arguments for an articulated model of lexical representation, in which a variety of properties are factored out. The logic

171

172　*Lexical Representation and Lexical Relatedness*

will be familiar to readers who are accustomed to lexicalist, constraint-based approaches to syntax, especially HPSG. The factorized properties are in large part motivated by the way in which they figure in defining systematic patterns of lexical relatedness. By 'lexical relatedness' we mean (following Spencer, 2013) relatedness between morphosyntactic word forms and between more abstract representations: lexemes. One important aspect of lexical relatedness and its relation to lexical representation proposed in Section 5.3 is the observation that words can be related to each other systematically along any of the main dimensions of this representation. This is explored in Section 5.4, which is based on Spencer (2013).

5.2 Individuating Lexemes

The problem of identifying or individuating lexemes is, in a sense, the obverse of the problem of defining relatedness between lexemes, and is of course a logical prerequisite to defining relatedness. We will make our discussion of the Lexeme Individuation Problem more concrete by casting part of it as a critical survey of proposals within the framework of HPSG, particularly the explicit proposals in Sag (2012) (SBCG).

5.2.1 Lexeme Individuation Problem

The simplest way of thinking of the Lexeme Individuation Problem is as follows: given two word forms, how can we determine whether they belong to the same lexeme or to two distinct lexemes? At first blush this might appear to be a trivial problem, since it seems to amount to no more than defining a characteristic function for the lexeme as an equivalence class defined over its word forms. However, we will see that there is in general no easy answer to this question. Where the problem is considered at all, the trivial solution is not necessarily adopted, and even when it is adopted, there remain non-trivial implications.

In traditional grammar, and in most approaches to morphology, a lexeme belongs to a particular part of speech; that is, it belongs to a particular lexical category. But we saw that some lexemes seem to have forms that belong to a distinct part of speech from the basic forms of that lexeme, the mixed categories. A major aspect of our treatment of noun–adjective hybrids centres on the difficulty of providing a phrase structure (c-structure) category label for such mixed categories and their projections. A noun–adjective hybrid has in part the distribution of an adjective but it retains some of the (distributional) properties of the base noun lexeme. Thus, standard techniques of grammatical analysis fail to assign it to a well-defined part of speech.

It might be thought that two representations define two distinct lexemes if they have distinct semantic content. In HPSG/SBCG this is made evident by the use of the Lexical Identifier (LID) attribute, which describes the class of word forms taken to belong to a single lexeme. In (1), Sag (2012, 84) explicitly defines the LID in terms of semantic representations.

(1)   LEXICAL-IDENTIFIER (LID) is used to individuate lexical items semantically; the value of LID is a list of semantic frames that canonically specify the (fine-grained) meaning of a lexeme ... this list is always singleton or empty.

In the remainder of this subsection we show that such semantic approach to lexemic individuation faces two empirical problems: (i) there are forms of a single lexeme that seem to differ semantically, and (ii) there are distinct lexemes that seem to have identical semantic representations.

Problem (i) is illustrated most clearly by systematic meaning-bearing argument structure alternations, notably causatives. These are often described as 'the causative form of verb V', suggesting that they are a form of the base verb lexeme, hence similar to inflection. However, causatives add a semantic predicate and a further argument to the base verb's representation. Similarly, as we mentioned in Chapter 1, some types of inherent inflection seem to add semantic content. This includes certain types of aspect or Aktionsart marking, semantic case marking, and comparative/superlative forms of adjectives (which also typically add clauses to the valence of the base adjective: *happier/*happy than we thought*).

Problem (ii) is illustrated trivially by perfect synonymy. However, that problem can easily be circumvented if we assume that the FORM attribute of a lexeme can serve as a kind of additional index. Thus, BIG/LARGE would be distinct lexemes by virtue of having different forms. More interesting, therefore, are cases in which two sets of word forms seem to be lexically related along the morphological and syntactic dimension and seem to share their semantic content, yet still belong to different lexemes. This is found in the relatedness type characterized as a 'transpositional lexeme' by Spencer (2013, 275, 360) (see also Spencer, 2016; Spencer and Nikolaeva, 2017).

A transpositional lexeme is a lexeme which has all of the properties of a transposition except that it does not seem to belong to the extended paradigm of its base lexeme, but rather appears to constitute a distinct lexeme in its own right. Examples are not hard to come by. In many European languages

174 *Lexical Representation and Lexical Relatedness*

we see property nominalizations derived from adjectives in which the original adjective base lexeme is opaque, as in the case of English *kindness, tallness, sincerity*, and so on. In its normal usage the word *sincerity* simply denotes the name of the property denoted by the adjective *sincere* and does not involve an added semantic predicate. It behaves solely like a noun and retains none of the properties of the original adjective, showing that it must be treated as a distinct lexeme. For example, it shows lexical opacity with respect to degree modification unlike its base adjective: *very sincere* but **very sincerity* (cf. *great/considerable sincerity*). We do not generally find property nominals of comparative or superlative forms of adjectives either (**tallerness/tallestness*). The nearest we get to such mixing in English is when complements to adjectives are inherited by nominalized forms: *her ability to solve this equation* (*she is able to solve this equation*), *his kindness to animals* (*he is kind to animals*), although even here we often find that the morphosyntax of the complement to the nominalization is different from that of the complement to the original adjective: *she is proud of her daughter's achievements* ~ *her pride in /*of her daughter's achievements*: the two-place adjective *proud* (*of NP*) is nominalized as *pride* (*in NP*), which retains none of the morphosyntax of the base adjective and which realizes the second argument of the base in a different way from the adjective. There thus seems to be no reason, given the typology of lexical relatedness we present in this chapter, why we should say that property nominalizations preserve the lexemic status of the base adjectives.

English has a number of other types of transpositional lexeme. In addition to property nominalizations, so-called 'action nominals' typically constitute transpositional lexemes (*destruction, arrival, amusement*, and so on). The *-ing* nominals are often ambiguous between a genuine verb-to-noun transposition and a transpositional lexeme reading. Thus, *their painting the ceiling* (*over wet plaster*) denotes the same event as *the painting/decoration of the ceiling* (*over wet plaster*), so that the word forms *painting/decoration* have exactly the same semantic content as the verb lexemes PAINT/DECORATE. However, it is only in the syntagmatically mixed variant (*their painting ...*) that we can speak of a transpositional nominalization. In the other examples we are dealing with transpositional lexemes, which show no verbal morphosyntactic properties at all.

A seldom-noted class of transpositional lexemes in English is formed from the *-ing* participles of transitive psychological state verbs. These provide a useful way of distinguishing between true transpositions and transpositional lexemes in that they are sometimes ambiguous between the two uses (Spencer, 2016). Thus, the adjective BORING, as in *He is a very boring lecturer*, behaves in all respects like a qualitative (gradable) adjective, and has all the hallmarks of being a distinct lexeme from the base verb lexeme TO BORE to which it is related derivationally. However, the adjective shares the same cognitive content as the base verb: *He is a very boring lecturer* means the same as *He is a lecturer who bores (people)* (either qua lecturer or simply by virtue of being a boring person who also happens to be a lecturer), and *a lecturer as boring as Dick* means *a lecturer who bores (people) to the same extent that Dick* does. The adjective BORING can be compared to the (true) participle form *boring* as in *the lecturers (*very) boring us most*. This means the same as *the lecturers who are the most boring (to us)*, in which we again see the distinct adjectival lexeme BORING. Again, the adjective BORING exhibits lexical opacity, in that it cannot take direct objects: **a lecturer as boring the students as Dick*. Contrast this with *a lecturer boring the students as much as Dick*. We can say that, as a participle, *boring* is an adjectival representation of the verb BORE. As a transpositional lexeme, *boring* represents a distinct lexeme, BORING, whose semantic representation is identical to the verb lexeme BORE from which it is derived. Moreover, the derivation of the lexeme BORING is based on a specific (essentially inflected) form of the base lexeme, not on the root or on some kind of derivational stem.

The two sets of problems just outlined demonstrate that we cannot rely on semantic representation to individuate lexemes, because it gives the wrong answer in both directions. In addition, transpositional lexemes show that we cannot always rely on the form of a word to guide us. Rather, each case of lexical (in)distinctness must be considered on its own merits, applying relatively uncontroversial tests for lexemehood where available (often these will be tests for word class).

In the next two subsections we will raise more general conceptual objections to the HPSG/SBCG implementation of lexemes, and we will ultimately reject that approach.[1]

5.2.2   Lexical Hierarchies

Within formal approaches to linguistics, HSPG/SBCG provides a particularly elaborated discussion of the nature of lexemes in their relation to parts of speech in unmixed and mixed categories. The kinds of type hierarchies assumed in that framework are also assumed in Ackerman and Nikolaeva (2013). However, while many of the constructions that Ackerman and Nikolaeva discuss are based on mixed categories, they explicitly leave to one side the analysis of such categories. We will therefore take up that question here.

---

[1] Fuller discussion of these questions is presented in Spencer (2017a).

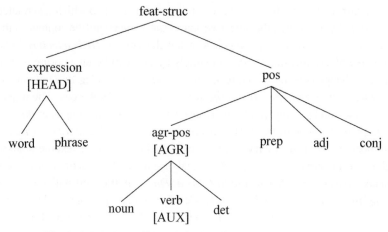

Figure 5.1 *Parts of speech hierarchy*

HPSG draws a distinction between word categories as parts of speech (*pos*) and word categories as types of lexemes (*lxm*). For concreteness, we will take as our point of departure the discussion of English in Sag et al. (2003, 61–62; 236–237). In Figure 5.1 we see a preliminary version of the part of speech type hierarchy proposed by Sag et al. for English (where 'feat-struc' stands for some feature structure). The hierarchy distinguishes two sorts of entity: expressions and part of speech (*pos*). The important part of the hierarchy from our perspective is that which defines *pos*. Sag et al., focussing on English grammar, assume that three categories are implicated in agreement constructions: nouns, verbs, and determiners. These form a distinct subtype, therefore. Of these, the verb subtype is uniquely associated with the auxiliary verb system. The type hierarchy is designed to allow such cross-classification by creating a new type wherever two subtypes share a feature.

Sag et al. contrast the *pos* hierarchy with the lexeme hierarchy, shown in Figure 5.2 (Sag et al., 2003, 237). This hierarchy unites the expression types shown in Table 5.1. The subhierarchy for the *const-lxm* subtype, that is, non-inflecting word types, is shown in Figure 5.3 (Sag et al., 2003, 242).

Finally, Sag (2012, 98) provides the sign hierarchy set out in Figure 5.4. From this we can see that the type *lexeme* is a subtype of *lex-sign* and hence a type of *sign*. An object of type *word* is an *overt expression* which inherits certain of its properties from the type *lex-sign*. (Notice that this hierarchy is not equipped to capture the fact that an object of type *word* is an instantiation of an object of type *lexeme*; indeed, the two types seem to be independent given this

Table 5.1 *Expression types in lexeme hierarchy*

constant lexeme	const-lxm
inflecting lexeme	infl-lxm
common-noun-lexeme	cn-lxm
count-noun-lexeme	cntn-lxm
mass-noun-lexeme	massn-lxm
verb lexeme	verb-lxm
strict-intransitive-verb-lexeme	siv-lxm
prepositional-intransitive-verb-lexeme	piv-lxm
transitive-verb-lexeme	tv-lxm
ditransitive-verb-lexeme	dtv-lxm
strictly-transitive-verb-lexeme	stv-lxm
prepositional-transitive-verb-lexeme	ptv-lxm

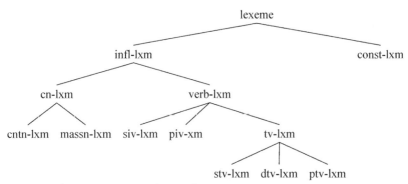

Figure 5.2 *Lexeme hierarchy*

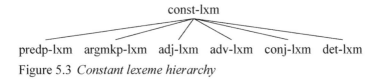

Figure 5.3 *Constant lexeme hierarchy*

hierarchy.) Since *lexeme* is a subtype of *sign*, any member of the *lexeme* type is a linguistic object, of the kind that has to be modelled by linguistic theory. We will shortly return to this point when we ask how lexemes are to be individuated and how they are to be related to the word forms that realize them.

How does the parts of speech hierarchy relate to the lexeme hierarchy in HPSG/SBCG? Sag et al. (2003, 245) explicitly discuss the difference between

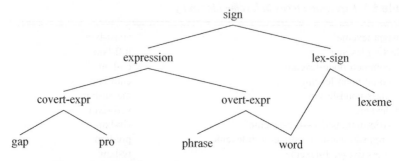

Figure 5.4 *Sign hierarchy*

the notions 'part of speech' and 'lexeme'. They say that the part of speech subtypes "specify which features are appropriate for particular categories of words and phrases". The lexeme subtypes "introduce constraints on what combinations of feature values are possible". For example, Sag et al. propose the constraint in (2) on entities of the type *adj-lxm* (adjective lexemes).

(2)
$$adj\text{-}lxm: \begin{bmatrix} \text{SYN} & \begin{bmatrix} \text{HEAD} & adj \\ \text{VAL} & \begin{bmatrix} \text{SPR} \ \langle X \rangle \\ \text{MOD} \ \langle [\text{HEAD } noun] \rangle \end{bmatrix} \end{bmatrix} \\ \text{ARG-ST} & \langle \text{NP}, \dots \rangle \\ \text{SEM} & [\text{MODE } prop] \end{bmatrix}$$

Constraint (2) states that a member of the subtype *adj-lxm* belongs to the part of speech 'adjective' ([HEAD adj]), that it modifies an expression whose part of speech is 'noun', that it expresses a proposition ([MODE prop]), and so on. Notice that two *pos* subtypes enter into the definition of this constraint, the first, [HEAD adj] defining the part of speech itself, and the second [MOD|HEAD noun] defining an adjective as the modifier of a noun.

From this example we can see that the notion of 'lexeme' is somewhat broader than the notion 'part of speech'. This is because *pos* labels are essentially labels for the lexical classes as traditionally defined in terms of distribution. The lexeme hierarchy, on the other hand, defines subclasses of word types on the basis of more abstract behavioural properties, especially those defined in the ARG-ST attribute or the SEM attribute, as in (2) above.

In our discussion of mixed categories in previous chapters we cast doubt on the wisdom of defining such categories in terms of (modified) part of speech classes from traditional grammar. Those objections carry over to the *pos* hierarchy. The first thing we will need to do, therefore, is to provide an alternative to the HPSG *pos* classification. We will restrict ourselves mainly to discussion of nouns and adjectives.

We begin with an observation about the hierarchy proposed by Sag et al. (2003) for English shown in Figure 5.1. Notice that there is a subtype of *pos*, the *agr-pos* subtype, which is intended to define all and only those word types which can be inflected, as indicated by the feature [AGR]. This works reasonably well for English, in that it has very little inflection and all members of an inflecting class of words (essentially nouns and verbs) can be considered to bear Head inflectional features, even if some inflected forms are identical to root forms (for instance, *sheep* as the plural of SHEEP). However, there are several points which are obscured by this description.

First, the characterization of the subtype *det* as *agr-pos* obscures the fact that only two members of the class actually inflect (THIS, THAT). Second, the auxiliary verbs include the modals, which in fact are non-inflecting. Third, from a cross-linguistic point of view it is very odd to partition word types into inflectable and uninflectable categories. The marginal status of demonstratives as inflecting, on the one hand, and of modals as non-inflecting members of the verb type, is amplified in many languages with richer morphology, where it is not uncommon to find words which simply do not inflect even though they have the same syntactic distribution as better behaved inflecting words of the same class. Thus, in Russian the noun *kenguru* 'kangaroo' and the adjective *bantu* 'Bantu' are uninflectable. Worse, we find degrees of (un)inflectability, as in Macedonian. In that language, native Slavic adjectives inflect for number and gender as well as definiteness: *nov* 'new.M.SG' *nova* 'new.F.SG', *novo* 'new.NEUT.SG', *novi* 'new.PL'. However, some adjectives (mainly loanwords from Turkish) only inflect for number: *kasmetlija* 'lucky.SG', *kasmetlii* 'lucky.PL', while others fail to inflect at all: *super* 'wonderful' (Friedman, 1993, 267).

The problem here is that we will make entirely the wrong predictions about (some aspects of) syntax if we take uninflectability to be a criterion for membership of the equivalent of the *agr-pos* subtype. Languages such as Russian and Macedonian have non-inflecting function words just like English (for instance adpositionals, conjunctions, adverbs, and particles of various types), but we do not want to relegate words like Russian *kenguru* or Macedonian *super* to the uninflecting classes (nor do we want to do this for English modals, at least in their finite uses).

What this means is that we must be careful to distinguish the morphological properties of individual lexemes or subclasses of lexemes from the syntactic properties of a class of lexemes. The *agr-pos* subtype has to be taken as

180   *Lexical Representation and Lexical Relatedness*

denoting a collection of word types which typically show morphological inflections of certain types (what in Chapter 6 we will call m-features). However, the real property shared by these word types is that they express appropriate sets of features referenced in the syntax, for instance agreement features, but also intrinsic properties such as the plural of a noun or past tense of a verb (what we will call s-features in Chapter 6).

5.2.3   *The Lexeme Concept in HPSG/SBCG – A Critique*

HPSG/SBCG draws an explicit distinction between linguistic objects such as phrases, word forms, affixes, and syllables, and descriptions of those objects. The objects themselves are approximated by models. A model of a linguistic object (model object) is a typed feature structure which specifies all the properties of that object. It is model objects that constitute the empirical domain of linguistic theory. A description, on the other hand, is a typed feature structure which gives a partial specification. Descriptions are therefore not objects or models of objects.

HPSG encodes derivational morphology in terms of feature structures. One way of conceptualizing a derivational rule, modelled as a feature structure of type *d-rule*, represents derivation in much the same way as the word formation rules of Aronoff (1976), as described by Sag et al. (2003, 74–83). We assume two attributes, INPUT and OUTPUT, where INPUT describes the base lexeme and OUTPUT describes the derived lexeme. Sag et al.'s (2003) discussion provides the analysis in Figure 5.5 for the Agent or Subject Nominalization (SN) process illustrated by DRIVE → DRIVER. Figure 5.5 represents the derivational process as a type of argument nominalization, in which the denotation of the derived noun is identified with the first/subject argument of the base verb. If we chose to represent the derivation as adding a semantic predicate (for instance, $\lambda x \lambda P[\mathbf{person}(x) \wedge P(x)]$ or some such) then the SEM attribute of the OUTPUT could be altered accordingly.

Sag et al. (2003, Ch 26) and Sag (2012) reconfigure the grammatical relationships, including morphologically defined lexical relatedness, in terms of constructions. Constructions in turn are represented as feature structures consisting of a MOTHER (MTR) attribute, of type *sign* and a set of DAUGH-TER attributes (DTRs), each of which is a list of signs (possibly empty or singleton). In the case of morphological relatedness governed by the rule types *i-rule* (inflectional morphology) and *d-rule* (derivational morphology) the MTR corresponds to the OUTPUT of Figure 5.5 and is of type *lexical sign*. This means that it is opposed to objects of the type *phrasal sign* and also objects

er-rule

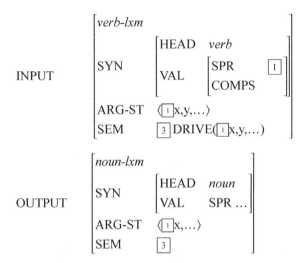

Figure 5.5 *SN process (for the suffix-*er*) expressed as INPUT/OUTPUT*

of the type *expression*. The DTR is a list of signs (by default a singleton list, because words are generally derived from individual words).

The model countenances multiple inheritance, so Sag et al. (2003, 473) propose a hierarchy in which the type *word* is simultaneously an *expression* and a *lex-sign*. Being an *expression* and *word* (that is, an inflected word form) it can appear as the leaf of a phrase tree. Being a *lex-sign*, a word can inherit various lexical properties, such as argument structure.

The feature structure describing a verb-to-noun derivation, such as the SN process, has the schematic form shown in (3).

(3) SN process (for the suffix-*er*) expressed as a construction

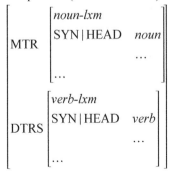

182   *Lexical Representation and Lexical Relatedness*

The principles of Lexical Integrity and lexical opacity are implicit in these representations. A derived lexeme (the value of the MTR attribute of a *d-rule* as shown in (3)) belongs to a different type from the DTR attribute, and this effectively means that it belongs to a different *pos*. There is no obvious way to represent the idea that a relational adjective (or any other true transposition) is at once a noun and an adjective syntactically, but with respect to different syntactic principles.

To capture such categorial mixing for deverbal nominalizations, Malouf (2000a,b) proposes enriching the type hierarchy so that the intermediate *pos* can be defined as the intersection of existing parts of speech. However, this modification is not in itself sufficient to capture the crucial relations. The problem is that there is no way, using just multiple inheritance, to capture the directionality or asymmetry implicit in transpositions. The relational adjective is the adjectival 'representation' of a noun (see Chapter 6) and so in an important sense it is essentially still a noun. On the other hand, a truly transpositional property nominalization would be the nominal representation of an adjective and hence essentially an adjective. This is the problem which we have already seen when discussing Malouf's account in Chapter 4.

Sag et al. (2003) analyse English *-ing* participles against the backdrop of their discussion of the *pos* and lexeme hierarchies. They capture the asymmetry of transpositions by treating participle formation as a kind of *d-rule* precisely because it involves a change in morphosyntactic *pos*. This means that they are committed to the claim that the word form *reading* in *the girl reading a book* is the invariant form of a lexeme READING, and hence a member of the non-inflecting *const-lxm* type. This *reading* belongs to a different lexeme from, say, *reading* in *the girl is reading a book*, which is the [VFORM:ing] of the inflecting lexeme (*infl-lxm*) READ on their account.

Given these preliminaries, we can now address the principal question: what kind of a representation is a dictionary (lexemic) entry? Specifically, is it a linguistic object in its own right? Related to this question is the relationship between lexemes, inflected words, and 'listemes'.

The listeme is the barest possible representation of a lexemic entry, but it is a description, not a modelled object. A listeme *licenses* modelled linguistic objects. This means that it places restrictions of what properties a modelled object or sign may have Sag et al. (2003, 105). Another way of characterizing the listeme is as "a lexeme description in the lexicon" (Sag et al., 2003, 107). Sag (2012) provides examples of representations of word forms from English (plurals, past tense forms), and in his Figure 6 (2012, 101), here reproduced as Figure 5.6, he gives the example of the lexeme LAUGH. Notice that this

5.2 Individuating Lexemes 183

representation actually seems to specify the word form *laughed*, in that it bears the feature [VFORM:psp]. It is worth citing Sag's (2012, 99) justification for this choice of representation:

> the value *psp* illustrated here ...represents an arbitrary choice – any value of VFORM would satisfy the requirements imposed by the *laugh* listeme. And each such choice gives rise to a family of well-formed FSs licensed by that listeme.

Note that Sag here appeals to the LAUGH listeme.

Sag (2012, 98) also introduces the notion of the lexeme into the model, giving it a special place in the type hierarchy of signs shown in Figure 5.2. Recall that the hierarchy defines the lexeme as a lexical sign, just like a word form. However, word forms appear as parts of syntactic phrases which can ultimately be pronounced, and so they count as linguistic expressions. A lexeme cannot be pronounced. This is not because it is some kind of 'covert expression', however (like *gap*, *pro* in Sag's type hierarchy). A lexeme is an altogether different kind of sign, in fact a unique type given the hierarchy in Figure 5.2.

The type *lexeme* plays a central role in SBCG, in that it is the starting point for all morphology (Sag is here following Paradigm Function Morphology (PFM) and related models). Inflection and derivation are modelled by means of morphological functions. An inflectional rule such as the English preterite (past tense) is modelled by a *preterite-cxt*, whose mother is the past tense form and whose daughter is the lexeme whose past tense form is being defined. A derivational rule is given by a construction whose mother is the derived lexeme and whose daughter is the base lexeme.

Sag (2012, 113) summarizes the morphological functions by saying that they express "the relation between the forms of two lexemes or the relation between the form of a lexeme and the form of a word that realizes that lexeme". This sounds like an expression of conventional wisdom in lexeme-based morphology, but it hides a serious conceptual flaw. This centres around the way that Sag's formulation uses the term 'form'. The problem is apparent from Sag's description of the lexeme LAUGH. He is obliged to provide this representation with an arbitrary Head inflectional feature specification, in effect defining not the lexeme as such but one of its inflected forms. This is because a lexeme is meant to be a modelled object, a subtype of *sign*, and a linguistic object must be fully specified. But the whole point of defining a lexemic level of representation is to abstract away from actual (concrete) word forms. This means that the lexeme is effectively a description, in fact a partial description, of the full set

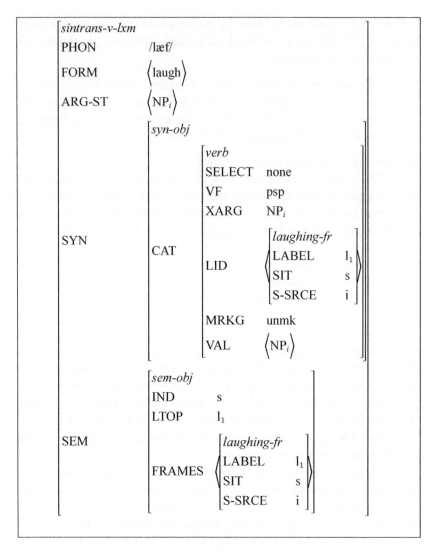

Figure 5.6 *Representation of the lexeme* LAUGH *(Sag, 2012, 101)*

of word forms. That is completely incompatible with Sag's type hierarchy and, indeed, with any coherent interpretation of the HPSG lexicon.

Given this reasoning, Spencer (2017a) proposes that we treat the lexicon as more than just a convenient descriptive fiction, as would be implied by a strict application of the object~description distinction. Rather, we should

5.2 Individuating Lexemes 185

take the lexicon to be a network of mentally represented (or representable) objects which can be defined and described by feature structures (FSs) just like (utterable and unutterable) linguistic expressions. By simply declaring a dictionary (lexemic) entry to be a kind of object we solve the immediate problem: the lexeme can remain a type of sign, and can be a supertype of other signs. Its unusual position in being partially underspecified is now reflected in the type hierarchy: only the expression type has to be fully specified, while a lexical sign may be only partially specified (*lexeme*), though when a lexical sign is also a subtype of *expression* (*word*) it, too, can, and must, be fully specified.

Now, once we admit the possibility of an underspecified entity as an object in the linguistic ontology, we are immediately faced with two sets of questions. The most general of these is: are there other linguistic objects which can be less than fully specified? Can *any* partially specified representation be interpreted as a modelled object? If so, then what is the content of the original object~description distinction?

It seems that we should not be allowed to postulate such objects except in very special circumstances. But if we admit lexemes as less than fully specified objects, what prevents us from postulating entirely arbitrary types? The simplest answer is to say that it is an architectural (i.e. stipulated) property of linguistic expressions that they be fully specified. However, whether this is really true may depend on how we perceive linguistic specification. Presumably, an object of type *word* such as *dogs* is to be regarded as a modelled object and not a description, even when, for instance, its intonation and other prosodic characteristics are not specified. But in the strictest sense a word form remains partially underspecified until its full phonetic realization is given. Indeed, the same is true of sentences, which can be uttered with a very wide variety of affective intonation contours even when realizing one and the same set of discourse or information-structure functions.

The second question is more immediately relevant: if we are to admit as an object a lexeme underspecified for its inflectional properties, how much further can we go with the underspecification? For instance, we might want to say that our lexeme LAUGH is underspecified for its inflectional properties by virtue of bearing the attribute values [TENSE:u, VFORM:u, SUBJAGR:u, ...] or whatever, where 'u' means 'not yet specified value', or we may wish to make the more radical proposal that LAUGH lacks the actual attributes [TENSE, VFORM, SUBJAGR, ...]. This may turn out to be little more than a matter of notational convention, but in a more radical vein we can ask why we cannot regard Sag's maximally underspecified 'listeme' as a default lexeme object. In other words, can we not adopt the underspecified lexemic entry model for dictionary entries?

186 *Lexical Representation and Lexical Relatedness*

We will see in Chapter 6 that this question assumes particular importance in defaults-based models of morphology such as PFM, where the lexeme concept finds its most elaborated implementation, and especially Generalized Paradigm Function Morphology (GPFM) (Spencer, 2013) where defaults define all aspects of lexical representation.

5.3   Lexical Representations

The question we address in this section is how to annotate a word's representation in such a way as to record our decision as to which word forms are members of a given lexeme. We will argue that any model of lexical relatedness is dependent on a suitably articulated model of lexical representation. We will then follow Spencer (2013) in adopting a rather simple model, which is close to standard lexicographic practice. Our factorization is minimal in the sense that it covers just those categories that we will need for investigating noun–adjective hybrids later in the book. This means we will be omitting a good deal of information at the level of semantics and pragmatics, for instance (finer grained definitions are possible, of course, and for some purposes no doubt essential).

5.3.1   Inflection/Derivation 'Continuum'

Although all modern morphologists accept that there is no clear dividing line between inflection and derivation, in practice morphologists who adhere to an inferential-realizational model of inflection (including us) implicitly have to accept such a distinction, much in line with earlier 'split morphology' proposals (Perlmutter, 1988; Anderson, 1992).

In general, relatedness between morphosyntactic words is mediated by the principles of inflectional morphology, which for our purposes we take to mean the revised model of PFM: PFM2 (Stump, 2016). A morphosyntactic word form such as *run* or *sheep* is more complex than a simple morphophonological form; rather, it is a pair consisting of the morphophonological form together with the set of morphosyntactic properties or features that it realizes. In other words, the morphosyntactic word is a cell in the realized paradigm (Stump, 2016) of a lexeme. A realized paradigm is a complete set of morphosyntactic properties defining the inflected forms of a given lexeme. In principle, this can include periphrastic forms (see Brown et al., 2012b), but we will ignore that refinement. Morphosyntactic word forms are therefore pairings which we can represent informally as ⟨*dogs*, pl⟩, ⟨*geese*, pl⟩, ⟨*sheep*, pl⟩. Where syncretism exists, such as with ⟨*sheep*, sg⟩, ⟨*sheep*, pl⟩, we therefore have two distinct (though closely related) morphosyntactic words.

Relatedness between lexemes is traditionally mediated by the rules and principles of derivational morphology, sometimes supplemented by a model of compounding.

Haspelmath's (1996) early and important discussion of category mixing provided a rule-of-thumb characterization of the inflection/derivation divide. He points out that inflection is typically associated with exhaustively paradigmatic organization and productivity, while derivation is typically "irregular, defective and unproductive" (Haspelmath, 1996, 47). However, these are not hard-and-fast properties so that the inflection/derivation distinction must allow for "gradience" and "fuzzy boundaries" and is represented as a "continuum".[2] He then proposes a statistical universal, which Bresnan and Mugane (2006, 221) call "Haspelmath's Generalization", as described in (4).

(4)   In words derived by *inflectional* word-class-changing morphology, the internal syntax of the base tends to be preserved.
      In words derived by *derivational* word-class-changing morphology, the internal syntax of the base tends to be altered and assimilated to the internal syntax of primitive members of the derived word-class.

We agree with the basic thrust of these proposals, especially where we have regular and productive morphology, in the sense that it is necessary to separate out properties such as category-changing from other properties that might be associated with inflection. Yet in practice the distinction is notoriously difficult to draw, with far too many patterns of lexical relatedness between canonical instances of inflection and derivation that prevent us from analysing any one of them as simply some kind of deviant variant of one or the other.

As Spencer (2013) demonstrates at great length, the standard, rather simple-minded, approaches to the inflection/derivation distinction appear inadequate for defining the myriad possible types of relatedness between words of different syntactic categories and the variety of their properties in the world's languages. It will be a very complex matter to enumerate all the attested types and distinguish patterns of commonality among them, and there is no reason to force all types of lexical relatedness into one or the other category. Even the more nuanced categories such as 'inherent/contextual inflection' or 'transposition' are difficult to apply in some instances. Inflection can have

---

[2] Taken literally, this should imply some metric mapped onto a continuous space defined over the real numbers, but we find it difficult to see what exactly this might mean for the grammars of individual languages as opposed to large-scale typological tendencies.

188   *Lexical Representation and Lexical Relatedness*

semantic effects, so even if a process adds to the semantic representation, we cannot guarantee that it will be derivational. Similarly, transpositions are processes which change word category and are hence traditionally taken to be derivational, but which (canonically) fail to add a semantic predicate and thus fail to create a new lexeme in this sense. Hence, there is no non-circular way of determining when a semantic category-changing morphosyntax is inflectional or derivational.

As Spencer (2013) argues, an important prerequisite for understanding the relationships between words is a carefully articulated descriptive framework for lexical entries of any kind. The core idea is that what is required in order to understand the mixed types is not a set of more or less traditional categories into which we have to shoehorn recalcitrant phenomena, but rather a clear statement of exactly what each construction involves and what properties of the base entry it preserves. The fact that those component properties cut across traditional categories of description means either that those categories represent a misanalysis or that it is a mistake to treat those descriptive categories as non-intersecting. With this understanding, canonical inflection and canonical derivation are merely two ends of a range of possible types of relatedness. Each intermediate type can be represented through adjusting lexical representations in an appropriate way, but this implies that the inflection vs. derivation distinction must hinge on a much more articulated view of lexical representations than is generally assumed.

5.3.2   *Factorizing Lexical Representations*

As discussed in Chapter 1, underlying our approach is the (fairly uncontroversial) presumption that there are three ways of thinking about a word: its meaning (denotation), its syntax (distribution), and its form (morphology). So the lexical entry of a lexeme generally has to record a variety of different types of information within the three broad categories of morphological form, syntactic distribution, and semantic representation. Spencer (2013) distinguishes four dimensions or attributes of lexical representation: FORM, SYN, SEM, and LI. These are shown schematically in (5) for the Russian noun KNIGA 'book'.

(5) Simplified lexical representation for the Russian noun KNIGA 'book'

$$\begin{bmatrix} \text{FORM} & \begin{bmatrix} \text{PHON} & |\text{kniga}| \\ \text{MORCLASS} & \text{Class 1} \end{bmatrix} \\ \text{SYN} & \begin{bmatrix} noun \\ \text{GENDER: f} \end{bmatrix} \\ \text{ARG-ST} & R \\ \text{SEM} & \begin{bmatrix} _{Thing} \lambda x.\mathbf{book}(x) \end{bmatrix} \\ \text{LI} & \text{KNIGA} \end{bmatrix}$$

The FORM attribute specifies morphosyntactic words, in effect representing the inflectional paradigm of a lexeme. We will assume that these word forms are defined by some kind of inflectional Paradigm Function (PF) as argued in Stump (2001) and refined in Stump (2016), though we will have cause to elaborate on Stump's conception of the PF somewhat when we come to consider transpositions and related phenomena. The FORM attribute specifies the basic form of the root of the lexeme together with the form of any unpredictable stems. However, one important subattribute of FORM defines the morphological class of a word, more generally the morphological class that a stem belongs to — for instance whether it is morphologically a noun and if so which inflectional class (declension) it belongs to, where appropriate.

The second attribute of the word, SYN, specifies its syntactic properties. Essentially, it indicates a word's syntactic class, i.e. it contains information which contributes to defining its distributional properties. Again, we can divide the SYN attribute into a number of subattributes. The most obvious of these is the lexical class of the word: noun, verb, adjective, and so on. However, as we pointed out in Chapter 1, the traditional notion of word class is seriously undermined by the kinds of intermediate categories that form the subject of this monograph, so we will ultimately follow Spencer (2013) in adopting a more nuanced approach to the question of lexical categories. For the present we will use the traditional labels, bearing in mind that these will be superseded.

One point that needs to be borne in mind is that a word's SYN category is usually considered to be in some sense identical to its morphological or FORM category. Now, in the literal sense of 'category' this can never be true: a word's morphological category is determined by its morphological properties, such as the way it inflects, while its syntactic category is determined by its privileges of occurrence within phrases. However, the two notions of category are obviously linked very closely. This is enshrined in Stump's (2016) revised model of PFM,

190 *Lexical Representation and Lexical Relatedness*

PFM2 (see Chapter 6, Section 6.3.1), by distinguishing, in addition to the realized paradigm of a lexeme, two abstract paradigms: a FORM paradigm defining purely morphological properties, and a CONTENT paradigm, whose features are visible to syntactic principles such as agreement and government, and which can be semantically interpreted (in some cases, at least). The two paradigms are related by a principle of paradigm linkage, which defaults to identity mapping but which can show a variety of significant mismatches such as syncretism, deponency, defectiveness, heteroclisis, and periphrasis. An alternative, largely equivalent, way of thinking of this linkage is to say that there is a single set of morphosyntactic properties or features but that they can be indexed as morphological (m-features) or syntactic (s-features). By default, a given feature fulfils both functions and therefore can remain unindexed. However, some of the features will be purely m-features and others will be purely s-features; and moreover, some m-features will map to non-default values of the s-features, and some s-features will map to non-default values of the m-features.

The second subattribute of SYN is the argument structure property, ARG-ST. We will take the position that all the major categories (in which we include N, V, A, P, Adv) have an argument structure. The level of argument structure is motivated as the interface between the syntactic representation and crucial aspects of the semantic representation. For instance, the ARG-ST of an adjective will include the (usually singleton) 'thematic' argument corresponding to the noun which the adjective modifies. Thus, the ARG-ST of the adjective TALL will include a variable 'x' which ultimately will be identified with the argument of a noun such as TREE. We will be following Spencer (2013) in proposing a somewhat articulated picture of ARG-ST and we will give details of this later in the book.

Other properties of the SYN attribute will include selectional (valency, collocational) properties, such as the type of clausal complement a predicate selects, or which cases it governs. The most important of these for our discussion will be the MOD feature, which defines the attributive modification relation.

The SEM attribute houses a conventional semantic representation of the kind familiar from works such as Levin and Rappaport Hovav (1994, 1995, 2005), Rappaport Hovav and Levin (1998), and many others, based on notions of Lexical Conceptual Structure (Jackendoff, 1990) or the similar but not identical notion of Semantic Form (Bierwisch, 1989, 2007). Following Jackendoff (1990), we type each simplex representation for an ontological class of *Thing*, *Event*, *Property*, or *Relation*. These correspond canonically to the word classes noun, verb, adjective, and preposition, though with many exceptions and mismatches.

5.3 *Lexical Representations*   191

Some morphologically represented types of relatedness involve addition of grammaticalized predicates or operators, and these can bring with them their own ontological categories. Thus, agent or subject nominals have roughly the denotation 'λxλy... **person**(x) ∧ **verb**(x,y,...)' and these shift the ontological category of the base verb lexeme (which canonically denotes an *Event*) to the category of *Thing*. Similitudinal adjectives derived from nouns (ontologically, *Things*) denote a *Property* with the meaning, roughly λxλyλδ.**similar_to**(x,y,δ), where y denotes a *Thing* and δ is some dimension of comparison ('x is similar to y with respect to δ').

Finally, we saw in Section 5.2 that given two words, one of the questions we must ask in an inferential-realizational model of morphology is whether they are members of the same lexeme or members of distinct lexemes. For this reason it is useful to postulate a fourth lexical property as a convenient way of recording this decision. Following Spencer (2013), we will make use of the fourth attribute, Lexemic Index (LI), in order to describe the class of word forms taken to belong to a single lexeme. The Lexemic Index is related to, but not identical to, properties such as the Lexical Index of Stump (2001) or the LID of Sag (2012) in HPSG/SBCG. Although it is deployed for a similar purpose to LID, it differs from it in a number of important ways. (In current versions of LFG the function of the LI is largely performed by the lexeme's PRED attribute, which effectively serves as simply the name for a lexeme (Spencer, 2015a)).

We understand the LI as an integer that uniquely identifies any ensemble of ⟨FORM, SYN, SEM⟩ attributes as realizing properties of a single lexeme. It is an attribute of each individuated lexeme, a unique identifier (for instance, a prime number). Hence it can best be coded as an attribute of the lexeme in the feature structure that represents the lexeme's lexical entry. In practice, we will use the base form of the lexeme in small capitals as the LI for that lexeme, supplemented by numerical indices where necessary (e.g. BANK1, BANK2). In the absence of reliable external criteria for lexemehood, the LI thus records our decision, for each word form, in respect of the Lexeme Individuation Problem: how do we know when two words are representatives of one and the same lexeme as opposed to representatives of two distinct lexemes?

Canonically inflected word forms of a lexeme all share the same LI, in that they are all forms of one and the same lexeme. By contrast, a canonically derived word has, by definition, a distinct LI from its base, because canonical derivation defines a new lexeme. We can then use the LI to separate out two broad types of lexical relatedness: within-lexeme (intra-lexemic) relatedness holds between lexical representations which share the same LI, while between-lexeme (inter-lexemic) relatedness holds between

192   *Lexical Representation and Lexical Relatedness*

representations which have distinct LIs. The LI will also play a crucial role for intermediate categories such as transpositions, which have the character both of inflection and derivation, and transpositional lexemes, which are lexemes that are distinct from their bases even though they do not differ in their semantic content. In Chapter 6 we will see how the LI can be deployed further in GPFM.

5.4   Lexical Relatedness

So far we have mostly discussed matters of lexical representation. We now turn to the question of representing the various types of lexical relatedness that words can contract with each other. Given our simple four-dimensional view of lexical structure, we can define a variety of types of lexical relatedness in more detail. Despite its simplicity, the model presented in the previous section will permit us to define a large number of relatedness types, including several that have no standard names and some which have scarcely been noted in the literature.

5.4.1   Dynamic and Static Relatedness

Taking 'relatedness' in the widest sense, there are two ways in which the corresponding attributes of two words can be related: they can be either different or identical. Two words are (non-trivially) related if at least one of their FORM, SYN, SEM, or LI attributes overlaps. By 'overlap' we generally mean that the content of at least one of these attributes for one word must subsume the content of the corresponding attribute of the other.

At the outset we should draw a distinction between 'static' relatedness and 'dynamic' relatedness. By dynamic relatedness we mean those relations that are 'live' in the language, in the sense that they are capable of giving rise to new words or word forms and can therefore license inflection and derivation. Completely regular inflection is a (trivial) example of dynamic relatedness: all the inflected forms of a lexeme are dynamically related to each other, and all forms realizing a particular morphosyntactic property or property set are dynamically related. Thus, the word forms {*dog, dogs*} are dynamically related, and so are all the plural forms of all count nouns in the language. By static relatedness we mean relations that hold between existing words or word forms in the lexicon. The characterization of relatedness has to be able to encompass both types, in part because the distinction itself is controversial and it is not entirely clear where the dividing line lies, even to those who accept the distinction.

One traditional type of lexical relatedness is defined over sense relations such as synonymy, homonymy, and hyper/hyponymy. For instance, two perfect synonyms (say, *big* and *large*) are related in the sense that they share the same semantic representation (modulo subtle connotations and collocational properties). In the default case this also means that they have the same syntax. However, their forms are entirely distinct. On the other hand, two homophones or homonyms have exactly the same set of forms but distinct semantics and (usually) distinct syntax. For instance, the verb GO as a locution verb (as in *She went "Whatever"*) is semantically unrelated to the verb GO as a verb of motion and has very different argument structure and syntactic properties, and yet they share exactly the same irregular morphology.

There are of course varying degrees of homonymy (though this fact is rather obscured in traditional, English-based descriptions). In one type the two lexemes share all their crucial FORM and SYN properties. The textbook example of the two nouns BANK is an instance, in that both are regular count nouns and their purely syntactic distribution is essentially identical. On the other hand, as a verb BANK can mean a variety of things, including 'put money into a bank' or 'rotate along a sagittal axis (of an aircraft)'. These are both verbs, but they have somewhat different argument structures so they do not entirely share the same SYN value. Finally, there are cases of homonymy illustrated by, say, the noun (river) BANK and the verb BANK with the sense 'to rotate (aircraft)'. Here, the relatedness is very weak, in that only the default (root, stem) forms of the lexemes are identical. Since one lexeme is a verb and the other a noun, their FORM attributes are clearly substantially different and overlap only accidentally in the form of the root. Indeed, they are no more or less related than the word forms *find* (root of the lexeme FIND) and *fined* (preterite/past participle of the verb root FINE).

Relatedness such as synonymy and homonymy are static relations that can be observed by inspection of the lexical entries of a language's lexicon, but they are not of general interest to the grammarian because they are not systematic and are not realized by regular morphology. A different type of static relatedness that is of potential importance to a grammatical description is illustrated by English pairs such as STAND~UNDERSTAND or TAKE~MISTAKE. Each member of the pair is unrelated semantically to the other, yet the second of each pair is based on an irregularly inflecting root whose inflection is identical to that of the first member: (*under*)*stood*, (*mis*)*took*, (*mis*)*taken*.

In English such examples are somewhat marginal, but the phenomenon is exhibited by many thousands of verb forms in languages such as German or Russian. The overwhelming majority of verb lexemes in Russian have a

194 *Lexical Representation and Lexical Relatedness*

complex root consisting of a prefix and a verb root which exists in other lexemes. For instance, the verb PRIPISAT' 'to ascribe' consists of the root *pis(a)* prefixed with *pri-*. The root occurs in many other verbs including the unprefixed verb PISAT', which has two functions: one as an atelic verb meaning 'to be engaged in writing activity' and the other as the imperfective form of the transitive telic verb NAPISAT' 'to write (something)'. Similarly, the prefix *pri-* occurs in hundreds of other verbs (along with about seventeen other prefixes). This pattern is typical for a large majority of Russian verbs. Also typical is the fact that in the verb PRIPISAT' neither the prefix nor the root can be ascribed any autonomous meaning. In particular, the *pis(a-)* stem does not realize any form of the meaning WRITE (x,y). In other words, most Russian verbs consist of two cranberry morphs, one of them drawn from a limited list of prefixes and the other a lexical stem which recurs in many other lexemes. Moreover, the prefixed verbs based on a given stem share FORM properties: the verb PRIPISAT' 'to ascribe' belongs to exactly the same conjugation as OPISAT' 'to describe', ZAPISAT' 'to note down, record', PODPISAT' 'to sign', VPISAT'SJA 'to blend into (reflexive verb)', and so on. Again, it is surely significant that the Russian lexicon has this property even though most of the verbs that exhibit it cannot be derived by any regular or productive process (though there are plenty of other regular/productive, that is paradigmatic, verb prefixation processes still alive in Russian).

Of even greater interest to grammatical theory, however, are those types of relatedness that are induced by paradigmatic word formation processes, what we called 'dynamic relatedness'. This type of relatedness is essentially the same as the notion of on-line relatedness discussed by Koenig (1999). This means morphology that is productive and hence which is used to expand the lexical stock in a rule-governed fashion, and not by deliberate coinings such as those found with blends, clippings, and other ad hoc, nonce instances of word creation.

5.4.2 *Types of Dynamic Relatedness*

So far we have seen two canonical types of dynamic relatedness between words under comparison (comparanda). The FORM attributes of the two comparanda differ in inflection only, while in derivation all four attributes differ. In addition to canonical types of dynamic relatedness, Spencer's model assumes that the factorized lexical properties of a word can be related to corresponding properties of another word in a completely free fashion. The model invokes a principle under which any combination of 'identical' or 'different' attributes can go

Table 5.2 *Lexical relatedness with SEM and LI attributes identical*

	A1	A2	A3	A4
FORM	–	Δ	Δ	–
SYN	–	–	Δ	Δ

towards defining a type of relatedness. This is enshrined in the Principle of Representational Independence (PRI), as described in (6) (Spencer, 2013, 139).

(6)   Principle of Representational Independence (PRI)
      The (four) components of lexical representation can be related to the corresponding components of other lexical representations independently

According to the PRI, if we continue to consider only the widest types of relationship between lexical attributes, we can distinguish $2^4 = 16$ distinct types of relatedness, according to whether corresponding attributes for the comparanda are identical or distinct. These are schematized in Tables 5.2 to 5.5. Some of these relations have traditional names, though most do not. Some of the forms of relatedness will be tangential to our discussion, so we will do no more than mention them. The question then arises as to which, if any, of the remaining logically possible types of relatedness are attested, and which, if any, represent regular and hence paradigmatic relations in the morphosyntax of any language. Spencer (2013) argues that very nearly all the logically possible types are in fact attested and that many of them figure in the productive morphology.

We will start with the cases where the SEM and LI attributes remain identical. In these tables the sign 'Δ' stands for 'attribute changed', and the sign '–' for 'attribute unchanged'. In Table 5.2, Type A1 is the identity relation, a trivial relation which holds between any word and itself. Type A2 is standard inflection. In the GPFM it is assumed that most inflection has no effect on the semantic representation of the base lexeme. This is reasonably clear in the case of Booij's contextual inflection (agreement, government), but it is also true of many instances of what Booij would treat as 'inherent' inflection, such as grammatical number, tense/aspect/mood, and many voice alternations. We assume a type A2 inflectional process whenever the inflection can be seen simply as realizing a feature value ([NUM:pl], [TNS:pst] or whatever).

Of the two remaining types in Table 5.2, A3 represents an important species of relatedness, the transposition. Transpositions represent a systematic type of

196   *Lexical Representation and Lexical Relatedness*

word formation that changes the form and syntax of the base but does not add a semantic predicate to SEM and does not change the LI. As is explained in some detail in Spencer (2005b, 2013), any major category can be transposed into any other major category. Assuming three basic lexical categories – verb (V), adjective (A), and noun (N) – we can envisage six logically possible basic types defined at the base level of syntactic word class (Beard, 1995, 178).

In the GPFM approach these are instantiated as follows. Verbs can be transposed into nominals and adjectives, V ⇒ N, A respectively. For V-to-N nominalizations this means an action or event nominal; for V-to-A transpositions we typically have the kinds of participles that can head participial relative clauses.[3] Adjectives can be transposed into property nominalizations and predicate adjectives, A ⇒ N, V respectively. A property nominalization names the property denoted by the adjective. This type is to be distinguished from nominalizations which have different denotations, such as things, since in that case we are dealing with derivational morphology which enriches the semantic content of the base lexeme. Finally, nouns can be transposed into adjectives and predicative nouns (i.e. nouns functioning as the predicate of a finite clause), N ⇒ A, V respectively. A transposition from N/A to V is found when the N/A takes verb inflections so as to form the head of a finite predication, to give the predicative form of the noun/adjective. A transposition from N to A is found when the N assumes the form of an attributive modifier. N-to-A transpositions result in a relational adjective, the main topic of this monograph.

The type represented by A4 is a transposition that is not expressed by a change in morphology (it is morphologically inert or m-inert in the terminology of Spencer (2005b, 2013)). A possible example is seen when a finite verb form heads a relative clause, as in Japanese. Spencer (2005b, 2013) suggests that such a verb might be regarded as having been shifted into the adjective category, so that it can function as an attributive modifier but without any change in its morphology or semantics (a morphologically inert participle in effect).

In the relatedness types illustrated in Table 5.3 we see a situation which is unexpected (and non-canonical): the two comparanda have different semantics but are still instantiations of a single lexeme. Type B1 is represented by

---

[3]   The term 'participle' in the description of some European languages is a little confusing because it often refers to a verb form which, while historically derived from a genuine transpositional participle, and often retaining some of the morphosyntax of an adjective, is used to form periphrastic inflectional forms, and is not necessarily used as an attributive modifier. This is true of passive participles in Germanic, Romance, Slavic, and other groups, for instance. Thus, in *The apple was eaten by Adam*, the form *eaten* is not a participle sensu stricto. Ideally, some other terminology should be invoked for such cases, such as 'departicipial converb' or similar.

Table 5.3 *Lexical relatedness with SEM attribute changed, LI attribute identical*

	B1	B2	B3	B4
FORM	–	Δ	Δ	–
SYN	–	–	Δ	Δ

words which show no difference other than in meaning. This is instantiated by systematic polysemy (in the sense of Apresjan (1974)) of the kind often discussed in the context of the Generative Lexicon (Pustejovsky, 1995). Thus, English words which denote containers, such as *bottle, box,* or *tin,* are systematically ambiguous between this reading and a reading which denotes the actual contents ('to drink an entire bottle (of milk)'). By definition systematic polysemy is not represented morphologically (if it were, it would be Type B2 relatedness), but in general it is a language-particular property and therefore has to be represented in the grammar of any language, as pointed out by Apresjan, Pustejovsky, and many others.

In type B2 the difference in meaning between base and derivate arises as the result of inflectional morphology and it represents a subtype of Booij's (1996) inherent inflection. Potential examples arc local or semantic cases with meanings such as 'inside N', 'from under the surface of N', 'because of N', and so on, and meaning-bearing argument structure alternations such as the causative, comparative/superlative forms of adjectives, and so on.

Another instantiation of type B2 is found with productive evaluative morphology such as the diminutive or augmentative. In evaluative morphology the lexeme (typically a noun, N) acquires an additional component of meaning, which in some cases is literally 'small/large N', but which is more generally evaluative: 'dear (little) N' or 'ugly (great) N'. In some languages such evaluative nuances are effectively inflection, in that they affect the pragmatic or discourse properties of the entire utterance. For example, the Russian word *kaša* 'porridge' has a diminutive form *kaška*, but when a speaker says *Dajte mne kašku* 'Give me (some) porridge', they are not asking for a small quantity of porridge but rather are supplying an emotional nuance of politeness or intimacy to the entire utterance. In this sense, the diminutive form certainly does not create a new lexeme and the evaluative morphology is closer to inflection than any other type of relatedness. At the same time, the evaluation implied by evaluative morphology very often affects solely the denotation of the evaluated word. Thus, in the Russian example in (7), the diminutive form

198 *Lexical Representation and Lexical Relatedness*

lačužka of *lačuga* 'hovel', bears the meaning 'small (and paltry)', while the augmentative form of *dom* 'house', *domišče*, bears the meaning 'large and (possibly) unattractive'.[4]

(7) Na meste   vetxix   lačužek   vyros
     on place.LOC old.GEN.PL hovel.GEN.PL.DIM grow.up.PST
     ogromnyj   domišče.
     huge.M.NOM.SG house[M].AUG
     'Where once there had been dilapidated little hovels there grew up an enormous great house.'

The parallel with inflection is particularly close in the case of *domišče* in that the augmentative form belongs to an inflectional class that is normally associated with neuter nouns, but the augmentative retains the masculine gender of the base *dom* (Spencer, 2013, 268).

Type B3 is a kind of lexical relatedness we do not normally expect to find. In this type, all the lexical attributes are changed except for the LI. This is therefore a kind of derivational morphology which does not define a new lexeme – a contradiction in terms under standard assumptions. On the other hand, we can also think of it as an unusual type of transposition, namely one which adds a semantic predicate to the lexeme's SEM representation, just as inherent inflection can be meaningful. This is what Spencer (2013) referred to as 'meaning-bearing transpositions'. Recall that a canonical transposition is non-meaning-bearing by default: it has the same semantic content as the base from which it is derived, as is the case in various nominalizations including English *-ing* gerunds.

Russian provides a marginal example of a meaning-bearing transposition, though not one which extends across the whole lexicon. A restricted number of Russian transitive verbs have a present passive participle in *-myj*: *razpoznavat'* 'recognize', *razpoznavae-myj*; *vozbudit'* 'arouse', *vozbudi-myj* (Wade (1992, 365–366) and Zaliznjak (2003) list about 300 such formations, though a good third of them are negated forms prefixed with *ne-* and thus do not count as separate examples). Although the participles can be used purely as non-past passive attributive forms of the verb (in technical or journalistic written registers at least), they are most commonly used with an additional modal meaning of possibility. Thus, *razpoznavaemyj* is better translated not as 'such that is being recognized' (an unexpected reading for an achievement verb) but rather as 'such that can be recognized', and *vozbudimyj* means 'capable of being aroused' (or in medical terminology 'sensitive') (Timberlake, 2004,

---

[4] This example is taken from the online version of Ushakov's dictionary, http://slovonline.ru/slovar_ushakov/b-4/id-13579/domishche.html, last accessed 29 November 2017.

5.4 *Lexical Relatedness* 199

349). These adjectives are therefore very close in meaning and function to *-able/-ible* adjectives in English and Romance languages, *-bar* adjectives in German, and so on. A similar phenomenon is observed with the passive voice in Punjabi (Bhatia, 1993; Smirnov, 1976), which is also almost always interpreted modally. In Chapter 8 we will discuss Selkup locative and similitudinal adjectives, a very clear example of transpositions which include additional semantic content (see also Spencer, 2013, Ch 10).

Type B4 is found when the derived word is of a different syntactic category from the base and is enriched with a semantic predicate, but is morphologically inert and remains a member of the same lexeme as the base. In Spencer (2013) it is argued that m-inert conversion of adjectives with the meaning 'property P' to personal nouns with the meaning 'person who has property P' can instantiate this relatedness type. Spencer dubs these '*Angestellte(r)*-nouns' from the German word for 'employee', which is a converted form of the passive participle of the verb 'to employ' used as a noun but retaining all the morphology of the original adjective. Superficially, the *Angestellte(r)*-nouns resemble nouns found in a number of languages that happen to inflect according to an adjectival rather than a nominal paradigm, usually because they are historically derived from adjectives although the link to the adjective is not (necessarily) transparent to speakers. As mentioned in Chapter 1, Russian has a good many nouns like that, and Spencer (2013) refers to them as '*stolovaja*-nouns'. But unlike the Russian *stolovaja*-nouns, the *Angestellte(r)*-nouns of German are formed by a productive regular process: in principle, any adjective capable of modifying a human referent could form an *Angestellte(r)*-noun, and the derivation *angestellter* 'employed' → *ein Angestellter* 'an employee' does not involve a change of LI. Hence, this type of static relatedness is of greater linguistic interest because it tells us something about the organization of the lexicon.

Before leaving this type we should distinguish it from the common situation in which a transposition itself undergoes derivation. For instance, in English a passive participle (transposition) can normally be used as an attributive or predicative adjective: *a frozen chicken, the chicken had been frozen in the deep freeze*. However, the participle *frozen* can then undergo semantic shift to mean just 'uncomfortably cold' as in *During the snow storm the poor chickens were so frozen that they all huddled together*. This type of relatedness is of interest, because the base for the derivation is an already modified form of the original base lexeme, but it is not an instance of meaning-bearing transposition.

In the types of relatedness illustrated in Table 5.4 we see a particularly non-canonical situation: the relatedness defines distinct lexemes but without

200 Lexical Representation and Lexical Relatedness

Table 5.4 *Lexical relatedness with SEM attribute identical, LI attribute changed*

	(C1)	C2	C3	C4
FORM	–	Δ	Δ	–
SYN	–	–	Δ	Δ

altering the semantic representation. This is a somewhat unexpected outcome, since semantic enrichment is a salient property of lexeme formation. Indeed, Type C1 is so unexpected that we have to rule it out as a possible type of relatedness, because it represents a situation in which we have two distinct lexemes that share all their properties. In a database this would be a duplicated entry. We assume that human lexica do not have duplicates.

In Type C2 we again see a type of static relatedness which is not instantiated in the grammar as such, namely perfect synonymy.[5] Synonyms are words which have the same SEM and SYN values, but they have (entirely) different forms and represent different lexemes: that is, they differ in their FORM and LI attributes. As mentioned above, this relatedness type is static in the sense that languages do not have productive morphological processes for creating pure synonyms.

Type C4 is a type of relatedness to which we will devote more detailed discussion in the next chapters. In this type we see what would appear to be a transposition: the morphosyntax of the derived entry is distinct from that of the base, but there is no meaning change. A true transposition has to be regarded as a form of the base lexeme; however, in Type C4 we see a transposition which is a distinct lexeme in its own right, that is, a transpositional lexeme. We have already seen examples of this type in Section 5.2.1 above and will discuss them more in Chapter 8 in the context of noun–adjective hybrids.

Type C3 would be a word comparable to C4 but derived by an m-inert process. This is bound to be an unusual type, given that morphological inertness is marked, and the C4 type is rare. If the reasoning of the previous paragraph is correct, then a hypothetical example would be an English deadjectival nominalization formed by conversion. We have not found an example of a morphologically inert transpositional lexeme, however, and will not consider it further.

We now turn to Table 5.5. In these types the two comparanda represent different lexemes and have distinct semantics.

---

[5] It has been argued that synonymy is an important part of lexical organization (Apresjan, 1974).

5.4 Lexical Relatedness 201

Table 5.5 *Lexical relatedness with SEM and LI attributes changed*

	D1	D2	D3	D4
FORM	–	Δ	Δ	–
SYN	–	–	Δ	Δ

Type D1 would be exemplified by two words which had the same form and syntax but different meanings and which instantiated different lexemes. As a static relationship (as opposed to a productive, paradigmatically driven relation) this is represented by non-systematic polysemy.

Type D2 represents derivation in which the syntax of a derived word is essentially the same as that of the base lexeme, what we might call 'syntactically inert derivation'. An example would be the derivation of negative adjectives by the addition of *un-* in English, as in English *un-happy*, or of nouns by the addition of *-hood* as in *boy-hood*. It can be difficult to distinguish such derivation from (inherent, meaning-bearing) inflection, or from evaluative morphology (our Type B2). For instance, when a language expresses negative polarity of a clause by head marking of the verb, we generally regard this as the realization of an inflection property [POLARITY:affirmative,negative]. By contrast, even if a process such as English *un-* prefixation is entirely productive and regular, we would tend to regard it as a form of derivation rather than inflection. It is not entirely clear what such decisions should be based on. In respect to *un*-prefixation we are unwilling to regard the negated word as an inflected form of the positive lexeme because the semantics of antonymy is very heterogeneous and rather different from clause-level polarity. On the other hand, if we consider the repetitive or iterative *re-* prefix, as in *re-write*, then we have derivation which is very close to Aktionsart inflection in other languages. And even the *un*-prefixation begins to look more like inflection when the base is a productively derived passive participle: *an unfinished meal* (≈ *a meal which has not been finished*), *an unopened letter*, and so on.

Type D3 is derivation that is m-inert. This is not the same as traditional conversion, which is a somewhat parochial phenomenon of little general interest. Rather, m-inert derivation represents a form of relatedness in which the derived lexeme retains all the formal properties of the base, including inflectional forms. Examples include nouns derived from adjectives or verbs which retain the adjectival declension or verbal conjugation of the base.

Type D4 is familiar as canonical derivation.

202　*Lexical Representation and Lexical Relatedness*

As was mentioned above, adjectives and nouns in Russian have clearly distinct inflectional paradigms. But there is an important subset of nouns which decline exactly like adjectives from which they are often historically derived, e.g. *skoryj* 'express (train) (masculine)' and *nasekomoe* 'insect (neuter)'. Such nouns include the *stolovaja*-type nouns, but they also include nouns which closely resemble the *Angestellte(r)*-nouns of German. Thus, from the adjective BOL′NOJ 'sick' we have the noun BOL′NOJ '(doctor's) patient'. As Spencer (2002) shows in some detail, the noun BOL′NOJ 'patient' in Russian is a distinct lexeme from the adjective BOL′NOJ 'sick'. The nouns, which have the SYN value of a noun but the FORM attribute of an adjective, are rather widespread in the language and their existence presumably makes it easier for speakers to coin new words by analogy. Such lexemes are common in English and other European languages: *the good, the bad, and the ugly, the (deserving) poor, the (seriously) injured, the most successful/least prepared, the first/last/seventh* (Arnold and Spencer, 2015).

The upshot of the survey in Spencer (2013) summarized here is that twelve of the fourteen logically possible and non-trivial types of coarse-grained lexical relatedness are reasonably well attested, and one of them may well be attested. Of the twelve relatively uncontroversial types, polysemy/ homonymy, and pure synonymy are not represented by regular, paradigm-driven rules or principles, and synonymy does not contribute to the expansion of the word stock in any sense, but all the rest may be attested as morphological processes to some degree or other. The significance of this (admittedly very coarse) typology of lexical relatedness is that it illustrates clearly the need to factorize the various dimensions of lexical representation, as is common in lexicalist or constraint-based models of grammar. It therefore provides a partial motivation for an articulated model of lexical representation.

Another crucial conclusion that must be drawn from considerations of lexical relatedness is that the traditional division of parts of speech is inadequate for characterizing the different word categories that we find in real lexica. Rather, there is a complex set of intermediate categories that cross-cut the traditional distinctions and which have important repercussions for the way we perceive the relationship between the lexicon, morphology, and syntax.

5.5　Conclusions

Since noun–adjective hybrids represent an intermediate type category, it is important to articulate how such intermediate categories can be represented in the lexicon. In this chapter we have outlined a view in which the lexicon is populated by bona fide linguistic objects and have offered a way of looking at two closely related questions: the structure of lexical representations and the kinds of relations that words (under various descriptions) contract with each other.

A key feature of the model of lexical relatedness proposed by Spencer (2013) and elsewhere and summarized here is the idea that lexical information is factorized, including information that is normally associated with morpholexical or morphosyntactic category. This is reflected in its most simple form by the way we have defined lexical relatedness. Given two words, we can ask in what ways, if any, they are related by asking what information they share, and what information is distinct in the two representations. We have described a broad four-dimensional definition of lexical representation in terms of morphological FORM, SYN(TAX), SEM(ANTICS), and a LEXEMIC INDEX (LI). The basic question when comparing two putatively related lexical items is now: do the items share the same FORM, SYN, SEM, LI values? We then ask: if they differ on one or more attribute, does the value associated with one lexical item subsume the corresponding value of the other lexical item? For instance, if two lexical items have different SEM values, can we write the SEM value of one of the entries as the SEM value of the other entry together with some added predicate?

Having surveyed the possible types of relatedness that this very crude and simple scheme permits, we have discovered that there is a whole host of types of lexical relatedness between canonical inflection and canonical derivation. Many of these intermediate types are very common (for instance, the pure transpositions), and many of them represent the type of category mixing which has posed severe problems for linguistic theory in the past. We have also noted that lexemes are related by type hierarchies, but the most important types of lexical relatedness will be characterized by a default inheritance hierarchy defined by a Generalized Paradigm Function, as we will discuss in Chapter 6.

6 Generalized Paradigm Function Morphology

6.1 Introduction

In this chapter we outline an explicit model of lexical and morphological relatedness couched within the general framework of inferential-realizational morphology, the Generalized Paradigm Function Morphology or GPFM (Spencer, 2013). We first summarize the basic architecture of the GPFM model, and then extend it by introducing the distinction between the FORM and CONTENT paradigms/features (Stump, 2016) that is essential for the description of many kinds of morphosyntactic mismatch, including some aspects of transpositions. We then explain the function of Morpholexical Signature and Default Cascade (Spencer, 2013), through which most of the properties of a lexical entry can be made to follow solely from a specification of ontological category.

The central feature of our treatment of transpositions will be the enriched notion of argument structure (ARG-ST), which includes not just thematic arguments but also what we call 'Semantic Function Roles' (after Spencer, 1999, 2013) – 'R', 'E', 'A*' – to mediate the semantics/syntax interface for nouns, verbs, and adjectives. These architectural preliminaries will set the scene for the characterization of (true) transpositions as 'representations' of a lexeme, which is captured by means of the morphosyntactic feature REPRESENTATION (Spencer, 2013, 2017b). One of the more puzzling aspects of true transpositions is that they seem to be a form of their base lexeme (say, noun) and yet inflect as though they were members of a different word class (say, adjective) – the 'paradigm-within-a-paradigm' problem (Spencer, 2017b). The extended GPFM model can provide a coherent description of this type of lexemic structuring. At the end of the chapter a brief comparison with Network Morphology will be offered.

6.2 Representing Lexical Relatedness in GPFM

As mentioned in Chapter 5, a limiting instance of dynamic relatedness is the relatedness between regularly inflected word forms of a single lexeme, namely the kind of relatedness defined by the Paradigm Function in Stump's PFM model. However, paradigmatic relatedness can cover the whole gamut of relatedness types up to and including canonical derivation. For this reason it makes sense to have a single formal device to capture dynamic relatedness, but one which can cut across the inflection/derivation divide without incurring incoherence. We achieve this by means of the Generalized Paradigm Function (GPF), a generalization of Stump's notion of (inflectional) Paradigm Function, which is meant to account for all types of lexical relatedness, including derivation (Spencer, 2013).

We have already seen that a lexical representation is factored into (at least) four components: FORM, SYN, SEM, and LI. Any two lexical items (word forms of a lexeme, derived lexemes and their bases, and so on) which are dynamically (paradigmatically) related to each other will be defined in terms of the GPF. We assume a set of features governing systematical relations, morphosyntactic property sets for inflection (for instance, 3sg, which informally represents the 3SG present indicative subject agreement forms of an English verb), and derivational features for derivation (for instance, a feature {SN}, which represents the Subject Nominalization process). For intermediate types of relatedness we may require more elaborated types of feature. Thus, as we show in Section 6.4, the complex set of transpositional relations can be described by a 'superfeature' of REPRESENTATION which takes values such as 'verb-to-noun', 'noun-to-adjective', and so on.

The GPF in fact consists of four functions defining values for each of the four lexical attributes. For simplicity we will use the same labels – FORM, SYN, SEM, LI – for these functions. These functions take as their domain pairs consisting of an LI (£), and a feature set, and they deliver a representation of some sort. In many cases one or other of the four functions will have no effect and the derived lexical item will inherit those properties from the base by default. This is guaranteed by the General Default Principle (GDP) (Spencer, 2013, 191), a variant of Stump's (2001) Identity Function Default, as shown in (1).

(1) General Default Principle: For any lexemic index £, for all attributes $ATTR_i$ of a representation $\{ATTR_i, \ldots, ATTR_n\}$, and for all feature sets $\{\sigma\}$, by default $GDP(\langle ATTR_i (£), \{\sigma\}\rangle)$ is evaluated as $ATTR_i (\langle£, u\rangle)$.

We give simple illustrations of (contextual) inflection in (2) and a verb-to-adjective transposition, that is a participle, in (3).

206 *Generalized Paradigm Function Morphology*

(2) Where Δ = {DRIVE, {3sg}}, GPF(Δ) =

$$\begin{bmatrix} \text{FORM} & \text{FORM}\langle\text{DRIVE, \{u\}}\rangle\text{ - s} \\ \text{SYN} & \text{(GDP)} \\ \text{SEM} & \text{(GDP)} \\ \text{LI} & \text{(GDP)} \end{bmatrix}$$

(3) Where Δ = {DRIVE, {prs.ptcp}}, GPF$\langle\rangle$ =

$$\begin{bmatrix} \text{FORM} & \text{FORM}\langle\text{DRIVE, \{u\}}\rangle\text{ - ing} \\ \text{SYN} & \text{Adj} \\ \text{SEM} & \text{(GDP)} \\ \text{LI} & \text{(GDP)} \end{bmatrix}$$

Spencer (2013, 347–348) proposes a way of representing deverbal participle transpositions in such a way as to make the argument structure of the SYN attribute of the participle subsume that of the base verb by introducing the notion of 'highest argument', but this refinement is not essential to our purposes here. For the FORM, SYN, and SEM functions the operation of the GPF will be fairly evident. For the LI function where a new lexeme is defined we will assume that, in paradigmatic word formation, the GPF defines a new LI on the basis of the base lexeme's LI. The SYN representation shown in (3) will be modified shortly so as to reflect the fact that the adjective is derived from a verb.

We now consider the question of how to identify distinct lexemes, and how to relate distinct lexemes to each other systematically by paradigmatic derivational morphology.

As mentioned above, we will follow Spencer (2013) in treating all forms of regular morphology, inflectional or derivational, by means of an extension of Stump's Paradigm Function. This, however, leads to an important descriptive problem. A typical Paradigm Function for defining an inflected word form of a lexeme is a mapping between a ⟨lexical index, Head inflectional features⟩ pairing and an output, a ⟨wordform, Head inflectional features⟩ pairing. Thus, for a noun plural in English we would have (informally) the function shown in (4).

(4) PF(⟨CAT, pl⟩) $\Rightarrow$ ⟨cats, pl⟩

However, this format will not do for derivation. Suppose we wish to derive the Subject Nominal lexeme DRIVER from the verb DRIVE. Assuming a derivational feature {SN} governing the Subject Nominal formation process, we would then obtain the function shown in (5).

(5)   PF(⟨DRIVE, {SN}⟩) ⇒ ⟨driver, {SN}⟩

There are two, related, problems here. First, we have not established that *driver* is a form of a distinct lexeme. If we were to apply the Paradigm Function strictly, then Stump's (2001, 45) Persistence of L-indexing principle would apply, guaranteeing that *driver* retains the L-index DRIVE. As we have seen, this is appropriate for transpositions but it is not appropriate for canonical derivation. The second problem is that we now have no obvious way of defining the inflectional paradigm of DRIVER itself. This is because, given the Paradigm Function shown in (5), the lexeme DRIVER does not really exist.

Before we present the solution to these problems, it will be helpful first to consider the nature of lexical semantic representations. There is a very obvious fact about lexical organization which is routinely ignored in theoretical discussion of lexical structure, namely the widespread existence of accidental polysemy. Polysemy is accidental when it is not mandated by the grammar of the language (in the broadest sense of 'grammar'). For instance, in English deadjectival verbs such as *thicken, widen, dry, centralize*, etc. are systematically ambiguous between a causative (transitive) and inchoative (intransitive) meaning, provided the derived verb's semantics is derived from the adjective's semantics. This type of polysemy is thus systematic, because it is part of the grammar of English. On the other hand, the majority of what lexicologists and lexicographers think of as polysemy is at best a vague, often metaphorical, relationship between meanings that is not coded in the grammar at all. For instance, the noun *head* has a variety of uses which are generally thought to be in some sense related: head of an animal; head of a nail; head of a queue; head of an institution such as the army, a department; the frothy upper part of carbonated drinks (especially beer); and so on. However, there is no principle of grammar or lexical organization in English which determines these meanings. They have arisen as a result of metaphor-induced semantic drift. In fact, it is extremely misleading to think of these meanings as reflecting 'polysemy' in any useful sense of that term. What we really have here is homonymy or homophony.

The main reason why lexicographers persist in calling such relatedness 'polysemy' is adherence to the doctrine of James Murray, the leader of the team that compiled the *Oxford English Dictionary* in the nineteenth century, according to which the main organizing principle for the dictionary is historical relatedness. This leads to well-known anomalies. For instance, the entry for

208 *Generalized Paradigm Function Morphology*

FAIR in the *Oxford English Dictionary* lists several submeanings: roughly, 'yellow coloured (of hair); just and reasonable (of a judgement, price, ...); moderate or averagely good; beautiful (of a female, obs.)'. All of these uses can be traced back to a single Middle English and Old English lexeme (unlike the 'fairground' or 'village market' meaning which has a different etymology). On the other hand, the verb LINE, as in 'to line the paper with a ruler', 'trees/demonstrators lined the streets', is a distinct headword from LINE, as in 'to line a jacket', because the former usage goes back to the Latin *linea* 'line', while the latter usage has an etymon related to English *lint*, *linen*. Clearly, Murray's 'historical principle' is no way to define semantic relatedness.

Given, then, that most polysemy is really homonymy, we are left with a large number of distinct lexical entries which have distinct meanings and which typically have distinct syntactic behaviour (especially in the case of verbs), but which nonetheless all share exactly the same morphological properties.

This is especially apparent when we look at verbs in a morphologically rich language such as Russian. Consider the verb ZAPISAT'. As already mentioned in Chapter 5, it is derived from the prefix *za-* and the verb PISAT' 'to write'. The four-volume dictionary of Russian (Evgen'eva 1985) defines the word ZAPISAT' under two headings. Under the first it gives the following meanings (slightly modernized in places):

(i) record in written form (report, thoughts, address, phrase, ...)
(ii) to record an acoustic signal on a permanent storage medium (vinyl disk, magnetic tape, CD, ...)
(iii) to include in a list or register: to register a child for a school, to enrol someone on a course, ...
(iv) to transfer property to someone (obs.)
(v) to cover with writing ('to fill a whole page with doodles')

The second headword simply lists the meaning 'to begin to write', a systematic ingressive use of *za-*.

The dictionary gives the following primary meanings for the base verb PISAT' 'write':

(i) reproduce symbols (letters, numerals, etc.) on e.g. paper
(ii) formulate text in writing
(iii) convey information in written/printed form
(iv) compose a text
(v) compose a piece of music
(vi) create a picture

6.2 Representing Lexical Relatedness in GPFM   209

To what extent do these meanings have entailments which are inherited by the different meanings of ZAPISAT'; that is, to what extent does Russian 'x zapisal y' entail 'x (na)pisal y/z' (where *na-* is a perfective prefix)?

Meaning (i) of the derived verb seems to share the entailments of meaning (ii). Indeed, it is not easy to distinguish the meanings of *zapisat' doklad/frazu/adres* from *napisat' doklad/frazu/adres* 'write a report/sentence/address', the simple perfective form of PISAT'. Meaning (v) also seems to have the entailments of meanings (i) and (ii), in that the page etc. has to have been covered by making an impression on the paper. Proper writing involves the deliberate reproduction of a linguistic or musical text; otherwise it is just doodling. But meaning in (v) can apply to doodling as well as to genuine writing. None of the other meanings, however, entail writing in any of the senses of the base verb (though it might often involve writing). Those meanings are therefore polysemous only in the historical sense. In terms of lexicology and lexical semantics they are homonyms. Innumerable further examples of such homonymy can be found with lexemes derived by prefixation from PISAT'.

Now, what is important for approaches to lexical morphology is the fact that every single entry for ZAPISAT', including the ingressive meaning, has exactly the same morphology, namely that of PISAT'. In the present tense the verbs conjugate as *-pišú, -píšeš', ..., -píšut*, the l-participle is *-pisál* and the passive participle is *-písannyj*. Formally speaking, all of the entries for ZAPISAT' are identical and all inherit their morphology from the base lexeme PISAT'. This fact has no doubt strengthened the treatment of these verbs as polysemous (though that does not explain the lexicographic practice of treating the ingressive as a distinct head word). Moreover, the same degree of morphological identity holds for all the prefixed derivates of PISAT' mentioned in Chapter 5, Section 5.4. Zaliznjak (2003) lists eighteen prefixed derivates, many of which are more 'polysemous' than ZAPISAT'.

How can we capture this formal identity across entirely distinct lexical entries? The solution proposed in Spencer (2013) is to treat the three major lexical attributes and their subcomponents as functions defined over a unique LI. Thus, for, meaning (i) of ZAPISAT', say, we will have LI 'ZAPISAT'1'. The set of inflected forms of this verb will be defined by the function shown in (6).

(6) $f_{form}(\langle \text{ZAPISAT'1, features} \rangle)$ = zapišú, zapíšeš', ...

The syntax of purely inflected forms (that is, not transpositions) is identical across those forms and is related to the semantics. Simplifying considerably, for the 'writing down a report/address/phrase' meaning, let us assume the semantic

210 *Generalized Paradigm Function Morphology*

representation in (7), from which by default we can define the syntactic representation in (8) (nothing hinges on the accuracy of these representations since their function is just to illustrate the formal system).

(7) $f_{sem}(\langle \text{ZAPISAT'1, all Head inflectional features}\rangle) =$
$\lambda e, x, y \, [\text{WRITE\_DOWN}(e, x, y)]$

(8) $f_{syn}(\langle \text{ZAPISAT'1, all Head inflectional features}\rangle) = \langle \text{SUBJ, OBJ}\rangle$

We can now abstract away from all Head inflectional features and define a general lexical entry for the verb as a function from the pairing of $\langle \text{LI, \{u\}}\rangle$ to semantic and syntactic representations, where $\{u\}$ is the empty set of features. Thus, more complete representations of (8) and (7) are shown in (9) and (10).

(9) $f_{sem}(\langle \text{ZAPISAT'1, \{u\}}\rangle) = \langle \lambda e, x, y \, [\text{WRITE\_DOWN}(e, x, y)], u\rangle$

(10) $f_{syn}(\langle \text{ZAPISAT'1, \{u\}}\rangle) = \langle \langle \text{SUBJ, OBJ}\rangle, \{u\}\rangle$

Next, we can define a basic STEM form for the verb ('STEM0', often equivalent to the traditional root of the lexeme) before any inflectional morphology has been applied, as shown in (11).

(11) $f_{form}(\langle \text{ZAPISAT'1, \{u\}}\rangle) = \text{STEM0}(\langle \text{ZAPISAT'1, \{u\}}\rangle) = \text{zapis-}$

In effect, then, a lexical entry is defined as an application of the GPF, but one defined over a pairing of a unique lexemic index, £, and the empty feature set, $\{u\}$: $\text{GPF}(\langle £, \{u\}\rangle)$.

Finally, we note that all the meanings and uses of ZAPISAT' share this morphology. This means that we can now define an all-encompassing f_{form} function over a set of LIs, as shown in (12).

(12) $f_{form}(\langle \text{ZAPISAT'1, ZAPISAT'2, ZAPISAT'3, ..., \{u\}}\rangle) =$
$\text{STEM0}(\langle \text{ZAPISAT'1, ..., \{u\}}\rangle) =$
zapis-

In a more complete morphological analysis of Russian we would circumscribe the prefix and define the FORM attribute over only the LI of the bare unprefixed verb PISAT', and then ensure that derivational morphology added the prefix to all inflected forms, for instance by deploying Stump's Head Application Principle.[1]

---

[1] There is one apparent counter-example to the claim that all derivates of PISAT' inherit its morphology, namely the verb *živopisat'* 'to describe in a particularly arresting and striking

6.2 Representing Lexical Relatedness in GPFM 211

This minor notational innovation has some far-reaching consequences. First, recall that we have been assuming a different status for the LI, namely as one of the attributes of a lexical entry. If that is still to be the case, then the LI must itself define a function, but one from pairings of LIs and features to LIs and features. This is not coherent. We therefore need to clarify the nature of the LI. First, we have the LEXEMIC INDEX function for any lexeme, f_{li}, which simply specifies which integer serves as the lexemic index. For instance, returning to the English lexicon, suppose that '59' is the LI of the verb DRIVE. Then the lexical entry for DRIVE will include the information shown in (13).

(13) $f_{li}(\langle 59, \{u\}\rangle) = \langle 59, \{u\}\rangle$

In other words, the f_{li} acts as a kind of identity function or General Default. It is not overridden by a set of values for {u} which define traditionally inflectional categories.

Consider now the English Subject Nominalization (derivational feature, SN) process which derives DRIVER from DRIVE, with which we opened this discussion. Here the GPF is defined over a derivational feature, {SN}. The GPF should give us a representation along the lines of that shown in (14).

(14)   Where $\Delta = \langle 59, \{SN\}\rangle$, GPF($\Delta$) =
$$\begin{aligned}
f_{form}(\Delta) &= \langle FORM\langle 59, \{u\}\rangle - er, \{SN\}\rangle \\
f_{syn}(\Delta) &= \langle N, \{SN\}\rangle \\
f_{sem}(\Delta) &= \langle [_{Thing} \lambda xarg\ \lambda arg2[PERSON(xarg)\ \wedge \\
&\qquad \exists e.DRIVE(e,xarg,arg2)]], \{SN\}\rangle \\
f_{li}(\Delta) &= DRIVER = 127 = \langle 59, \{SN\}\rangle
\end{aligned}$$

The f_{form} function tells us to add -er to the base form of DRIVE. The f_{sem} and f_{syn} functions define the new semantic and syntactic representations. The f_{li} function defines a new LI (recall this is a new integer, say 127).

If the Subject Nominalization process is a fully productive, regular, and hence paradigm-driven process (in the sense of Spencer (2013)), we can make better sense of the f_{li} function in (14) by assuming that the LI itself may be a complex entity rather than a simple integer. Suppose we say that any regular derivational feature such as SN itself defines a function (call it f_{SN}) which takes permissible value of the LI and delivers a (unique) distinct LI.[2] In this way the

---

fashion, paint a vivid picture of'. This verb belongs to the default conjugation class exemplified by *delat'* 'do': *živopisúju* (1SG) and not **živopišú*. However, this is easily explained, because *živopisat'* is derived not from the verb *pisat'* directly but from the noun *živopis'* '(figurative, non-abstract) painting'.

[2]   We can still define the LI as an integer if we assume that the SN feature imposes something like a Gödel numbering.

212 *Generalized Paradigm Function Morphology*

LI itself records, so to speak, a shadow of the derivational history of the new lexeme. Thus, the LI of DRIVER will be $f_{SN}(DRIVE)$ (=$f_{SN}(59)$ = 127, say), given by the function f_{li} shown in (15).

(15) $f_{li}(\Delta) = \langle f_{SN}(DRIVE), \{SN\}\rangle$

We now assume a simple notational principle for defining the GPF in the case of morphology which changes the LI: the Derived Lexical Entry Principle (Spencer, 2013, 191–195, 200). Given a GPF($\langle £, \delta\rangle$), such that $f_{li}(\langle £, \delta\rangle)$ = $\langle f\delta(£), \delta\rangle$, then GPF($\langle £, \delta\rangle$) $\equiv$ GPF($\langle f\delta(£), \{u\}\rangle$). In other words, the principle states that the GPF defines the lexical entry for the lexeme with LI $f_{\delta(£)}$. Thus, we can rewrite (14) as (16), using the mnemonics DRIVE and DRIVER for lexemic indices.

(16) Where Δ = $\langle DRIVE, \{SN\}\rangle$, then Δ' = $f_{SN}(DRIVE)$ and GPF(Δ) =

$f_{form}(\Delta)$ = $\langle f_{form} (\langle DRIVE, \{u\}\rangle)$ - er, $\{SN\}\rangle$

$f_{syn}(\Delta)$ = $\langle N, \{SN\}\rangle$

$f_{sem}(\Delta)$ = $\langle [_{Thing} \lambda xarg \lambda arg2 [PERSON(xarg) \wedge \exists e$
     $DRIVE(e,xarg,arg2)]], \{SN\}\rangle$

$f_{li}(\Delta)$ = Δ' (= DRIVER)

and GPF(Δ)   =   GPF(Δ') =

$f_{form}(\Delta')$ = $f_{form}(\langle f_{SN}(DRIVE), \{u\}\rangle)$ =
     $f_{form}(\langle DRIVER, \{u\}\rangle)$

$f_{syn}(\Delta')$ = $\langle N, \{u\}\rangle$

$f_{sem}(\Delta')$ = $\langle [_{Thing} \lambda xarg \lambda arg2 [PERSON(xarg)$
     $\wedge \exists e\ DRIVE(e,xarg,arg2)]], \{u\}\rangle$

$f_{li}(\Delta')$ = Δ' (= DRIVER)

Since GPF(Δ') defines a new lexical entry, it will now be available for inflection. Spencer (2013), provides mechanisms to ensure that all and only the inflecting derivates get inflected, and in the right manner.)

In principle, the output of one of the component functions of the GPF could be entirely different from its input. Indeed, this is required for describing suppletive inflection forms such as *go~went* or (less commonly) suppletive derivational forms such as *fly (an aircraft)~pilot* (cf. *drive~driver*). For the static types of relatedness we often find such suppletive functions over SYN or SEM attributes, of course. However, in the overwhelming majority of cases of paradigmatic/dynamic relatedness, the FORM and SEM functions define a more intimate type of relatedness. The FORM attribute of the derived word will usually involve some identifiable modification of (some part of) the FORM attribute of the base, and likewise the SEM attribute of the derived word will itself be formally related to the SEM attribute of the base. In the simplest cases, of course, we have a directional, incremental relationship, in that the FORM/SEM attributes of the derived word wholly contain (some instance of) the FORM/SEM attributes of the base. This is how canonical inflection and derivation are described by Corbett (2010), for instance. The relation between the uninflected root *drive* and the 3SG form *drives* is a canonical relation for FORM attributes. Similarly, the relation between the uninflected root form *drive* and the uninflected root form *driver* of the lexeme DRIVER is also canonical, as is the relation between the SEM attributes, in that the semantics of DRIVER is that of DRIVE enriched with the semantic predicate PERSON WHO (drives). When we consider paradigmatic relatedness, governed by grammatical principles, there is an asymmetry: suppletion in form is still compatible with paradigmatic relatedness, but suppletion in content/meaning is not compatible with paradigmatic relatedness, even if the formal relationship between the two related words is entirely transparent. It is in this sense that lexical morphology is semantically driven.

6.3   Lexical Categories

In this section we cash out our promise to provide a further factorization of lexical representations, largely focussing on those attributes that are relevant for the syntactic properties of a lexeme: the SYN attribute. Although some of these properties are mirrored in morphological form (the FORM attribute) in many languages, in general SYN properties are different in kind from FORM properties even for languages with relatively complex morphologies such as Russian. We discuss these differences against the backdrop of a distinction between m-features (for 'morphological features') and s-features (for 'syntactic features'), briefly mentioned in Chapter 5, or the FORM paradigms and CONTENT paradigms of Stump (2016). These distinctions will be extended in various ways in accounting for the morphosyntax of mixed categories. The section concludes with remarks about the Default Cascade alluded to above, under which a great many of the properties of any lexeme are predictable from very general semantic properties, often going no further than the basic ontological category (a version of the notional definition of parts of speech).

214   *Generalized Paradigm Function Morphology*

6.3.1   FORM/CONTENT Paradigms

We have already mentioned the distinction drawn by Stump (2016) in the PFM2 model between different conceptions of paradigm. The most concrete type of paradigm is the realized paradigm. This is a listing of each inflected form of a lexeme paired with the set of features of morphosyntactic properties that it realizes, for instance, {⟨/dog/,sg⟩, ⟨/dogz/,pl⟩} for DOG or {⟨/ʃi:p/,sg⟩, ⟨/ʃi:p/,pl⟩} for SHEEP. That paradigm is derived by application of the Paradigm Function to the set of cells in the FORM paradigm. This consists of a set of pairings between the appropriate root or stem form of the lexeme and the morphosyntactic properties expressed, as in {⟨/dog/,sg⟩, ⟨/dog/,pl⟩} for DOG, {⟨/ʃi:p/,sg⟩, ⟨/ʃi:p/,pl⟩} for SHEEP. Finally, the CONTENT paradigm consists of a set of pairings between the lexeme's index and the morphosyntactic properties expressed, as in {⟨DOG,sg⟩, ⟨DOG,pl⟩}, {⟨SHEEP,sg⟩, ⟨SHEEP,pl⟩}.

The FORM paradigm is projected from the CONTENT paradigm by paradigm linkage and mediated by two additional functions: the property mapping function, ***pm***, and the Correspondence function, ***Corr***. Both functions default to the identity function, so that, *ceteris paribus*, the FORM paradigm is isomorphic to the CONTENT paradigm. Consider, however, the case of a typical mismatch. In Russian, the accusative form (singular or plural) of one set of nouns (masculine gender animates of Class I, such as SLON 'elephant') is identical to the genitive, while for non-animates the accusative syncretizes with the nominative case. Thus we have *slon* 'nom sg', *slony* 'nom pl', *slona* 'acc/gen sg', *slonov* 'acc/gen pl', but for ZAKON 'law' we have *zakon* 'nom/acc sg', *zakony* 'nom/acc pl', *zakona* 'gen sg', *zakonov* 'gen pl'. The syncretisms can be captured by setting up a ***pm*** function which instructs the grammar to treat the two CONTENT paradigm cells ⟨ELEPHANT, {acc, (sg/pl)}⟩ as though they corresponded to the FORM paradigm cells ⟨|*slon*|, {gen, (sg/pl)}⟩ and the two CONTENT paradigm cells ⟨LAW, {acc, (sg/pl)}⟩ as though they corresponded to the FORM paradigm cells ⟨|*zakon*|, {nom, (sg/pl)}⟩. This is part of the definition of paradigm linkage for Russian.[3]

In the examples of mismatch analysed by Stump (2016), the same set of morphosyntactic properties or features is deployed in both types of paradigm (the principal exception is the inflectional class feature, found solely in FORM

---

[3]   More formally, for *slon*, say, we have ***pm***({CLASS:I, GENDER:m, ANIMATE:yes, CASE:acc}) = {CLASS:I, GENDER:m, ANIMATE:yes, CASE:gen}. Where N is a noun lexeme's index and σ is a feature set containing {CLASS:I, GENDER:m, ANIMATE:yes, CASE:acc}, and where τ = σ/Case:gen and Z is the root of N, then the CONTENT paradigm cell ⟨N,σ⟩ is realized by a word form defined by the PF(⟨N,σ⟩) = PF(***Corr***(⟨N,σ⟩)) =PF(⟨X, ***pm***(σ)⟩) =PF(⟨X,τ⟩) =PF(⟨|slon|,τ⟩) ={*slona, slonov*}.

6.3 Lexical Categories 215

paradigms). However, there are well-attested instances in which the FORM paradigm has to be defined in terms of featural oppositions not found in the CONTENT paradigm. In other words, the FORM paradigms sometimes have to be defined in terms of purely morphological, that is morphomic, features. These morphomic, FORM paradigm-only, features are the m-features of Sadler and Spencer (2001), as distinct from the s-features found solely in CONTENT paradigms.

As a simple illustration of the need to distinguish m-/s-features, consider the Russian tense-aspect system (for further details on this see Spencer, 2017b). Russian distinguishes present, past, and future tenses, with standard time-anchored interpretations. It also distinguishes a category of aspect: all verbs are either perfective (very roughly, having a telic or bounded interpretation) or imperfective (atelic/unbounded). Transitive verbs denoting bounded eventualities obligatorily distinguish the two aspects. There is therefore an inflectional property [ASPECT:{ipfv,pfv}]. Verbs in the imperfective form distinguish [TENSE:{prs,pst,fut}] tense forms while verbs in the perfective lack a present tense and express only [TENSE:{fut,pst}].

In the imperfective, present tense is expressed morphologically; thus from the lexeme DELAT· 'make, do', we have *delaj-u, delaj-eš'*, ..., 'I make, am making; thou makest, art making, ...'. The future form is expressed periphrastically with the (unique) synthetic future form of 'be' and the (imperfective) infinitive: *budu delat', budeš' delat'*, ... 'I will make/be making, etc'. Verbs in the perfective aspect, however, express future tense synthetically, but using the same morphology as that found with imperfective present tense verbs. Thus the perfective stem corresponding to *delat'* is prefixed with *s-*, as in *sdelat'*, and its future has the form *s-delaj-u, s-delaj-eš'*, etc. Exactly the same pattern is found with all aspectually paired verbs. Thus, *uronit'* (perfective), *uronjat'* (imperfective) has the future tense *uronju*, ... (perfective)/*budu uronjat'* (imperfective), where the endings for the perfective future are identical to those of the imperfective present of the verb *zvonit'* 'ring, call' (both verbs are standard exemplars of the regular second conjugation). These patterns are illustrated in Table 6.1, which shows (one possible interpretation of) the CONTENT paradigm, and Table 6.2, which shows which formal contrasts are actually observed in the Russian verb forms.

The Russian present/future distinction demonstrates very clearly the need to distinguish m-features from s-features. Ignoring the past tense for the moment, the s-feature inventory has to include the specifications s-[TENSE:{prs,fut}]. However, the m-feature inventory does not include a [TENSE:fut] specification at all: in the imperfective, s-[TENSE:fut] is expressed periphrastically, while in

216　*Generalized Paradigm Function Morphology*

Table 6.1 *Russian verb CONTENT paradigm for* UDARJAT′/UDARIT′ *'hit'*

aspect	imperfective	perfective
INFINITIVE	udarja-t′	udari-t′
GERUND	udarjaj-a	udari-v(ši)
IMPERATIVE	udarjaj(te)!	udar′(te)!
TENSE		
present	udarjaj-u, -eš′, …	<none>
future	bud-u, -eš′, … udarjat′	udar-ju, -iš′, …
past	udarja-l, -a, -o, -i	udari-l, -a, -o, -i
CONDITIONAL	udarja-l, -a, -o, -i + by	udari-l, -a, -o, -i + by
PASSIVE	udarjat′-sja, etc.	(byl) udaren, -a, -o, -y

Table 6.2 *Russian verb FORM paradigm for* UDARJAT′/UDARIT′ *'hit'*

aspect	imperfective	perfective
INFINITIVE	udarja-t′	udari-t′
GERUND	udarjaj-a	udari-v(ši)
IMPERATIVE	udarjaj(te)!	udar′(te)!
TENSE		
present/future	udarjaj-u, -eš′, …	udar-ju, -iš′, …
LPTCP	udarja-l, -a, -o, -i	udari-l, -a, -o, -i
REFLEXIVE	udarjat′-sja, etc.	<none>

the perfective the future is expressed morphologically, but using forms which are identical to the present tense forms of the imperfective.[4]

Even the future auxiliary form of 'be', *bud-u, bud-eš′*, … conforms to that generalization, in the sense that its endings are identical to the present tense endings of an imperfective first conjugation verb such as DELAT′. Thus, we must say that the synthetically inflected forms distinguish only the m-feature value [TENSE:prs]. Strictly speaking, therefore, the [ASPECT:ipfv, TENSE:fut] cells of a lexeme's paradigm are only defined at the level of s-features, in the CONTENT paradigm.

---

[4]　In some verbs the m-/s-feature distinction is particularly clear. Thus, the verb *sxodit′* is derived from the base form *xodit′* 'to go (on foot)' by the prefixation of *s-*. When *sxodit′* means 'to go (and come back)' it is perfective. However, it is imperfective when it means 'to go down; to leave; to go from the surface of' (perfective *sojti*). But in both cases *sxodit′* inflects in the same way (and in the same way as the imperfective verb *xodit′*).

6.3 Lexical Categories 217

These examples illustrate several important points about the architecture of morphology. First, they demonstrate the priority of CONTENT paradigms (s-features) over FORM paradigms (m-features). The FORM paradigms merely provide (some of) the morphological building blocks necessary for expressing the full repertoire of grammatical distinctions a language makes. Periphrastic (and clitic) constructions by definition allow for a greater number of distinctions than purely synthetic forms. But in addition, combinations of m-features may express contrasts which cannot be predicted from mere inspection of forms, as in the case of future tense perfective aspect forms, which are realized by a paradigm whose default meaning is to realize present tense forms. It is for this reason that Stump defines FORM paradigms as a projection from CONTENT paradigms.

The Russian tense system illustrates another important point about the special status of FORM paradigms. Since Aronoff (1994), morphologists have recognized a morphomic level of organization. Aronoff's original demonstration concerned stem forms in Latin which cannot be associated with any particular sets of morphosyntactic properties. Those stems, he argued, are therefore just forms identifiable solely by an arbitrary index: STEM0, STEM1, etc. Stump (2001) further demonstrates that in Sanskrit there are morphophonologically defined stem types which correspond to morphomic, that is purely morphological stem types, but only imperfectly, so that it is not possible in general to define either set in terms of the other without taking into account which class of lexeme is being described and which part of the paradigm is being defined. The concept of the morphome has been extended in an important series of papers by Maiden (for instance, Maiden, 1992, 2005, 2012) on Romance conjugation and its history. Maiden observes that patterns of stem alternation and other features of inflection can be described over disparate parts of Romance verbs, unifying within a single language such non-natural classes as {1sg, 3pl}, {2pl, 3pl}, {1sg present indicative, present subject – all person/numbers}, and others. These patterns, which often have their origins in now defunct phonological alternations at much earlier stages of the Romance group's development, have been remarkably robust over time and seem, therefore, to reflect linguistic generalizations that are somehow available to those acquiring the language.[5]

---

[5] Round (2015) has a very useful survey and typology of the different kinds of morphomicity that have been described in the literature. He distinguishes rhizomorphomes, which are essentially morphomic stems, metamorphomes of the kind Maiden describes, and a third type, meromorphomes, which are found when a single affix expresses a variety of disparate morphological functions.

218   *Generalized Paradigm Function Morphology*

Table 6.3 *Past tense forms of Russian* UDARIT′ *'hit'*

singular	
masculine	udaril
feminine	udaril-a
neuter	udaril-o
plural	udaril-i

As is pointed out by Spencer (2017b), the Russian past tense is also a morphomic category. This tense is expressed in the same way for both aspects by means of the 'l-participle', so called because its exponent for most verbs is a suffix *-l*: *(s)dela-l, (po)zvoni-l, uroni-l, uronja-l*, etc. The l-participle originated historically as a resultative participle which combined with the 'be' copula/auxiliary to form a perfect series of tenses comparable to the English perfect (and still found in Bulgarian/Macedonian, for instance). Being a participle, the l-form agreed with its subject NP in the manner of an adjective for number, and in the singular for masculine/feminine/neuter gender, but not for person. In some Slavic languages (West Slavic, Slovene, Serbian-Croatian) the auxiliary + l-participle has been reinterpreted as a simple past tense, just like its counterpart in spoken French. In Russian, however, grammaticalization went a stage further with the loss of the present tense forms of BE. The result is that the l-participle is now the sole exponent of the past tense, preserving, nonetheless, its original adjectival agreement inflections. This is illustrated in Table 6.3.

At this stage we might simply conclude that the l-suffix has now been reanalysed as a marker or exponent of [TENSE:pst]. However, this is not correct. Russian has a mood that is signalled periphrastically: the clause has to contain the particle *by* in some place other than the absolute initial position and the verb has to then appear in the l-participle form (glossed as LPTCP in the examples in (17)).

(17)   a. Ty by sdelal   bol′šuju ošibku
           you BY make.LPTCP big   mistake

      b. Ty sdelal   by bol′šuju ošibku
          you make.LPTCP BY big   mistake

      c. Bol′šuju ošibku ty by sdelal
          big   mistake you BY make.LPTCP

6.3 Lexical Categories   219

    d. Ty bol´šuju ošibku by sdelal
        you big   mistake BY make.LPTCP

    e. Ty bol´šuju ošibku sdelal   by
        you big   mistake make.LPTCP BY
        'You would be making a big mistake.'

The mood cannot be related semantically to the past tense, and in any case the l-participle is also found after non-past, non-conditional subordinating conjunctions which happen to be formed historically from the *by* particle: *čtoby* 'in order to', *kak by* 'lest', as shown in (18) and (19).

(18)   Otkroem okna,   čtoby   kraska vysox-l-a
            lets.open windows in.order.that paint[F] dry-LPTCP-F.SG
            'Let's open the windows for the paint to dry'

(19)   Ja bojus´, kakby ty   ne uspe-l-a   doexat´ zavtra
            I fear   lest   you[F] not succeed-LPTCP-F.SG arrive   tomorrow
            'I'm afraid you might not get there in time tomorrow'

What this fragment of Russian grammar tells us is that there is a grammatical construction based on inflected forms of the l-participle, which are disparate and cannot be put into direct unique correspondence with any specific morphosyntactic property. In other words, we are dealing with a morphome. At the level of the CONTENT paradigm (i.e. for us, the level of SYN features) there is no correspondent for the l-participle. At the level of the FORM paradigm we must simply record that verbs have a form, describable using the arbitrary feature label [VFORM:lptcp], called up by the grammar to realize CONTENT paradigm properties such as s-[TENSE:pst], s-[MOOD:cond] or when defining the (tenseless) forms of complement clauses introduced by *čtoby*, *kak by*.

A partial summary description of the Russian conjugation system is shown in Table 6.4. This is not intended as a definitive analysis (we could streamline it in various ways and some of the categories would require detailed justification). Our purpose is to show that by no means all of the verbal categories of the language are reflected directly in morphology. There seems to be no way that we could define a set of features that would be able to cover both syntactic constructions and morphological form. This is in part because there are a number of morphological categories which are purely morphological, that is morphomic. This, of course, poses an inherent challenge to anyone who believes that it is possible to account for all morphology by purely syntactic means.

220 *Generalized Paradigm Function Morphology*

Table 6.4 *CONTENT/FORM feature arrays for Russian verbs*

CONTENT feature array	
aspect	{ipfv,pfv}
VFORM	INFINITIVE
	TENSE:{prs, fut, pst}
	IMPERATIVE:{sg, pl}
	CONDITIONAL:{yes, no}
REFLEXIVE	{yes, no}
AGRSUBJ	PERSON:{1, 2, 3}
	NUMBER:{sg, pl}
	GENDER:{m, f, n}
VOICE	{ACTIVE, PASSIVE}
REPR	{⟨V,A⟩, ⟨V,Adv⟩}

FORM feature array	
aspect	{ipfv,pfv}
VFORM	INFINITIVE
	TENSE:{prs-fut}
	IMPERATIVE:{sg, pl}
	LPTCP
REFLEXIVE	{yes, no}
AGRSUBJ	PERSON:{1, 2, 3}
	NUMBER:{sg, pl}
	GENDER:{m, f, n}
REPR	{⟨V,A⟩, ⟨V,Adv⟩}

We can conclude that all the logically possible types of mismatch between m-features and s-features are attested, as schematized in Figure 6.1.

	CONTENT		FORM
(1)	s-F	$\nrightarrow$	$\emptyset$
(2)	$\emptyset$	$\nleftarrow$	m-F
(3a)	s-F(α)	$\rightarrow$	m-F(α)
(3b)	s-F(α)	$\rightarrow$	m-F(β)/m-G(α)/m-G(γ)

Figure 6.1 *Mismatches between m-/s-features (FORM/CONTENT paradigms)*

In Case (1) we see a situation in which some SYN/CONTENT feature F fails to have any FORM correspondent. This is typical of periphrastic constructions, such as the Russian imperfective future tense, but we have seen that it is also true of the Russian past tense: the feature s-[TNS:pst]

6.3 Lexical Categories 221

has no corresponding value m-[TNS:pst]. Similarly, there is no m-[TNS] correspondent of s-[TNS:fut], since even the non-periphrastic perfective future is realized by forms which bear the m-feature specification m-[TNS:prs].

In Case (2) we see a morphomic feature, F. The morphomic properties are precisely those m-features which fail to have any SYN correspondent. The Russian m-[VFORM:l-ptpc] specification is a case in point.

In Case (3b) we see the kind of mismatch found with syncretism, deponency, and similar mismatches. A feature specification s-F(α), whose default FORM specification is m-F(α) (Case 3a), may map to a different value, say β, of F under certain conditions, or it may map to the α value of a different feature, G, or it may map to an entirely different value of an entirely different feature, G(γ). Thus, a deponent verb marked s-[VCE:act] may map to m-[VCE:pass] (F(β)). In many languages, subject or object agreement on certain verb forms is mediated by morphology which is derived from possessor agreement inflection on nouns. Thus, we may find that a particular verbal person/number combination is realized by the FORM possessor agreement feature for that combination (G(α)). The Russian s-[TNS:pst] property is realized by a FORM feature m-[VFORM:lptcp], which does not even have an s-feature correspondent (G(γ)).

6.3.2 MORSIG

For any inflecting language we need to be able to declare the set of features for which a given lexeme inflects. Normally, such a declaration or signature is taken to be a kind of meta-statement or meta-constraint rather than a property of individual linguistic objects such as words, phrases, or lexemes. However, in the GPFM model this declaration is coded as an attribute of the lexeme's lexical representation, the MORPHOLEXICAL SIGNATURE (MORSIG). The reason for this is that a good deal of lexical morphology can be traced back to differences in the inflectional potential of a lexeme or a subset of a lexeme's word forms. The MORSIG attribute is normally (but by no means always!) shared across the FORM and SYN attributes. We will deploy it to encode the FORM/CONTENT paradigm distinction. Spencer (2017b) uses the distinction, together with the m-feature/s-feature distinction, in his analysis of Russian participles, and we will extend that analysis to the case of relational adjective transpositions in further chapters.

The MORSIG attribute is a property of lexemic entries. It governs the operation of the PF in the sense that the PF can only be defined for a given lexical entry if that entry's MORSIG includes the feature set which the PF realizes.

However, for the great majority of lexemes the MORSIG specifications are provided by default. In Spencer (2013) the MORSIG attribute is treated as a property of the FORM attribute and consists simply of an enumeration of those properties which define the 'realized paradigm' of a lexeme. For instance, suppose we have a language in which nouns inflect for number [NUM:{sg,pl}] and possessor agreement [AGRPOSS:{[PERSON/NUMBER:{1sg,1pl,2g, ...}]}]. Then the MORSIG attribute will supply precisely those properties, as shown in (20).

(20) Hypothetical MORSIG attribute of FORM

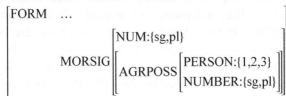

When we adopt the PFM2 model with its distinction between FORM/CONTENT paradigms, it becomes necessary to treat MORSIG as a property of the SYN attribute, as well as the FORM attribute (Spencer, 2017b). Although the two sets of features are identical in the default case, the distinction between them is motivated by the mismatches we have seen.

The most direct way to code this would be to duplicate the MORSIG attribute in both the FORM and the CONTENT paradigms, that is in the FORM and SYN attributes of the lexical entry. We could then assume a mapping from the SYN|MORSIG attribute to the FORM|MORSIG attribute, performing the role of Stump's *Corr* function. For the default mappings between SYN MORSIG and FORM MORSIG perhaps the simplest way of representing the two sets of features is to follow the lead of Sadler and Spencer (2001) in assuming that the two feature types are identical in the default case, but that they can be typed as m- or s-features (Stump (2002) assumes they are by default identical). A feature label that lacks a type designation can then be taken to be both m-feature and s-feature. By making use of the notion of re-entrancy, we can notate the m-/s- neutral type feature by writing it as a value of, say, the SYN|MORSIG attribute and tagging it in the FORM|MORSIG attribute, as indicated in (21).

(21) FORM/CONTENT feature as re-entrant attribute

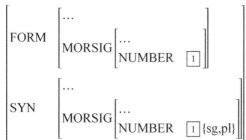

Some care is needed in formulating **Corr**. We need to distinguish s-features (specifications) which have no m-correspondents at all, but it is not sufficient simply to partition them off in some way and declare them out of the range of **Corr**. This is because some s-feature specifications may have FORM correspondents which are not the default value. Thus, the feature specification s-[TNS:fut] has no m-correspondent, but for perfective verbs the **Corr** function must map that specification to appropriate person/number forms of the m-[TNS:prs] correspondent. The most direct way of coding the **Corr** function is therefore to permit certain (combinations of) s-feature specifications to map to a null output, or to the value 'undefined'. The existence of morphomic (FORM-only) features shows that the definition of MORSIG cannot be stated purely in terms of a declaration of s-/CONTENT features together with the **Corr** function. Rather, the FORM MORSIG attribute needs to be supplemented with feature specifications which in part will be defined rather narrowly by other aspects of lexical representation.

In further sections and chapters we will see that the MORSIG attribute plays a crucial role in defining transpositions and is a very convenient way of encoding the mixing of inflectional properties. For instance, when a noun lexeme appears in its adjectival representation as a relational adjective, it acquires the MORSIG properties of an adjective while retaining some of the MORSIG properties of the original base noun lexeme.

6.3.3 Semantic Function Roles

Recall from Chapter 4 that we are working within a single projection model of mixed categories, so we need to be able to describe the categorial mixing at the level of lexical representations. One of the recurrent questions raised by the kinds of noun–adjective hybrid construction we are investigating is how to characterize the lexical category of the hybrid. A particularly difficult question is what category label we give to the mixed category in phrase

224   *Generalized Paradigm Function Morphology*

structure (c-structure) representations. We bypass that problem by defining the crucial aspect of the lexical categorization in terms of an enriched conception of argument structure.

First, we can represent the meaning of a lexeme as a simple formula in predicate calculus. We will assume that meanings are combinations of predicates with ontological typing. We will consider only *Thing*, *Event*, and *Property* types, which were introduced informally in Chapter 1. In most cases the predicates are constants, such as $TREE(x)$, $TALL(x)$, $BREAK(x,y)$. In other cases we will assume a modest degree of lexical decomposition. This is especially the case with morphologically complex representations. Thus, we will assume that a Subject Nominalization such as DRIVER has a semantic representation which includes not only the verbal predicate $[_{Event} DRIVE(x,y)]$ but also (as its semantic head) the predicate $\lambda x[_{Thing} PERSON(x)]$. When these are combined to provide the semantic representation of DRIVER, we obtain $\lambda x,y[_{Thing}[_{Thing} PERSON(x)] \wedge [_{Event} DRIVE(x,y)]]$. In fact, we will assume a slightly more elaborated representation of eventive predicates. Such predicates include an argument, e, denoting the event itself (following Higginbotham, 1985; Bierwisch, 1989; Wunderlich, 1996; Sag, 2012; Sag et al., 2003): $\lambda e,x,y[_{Thing}[_{Thing} PERSON(x)] \wedge [_{Event} DRIVE(e,x,y)]]$.

We could then represent the syntactic properties of a lexical entry by means of a two-tier representation. On one tier we provide a basic lexical category label. On the other tier we provide a representation of the lexeme's ARG-ST. In the simplest cases this gives us the representations shown in (22).

(22)   Noun (simple):   CAT:N
                                               $\langle x \rangle$

       Noun (inalienably possessed):   CAT:N
                                               $\langle x,y \rangle$

       Adjective (intransitive):   CAT:A
                                               $\langle x \rangle$

       Adjective (transitive):   CAT:A
                                               $\langle x,y \rangle$

       Verb (monotransitive):   CAT:V
                                               $\langle x,y \rangle$

       Preposition: CAT:P
                                               $\langle x,y \rangle$

6.3 *Lexical Categories* 225

Interfaced with syntactic models such as HPSG or LFG we might want to enrich such representations, at least for verbs and adpositionals, by adding grammatical function information: ⟨SUBJECT, OBJECT⟩. However, we will assume that this information will be recoverable from the lexical representations we posit. The ARG-ST representation reflects the interface between semantics and syntax, and is often referred to as the syntactic reflex of semantics. What this means is that we can project the argument structure directly from the semantic representation. Thus, a transitive verb has two argument positions because it is semantically a relation between two variables. Adjectives are typically intransitive, so the highest argument is usually the only argument: **tall**$\langle x \rangle$. There are also transitive adjectives, such as *proud*, for which it is important to distinguish the highest argument, **proud**$\langle x \langle y \rangle \rangle$.

However, we will take a somewhat different view on category labelling, given the canonical approach we described in Chapter 1. We will assume that the categorial labels, too, can be projected in the default case from the ontological type of the head of the semantic representation, much as proponents of prototype models of word classes argue.

In a number of frameworks it is common to identify additional roles called 'Semantic Function Roles', abbreviated here to 'SF roles' (see Spencer, 1998, 1999, 2002, 2005b, 2010a, 2010b, 2013). The SF roles are the components of argument structure whose values essentially correspond to the traditional parts of speech supplied by canonical content (Chaves, 2014). Following Spencer (1999, 2013) and a long tradition in descriptive semantics, we assume that the two major categories of noun and verb are associated with the SF roles 'R' (for Reference) and 'E' (for Eventuality), respectively. In addition, we will assume that an attributive modifier has its own SF role, represented as 'A*' (for Attribute), where the '*' indicates the property of being coindexed with the R role of a noun. This will be elaborated in Chapter 7. Additionally, we can perhaps assume a 'Relation' role, 'Rel', for prepositions.

In the defaults-based architecture we adopt, SF roles can be specified in most cases by inspection of the ontological type of the word as found in its semantic representation (the value of its SEM attribute). This can be thought of as a defaults-based interpretation of the notional theory of parts of speech discussed in Chapter 1. The idea can be implemented by assuming that a default mapping defines the SF role of a lexeme directly from its ontological category: *Thing* maps to R, *Event* maps to E, *Property* maps to A*, and *Relation* (as expressed by prepositions, semantic cases, and similar devices) maps to 'Rel'.

226 *Generalized Paradigm Function Morphology*

When we consider inter-lexemic relatedness in the GPFM model, the SYN function has to specify the syntactic category of the output. This principally means specifying the SF role. Most of the relevant morphosyntactic properties of the lexeme are projected from the SF role. For simplex categories there is thus no reason to provide any additional N, V, A, ... label. The revised lexical category descriptions for major parts of speech with their SF roles are illustrated in (23).

(23) Syntactic representation for basic parts of speech with SF roles

Noun	SF: R
simple:	$\langle x \rangle$
inalienably possessed:	$\langle x,y \rangle$
Adjective	SF: A*
intransitive:	$\langle x \rangle$
transitive:	$\langle x,y \rangle$
Verb (monotransitive)	SF: E
	$\langle x,y \rangle$
Preposition	SF: Rel
	$\langle x,y \rangle$

Mixed categories are defined as having elaborated, compound SFs. This is discussed further in Section 6.4.

6.3.4   The Default Cascade Principle

As we outlined in Section 6.2, the GPFM model takes seriously the idea that the grammatical properties of a word are defined in the default case by its basic meaning. In the GPFM model these default relationships are captured by the Default Cascade Principle (Spencer, 2013, 191–195), which essentially states that lexical properties are projected from ontological class to syntactic specifications and that these are projected to morpholexical specifications. For the Default Cascade to operate, it is important that the relevant properties be underspecified in the lexical representation. This means that the defaults can be overridden in cases of mismatch.

In cases of relatedness which do not affect the SYN attribute at all (such as most traditional cases of inflection), there is no specific statement relating to the SF role and it is therefore preserved from the base lexeme's representation by default. In contrast, canonical derivational morphology induces a complete change in a lexeme's representation, in the sense that all four attributes are non-trivially affected, but some aspects of the derived lexical representation are redundant, in that they can be projected from the derived lexeme's semantic representation. According to the Derived Lexical Entry Principle and the Default Cascade Principle, canonical derivation underspecifies the basic morphological and syntactic specification of the derived word. Thus, if the process derives, say, a noun from a verb, the FORM and SYN representations that define the base verb are despecified by the derivational process. According to the Derived Lexical Entry principle, this is a consequence of the fact that the LI is non-trivially changed. The SYN attribute is then defined by the Default Cascade Principle by projecting the syntactic category from the ontological category. For instance, the derived word of the SEM category *Thing* is realized as a noun. This in turn is realized in the FORM attribute as a member of the morphological noun class. In principle, these defaults can be overridden, but then the resulting derivation ceases to be canonical derivation and represents one of the other, intermediate, types of lexical relatedness.

There are two types of mismatch attested between the SF role and morphosyntactic properties. The first is the systematic set of mismatches found with transpositions and related types of paradigm-driven morphology (including, perhaps, some types of derivation). We will address transpositions in Section 6.4. The second are lexicalized types, a number of which are discussed in detail in Spencer (2013). Russian *stolovaja*-nouns, for instance, are nouns syntactically (Semantic Function Role R) which belong to an adjectival inflection class, while many languages have nouns which take the form of finite verbs (for instance, the 'descriptive noun' of Navajo, found also in many other unrelated indigenous American languages).

As for the mismatches between SF roles and ontological types, default mappings can be overridden either by lexical stipulation or by some kind of morpholexical rule or principle. For instance, there are a number of nouns such as *trip, party, concert, lecture* that denote events, and hence collocate with predicates and modifiers that semantically select event denotations (*The five hour concert took place last night*). To prevent such nouns being incorrectly classified as verbs by default mapping, we need to prespecify the SF role, as shown in (24).

(24) $f_{syn}(\langle \text{TRIP},\{u\}\rangle) \Rightarrow$ Semantic Function Role R

Similarly, we may wish to argue that a noun such as BEAUTY denotes a property even though it is not an adjective. In that case its lexical entry will specify the SF role R. This will mean that BEAUTY and BEAUTIFUL will have the same SEM

228   *Generalized Paradigm Function Morphology*

representation, say, $\lambda x[_{\text{Property}}$ BEAUTIFUL$(x)]$, but that BEAUTY is lexically specified as a noun. In effect, this means taking BEAUTY to be the property nominalization of BEAUTIFUL, so that BEAUTY bears the same lexical relation to BEAUTIFUL that KINDNESS bears to KIND, as shown in (25).

(25)   a very kind/beautiful person ⇔ a person of great kindness/beauty

Given our three major parts of speech, we might expect four other types of mismatch, as shown in (26).

(26)   Mapping between ontological class and SF role

    R
    Default: Thing   *tree, idea*
    Mismatch: Event   *trip*
    Mismatch: Property   *beauty, sloth, pride*

    E
    Default: Event(uality)   *run, hit, give*
    Mismatch: Thing   ⟨absent in English?⟩ Navajo 'descrip-
                             tive nouns', etc.
    Mismatch: Property   *shine, exceed, excel, suffice, belet'*
                             (Russian 'to be/appear white')

    A
    Default: Property   *tall, proud, difficult*
    Mismatch: Event   *current* (the current situation)
    Mismatch: Thing   *the poor, the injured, red* ('there's too
                          much red in this wallpaper')

It is not difficult to find apparent instances of these mismatches in English, but the great majority of them seem to involve derivational morphology (including conversion) from a lexeme of the default category. Thus, a verb such as TO HAMMER is not an instance of a *Thing* word prespecified as [Semantic Function Role E]. Rather, it is the result of a widespread process of denominal verb formation from the pre-existing noun. This process changes the SEM representation (to something like 'act on some object O_1 with an object O_2 in a manner similar to that in which one would act on O_1 with a hammer'), which also changes its ontological category. What we need to find is a basic, simplex (underived) verb with something like the meaning 'to be a NOUN', in the absence of a lexeme NOUN which would serve as the derivational base for the verb lexeme. It is not easy to find such examples.

Likewise, it is hard to find instances of a *Property* word being realized as a verb in English (though in languages which have only a weakly distinguished category of adjective, or no such category in the first place, it is normal of course for property concepts to be expressed by words which are grammatically stative verbs). Possible examples of such property-verb mismatches would be verbs such as SHINE, GLEAM, GLISTEN, which arguably denote (physical) properties of their subjects, but which do not seem to be derived from basic adjectives (unless, perhaps, we were to say that SHINE derives from SHINY, rather than the other way around).[6]

We saw in Chapter 1 that the category of adjective is less well attested cross-linguistically, and it seems clear that there are some languages which lack it altogether. It should not be surprising, therefore, that, cross-linguistically, it is difficult to find examples of *Thing* or *Event* words being realized as adjectives. Again, it is not difficult to find, say, adjectives which have been converted from *Thing* words (for instance, a number of colour terms such as ORANGE); the task is to find a word which is ontologically a *Thing* but which is only used in the language as an adjective, and such examples are rather elusive. The same is true of adjectives derived from *Event* words. It is rather difficult to imagine the adjectival equivalent of *trip*-words.

Despite the mismatches, using only a very crude characterization of a lexeme's ontological type a good deal of lexical information can generally be predicted. Indeed, all in all it turns out to be quite difficult to find genuine mismatches between the ontological category and the grammatical category of simplex words. This conclusion complements the observation that the semantic array of arguments/participants associated with a predicate is, by default, associated with specific syntactically defined argument structure types. On a more general note, the approach to word categorization introduced in this section owes a great deal to work based on the notion of prototypes found in the typological literature (see Chapter 1). However, we do not use the notion of prototype. Instead, we would argue that the key notion here is that of 'Morpholexical Coherent Lexical Entry' (Spencer, 2005b), a notion which belongs rather to the framework of Canonical Typology (see the contributions to Brown et al. (2012a) and for an overview, see Bond, 2019). Space does not permit us to expand on this point here, however (see Nikolaeva and

---

[6] Another candidate might be the verb REJOICE, related to JOYFUL.

230   *Generalized Paradigm Function Morphology*

Spencer (2012) for some preliminary discussion in the context of possessive constructions).

6.4   Transpositions in GPFM: The Feature [REPRESENTATION]

A central feature of the canonical approach to lexical representations is that in practice lexical representations are very frequently 'mixed', in the sense of deviating from the canonical ensemble of properties found with canonical nouns, verbs, and adjectives. In Chapter 1 we distinguished the notions of syntagmatic and paradigmatic categorial mixing. Much of the interest of the noun–adjective hybrids we are concerned with in this book lies in their syntagmatic properties, but before we address that issue in Chapter 7 it is necessary to summarize briefly what types of paradigmatic mixing we find. The most important paradigmatically mixed category (which in practice also exhibits syntagmatic mixing) is the transposition.

From the relatively little literature devoted to the morphosyntax of transpositions it is clear that, in general, a transposition is marked in part by the acquisition of the output category's features and simultaneously, but independently, by the loss of the input category's features. As mentioned in Chapter 1, this is evident from Malchukov's (2004, 2006) cross-linguistic surveys of deverbal nominalizations. These surveys confirmed that input/output features are respectively lost/gained in broad conformity with Bybee's (1985) Relevance Hierarchy, though it does not seem to be possible to advance any entirely robust implicational universals. For this reason we will content ourselves with a minimally restrictive characterization of the morphosyntactic consequences of transposition until more detailed typological work enables us to draw firmer conclusions.

Transpositions pose particular problems for models of lexical relatedness and morphosyntax because they share some of the properties of inflection and some of the properties of derivation. One important, but underappreciated, problem for morphology is that, in inflecting languages, the transposition belongs to the same paradigm as the basic lexeme, and yet it inflects like a member of a different lexical class. Spencer (2017b), discussing the participle system in Russian, refers to this as the 'paradigm-within-a-paradigm problem' (we could also call it the 'lexeme-within-a-lexeme' problem). Thus, Russian participles are verb forms which modify a head noun in the manner of an attributive adjective and which inflect for agreement ('CONCORD') properties (number, gender, case of the noun modified) exactly like adjectives.

6.4 Transpositions in GPFM: The Feature [REPRESENTATION]   231

Another important point apparent from even a cursory look at transpositions in general is that we cannot expect a transposition to inherit all of an output category's properties. In some cases it is easy to identify independent (i.e. semantic) reasons for this. Thus, participles do not typically derive from predicates which denote gradable property concepts, so we do not expect them to take degree modifiers or to appear in comparative/superlative forms. But on the other hand, it is not uncommon to find a language that permits nouns or adjectives to appear in predicative forms which only inflect for a subset of the output verbal properties, often excluding TAM inflections, for instance. This is true of the Chukotkan languages (Chukchi, Dunn (1999), Koryak, Žukova (1972), Alutor, Kibrik et al. (2004)), and also of Kolyma Yukaghir (Maslova, 2003). In those languages, the only way to express the full set of verbal categories with a predicative nominal is to use a distinct copular construction (effectively a periphrastic transposition). By contrast, a number of Samoyedic languages, notably Tundra Nenets, permit a variety of verbal categories to be expressed on a predicative noun, including tense and evidentiality.

Spencer (1999) develops a descriptive framework for handling non-canonical categories by proposing a simple calculus for describing transpositions in terms of SF roles. A virtue of the notation of SF roles is that it provides a transparent representation of categorial mixing. Transpositions result from an enrichment of the SF role array. A transposition differs from a simplex category in that it has a compound SF role, in which the SF role of the derived category is added to that of the base. Thus, if the ARG-ST structure representation of a typical verb is $\langle E\langle x, \ldots \rangle\rangle$, where '$\langle x, \ldots \rangle$' is a string of thematic arguments, then an action nominal will have a compound SF role giving the ARG-ST representation $\langle R \langle E\langle x, \ldots \rangle\rangle\rangle$, and a participle will have a complex SF role giving $\langle A\langle E\langle x, \ldots \rangle\rangle\rangle$.

As mentioned in Chapter 4, the directionality of transpositions is asymmetrical. The useful distinction drawn by Haspelmath (1996) between 'external' and 'internal' syntax requires us to be able to distinguish 'embedded' SF roles from the 'outer' SF role. The outer role determines external syntax and the inner, embedded role distinguishes internal syntax. In order to reflect the nature of syntagmatic mixing, the transposition must guarantee that it is the highest, 'outermost', SF which determines the external syntax of the transposition. Otherwise, it will not be possible to distinguish between, say, a relational adjective (noun-to-adjective transposition) and a property nominalization (adjective-to-noun transposition). The most straightforward way to achieve this is to assume that it is the outer role which determines

232　*Generalized Paradigm Function Morphology*

the principal morphosyntactic properties of a word by default, and that the preserved properties are stipulated.

Consider a language in which verb phrases are regularly used as attributive modifiers, headed by participial forms of the verb, corresponding roughly to English expressions such as *a falling tree, the girl quietly singing a song, a present given to the children by Grandmother*. A deverbal participle is formed by adding the A* role to the argument structure representation of the original verb, but retaining the E role. That E role is then able to license, on a language-by-language basis, various aspects of the original verb morphosyntax. For instance, the participle may express voice, aspect, or tense information. We therefore obtain representations along the lines of those shown in (27).

(27)　verb-to-adjective transpositions

    a.　*a falling tree*

       $\text{fall}\langle A^*_x \langle E \langle x \rangle \rangle \rangle \text{ tree}\langle R^* \rangle$

    b.　*the girl quietly singing a song*

       $[\text{sing}\langle A^*_x \langle E \langle x \langle y \rangle \rangle \rangle \rangle \wedge \text{quietly}(E) \wedge \text{song}\langle R_y \rangle] \text{ girl}\langle R^* \rangle$

    c.　*a present given to the children by Grandmother*

       $[\text{give}\langle A^*_y \langle E(x) \langle \langle y \langle z \rangle \rangle \rangle \rangle \rangle \wedge \text{children}\langle R_y \rangle \wedge \text{Grandmother}\langle R_x \rangle]$
       $\text{present}\langle R^* \rangle$

The examples in (27) include additional participants whose exact representation we leave inexplicit. The idea is straightforward, however. Thus, in (27c) we have a passive participle, indicated by suppression of the subject role 'x', shown in parentheses. This leaves the direct object role 'y' as the highest argument and it is this to which the A* SF role is linked. The A* role is coindexed with the R role of *present*. This effectively identifies *present* as the direct object ('y' argument) of the predicate *give*. The additional arguments in the participial phrase express the 'z' indirect object argument and the suppressed subject argument respectively. It is a parochial fact about English that the A* role can be overlaid onto an eventive predicate which has the form of a passive. It is also a parochial fact about English that mood and tense information are lacking in the participles.

There is an important sense in which this notation allows us to sidestep the tricky question of exactly which part of speech a participle belongs to. In some respects it is an attributive adjective while in other respects it remains a verb (expressing verbal arguments and being modified by eventive adverbials, for instance). Given that we have a clear description of this categorial mixing in the

6.4 Transpositions in GPFM: The Feature [REPRESENTATION] 233

SF role array, there is no need to worry about whether to label such a category as 'V' or 'A', or as something else, in phrase structure representations. Indeed, provided that phrase structure has access to the SF role array terminals there is no need to provide any categorial label whatsoever.

The proposals in Spencer (1999) are very programmatic in the sense that they do not address the paradigm-within-a-paradigm problem. This is touched on, but not resolved, in Spencer (2013), where it is proposed that transpositions can be defined in terms of a Head inflectional feature [REPRESENTATION], following the terminology of Smirnickij (1959) and adopted also by Haspelmath (1996). This proposal is taken up in detail in Spencer (2017b).

Let us assume that the grammar includes a feature [REPRESENTA-TION:{no, yes:$\langle\langle K,\Lambda\rangle,\sigma\rangle$}] (abbreviated [REPR:{no, yes:$\langle\langle K,\Lambda\rangle,\sigma\rangle$}]). The feature has the value 'no' when the basic form of a lexeme is inflected. The 'yes' value is itself a set-valued attribute, taking a specification of the input/output categories, together with a specification, σ, of any other construction-specific properties. For simplicity of exposition we will take a specification [REPR:no] as read, so that failure to mark the REPR feature for a given lexeme will be taken to mean 'basic category' for those lexemes whose MORSIG specifies a positive value of the REPR feature. We will therefore adopt the notational convention that [REPR:$\langle\langle K,\Lambda\rangle,\sigma\rangle$] is equivalent to [REPR: yes:$\langle\langle K,\Lambda\rangle,\sigma\rangle$]. We return directly to the question of what we mean by 'category K, Λ' in this connection. The term σ is a feature set defining further properties of the transposition. For example, Latin participles fall into distinct declension classes: the passive participle belongs to Declension 1/2, while the present active participle falls into Declension 3. Where such details are irrelevant we will omit them and refer only to the feature [REPR:$\langle K,\Lambda\rangle$].[7]

We must also take into account the fact that in any transposition the derived, mixed, category may share some of its morphosyntax with the base category, K, (for instance, Verb) and some of its morphosyntax with the derived category, Λ, (for instance, Adjective). We must therefore ensure that our descriptive apparatus is able to make the relevant distinctions in a coherent fashion.

For standard cases of transposition the salient fact is that the transposed output is inflected as a different part of speech from the base lexeme, so that a participle is inflected as an adjective, not as a verb. This means that part of the paradigm of a verb inherits some of its inflectional properties,

---

[7] Another way of encoding these distinctions would be to set up a privative feature [REPR:$\langle\langle K,\Lambda\rangle,\sigma\rangle$], which applies only when a transposition is defined. We will assume nothing hinges on these implementational decisions.

234   *Generalized Paradigm Function Morphology*

i.e. its MORSIG, from the adjective category. In Spencer's (2017b) treatment of Russian participles the feature specification [REPR:⟨⟨V,A⟩,σ⟩] defines the compound SF role which characterizes participles ⟨A*ᵢ⟨E⟨xᵢ, …⟩⟩⟩ over the lexemic representation of the verb. (For verbs with the default semantics of an event, this function specifies an otherwise underspecified SF role value. For verbs with non-default semantics, such as BELET′ 'to be white', it overrides the lexical SF role specification.) The principles of default specification for lexical representations (the Default Cascade) then specify the MORSIG of the participle as that of an adjective, though with certain verb properties, voice and aspect, as enumerated in the σ feature set. The function defining the participle also preserves the base verb's thematic argument structure, selection properties, quirky case marking where appropriate, and so on.

The participle function specifies the adjectival properties for which the participle inflects – in Russian, the concordial properties of gender, number, and case. However, it leaves the attributes themselves underspecified: CONCORD:{[GENDER:u], [NUMBER:u], [CASE:u],}. The entry for a participle therefore looks exactly like that of a yet-to-be inflected adjective. This underspecified representation is the 'paradigm-within-a-paradigm' or 'lexeme-within-a-lexeme'.

6.5   Excursus: Comparison with Network Morphology

Brown and Hippisley (2012, Ch 7) also extend the proposals of Stump (2001) but within the somewhat different architecture of Network Morphology. In large part the aims of Network Morphology are the same as those of Stump's PFM and its extension GPFM.

In Network Morphology lexical relatedness is coded in terms of default inheritance hierarchies implemented in the programming language DATR. These hierarchies play the same role as the Paradigm Function in PFM. For instance, in PFM we would capture English regular plural formation by stating that, by default, if X is the root form of a noun lexeme, then the plural is defined by the function $PF(X,\{plural\}) = Xz$. In Network Morphology we set up a word structure hierarchy whose root is W (for morphological word) and which has various dependents, including the node N for nouns. Individual noun lexemes are dependents of the N node. A noun such as TABLE includes a piece of information in its lexical entry represented in Network Morphology as shown in (28).

(28)   ⟨⟩ = = NOUN

6.5 Excursus: Comparison with Network Morphology   235

This equation states that the lexical entry concerned inherits by default all its grammatical information from the node NOUN. That node will include the information that there is a plural form and that that form consists of whatever the lexeme's root is, concatenated with the /z/ suffix.

Both Network Morphology and GPFM define (canonical) derivation by adopting a default inheritance version of Aronoff's (1976) conception of word formation rules (WFRs). Aronoff proposed that a WFR such as that which derives DRIVER from DRIVE is essentially a mapping which defines a new form (by affixation) and a new meaning, by addition of a semantic predicate. The Aronovian WFR can be treated as a generalization of the realization rules which define the Paradigm Function for inflection.

Brown and Hippisley illustrate their basic approach to derivation by considering the Russian words for *to read* and its derivate *reader*, though the essentials can be illustrated by considering our earlier English example of DRIVER derived from DRIVE.

In their Network Morphology account, a derived word inherits certain properties from the base and overrides others (Brown and Hippisley, 2012, 253). This is coded in terms of the lexeme-formation template (LFT), corresponding to a WFR. The set of LFTs defines another hierarchy which is distinct from both the inflectional hierarchy and the lexeme hierarchy. Derived lexemes can inherit orthogonally from the LFT hierarchy, as well as from other members of the lexeme hierarchy. Where the LFT defines most of the properties of the derived word we have canonical derivation, and deviations from canonicity will therefore be found where some of the properties of the derived word are inherited from the base lexeme. Thus, we can assume a LFT as shown informally in (29a) and slightly more formally in (29b) (modelled on the corresponding formation for Russian in Brown and Hippisley (2012, 255, 256)).

(29)   Schematic LFT for -er Subject Nominals

    a. WFR_ER:
        FORM [base stem]-er
        SYN Noun (i.e. $\langle R \rangle$)
        SEM 'person who [SEM(BASE)]'

    b. WFR_ER:
        $\langle \rangle$ == NOUN
        $\langle$gloss$\rangle$ == $\lambda x[\text{PERSON}(x) \wedge \text{"[SEM(BASE)}(x)]\text{"}]$
        $\langle$stem$\rangle$ == "$\langle$STEM0(BASE)$\rangle$" er$\rangle$

236   *Generalized Paradigm Function Morphology*

Derived *-er* Subject Nominals such as DRIVER will now inherit most of their content from the node WFR_ER as in (29b), and will supply the base form and the base meaning from an appropriate node in the lexeme hierarchy (in this case from the node DRIVE defining the lexeme DRIVE). In effect, this is a Network Morphology instantiation of Stump's (2001, 257) notion of derivational paradigm.

It is beyond the scope of this study to examine Network Morphology in detail. Thus far, Network Morphology and PFM (in its generalized form, GPFM) operate in parallel, with interchangeable implementation. However, it should be emphasized that there are also important differences between the specific proposals of Brown and Hippisley and the GPFM model.

Brown and Hippisley provide a brief survey of certain types of non-canonical derivation, namely what they call conversion, transposition, and category-preserving derivation. The first of the non-canonical types they discuss is (traditional) conversion, as illustrated by pairs such as *(a) hammer ~ to hammer*. Now, conversion is essentially standard derivation but without any overt morphological marker of the derived derivational category. Rather, the base of the derived lexeme is identified with that of the base lexeme.

Category-preserving derivation is illustrated by the Russian diminutive formation. The Network Morphology account is broadly congruent with the GPFM account of similar facts provided in Spencer (2013, 265–270). However, Spencer argues that expressive morphology gives rise to two types of output: in many cases the expressive derivation is a novel lexeme, often with idiosyncratic semantics (and hence not fully paradigmatic). This type is just a variant on idiosyncratic derivation generally. The more interesting type is paradigmatic, but it does not define a novel lexeme; rather, it serves as an instance of meaning-bearing morphology which is realized by a change in form, but not a change in syntactic representation – an instance of Type B2 relatedness as described in Chapter 5. On Brown and Hippisley's model all evaluative morphology seems to be handled by orthogonal inheritance from the lexeme hierarchy, which means that the diminutive form of a word has to be treated as an independent lexeme (rather than the diminutive form of a base lexeme). It is not clear how the Network Morphology account would capture the idea that this type of evaluative morphology is effectively a non-canonical, meaning-bearing inflection and not derivation.

A similar problem in a more serious form is seen in Brown and Hippisley's account of transpositions. They note that a transposition involves a change in the morphological form and syntactic category of the base without the addition of a semantic predicate, but they still treat transpositions as a kind

6.5 Excursus: Comparison with Network Morphology   237

of derivation. However, as argued extensively in Spencer (2013), there are several sorts of transposition. The standard (one might say canonical) type of transposed lexical entry inherits its semantic content and also its Lexemic Index from its base, and thus is closer in kind to inflection than derivation. We will see later in Chapter 8 that there are transpositions that share most of the properties of inflection but which add a semantic predicate to the lexical representation. On the other hand, in languages like English and Russian there are transposition-like derivations illustrated by relational adjectives. In contradistinction to a number of languages, these relational adjectives behave like autonomous lexemes and not like forms of the base noun lexeme in any way. The differences are particularly visible when we consider the phenomenon of syntagmatic category mixing in Chapter 8. They are easily accounted for if we distinguish true transpositions from transpositional lexemes, the novel type of lexical relatedness between two distinct lexemes, in which a derived lexeme is morphologically marked and syntactically distinct from its base, but its SEM value is non-distinct from that of the base lexeme (see Chapter 5, Section 5.2.1 and Chapter 8 for further discussion).

The crucial property of the Network Morphology architecture which gives rise to the problems with evaluative morphology, just noted transpositions, and other types of categorial mixture just noted is that there is no obvious way of distinguishing the notion of 'two distinct lexemes' from 'two forms of a lexeme'. Now, it may be that this distinction is illusory, but in that case it is hard to see how the network of lexical relations could make the kinds of distinctions that are explored in detail in Spencer (2013) and which rely crucially on the notion of 'distinct lexeme' vs. 'form of lexeme'.

Note also that Brown and Hippisley (2012, 261) explicitly limit the range of non-canonical types of lexical relatedness by assuming a biconditional implication: the syntactic category must be defined either by the base lexeme's lexical representation or by the LFT (word formation rule), but not both. This makes sense when syntactic categories are defined as privative (unary) features, as implied by labels like 'NOUN' and 'VERB'. However, this is not necessarily the case for models of syntax in which categories are fractionated into features such as [±N, ±V], and it is certainly not the case in the model of GPFM, in which the syntactic category of a word might be a complex object resulting from a combination of SF roles, as described above.

Despite a number of important differences in implementation, the Network Morphology approach to derivation and similar types of lexical relatedness is closely allied to the GPFM model. This is to be expected, since GPFM arises from Stump's PFM model, and PFM and Network Morphology have been

238   *Generalized Paradigm Function Morphology*

developed in close conjunction with each other. Moreover, we would anticipate that our proposals here (and likewise the proposals of Spencer, 2013) could in principle be coded using the formalism of Network Morphology. However, to do that it would be necessary to introduce the notion of Lexemic Index into the DATR-encoded Network Morphology formalism. We leave that possibility for future research.

6.6   Conclusions

In this chapter we have presented a model of lexical relatedness in which a central role belongs to the Generalized Paradigm Function (Spencer, 2013), a development of the notion of Paradigm Function (Stump, 2001), but extended to cover all four of the principal attributes of a lexical representation and not just the FORM attribute. We discussed how the model handles both canonical cases of relatedness and various kinds of mismatches. Mismatches are particularly obvious in the case of transpositions, which account for a good many of our noun–adjective hybrids.

Given our background discussion, we were in a position to capture the idea that transpositions, such as (true) participles are the adjectival 'representation' of the base verb lexeme and not distinct lexemes/dictionary entries in their own right. Treating transpositions as part of the base lexeme's paradigm, however, raises an important question, the 'paradigm-within-a-paradigm' or 'lexeme-within-a-lexeme' problem: how can we account for the fact that a verb has word forms in its paradigm which inflect exactly like adjectives? We have followed Spencer's (2017b) analysis of Russian participles in introducing the feature REPRESENTATION. This triggers a set of default procedures under which the Morphological Signature of the representation of the transpositional forms is enriched and modified so as to reflect the newly acquired adjectival features along with any features of the base lexeme that are inherited by the transposition. These include, for instance, verbal aspect in the case of Russian participles and, as we will see in the case of Selkup relational adjectives, possessor agreement.

This model will be elaborated in Chapter 8, where we will show that this treatment of lexical representation and the lexical relatedness between transpositions and the base lexeme's forms permits a principled way of handling many types of the noun–adjective hybrids. But before we do this, in Chapter 7 we will sketch an initial model of modification, since we need to tie our lexical representation to syntactic construction types, and the concept of attributive modification is central to such an analysis.

7 Attributive Modification in Lexicalist Morphosyntax

7.1 Introduction

In Chapter 2 we looked briefly at the way that we can express the basic adnominal modification relation using very simplified semantic representations. Our discussion provided a generic semantic sketch of a kind which is neutral with respect to syntactic model. However, in order to explore the complexities of the mixed category constructions that we have already described, we will need to be more explicit about syntactic organization. For this reason, in this chapter we will outline an informal syntactic implementation of our ideas broadly within the HPSG framework (enriched with certain elements from LFG, as well as some of the Construction Grammar theoretic devices of SBCG).

Section 7.2 summarizes existing assumptions on nominal phrase structure based primarily on the HPSG literature. In Section 7.3 we will return to the GPFM model of Spencer (2013) and sketch the way in which the representations developed in Chapters 5 and 6 can be coded in HPSG in such a way as to permit us to investigate the syntactic behaviour of noun modifiers. We should stress, though, that the purpose of our implementation is not to argue for a specific HPSG (or SBCG) analysis of attributive modification (though our suggestions may well be of value in such discussions). Rather, we aim to provide a model for relating our lexical representations to a syntactic representation which is explicit enough to allow us to convey the salient problems posed by categorial mixing. Section 7.4 discusses our approach to the syntax of the $\mathcal{R}$ relation that is crucially involved in many modification-by-nominal-concept constructions.

7.2 Nominal Syntax

Before we present our own approach to nominal syntax, we first have to decide whether to adopt an analysis under which the noun is the head of the nominal phrase or the determiner (or, indeed, some other functional element). We will briefly survey these alternatives and then discuss how attributive modification is represented in HPSG.

7.2.1 Approaches to Nominal Phrase Structure

The typical nominal phrase is based on a lexical noun modified by various elements. After the appearance of Chomsky (1970) it became customary within most formal models of syntax to adopt the 'X-bar' schema for phrasal categories. The simplest form of this schema is shown in (1).

(1)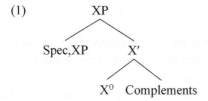

If X=Noun, then the simplest way of representing a nominal phrase will be as shown in (2).

(2)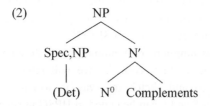

The complements to a noun will normally be arguments, but only if the noun has a non-trivial argument structure. This is true of deverbal nominalizations, a category that has been intensively studied from this point of view: see the examples in (3).

(3)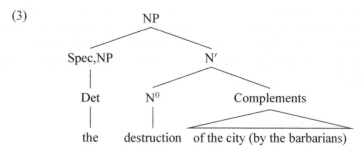

From our perspective a more interesting case is that of the relational noun, such as *daughter-of* or *corner-of*, as shown in (4).

(4)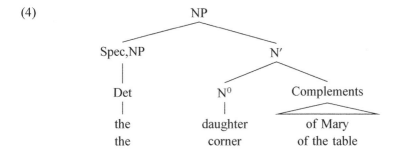

We could analyse 'semantic' arguments that are implicit in the meaning of the noun, but which do not have the status of fully fledged arguments, in the same way, as shown in (5).

(5)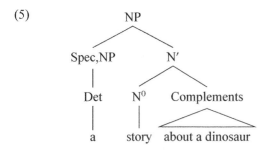

By extending the notion of 'complement' somewhat, we might also propose representations such as those in (6).

(6)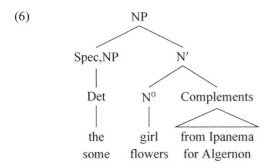

A number of proposals exist in the literature for describing nominal phrases using this basic X-bar schema, starting with Jackendoff (1977).

A different approach to the structure of nominal phrases is the DP hypothesis. Since Chomsky (1986), it has been common in Mainstream

242   *Attributive Modification in Lexicalist Morphosyntax*

Generative Grammar to assume that the most important heads in syntactic structure are functional heads (including inflections) and that phrases headed by lexical items are complements to those heads. Thus, clausal structure is built around a sequence of heads representing clause-level properties (whose names are typically written with initial capitals). Originally, these properties were Infl(ection) (I) and the Complementizer (C), the functional head of the clause itself – an important category in this framework, though one with unclear semantic import. Later, these heads became split into more specific types such as tense, mood, aspect, and even relational categories realizing contextual inflection such as the clause-level agreement properties of AgrS (subject agreement) and AgrO (object agreement). In addition, the set of functional heads was enriched with various discourse properties such as Topic and Focus (the so-called 'split-CP hypothesis'; see Rizzi, 1997).

In parallel, the DP hypothesis is based on the idea that nominal phrases are projections of functional heads and that lexical items, such as nouns and their immediate projections, are merely complements to those functional heads. In particular, it has been claimed that nominal phrases are built around the functional properties of Number (Num), Case (K), and various (in)definiteness features (D), as well as properties such as Possession (Poss). The DP hypothesis further postulates that nominal phrases are headed by the D head as opposed to a noun. According to one view, DP is a universal projection regardless of the presence/absence of overt articles in a language, but in languages that lack articles the D head is not pronounced (e.g. Progovac, 1998; Pereltsvaig, 2007). Others have claimed that languages differ in whether they instantiate the DP structure (e.g. Baker, 2003; Bošković, 2008; Despić, 2013).

Some authors within Mainstream Generative Grammar have argued for a complete parallelism between clause (CP) structure and nominal phrase (DP) structure. Szabolcsi (1987, 171), for instance, proposes the structure shown in Figure 7.1 for the Hungarian nominal phrase *(az) a Péter minden kalapja* 'every one of Peter's hats' (see also Szabolcsi, 1994; Zimmermann, 1993; Alexiadou et al., 2007, 136), in which the possessor is effectively treated as the 'subject'. Here 'IN' corresponds to the 'Infl' (I) node and 'CN' corresponds to the 'C' node. Some authors, including Alexiadou et al. (2007, 130ff), Giusti (2008), Lecarme (2008), and Haegeman (2010), detail further studies which extend the parallelism between clause structure and nominal structure.

For our purposes, however, it is very difficult to evaluate these proposals. The conception of clause structure differs from author to author and changes somewhat drastically within a short space of time. It is therefore all but

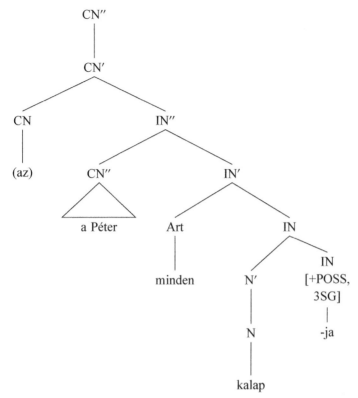

Figure 7.1 *Szabolcsi's analysis of the Hungarian nominal phrase*

impossible to ascertain a typical or generic analysis within this kind of framework, even for well-studied languages such as English or Romance languages. For the languages which we focus on, which have a much poorer descriptive history, this makes it well-nigh impossible to establish any kind of correspondence or correlation to the kinds of structures illustrated in Figure 7.1. It is noteworthy that the most exhaustive, theoretically informed descriptive grammar of English to date, Huddleston and Pullum (2002), explicitly rejects the DP analysis even for English.

Moreover, we have yet to see any strong independent motivation for the collection of assumptions that motivate the cartographic family of approaches to syntactic structure (for further discussion of this point see Ackerman and Nikolaeva, 2013, Ch 1). On the contrary, we find it convenient, both descriptively and theoretically, to factorize questions of constituency (where they can be identified), linear order, logical scope, grammatical function, and

244 *Attributive Modification in Lexicalist Morphosyntax*

semantic contribution just as is done in lexicalist or constraint-based models such as LFG, HPSG, or Construction Grammar. We will therefore leave to one side further consideration of the Mainstream Generative Grammar approaches to nominal syntax and opt for a somewhat traditional view on nominal phrase structure, similar in many respects to that adopted in Huddleston and Pullum (2002) for English, but applied cross-linguistically. For the sake of convenience we will refer to nominal phrases as 'NP' where we are considering the structure and role of attributive modifiers. As far as we can tell, nothing in our exposition hinges on adopting an NP analysis as opposed to the DP analysis of Mainstream Generative Grammar, LFG, and other frameworks. However, we regard the analysis of nominal phrases in which the nominal syntagma is a projection of a lexical head, NP, and the determiner system is the specifier of the NP, as the simplest. Where we wish to compare and contrast attributive modification with possessive constructions, the DP analysis raises descriptive barriers that we do not necessarily encounter with the NP analysis.

This is essentially the solution adopted by HPSG. In our analysis of noun–adjective hybrids in Chapter 8 we will also in part rely on the HPSG-style approach to attributive modification, which we discuss in the next sections in more detail.

7.2.2   *Attributive Modification in HPSG*

An interesting question arises at this point: how is attributive modification represented? There is rather little explicit discussion of how to represent attributive modification of a noun by an adjective or similar category. While there is a fair deal of discussion of the semantics of attributive modification (see the references cited in Chapter 2), in Mainstream Generative Grammar most work on syntax concentrates on the placement of different types of adjectives within the nominal phrase (Alexiadou et al., 2007; Cinque, 2010; Cabredo Hofherr and Matushansky, 2010, among others). In lexicalist theories the morphosyntactic aspects tend to be handled in a somewhat superficial manner, say by assuming an attribute such as MOD(ifier) (in HPSG) or ADJUNCT (in LFG) and linking these features to some standard set-theoretic interpretation of adjectives as predicates.

In earlier versions of HPSG (Pollard and Sag, 1994) attributive modification of a head noun is mediated through a MOD attribute. This attribute is a value of the VAL(ENCE) feature, along with other categories that (loosely speaking) define combinatorial properties of heads, namely a set of specifiers (SPR) and complements (COMPS) governing which words and phrases a

7.2 *Nominal Syntax* 245

head combines with. In the standard HPSG models this attribute is to be distinguished from the closely related ARG-ST, attribute which provides a listing of the arguments a given lexeme can potentially combine with. It is not obvious what the implicational relation should be between the SYN, VAL, and ARG-ST attributes. On the one hand, one could imagine that VAL would be a value of ARG-ST, which itself is a value of the SYN|HEAD attribute. On the other hand, Sag et al. (2003, 205) treat ARG-ST as distinct from the SYN attribute, and we will follow that lead.

The MOD attribute permits us to describe the modification of any category by any other category in principle (Pollard and Sag, 1994). It takes as its value a (possibly) empty list with at most one member, specifying the type of phrase modified by that expression. Thus, for adjectives we have the AVM [MOD ⟨NP⟩]. This MOD attribute will be shared by any word or phrase that can serve as an attributive modifier, including clauses (such as finite relative clauses), clause-like participial modifiers, and PP modifiers.

A particularly clear instance of the application of MOD is seen in Sag et al.'s (2003) very detailed and explicit introduction to the HPSG account of English. They propose a Head-Modifier Rule (Sag et al., 2003, 145, 146) whose 'near final' version is shown in (7).

(7) Head-Modifier Rule (after (Sag et al., 2003, 146, ex. (29)))

$$[\textit{phrase}] \quad \rightarrow \quad H\,\boxed{1}\left[\text{VAL}\left[\text{COMPS}\,\langle\,\rangle\right]\right]\quad\left[\text{VAL}\begin{bmatrix}\text{COMPS}\,\langle\,\rangle\\\text{MOD}\,\langle\,\boxed{1}\,\rangle\end{bmatrix}\right]$$

This rule permits a head H to be followed by a word/phrase with the attribute VAL|MOD ⟨ $\boxed{1}$ ⟩ tagging the head word which it modifies. The modification property is inherited by the mother of the head daughter by virtue of the Head Feature Principle.

This version is 'near-final' in that it does not account for *tough*-adjective constructions (*This book seems easy to read*). For this class of adjectives Sag et al. (2003, 441) introduce a variant of the GAP attribute used for handling long-distance dependencies (such as those found in relative clauses). However, it is also non-final in that it fails to license prenominal adjectives.[1] Similarly, a German-language introduction to HPSG by Müller (2007) contains very little about attributive modifiers, even though their syntax in German is in some ways

[1] The matter is addressed in their Chapter Five, Problem 1 (p. 161, with additional discussion in Chapter Eight, Problem 2, pp. 265–266), where the reader is encouraged to postulate a binary feature [POST-HEAD{+,−}] to distinguish the two positions.

246 *Attributive Modification in Lexicalist Morphosyntax*

richer than that in English. Müller (2007, 75) defines a Head-Adjunct Structure, as shown in (8).

(8) Müller's Head-Adjunct Structure

$$\begin{bmatrix} \text{HEAD-DTR} & \boxed{1} \\ \\ \text{NON-HEAD-DTRS} & \left\langle \begin{bmatrix} \text{CAT} \begin{bmatrix} \text{HEAD}\,|\,\text{MOD} & \boxed{1} \\ \text{SUBCAT} & \langle\rangle \end{bmatrix} \end{bmatrix} \right\rangle \end{bmatrix}$$

The main point of Müller's (2007, 75) discussion is to establish that PPs inherit the HEAD|MOD N′ property from the P's lexical entry, so that *in der Speisekammer* ('in the larder') can modify *(die) Wurst* ('(the) sausage') but *in* 'in' on its own cannot (**die Wurst in* 'the sausage in'). The representation for 'in the larder' is shown in (9).

(9)

$$\begin{bmatrix} \text{PHON} & \langle \textit{in the larder} \rangle \\ \\ \text{CAT} & \begin{bmatrix} \text{HEAD} & \begin{bmatrix} \text{MOD N}' \\ \textit{Prep} \end{bmatrix} \\ \\ \text{SUBCAT} & \langle\rangle \end{bmatrix} \end{bmatrix}$$

This representation seems to suggest that adpositionals always have the function of modifying N′, so we have to assume a construction or lexical rule which adds the MOD attribute to the VAL attribute of any adpositional that can head a PP modifying a noun. In other words, while Sag et al. (2003) represent the MOD feature as a value of the HEAD attribute, Müller takes it to be a value of the VALENCE attribute.

In sum, there is as yet no full consensus in the literature as how best to describe attributive modification in the HPSG/SBCG framework. However, the general picture is clear: attributive modifiers, whether lexically adjectives or some other part of speech, have a MOD feature in their syntactic array. This feature is defined in such a way as to constrain the attributive modifier to combine with a noun. In the case of simple modifiers with intersective semantics, the meaning of the combination is simply the unification of the meanings of the components. For an adjective, this means that the lexical meaning can be represented as including a place holder for the modified noun. If we say that the variable P ranges over noun properties, then the meaning of an adjective whose lexical content is $\lambda x.\textbf{adjective}(x)$ will be the standard $\lambda x \lambda P[\textbf{adjective}(x) \wedge P(x)]$.

7.3 A Model of Attributive Modification

In this section we show how the framework sketched in Chapter 6 can be implemented in our version of HPSG/SBCG. The GPFM model of lexical relatedness makes a number of assumptions which differ from the standard assumptions normally found in the HPSG literature. In particular, an important difference between GPFM and HPSG (or LFG, or standard versions of Mainstream Generative Grammar) is found in the treatment of major lexical categories. However, we believe that the commonalities between GPFM and HPSG are sufficient to allow us to deploy HPSG techniques to advantage.

7.3.1 The A* Semantic Function Role

To a large extent the semantics of attributive modification is orthogonal to our concerns in this book. However, it will be essential to be as explicit as possible about the way we represent the idea of an attribute modifying a noun. This is because the attributes and nouns we have been discussing do in many cases have non-canonical properties, and in particular they exhibit mixing of part of speech properties.

We will first need to consider two crucial properties of (canonical) nouns and adjectives. We mentioned in earlier chapters that a noun is a predicate that serves to pick out individuals or sets of individuals corresponding to the ontological class of *Thing*. Syntactically, this means that a (common) noun in many languages has to be associated with a specifier of some kind, SP[...], serving to ensure that the phrase which the noun heads is (or can be) referential. Adjectives lack such a specifier but are canonically associated with a specifier-like functional category which we can call Degree (DEG[...]).

The leading idea of the present analysis derives from the common assumption (summarized in Chapter 2, Section 2.2) that the canonical function for an adjective is that of an attributive modifier expressing a property. As mentioned in Chapter 6, a key feature of this analysis is the A* SF role, since its function is to mediate attributive modification. Thus, the lexemes which bear this role are the canonical attributive modifiers: adjectives. Given the additional attribute of the SF role, attributive modification can be notated by coindexing the A* role with the R role of the modified noun, as shown in (10) and (11) (Spencer, 2002, 2013, 34).

(10) Argument structure for attributive modification
      $\langle A^*_x \langle x, \ldots \rangle \rangle$ noun$\langle R^* \rangle$

248   *Attributive Modification in Lexicalist Morphosyntax*

(11)   a.   tall tree

   $\text{tall}\langle A^*_x\langle x\rangle\rangle\ \text{tree}\langle R^*\rangle$

   b.   man proud of (his) car

   $\text{proud}\langle A^*_x\langle x\langle\text{car}\langle R\rangle\rangle\rangle\rangle\ \text{man}\langle R^*\rangle$

In (12) we see the basic schema for the semantic interpretation of modification by (canonical) adjective:

(12)   modification-by-adjective:

   $A^*_x\langle x\langle\ldots\rangle\rangle\ \langle R^*\rangle \rightarrow \lambda x[\textbf{adjective}(x,\ldots) \wedge \textbf{noun}(x)]$

This assumes intersective semantics, of course, and ignores all the well-known puzzles associated with attributive adjective modification.

   If we make standard assumptions about the semantic representations of words such as *tall*, *tree*, *proud*, *car*, then these will be one- or two-place predicates, roughly as shown in (13).

(13)   Basic semantic representations

   a. $\lambda x.\textbf{tall}(x)$

   b. $\lambda x.\textbf{tree}(x)$

   c. $\lambda x\lambda y.\textbf{proud}(x,y)$

   d. $\lambda x.\textbf{car}(x)$

The simplified representation of *man proud of (his) car* (ignoring the possessor *his*) will then be along the lines shown in (14).

(14)   Semantic representation of *man proud of (his) car*

   $\lambda x\exists y[\textbf{proud}(x,y) \wedge \textbf{man}(x) \wedge \textbf{car}(y)]$

The highest, 'x', argument of **proud** is linked to the adjective's A* role. In the examples given, the modified nouns themselves are intransitive, but there are inalienably possessed nouns that are transitive (divalent), typically kin terms and body parts: $\lambda x\lambda y.\textbf{daughter}(x,y)$, $\lambda x\lambda y.\textbf{leg}(x,y)$. We will adopt the convention that the highest, 'x', argument denotes the possessee, the entity referred to by the noun, while the second, 'y', argument denotes the possessor. When such nouns are modified, we will likewise assume that the highest argument of the noun is linked to the R role of the noun. Thus, the 'x' role of $\lambda x\lambda y.\textbf{daughter}(x,y)$ will be linked to the R SF role. Attributive modification, then, will ultimately give rise to a representation such as that shown in (15) (after λ-conversion from the more complex, but properly typed, expressions):

(15) Semantic representation of *mother, proud of (her) daughter* (ignoring the possessor *her*)

$\lambda x \exists y [\mathbf{proud}(x,y) \wedge \mathbf{mother}(x,y) \wedge \mathbf{daughter}(y,x)]$

The schema assumed so far presupposes that an adjective (phrase) modifies a noun head rather than modifying, say, a noun phrase determiner phrase, or smaller intermediate phrasal unit (see also the analysis in Ackerman and Nikolaeva (2013), for instance their Figure 28, p. 202, discussed below in Section 7.3.3). We will later wish to compare modification-by-adjective in standard syntactic representations with modification-by-adjective inside compounding constructions. That comparison would be made rather difficult if we assume that adjectives modify NP or DP denotations rather than N denotations. Thus, we mentioned in Chapter 3, Section 3.3 that in Chukchi, nouns incorporate attributive adjectives, in some contexts obligatorily, without changing the meaning of the attributive construction. The adjective–noun compounds are word forms, not phrases, so it is clear that the attributive relation has to be defined at the level of words.

7.3.2 Adjectives as Lexical Categories

In Chapter 5 we discussed the way in which lexical categories and parts of speech are coded in HPSG (and SBCG). We now return to those questions in the light of the approach to lexical representation and lexical relatedness proposed in the GPFM model. The relevant question to ask is what role a part of speech hierarchy will play in our analysis and what form that hierarchy should take.

Recall from Chapter 6 that in GPFM there would appear to be no need for the traditional category labels 'N', 'V', 'A', 'P'. This is because the notion 'lexical category' is factorized into various components, but the most basic description is defined by the SF role, part of the argument structure of the lexeme. We mentioned in Chapter 6, Section 6.3 that, by using the SF role value to define the basic lexical category of a word, we can eliminate redundancy in representations. Now, under normal circumstances redundancies are tolerated in HPSG representations. This is obvious from the fact that different aspects of a word's complementation repertoire are represented in no less than four places in the representations we are assuming (VAL, ARG-ST, F-STR, and RESTR). However, in earlier chapters we detailed extensively the kinds of difficulties that arise when we try to accommodate mixed lexical categories in a descriptive scheme that operates in terms of traditional category labels. One conclusion that

250 *Attributive Modification in Lexicalist Morphosyntax*

can be drawn from that discussion is that the traditional labels do no more than get in the way (see Spencer, 1998, 1999, 2013; see also Kenesei, forthcoming).

We will therefore adopt a more nuanced approach to lexical categories, deploying the descriptive apparatus of HPSG and GPFM but without appeal to descriptions such as [SYN|HEAD|CAT N] or to heads defined in terms of a *pos* subtype such as [HEAD adj]. In developing our representations we will be following in part very similar suggestions made independently of our own work by Chaves (2014), who explicitly proposes a category-less model of SBCG, partly on the basis of category mixing in deverbal nominals, the 'NP squish' of Ross (1973), and partly on the basis of coordination, leftwards extraction, and other syntactic processes which seem to be partially blind to strict lexical categorization.

As discussed in the previous chapter, in the GPFM model a lexical entry consists of four attributes: FORM, a specification of the inflected word forms of the lexeme; SYN, a specification of the word class, argument structure, and selectional/collocational properties of the lexeme; SEM, a semantic representation loosely based on Jackendoff's Lexical Conceptual Structure; and LI, a unique integer individuating each lexeme. Each of these attributes is defined by a function relating a pairing of ⟨LI, features⟩ to an output representation.

Of these attributes, SYN and SEM correspond largely to HPSG's corresponding attributes. For the present we will leave aside the SEM attribute since our representations are essentially a simplification of the standard HPSG representations, eliminating details which are not relevant to our discussion. The FORM attribute includes morphological information most of which is found in the SYN|HEAD attribute in HPSG. However, GPFM draws a distinction between morphological properties (m-features) and syntactic properties (s-features) defining respectively FORM and CONTENT paradigms in Stump's (2016) terms. In the default cases there is an isomorphism between the m-features and the s-features, but they are distinguished because there are numerous instances of mismatch, many of which are explored in Spencer (2013). The various morphology-related properties found in standard HPSG tend to conflate m- and s-features, so we will propose a slight extension of HPSG practice here to include the m-features in the FORM attribute, mirrored to a large extent by s-features in the SYN|HEAD attribute.

We illustrate in (16) the basic structure of a lexeme for the English adjective BLACK, and its Russian translation, ČORNYJ.

7.3 A Model of Attributive Modification 251

(16)   Basic representation for English BLACK, Russian ČORNYJ

$$\begin{bmatrix} \text{FORM} & [/\text{blæk}/, /\text{ʧɔrnɨj}/] \\ \text{SYN} & [\ldots] \\ \text{SEM} & \begin{bmatrix} \textit{Property} \\ \lambda x.\textbf{black}(x) \end{bmatrix} \\ \text{LI} & \text{BLACK} \end{bmatrix}$$

Given the framework developed in Chapter 5, we can also represent these entries as the list in (17).

(17) $f_{form}(\langle\text{BLACK}, \{u\}\rangle) = \text{STEM0}(\langle\text{BLACK}, u\rangle), \ldots = /\text{blæk}, \text{ʧɔrnɨj}/$
        $f_{syn}(\langle\text{BLACK}, \{u\}\rangle) = [\ldots]$
        $f_{sem}(\langle\text{BLACK}, \{u\}\rangle) = [_{Property} \lambda x.\textbf{black}(x)]$
        $f_{li}(\langle\text{BLACK}, \{u\}\rangle) = \text{BLACK}, \text{ČORNYJ}$

Using the notational conventions of Spencer (2013), we can then represent the entry as shown in (18), in which the LI is treated as a re-entrant property of the FORM, SYN, and SEM attributes.

(18)   Lexical representation for English BLACK, Russian ČORNYJ with LI attribute of FORM, SYN, SEM attributes

$$\begin{bmatrix} \text{FORM} & \begin{bmatrix} \text{LI} \boxed{1} \\ /\text{blæk}/, /\text{ʧɔrnɨj}/ \end{bmatrix} \\ \text{SYN} & \begin{bmatrix} \text{LI} \boxed{1} \\ \ldots \end{bmatrix} \\ \text{SEM} & \begin{bmatrix} \textit{Property} \\ \text{LI} \boxed{1} \\ \lambda x.\textbf{black}(x) \end{bmatrix} \\ \text{LI} & \boxed{1}\,\text{BLACK} \end{bmatrix}$$

The Russian adjective belongs to a specific declensional class and inflects for case, number, and gender, and so these m-properties need to be specified in its lexical entry. These properties are mirrored in the SYN attribute in that they are responsible for expressing syntactic agreement with a head noun or with the subject of a predicatively used adjective. In the case of Russian then, we need to expand both the FORM and SYN representations.

252 *Attributive Modification in Lexicalist Morphosyntax*

The FORM attribute needs to specify a root or STEM0 form, from which inflected word forms can be derived by the operation of regular inflectional morphology.[2] It also needs to define the inflectional class (here denoted by '1/2', indicating the default class for adjectives). Finally, for any particular fully inflected word form we need to specify which features it realizes in its paradigm. These are the m-features, which we will label MORCASE, MORNUM and MORGENDER. This is illustrated in (19).

(19) Elaborated lexical entry for Russian ČORNYJ 'black'

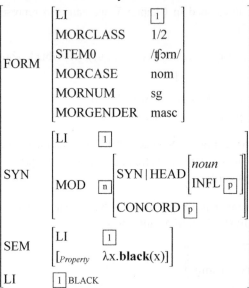

The representation in (19) imports the standard MOD attribute which provides a slot for the head noun which the adjective modifies and with which it agrees (in Russian). Agreement is indicated by the CONCORD attribute of MOD. This is tagged with the INFL attribute for the head noun, which will serve as the modifiand of the adjective when the adjective is combined with a suitable noun.

We will now consider the way that lexical categories are defined in the GPFM model, focussing on adjectives.

A noun is a word with the semantic function role R and an adjective has a semantic function role A*. As we saw in Section 7.3.1, this role is linked

---

[2] The value of the FORM|STEM0 attribute corresponds to the value of the PHON attribute familiar from HPSG lexical representations. We occasionally use PHON as a shorthand for FORM|STEM0.

7.3 *A Model of Attributive Modification* 253

to the first or highest argument of the attributive modifier. Spencer (2013) indicates ways in which the SF role of a word can be represented as the value of an argument structure attribute (abbreviated variously as A-STR, ARG-ST, ARG-STR) in LFG representations. Here we will adopt essentially the same device. We will follow Ackerman and Webelhuth (1998) and Ackerman and Nikolaeva (2013) in assuming that the SYN attribute of a word includes a variety of ways of representing complementation, each corresponding to slightly different morphosyntactic or syntactico-semantic notions.

An adjective such as BLACK or Russian čornyj has an argument structure in that it combines with a noun head. In the GPFM model its argument structure includes the semantic function role A*. The example in (20) shows that the adjective's representation needs to be enriched to accommodate this ARG-ST attribute. In HPSG terms, this means that we assume an attribute SFROLE as a value of the ARG-ST attribute. A noun is a lexeme whose ARG-ST attribute has the value [SFROLE R], while an adjective is a lexeme whose ARG-ST attribute has the value [SFROLE A*]. Now, there are occasions in HPSG grammars of particular languages when direct reference is made to major lexical classes. In the representations in (19) and (20) an attributive modifier is (understandably) defined as a lexeme which has a [SYN|VAL|MOD] attribute whose value is [HEAD *noun*]. How can we capture this insight without appeal to a class of nouns?

(20) Lexical representation of BLACK

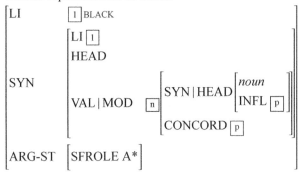

One possibility (which would require least rewriting of existing HPSG grammars) would be to define a different type hierarchy for major categories, but using the semantic function role labels as names instead of traditional labels. Thus, we might have types *r-cat, a*-cat, e-cat, rel-cat* for *noun, adjective, verb, adpositional* respectively. However, this could not be a genuine solution to the problem of category mixing because we would still have to define new subtypes

254 *Attributive Modification in Lexicalist Morphosyntax*

for the mixed categories, and we would encounter exactly the problems we revealed in Chapter 4. What we need is an analysis of parts of speech which makes direct appeal to the SF role itself. Thus, we would replace the value of the MOD attribute in (19) and (20) with the value [ARG-ST|SFROLE R]. This would account for straightforward cases without category mixing.

Suppose, however, we have a derived denominal adjective whose base noun can still be modified by a noun-selecting attribute, as in the examples from Tundra Nenets, Georgian, and other languages discussed in Chapter 3. Consider again the Tundra Nenets example in (21).

(21) Tundra Nenets noun–adjective mixed category

pər'id'en'a-q sarm'ik°-rəxa-x°h wen'ako-x°h
black-PL   wolf-SIM.A-DU   dog-DU
'(two) dogs (looking) like black wolves'

The word *sarm'ik°-rəxa-x°h* has the external syntax of an attributive adjective, agreeing in (dual) number with the head noun. This means that *sarm'ik°-rəxa-x°h* is a type of adjective, and hence bears the value [ARG-ST|SFROLE A*]. However, the base lexeme *sarm'ik°* 'wolf' is modified by the adjective *pər'id'en'aq* 'black' (which even agrees in number with the uninflecting noun base). This implies that the form *sarm'ik°-rəxa-x°h* has the value [ARG-ST|SFROLE R].

The similitudinal adjective in Tundra Nenets is an instance of a transposition (though admittedly one which is associated with the addition of a semantic predicate, a 'meaning-bearing transposition'). The whole point of the SF role as introduced in Spencer (1999) is to permit us to define mixed categories of this sort in a systematic way. We saw in Chapter 6 that a transposition is characterized by a compound SF role. In this instance it can be represented as $\langle A^*\langle x\langle R\rangle\rangle\rangle$, where 'x' represents the (external) argument of the derived adjective. In terms of the attribute-matrix representations developed so far, we can simply write this compound SF role as [ARG-ST|SFROLE $\langle A^*\langle R\rangle\rangle$] (the external argument will be the value of a different ARG-ST subattribute).

As discussed in Spencer (2013), the 'outer' SF role will define the external syntax (in the sense of Haspelmath (1996)), but the 'inner' SF role is still accessible to certain aspects of syntactic organization. Exactly how accessible and how that accessibility is encoded in the grammar will be discussed in Chapter 8. For the present we just need to note that the type *adj-lxm* can be defined as a lexeme with the value [ARG-ST|SFROLE A*], while in Tundra Nenets (though not necessarily in other languages) the MOD attribute for adjectives such as BLACK can be defined over words bearing the attribute value

[ARG-ST|SFROLE ⟨(A*)⟨R⟩⟩] (where the notation is intended to be interpreted as '[ARG-ST|SFROLE ⟨A* ⟨R⟩⟩] ∨ [ARG-ST|SFROLE ⟨R⟩]').

7.3.3 The Attributive Modifier Rule

We now turn to the question of how exactly attributive modification can be represented in our version of the HPSG approach, partly taking our lead from the recent discussion in Ackerman and Nikolaeva (2013). We saw that in the GPFM framework, mediating attributive modification is the main point of the A* semantic function role. In HPSG, however, modification is represented by the MOD attribute. Therefore, we need to ensure that the MOD attribute and the [SFROLE A*] are appropriately related to each other.

The simplest approach is to assume a principle according to which any lexeme which has the value [SFROLE A*] also has the value [VAL|MOD 1][ARG-ST| SFROLE R], where the tag 1 indicates that the modified head is identified with the (first) argument of the adjective. This is the Attributive Modifier Rule, which in effect can be thought of as an HPSG implementation of the rather vague syntactic scheme hinted at in Spencer (2013).

(22)   Attributive Modifier Rule

$$
\begin{bmatrix} word \\ \text{ARG-ST} \begin{bmatrix} \text{SFROLE}_e & \text{A*} \\ \text{ARG1} & \boxed{1} \\ (\text{ARG2} & ...) \end{bmatrix} \end{bmatrix} \rightarrow [\text{VAL|MOD} \boxed{1} [\text{ARG-ST|SFROLE R}]]
$$

Let us now consider the model of attributive modification developed by Ackerman and Nikolaeva (2013) in their analysis of what they call 'possessive relative clauses' in Tundra Nenets and other languages. Ackerman and Nikolaeva deploy the HPSG Modifier-Head Construction, which we will discuss in detail before we show how to integrate their approach with the GPFM approach.

The Modifier-Head Construction is defined between a noun and an attributive modifier (canonically, an adjective) whose lexical representation specifies that it selects a noun head to modify. The basic construction is illustrated schematically in Figure 7.2, a simplified representation of the phrase *serako ti* 'white reindeer' (Ackerman and Nikolaeva, 2013, Figure 28, p. 202). In the interests of perspicacity we have replaced their labels 'ROLE1, ROLE2' for the ℜ relation with the labels 'TARGET (TGT), RESTRICTOR (RCTR)', which

256   *Attributive Modification in Lexicalist Morphosyntax*

we will also employ in our analysis of the $\mathcal{R}$ relation in the next section.[3] Note that the phrase as illustrated combines two objects of the type *word* (see the discussion above, Section 7.3.1).

In Figure 7.2 the PHON attribute is a representation of the phonological form of the word. In a complete description this form will be defined in part by the lexeme's basic lexical representation and in part by the rules of inflectional morphology of the language. We will simplify for the moment and take these phonological forms as read.

The SYN attribute of the adjective defines two main properties in Figure 7.2, both of them HEAD properties (and hence they will also be properties of any phrase headed by the adjective). First, it defines the *pos* (*part of speech*) of the word as adjective.[4] Second, it defines a MOD attribute. Because of this specification, an adjective is constrained to combine with another word of the appropriate kind, namely an object whose SYN|HEAD is specified as type *noun*.[5]

Two further syntactic attributes relating to complementation types are distinguished in Ackerman and Nikolaeva's account F-STR and the ROLE values of the SEM|RESTR attribute. The F-STR attribute can be thought of as an HPSG representation of LFG's f-structure projection and lists the grammatical functions associated with a head: that is, whether the head combines with expressions realizing the role of SUBJECT, OBJECT, POSSESSOR, and so on. The ROLE attribute is a semantic argument. By default, it is possible to read the ARG-ST list from the list of ROLEs.

The SEM attribute is a representation of the meaning of the adjective. In the model of HPSG adopted by Ackerman and Nikolaeva, lexical meaning is represented as a set of constraints defined by the attribute RESTR(ICTION) which restrict the meaning of the adjective to denoting the set of things which bear the semantic relation denoted by the adjective. Ackerman and Nikolaeva

---

[3]   Throughout we silently correct various minor typographical infelicities in the AVMs provided by Ackerman and Nikolaeva. Where appropriate we also re-tag some of the representations in the interests of clarity.

[4]   Ackerman and Nikolaeva assume traditional parts of speech type labels for words. Given our assumptions these are probably no longer necessary, but for transparency and for ease of comparison with Ackerman and Nikolaeva's analyses we will retain them in our AVMs.

[5]   We ignore the question of predicative uses of adjectives. Adjectives used predicatively enter into one of two construction types cross-linguistically. Either they take verb-like inflection (subject agreement, tense marking, and so on) not found on attributive adjectives, or they combine with a copular verb expressing verbal features. On the current model, the first type would be a straightforward transposition from adjective to verb, while the second would be a periphrastic transposition. See Ackerman and Webelhuth (1998) for further discussion of the grammatical relation 'predicate' in constraint-based grammar.

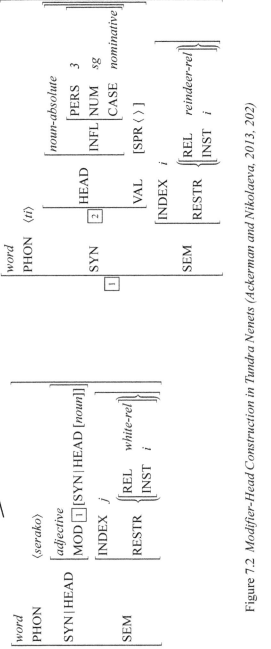

Figure 7.2 *Modifier-Head Construction in Tundra Nenets (Ackerman and Nikolaeva, 2013, 202)*

258 *Attributive Modification in Lexicalist Morphosyntax*

do not mention the Lexical Identifier (LID) and it seems to play no role in their analysis.

Tundra Nenets adjectives show (optional) concord for case, number, and possessor agreement features. In Figure 7.3 we reproduce a variant of Ackerman and Nikolaeva's (2013, 204) Figure 30, showing the feature structure for the expression given in (23), ignoring the optionality. Note that Ackerman and Nikolaeva assume that possessed nouns are type-shifted to *noun-possessed* and that they thereby acquire the SYN attributes [F-STR[POSS-or, POSS-ee]] and the SEM attribute [RESTR[REL $\Re$]]. Agreement itself is coded by the attribute CONCORD on the adjective, tagged $\boxed{2}$ in Figure 7.3, to those INFL features of the head noun which serve as the target of agreement.

(23) serako-m-t°   te-m-t°
      white-ACC-2SG reindeer-ACC-2SG
      'your white reindeer (ACC)'

The final question concerns the semantics of attribution. For simplicity of exposition we will follow Ackerman and Nikolaeva (2013) and avoid the traditional puzzles posed by beautiful dancers or alleged criminals, and will consider ordinary adjectives with intersective semantics, under which the SEM attribute of the adjective is essentially unified with that of the head noun. More precisely, the RESTR attributes, tagged $\boxed{\text{mod}}$, $\boxed{\text{head}}$ in Figure 7.3, are unified. Thus, the mother NP node's RESTR attribute will contain the values {REL *white-rel*, REL *reindeer-rel*}, corresponding to the logical form λx[**white**(x) ∧ **reindeer**(x)] (Ackerman and Nikolaeva, 2013, 202).

7.4   The Syntax of the $\Re$ Relation

We now make explicit certain assumptions about the contextually/ pragmatically specified $\Re$ relation, which is a crucial part of the interpretation of modification-by-noun (including relational adjectives) as well as many possessive constructions. Given our discussion of the nature of the $\Re$ attribute in previous chapters, we now turn to the way it can be deployed in lexical representations.

7.4.1   The $\Re$ Relation in Modification-by-Noun

A characteristic of modification-by-nominal-concept constructions is coercion or type-shifting: a noun ceases to have its normal referential function and instead functions as an attributive modifier, as though it had been turned into

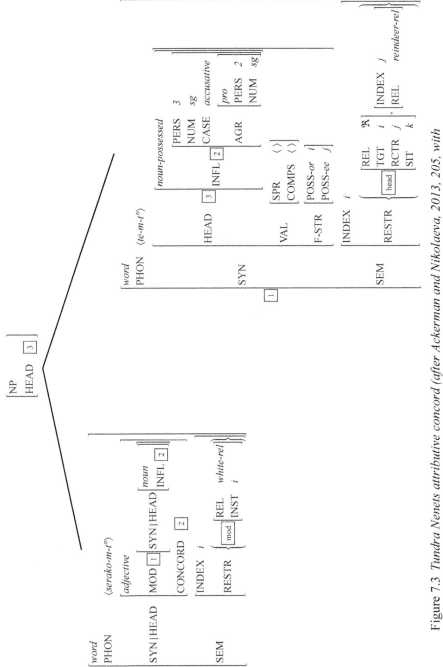

Figure 7.3 Tundra Nenets attributive concord (after Ackerman and Nikolaeva, 2013, 205, with slight corrections)

260 *Attributive Modification in Lexicalist Morphosyntax*

an adjective. The constructions share the semantic property of expressing the $\mathfrak{R}$ relation between modifier and head. The intuition is that, for instance, in a non-lexicalized compound such as *reindeer soup* the denotation of the head noun, *soup*, is restricted to the set of types of soup bearing the $\mathfrak{R}$ relation to the concept denoted by *reindeer*. In this respect the modifying (non-head) noun behaves like a canonical intersective attributive modifier. Stated in these terms, we can see that $\mathfrak{R}$ is clearly an asymmetric two-place relation between two semantic roles. We will call the role expressed by the head noun the TARGET role and that expressed by the modifier the RESTRICTOR role. The latter can be expressed, for instance, by a bare noun or noun stem (in compounding constructions), or by an NP or PP (typically in possessive constructions). We will take the first argument of $\mathfrak{R}$ to be the TARGET and the second argument to be the RESTRICTOR: $\mathfrak{R}$(TGT,RCTR). Thus, *reindeer soup* will correspond to the representation $\mathfrak{R}$(**soup,reindeer**).

The first question we need to ask is: where is the $\mathfrak{R}$ relation represented? There are three logical possibilities:

(i) it can be added to the semantic representation of the head noun, and thence shared as a head feature with the NP as a whole

(ii) it can be added to the semantic representation of the modifier noun and thence combined with the semantics of the head by some appropriate principle, just as the semantic attribute of a qualitative adjective is combined with the noun's semantics

(iii) it can be introduced as a constructional meaning to the semantic attribute of the NP node

The three possibilities are illustrated in Figures 7.4 to 7.6.

In Figure 7.4 the head noun's SEM attribute has been enriched to include the $\mathfrak{R}$ attribute, which is inherited by the NP along with the meaning of the head noun itself. In Figure 7.5, by contrast, we see that it is the modifier expression which bears the $\mathfrak{R}$ attribute, along with its own lexical meaning. In the SEM attribute of the NP this is combined by simple set theoretic union with the SEM attribute of the head noun. In Figure 7.6 we see the constructional analysis: the $\mathfrak{R}$ attribute is not associated with either of the daughters; rather, it is introduced by the construction itself.

The structure in Figure 7.4 is congruent with that normally assumed for possessive constructions, as we will see later. The structure in Figure 7.5 locates the $\mathfrak{R}$ relation on the modifier itself, making the $\mathfrak{R}$ relation congruent with the semantic contribution of a canonical attributive adjective. It is

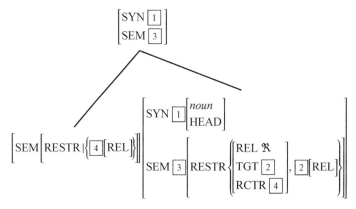

Figure 7.4 $\mathcal{R}$ *on head*

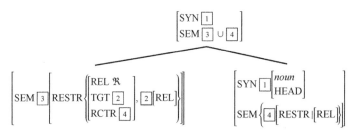

Figure 7.5 $\mathcal{R}$ *on modifier*

therefore the construction we would expect to find, *ceteris paribus*, with denominal adjectives, including relational and possessive adjectives.

The constructional analysis of Figure 7.6 is not one which is normally advocated in the HPSG literature, but it is explicitly permitted in SBCG. Thus, Sag (2012, 146, fn. 88), appealing to the formalism of Minimal Recursion Semantics (MRS), introduced in Copestake et al. (2005), comments: "there is a further feature CONSTRUCTION-CONTENT, whose value is a possibly empty list of frames that is also included in the mother's FRAMES list. This treatment …systematically allows for constructional meaning."

Following Spencer (1999) (see also Nikolaeva, 2008), we will deploy the construction type in Figure 7.5 for relational/possessive adjectives. This captures the idea that the relation defined by $\mathcal{R}$ is a lexical property of the relational or possessive adjective itself. However, for compounds such as

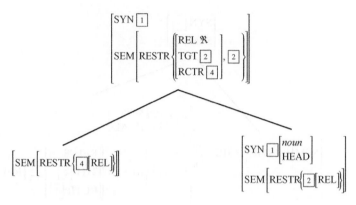

Figure 7.6 $\mathcal{R}$ on NP

preposition phrase we adopt the constructional analysis of Figure 7.6. The basic structure for a compound noun is shown in Figure 7.7, simplifying considerably and including only crucial information (we use the type *noun* as a shorthand for the [SFROLE R] specification of the ARG-ST attribute). Each noun contributes its own semantics to the construction as a whole and the compound defines the $\mathcal{R}$ relation between the head and its modifier.

For denominal adjectives, as in the case of (standard) adjectives, we can simply assume that the semantic representations of the two daughters are unified, as shown in Figure 7.5. In terms of λ-expressions this means that we can assume the kinds of representations shown in (24) in simplified form for the expression *prepositional phrase*.

(24) *prepositional*: $\lambda P \lambda x \exists \mathcal{R} \exists y [P(x) \wedge$ **preposition**$(y) \wedge \mathcal{R}(x,y)]$
 phrase: $\lambda z.$**phrase**(z)
 prepositional phrase:
 $\lambda P \lambda x \exists \mathcal{R} \exists y [P(x) \wedge$ **preposition**$(y) \wedge \mathcal{R}(x,y)](\lambda z.$**phrase**$(z))$

The λ-expression for the whole phrase now reduces to the version shown in (25), which has the desired interpretation 'the property of being a phrase, x, such that there is a preposition y bearing the RESTRICTOR relation $\mathcal{R}$ to the TARGET x'.

(25) $\lambda x \exists \mathcal{R} \exists y [[\lambda z.$**phrase**$(z)](x) \wedge$ **preposition**$(y) \wedge \mathcal{R}(x,y)] =$
 $\lambda x \exists \mathcal{R} \exists y [$**phrase**$(x) \wedge$ **preposition**$(y) \wedge \mathcal{R}(x,y)]$

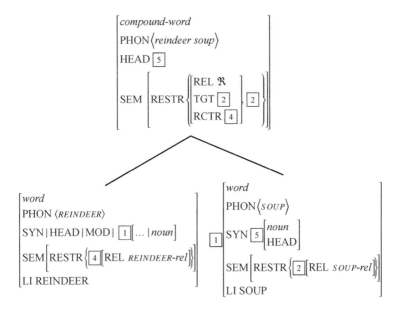

Figure 7.7 *Structure for the N-N compound* reindeer soup

Since relational adjectives are adjectives, we expect them to inherit the basic morphosyntax of attributive modifiers as just illustrated. However, we need to ensure that the adjective establishes the ℜ relation between the denotations of the head noun and the base noun lexeme of the relational adjective. The natural way to do this is to introduce the ℜ relation as part of the SEM|RESTRICTION attribute for the adjective. This means that we need an additional stipulation in the Attributive Modifier Rule, but one solely for relational adjectives. In the case of transpositional lexemes such as MARINE, this rule serves as a static constraint on lexical representations, but it also has to be deployed as part of the GPF defining genuinely transpositional relational or possessive adjectives, such as those of Chukchi.

Thus, when the morphology takes a noun and derives the adjectival transposition or 'representation' of that noun, the Attributive Modifier Rule has to come into play so as to ensure that the derived word has the external syntax of an adjective. In that event, the rule as formulated in (22) is not sufficient, because the adjective formation process introduces an external argument co-referenced to the modified head. We can therefore revise the Attributive Modifier Rule so as to make explicit reference to the highest

264   *Attributive Modification in Lexicalist Morphosyntax*

	SEA	MARINE
FORM	sea	marine
SYN	R	A*
SEM	$[_{Thing}\ \lambda z.\textbf{sea}(z)]$	$[_{Property}\ \lambda P\lambda y \exists \mathcal{R} \exists x\ [[_{Thing}\ P(y)] \wedge$
		$[_{Thing}\ \textbf{sea}(x)] \wedge \mathcal{R}(x,y)]]$
LI	SEA	MARINE

Figure 7.8 *Lexical representations of* SEA, MARINE

thematic argument of the adjective, as shown in (26) (cf. the analysis of Russian participles in Spencer, 2017b).

(26)   Attributive Modifier Rule (revised)

$$\begin{bmatrix} word \\ \text{ARG-ST [SFROLE A*]} \end{bmatrix} \quad \rightarrow$$

$$\begin{bmatrix} \text{VAL}\,|\,\text{MOD} & \boxed{1}\,[\text{ARG-ST}\,|\,\text{SFROLE R}] \\ \text{ARG-ST} & \begin{bmatrix} \text{ARG1} & \boxed{1} \\ \ldots & \end{bmatrix} \end{bmatrix}$$

In addition, we have to define the meaning of the modifier-head combination in terms of the $\mathcal{R}$ relation. We will show this for the English expression *marine animal*. We take MARINE to be an instance of a suppletive relational adjective (of the kind studied in detail by Koshiishi (2011)). It is therefore a transpositional lexeme, semantically related to SEA by virtue of the fact that it additionally encodes the $\mathcal{R}$ relation established between 'sea/marine' and the modified head noun. This is illustrated in Figure 7.8, in which the lexical representations of SEA and MARINE are presented for comparison.

A relational adjective from a noun, **N**, has the representation shown in (27), so that the attributive form of MARINE shown in Figure 7.8 is given in (28).

(27) $[_{Property}\ \lambda P\lambda x \exists \mathcal{R} \exists y[P(x) \wedge \textbf{N}(y) \wedge \mathcal{R}(x,y)]]$

(28) $\lambda P\lambda x \exists \mathcal{R} \exists y[P(x) \wedge \textbf{sea}(y) \wedge \mathcal{R}(x,y)]$

In the framework developed by Ackerman and Nikolaeva (2013) we can give the partial lexical representation shown in Figure 7.9 for MARINE.

The expression *marine animal* means 'animal which has some contextually defined relation to the concept of "sea" (including one that lives in the sea)'. This interpretation is illustrated in Figure 7.10.

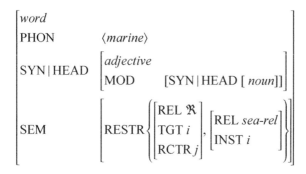

Figure 7.9 *Partial lexical representation of* MARINE *after Ackerman and Nikolaeva (2013)*

Let us now consider the synonymous N-N compound. According to Spencer (1999), the meaning relations between the elements of a standard N-N endocentric compound are given constructionally; they are not associated with any specific element of that compound. This means we should model such compounds as constructions. The compound construction is sketched schematically in Figure 7.11.

The compound construction can apply to a pair of nouns such as SEA and ANIMAL to give a compound word in which SEA functions effectively like the relational adjective MARINE, except that it is phonologically identical to (the base form of) SEA. In that way we can coin the compound *sea animal*, one of a number of compounds which seems to alternate freely with the relational adjective MARINE: *sea/marine defences, wall, life, etc.*

An alternative to the constructional approach is to define a rule which has the consequence of 'temporarily' redefining a noun as an adjective, but without any concomitant morphological expansion and hence without the morphosyntax of an adjective. This can be achieved by a process of on-line retyping (Koenig, 1999). We assume a lexical rule that can apply to any word of the type noun and which has essentially the same effect as the Attributive Modifier Rule. We may label this the Modification-by-Noun Rule. This is illustrated in Figure 7.12. Here [2] is the RESTR attribute of the lexeme whose ARG-ST is [1]. The rule adds the A* role to the SFROLE attribute of the noun, effectively defining an m-inert noun-to-adjective transposition. The advantage of formalizing the compound construction as an online lexical rule would be that it might make it easier to restrict the dependent noun to the form of the uninflected base. This would leave open the question of how to deal with the

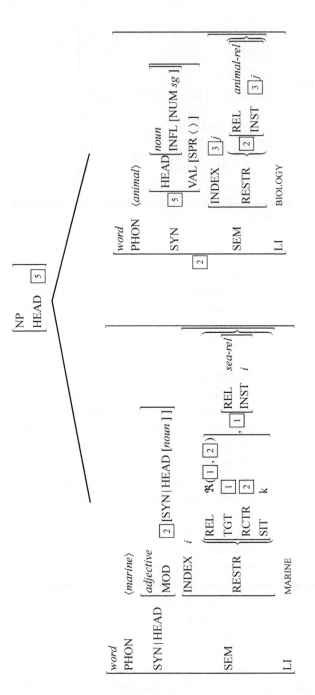

Figure 7.10 *Structure for the marine animal*

7.4 *The Syntax of the* ℜ *Relation* 267

(typologically infrequent) cases of compounding which do permit, e.g., case or number marking on the dependent noun. However, we can easily write such a restriction into language-specific instantiations of the Modification-by-Noun Rule by restricting the FORM attribute of the dependent to the base form (or, indeed, some special combining form).

A further reason for adopting the *cpd-cxt* is that it leaves open the possibility of treating other types of compounding as instances of the Modification-by-Noun Rule. In Chapter 8 we discuss compounds in Tundra Nenets whose dependent noun optionally takes adjective-like agreement with the head, and argue that in just such a case it makes sense to encode the adjectival behaviour (including its optionality) as the consequence of online application of the Modification-by-Noun Rule.

7.4.2 *The* ℜ *Relation in Possessive Constructions*

A number of our examples of noun–adjective hybrids are based on possessive adjectives (PossA). These resemble relational adjectives in that they do not add a semantic predicate to the base noun lexeme from which they are derived. However, they enter into constructions which are congruent with possessive constructions in other languages, or elsewhere within the same language, and this means that they define a relation not between a modifying noun and a head but between a modifying NP and the head. Before we can discuss possessive adjectives, however, we need to make explicit certain assumptions about possessive constructions generally. The problem of possessive adjectives will compel us to rethink a number of standard assumptions that are made in the literature (including assumptions we have ourselves espoused in earlier work).

As we have argued extensively in Chapter 2, the nature of the possessive construction depends crucially on the semantics of the possessed noun. Some classes of nouns are inherently relational and imply a two-place argument structure. Thus, kin terms, body parts, and other meronyms entail a possessor: *Mary's* <u>mother</u>, *the bird's* <u>wing</u>, *the* <u>corner</u> *of the table*. This is the familiar situation of inalienable possession. The natural way to represent inalienable possession in the current framework is shown very schematically in Figure 7.13 for the expression *the bird's wing*.

By contrast, alienable possession is a relation between two one-place nominal concepts: *Mary's book, the bird's nest*. The concepts of *book* and *nest* do not entail the existence of Mary or even a bird, and in general the semantic relation between the two noun concepts is the contextually specified ℜ relation,

268 *Attributive Modification in Lexicalist Morphosyntax*

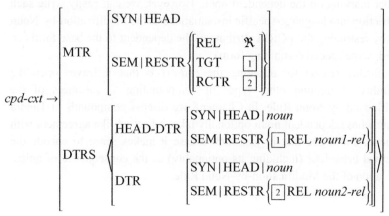

Figure 7.11 *The compound construction*

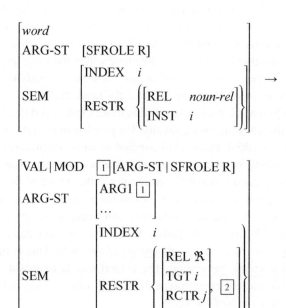

Figure 7.12 *The Modification-by-Noun Rule*

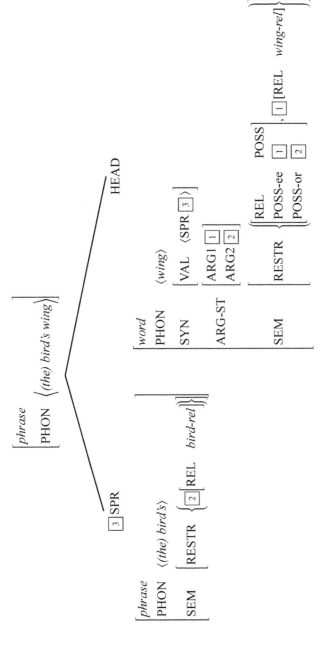

Figure 7.13 *Inalienable possession*: the bird's wing

270 *Attributive Modification in Lexicalist Morphosyntax*

$$
\begin{bmatrix}
abs\text{-}noun \\
\text{PHON } \langle book \rangle \\
\text{SEM | RESTR |} \{ [\text{RELN } book\text{-}rel] \}
\end{bmatrix} \quad \rightarrow
$$

$$
\begin{bmatrix}
noun\text{-}possessed \\
\text{PHON } \langle book \rangle \\
\text{SEM | RESTR |} \left\{ \begin{bmatrix} \text{RELN} & \text{POSS} \\ \text{POSS-ee} & \boxed{2} \text{ POSS-or} \end{bmatrix}, \boxed{2}\, book\text{-}relf \right\}
\end{bmatrix}
$$

Figure 7.14 *Defining the* noun-possessed *subtype*

just as with N-N compounding. Indeed, one can think of alienable possession constructions as 'modification-by-NP'.

The standard approach to alienable possession in lexicalist frameworks is, in effect, a generalization of inalienable possession. In HPSG, a subtype of the type *noun* is defined, *noun-possessed*, which differs from the plain unpossessed noun (of subtype *absolute-noun*) solely by having the POSS relation as part of its semantics (Ackerman and Nikolaeva, 2013, 166). The *noun-possessed* can then enter into some variant of a *possessor-cxt*, in which the possessor role is expressed by an NP in the specifier position. This construction is illustrated schematically in Figure 7.14.

As mentioned in Chapter 2, Section 2.3.2, a similar approach to alienable possession is adopted in LFG. In particular, recall that Bresnan (2001) proposed that the f-description [PRED: 'book'] becomes [PRED: 'book⟨↑POSS⟩'] (Spencer, 2013, 320–321).

The approach in which it is the possessum which is type-shifted works well enough for simple cases in which the possessor is marked, for example by an adposition such as *of*, genitive case, or similar morphosyntactic devices. We illustrate this from Ackerman and Nikolaeva's (2013) representation of the Tundra Nenets phrase 'Wera's reindeer' seen in Figure 7.15. Ackerman and Nikolaeva deploy the same representational schema for possessor agreement with covert pronominals, as shown in Figure 7.16 for the Tundra Nenets phrase 'my reindeer'.

However, questions arise when we look at other construction types expressing the possessive relationship. Specifically, how should we represent the possessive relation when it is expressed by means other than a phrase

$$\left[\begin{array}{ll} phrase \\ \text{PHON} & \langle Werah\ ti \rangle \end{array}\right]$$

NP   N

$$\left[\begin{array}{ll} phrase \\ \text{PHON} & \langle Werah \rangle \\ \text{SYN} & \left[\text{HEAD}\ \left[\begin{array}{l} noun\text{-}absolute \\ \text{INFL}\ \left[\begin{array}{ll} \text{NUM} & sg \\ \text{PERS} & 3 \\ \text{CASE} & genitive \end{array}\right] \end{array}\right]\right] \\ \text{SEM} & \left[\begin{array}{ll} \text{INDEX} & i \\ \text{RESTR} & \left\{\left[\begin{array}{ll} \text{REL} & Wera\text{-}rel \\ \text{INST} & i \end{array}\right]\right\} \end{array}\right] \end{array}\right]$$

$$\left[\begin{array}{ll} word \\ \text{PHON} & \langle ti \rangle \\ \text{SYN} & \left[\begin{array}{ll} \text{HEAD} & \left[\begin{array}{l} noun\text{-}possessed \\ \text{INFL}\ \left[\begin{array}{ll} \text{NUM} & sg \\ \text{PERS} & 3 \\ \text{CASE} & nominative \\ \text{AGR} & none \end{array}\right] \end{array}\right] \\ \text{VAL} & \left[\text{SPR}\ \langle \text{NPgen}_i \rangle\right] \\ \text{F-STR} & \left[\begin{array}{ll} \text{POSS-}or & i \\ \text{POSS-}ee & j \end{array}\right] \end{array}\right] \\ \text{SEM} & \left[\begin{array}{ll} \text{INDEX} & j \\ \text{RESTR} & \left\{\left[\begin{array}{ll} \text{REL} & \mathfrak{R} \\ \text{ROLE1} & i \\ \text{ROLE2} & j \end{array}\right],\ \left[\begin{array}{ll} \text{REL} & reindeer\text{-}rel \\ \text{INST} & j \end{array}\right]\right\} \end{array}\right] \end{array}\right]$$

Figure 7.15 *Syntactic structure of* Werah ti *'Wera's reindeer' (adapted from Ackerman and Nikolaeva, 2013, 175, Figure 10)*

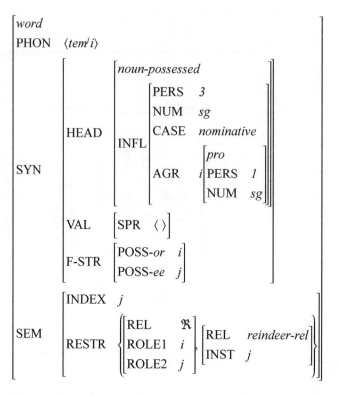

Figure 7.16 *Ackerman and Nikolaeva's (2013, 198) structure for Tundra Nenets possessed noun* tem^{j}i *'my reindeer'*

in SPR position? This includes N-N juxtaposition, i.e. in a compound, as well as PP complements. Further, how should we represent possessors expressed as adjectives, i.e. the PossA construction? For instance, how do we represent the semantics of the possessor and the possessum in the Russian PossA expression *mamina ruka* 'Mummy's hand', in which the PossA agrees with its head noun in number, gender, and case, just like a qualitative adjective?[6]

On the one hand we want the PossA to inherit its agreement morphosyntax and its linear placement from the attributive adjective construction. The PossA in Russian, for instance cannot be analysed as an SPR, since it has an entirely

---

[6] This question is of wider relevance in the case of pronominal possessors. We often find that these have adjectival morphosyntax, for instance, adjectival agreement, even in languages for which the PossA construction itself is marginal or non-existent, as in Latin and Romance languages, German, and others. See later in this section.

different distribution from specifiers such as demonstrative adjectives. On the other hand, it must also inherit its principal semantic effects from the standard possessive construction.[7]

Recall that we have argued that there are three types of morphosyntactic representation which could capture the ℜ relation between TARGET *book* and RESTRICTOR *Mum's* in an expression such as *Mum's book*. The ℜ can be associated with the TARGET argument, as in Ackerman and Nikolaeva's (2013) account and other standard accounts (see Figure 7.4), or it can be associated with the construction as a whole (Figure 7.6), or it can be associated with the RESTRICTOR, 'Mum' (Figure 7.5). This last representation is appropriate precisely when the RESTRICTOR argument is specially marked as a modifier/possessor. This means that we can assign the [REL ℜ] specification to the RESTRICTION attribute of the genitive case-marked noun in a typical possessive construction. Thus, the representation for 'Wera's reindeer' will now be that shown in Figure 7.17.[8]

This analysis obviates the need to type-shift the possessum, so we dispense with the label *noun-possessed*. It is not clear whether we would ever need to retype the genitive-marked noun (as, say, *noun-possessor*), so we leave it as type *noun*. In any case the crucial information is the [ARG-ST|SFROLE] specification. For the 'pro-drop' cases of the kind illustrated in Figure 7.16 we can assume a covert (empty) pronoun bearing the ℜ attribute.

There are languages with possessor agreement in which the possessor receives no special marking at all. This is the case with one of the possessive constructions in Hungarian: *a Péter ház-a* DEF Péter house-3SG.POSS 'Peter's house'. Such constructions might suggest that it is the agreement morphology on the possessum (TARGET) itself that realizes the ℜ relation, giving an analysis just like the standard type-shifting to possessed noun account. However, a purely constructional analysis might equally be appropriate.

Indeed, in some languages neither the possessor nor the possessum receives any morphosyntactic marking and the construction is realized by pure juxtaposition for both alienable and inalienable possession (Nichols and Bickel, 2013). This is true of Indonesian, for instance (Sneddon, 1996), as shown in (29). In (29a) we see an NP/DP alienable possessor phrase, while in (29b) we see a

---

[7] In a sense this is the mirror image of the problem addressed in Ackerman and Nikolaeva (2013), who describe a fundamentally attributive construction, the relative clause, which inherits properties of the possessive construction.

[8] This analysis is essentially an elaboration of Nikolaeva's (2008) Construction Grammar analysis of Tungusic proprietives.

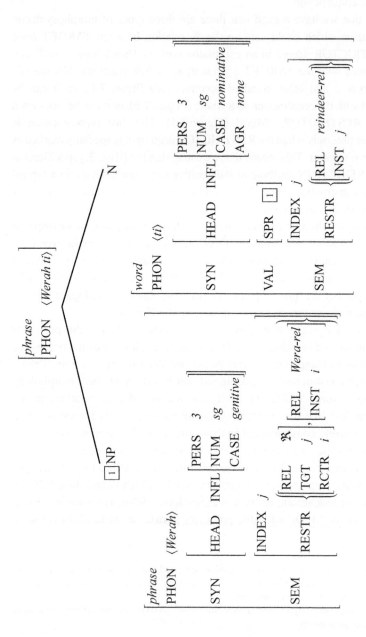

Figure 7.17 Revised syntactic structure for Werah ti 'Wera's reindeer'

7.4 *The Syntax of the* ℜ *Relation* 275

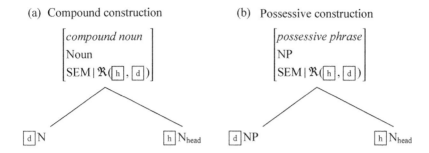

Figure 7.18 *Compound and possessive construction by juxtaposition*

full NP/DP, *rumah kecil itu* serving as a juxtaposed, presumably inalienable, possessor (Indonesian lacks nominal morphology).

(29) a. pemilik hotél ini
       owner hotel this
       'the owner of this hotel'

    b. pintu rumah kecil itu
       door house small this
       'the door of the small house'

Such considerations imply that we must say that the constructional format, in which the ℜ relation is defined only at the level of the 'mother' of the construction, applies to either Figure 7.18(a) or (b). In other words, we can propose a constructional analysis not only for compounding cases in which the dependent is a bare noun (or a modifier-modified 'small construction' such as [N N] or [A N], as in [[*American history*] *teacher*]), but also for true possessive constructions in which the dependent is a fully-fledged phrase occupying the [specifier, NP] position, such as *this hotel* in (29a). In fact, *ceteris paribus*, this is what we would expect in any case.

A further implication of our analysis is that there is no single representational format universally applicable to all cases of alienable possession. This is a simple consequence of the fact that languages differ significantly in the morphosyntactic devices they use to express the modification-by-nominal-concept generally, and possession in particular, as we illustrated in some detail in Chapter 2. Again, this should not be surprising, especially given the fact that

276 *Attributive Modification in Lexicalist Morphosyntax*

there is no valid universal characterization of the pre-theoretical (descriptive) term 'possessive construction'.[9]

Now, the adjectival representations of nominal specifiers pose interesting questions of description. The PossA lexical type is problematical in any framework for conceptual reasons. Recall that a possessor is (canonically) a referring expression, and hence should be realized by an NP, not by a bare noun. However, it is extremely non-canonical for an adjective to take nominal determiners/specifiers without itself being converted into a noun. Thus, the nature of nominal morphosyntax conspires against PossAs, it would seem. Indeed, for this reason it is difficult to see how an adjective can possibly serve as the possessor of a head noun, whether it expresses alienable possession or inalienable possession.

When we examine the distribution of possessive adjectives across the lexicon, however, we observe that they are often greatly favoured, or even restricted to, certain classes of noun, particularly kin terms and proper names. Moreover, a possessive adjective construction is particularly common with pronominal possessors, and it is found even in languages which otherwise lack a systematic PossA construction. It is very unusual for derivational morphology to apply to these classes, especially pronouns and proper names of course, which further strengthens the case against possessive adjective formation being a type of derivational lexeme formation.

Slavic languages such as Russian are especially interesting in this regard: just as in Latin, third person possessive pronouns are typically homophonous with the genitive case of the pronoun, while the first and second person forms, along with the reflexives (which neutralize person/number distinctions) are adjectival (the same pattern is found in Rumanian, but not in other Romance languages). In Standard Bulgarian/Macedonian, as in modern Romance languages, third person pronouns are also adjectival. However, the adjectival possessive pronouns alternate with a possessive construction in which the pronominal possessor is expressed by a dative clitic form, as shown in the Bulgarian examples in (30).

(30) a. texn-a-ta   kniga
          3PL.POSS-FEM.SG.AGR-DEF.FEM.SG.AGR book[FEM.SG]

      b. kniga-ta   im
          book[FEM.SG]-DEF.FEM.SG.AGR 3PL.POSS.DAT.CLITIC
          'their book'

---

[9] We find it instructive that some descriptive grammars seem to avoid the term 'possessive construction' precisely where there is no real boundary between alienable possession and other types of modification-by-nominal-concept.

7.4 The Syntax of the $\mathcal{R}$ Relation   277

The possessive pronouns thus present a particularly clear illustration of the way that morphosyntax variation can be tolerated even within a single (very small) category.

What these classes of words have in common is that they are all intrinsically specified; indeed, in the default case they are inherently definite. They thus behave semantically as though they were determined/specified NPs and can therefore readily realize the possessor function.

We have said that the PossA lexical type is comparable to the relational adjective type (RA). Given that, we would expect it to behave semantically in the same way. In our analysis of *prepositional phrase* we argued that the RA has essentially the same properties as an ordinary adjective except that its meaning is a combination of the base noun's meaning and that of the $\mathcal{R}$ relation. Since the PossA also expresses the $\mathcal{R}$ relation (in its alienable possession interpretation, at least), we would expect it to have exactly the same logical form as other relational adjectives as shown in (31).

(31) Where **m** is a constant denoting 'Mum/Mama'

Mum's/mamin-: $\lambda x \lambda P \exists \mathcal{R}[\mathcal{R}(x,\mathbf{m}) \wedge P(x)]$

book: $\lambda y.\mathbf{kniga}(y)$

mamina kniga 'Mum's book':
$\lambda x \lambda P \exists \mathcal{R}[\mathcal{R}(x,\mathbf{m}) \wedge P(x)](\lambda y.\mathbf{kniga}(y)) =$
$\lambda x \exists \mathcal{R}[\mathcal{R}(x,\mathbf{m}) \wedge (\lambda y.\mathbf{kniga}(y))(x)] =$
$\lambda x \exists \mathcal{R}[\mathcal{R}(x,\mathbf{m}) \wedge \mathbf{kniga}(x)]$

The reduced λ-expression in (31) now has the desired interpretation.

Finally, we must ensure that the $\mathcal{R}$ relation on the dependent NP is integrated into the possessive construction's semantics, so that the TARGET argument is correctly identified as the possessed head. We can therefore assume a variant of the Modifier-Head Rule (or construction) to ensure that the TARGET role is identified with the head noun.

However, difficulties arise with inalienable possession. We are assuming a representation for relational nouns which includes an existential commitment to a possessor for the noun. Thus, Russian *sestra* 'sister' will have the logical form $\lambda x \exists y.\mathbf{sister}(x,y)$. Such a noun can easily be modified by a qualitative adjective such as *tall*: $\lambda z \lambda P[\mathbf{tall}(z) \wedge P(z)]$, as in *(someone's) tall sister*: $\lambda z \lambda P[\mathbf{tall}(z) \wedge P(z)]([\lambda x \exists y.\mathbf{sister}(x,y)])$. This converts to $\lambda z[\mathbf{tall}(z) \wedge [\lambda x \exists y.\mathbf{sister}(x,y)](z)] = \lambda z[\mathbf{tall}(z) \wedge \exists y.\mathbf{sister}(z,y)]$. However, if we apply the representation of the

278 *Attributive Modification in Lexicalist Morphosyntax*

Russian PossA *mamina* to that of *sestra* to derive the meaning of *mamina sestra* 'Mum's sister', we obtain: $\lambda z\lambda P\exists\Re[\Re(z,\mathbf{m}) \wedge P(z)]([\lambda x\exists y.\mathbf{sister}(x,y)])$. This converts to $\lambda z\exists\Re[\Re(z,\mathbf{m}) \wedge \exists y.\mathbf{sister}(z,y)]$, which corresponds to the property of being (someone's) sister and being the TARGET role of the $\Re$ relation, whose RESTRICTOR is 'Mum'. But this fails to identify the TARGET argument, 'x', supplied by the possessive adjective *mamina* with the possessor argument, 'y' of the relational noun *sestra*.

In fact this problem is not unique to possessive adjective constructions. The same problem will arise if the relational noun's possessor is realized by a specifier or a complement: *sestra mamy* 'the sister of Mum'. What seems to be required here is a constructional definition of inalienable possession under which the TARGET role and the RESTRICTOR role are explicitly equated with the POSSESSED/POSSESSOR roles in the relational noun's argument structure. Since this study is not focussed on possessives, we will simply assume such a construction without further comment. It will not affect our account of the morphosyntax of noun–adjective hybrids in any case.

7.4.3 The Possession-Modification Scale Again

The discussion of possessive constructions, however, brings us back to a claim discussed earlier in Chapter 2 in the context of a typology of possessive and modification constructions. There we argued for a Possession-Modification Scale (following Nikolaeva and Spencer, 2012), against the background of a Canonical Typology approach to the problem.

Recall that there are a good many constructions in which a noun denotation is modified by a nominal concept, and that these constructions overlap with canonical attributive modification. Specifically, we can contrast inalienable possession, which realizes the possessor argument through a process of 'modification/specification-by-NP/DP' (case D in Chapter 2) with modification by attributive (qualitative) adjective (case A in Chapter 2), in which the adjective brings its own semantic predicate to be combined with that of the head noun. But between these poles we find two important intermediate types: the modification-by-noun construction (case B) and alienable possession (case C).

The morphosyntactic constructions that can realize these four types are very varied as we have seen, but in Chapter 2, Section 2.5 we observed that languages tend to deploy non-standard, non-default morphosyntax for nominal modification/specification in a characteristic way, respecting the Possession-Modification Scale. If a language, say, expresses inalienable possession using the PossA encoding strategy as its

7.4 The Syntax of the ℜ Relation 279

principal construction, then it will use such a strategy for alienable possession and for modification-by-nominal-concept. Conversely, if a language uses a genitive or adpositional strategy for modification-by-nominal-concept, then it will use that strategy for both alienable and inalienable possession.

We propose that in its present form the scale can be thought of as representing cross-linguistic tendencies in the semantic structure of adnominal modification and providing an empirically testable tool for studying meaning variations across languages. Having focused on those aspects of modification and possession that have to be regarded as systematically related, we are now in the position to highlight those of their properties which regularly pattern together.

First, it is of course very common cross-linguistically to find alienable and inalienable possession grouped together. This follows from the semantic commonalities between all possessives discussed in Chapter 2. Informally, all possessives were taken to be based on some kind of semantic prototype in which the possessor serves as the cognitive reference point for the conceptualization of the possessed and deviations are a matter of degree. For us, this implies that alienable possession shares with inalienable possession the property that the modifier/specifier is canonically referential, and hence an NP/DP. The problems posed by the two types of possession are slightly different, in that with alienable possession we have a head noun which does not intrinsically have a possessor argument. Nevertheless, we saw in the previous section that it must clearly acquire such an argument at some level of representation, and that argument can even be discharged by a word of entirely the wrong category in the case of possessive adjectives.

Modification-by-noun is typically (indeed, canonically: Spencer (2019)) realized by juxtaposition of a non-referential bare noun modifier realizing the RESTRICTOR role of the ℜ relation. At the same time, we saw earlier that the effects of the modification-by-noun construction can sometimes be realized by a construction normally associated with possessives: *children's literature/clothing/furniture* (vs. *child seat*). Especially common are languages that treat modification-by-noun and alienable possession as one and the same construction type, ambiguous between these two interpretations. It is then important to see how modification-by-noun differs from alienable possession and how they are alike. This was discussed in some detail within the Canonical Typology framework in Nikolaeva and Spencer (2012) and in Chapter 2. Speaking very roughly, alienable possession shares with modification-by-noun the property of expressing the semantically unspecified

280   *Attributive Modification in Lexicalist Morphosyntax*

but contextually/pragmatically determined $\mathcal{R}$ relation between two entities, the TARGET and the RESTRICTOR. In both cases, the $\mathcal{R}$ relation can be taken to be either a lexical property of the RESTRICTOR (e.g. RA or the genitive) or a constructional property of the phrase as a whole.

However, as first mentioned in Chapter 2, one essential difference between modification-by-noun and alienable possession is that in the former the RESTRICTOR tends to be non-referential – that is, N or perhaps NP, rather than DP – unlike possessors. Baker (2003, 198), for instance, claims that the referential index of a nominal modifier is deactivated because of its syntactic position in the phrase. In this sense a nominal modifier is a non-referential counterpart to the alienable possessor, as in *child's seat*. Thus, while the expression *a ghost's train* denotes a train with some contextually defined relation (e.g. ownership) to some (actual) ghost, *a ghost train*, with modification-by-noun, simply describes a type of train without even committing us to the existence of ghosts, leave alone specifying some particular train-owning ghost. The difference is readily understandable when we note that the modification-by-noun construction, by its nature, can establish a relation only between the denotation of the head noun and a common noun denotation, which by definition is non-referential. The possessive construction, on the other hand, establishes a relation between the head noun denotation and that of a possessor realized as a determined NP/DP, hence (potentially) referential. As a result, it comes as no surprise that many languages choose to grammaticalize this difference.

We have also seen that many languages group together modification-by-noun and canonical attributive modification by employing essentially the same encoding strategy. In the case of RAs, for instance (whether true transpositions or transpositional lexemes), the modification-by-noun type meaning is expressed as an adjectival representation of the modifying noun. Our analysis effectively treats them as nouns which have been type-shifted or coerced into becoming adjectives, while retaining their essentially nominal semantics.

The semantic similarity between modification-by-noun and canonical attributive modification lies in the fact that both types involve set intersection, where the denotation of the dependent identifies a certain subset in the denotation of the head noun. But canonical attributive modifiers tend to be some kind of adjective, hence the split observed in many languages. The whole point of having a class of adjectives is to allow the grammar to ascribe properties to nouns. This cannot be the point behind modification-by-noun because the noun has as its canonical function reference to entities, not to (gradable) properties, and the relation between the modifier and head is not defined by an intrinsic meaning of the modifier itself.

7.4 *The Syntax of the* ℜ *Relation* 281

In sum, encoding strategies employed to express relevant constructional meanings exhibit monotonicity along the Possession-Modification Scale because the neighbouring points are semantically close. This idea is in part similar to some of the research within traditional functional typology with its reliance on implicational statements, and shows particular convergence with semantic maps (Haspelmath, 2003; Croft, 2003, 133ff, among others) because it condenses a number of individual statements about possible shared forms into a single cross-linguistic representation. The thinking behind this method is that different subcategories of meaning do not represent an unordered set: polyfunctionality of form only occurs when they are sufficiently similar. Similarity is illustrated by the topological closeness of the nodes representing submeanings, so conceptual proximity is reflected in spatial proximity. If points are non-adjacent, there will only be a form that expresses them both if it also takes in a complete sequence of intermediate points in between. This approach allows the derivation of a number of implicational statements and demonstrates a close connection between synchronic studies of polysemy, on the one hand, and grammaticalization theory and diachronic studies of semantic change, on the other hand. Semantic maps can be used to illustrate the direction of change within a given domain. Whenever the domain covered by some marker on a map changes, the relevant developments can only affect neighbouring nodes. A semantic development from X to Y will always involve an intermediate stage of polysemy, with both meanings X and Y available for the same form.

Most semantic maps deal with polyfunctional exponents realizing categories such as, e.g., case, tense, or modality. Our approach differs from this traditional method, since we have studied morphosyntactic constructions rather than individual exponents and have defined the form of the construction in terms of what we have referred to earlier as 'encoding strategy'. Perhaps even more importantly, a classical semantic map is a two-dimensional representation of functions in conceptual space that are linked by many connecting lines and form a complex network. Compared to the multidimensional maps of many studies, our one-dimensional scale may seem a rather meagre affair. There is a good reason for this. The kind of semantic affinity which gives rise to our implicational scale is different from the usually studied types of semantic effects. A fair amount of research has been devoted to polysemy in which a given morphosyntactic construction with a core meaning (such as, say, a reflexive verb) undergoes semantic drift and acquires a host of polysemous or homonymous usages. In our case, the effect of semantic relatedness is the precise opposite: a single semantic thread runs through our four construction

282 *Attributive Modification in Lexicalist Morphosyntax*

types, namely the poorly understood notion of 'modifier of a noun'. This semantic core serves to restrict encoding strategies that can be found across the four types. Such semantically driven restrictions across morphosyntactic expressions are a phenomenon which has not been widely discussed in the typological literature, but it is a line of inquiry which we believe may prove very fruitful if applied to a greater variety of construction types.

Finally, although the Possession-Modification Scale makes predictions which hold up reasonably well cross-linguistically, there are some respects in which it is not fully satisfactory as a typological generalization. The main problem with the scale is that discussed in Chapter 2, Section 2.5.7, namely counterexamples to the scale's monotonicity requirement that arise from constructions using pure juxtaposition. On the current set of assumptions those are just the constructions for which we would provide a genuinely constructional analysis, locating the $\mathfrak{R}$ attribute on the mother node and not on either of its daughters. It is therefore possible that it is this representational property that gives rise to the violations of the scale.

One possibly relevant consideration is that juxtaposition is not inherently oriented towards the possession/modification distinction, unlike dedicated morphosyntactic constructions such as genitives or adjective agreement, which appear to be canonical expressions for possession and modification, respectively (Nikolaeva and Spencer, 2012). Juxtaposition (or specific word orders generally) is, in an important sense, construction-neutral. It is just one aspect of the more general phenomenon of expression by syntactic structure as it does not rely on anything other than what all languages have to have, namely linearized sets of words. Simple linear adjacency can be used to express more or less any relationship, and without some language-specific convention it is not even possible to identify which element is the head and which the dependent. Moreover, it is completely independent of grammatical category. In this sense it is the default encoding strategy for any grammatical relation and is likely to be historically primary. Thus, juxtaposition can appear unpredictable from the point of view of our implicational scale for expressing any type of semantic function, ranging from inalienable possession to either type of modification.

7.5   Conclusions

In this chapter we have laid out our basic assumptions about the structure of nominal phrases, paying particular attention to the (usually scant) discussion of attributive modification. The chapter presented a descriptive framework which can, in principle, be easily adapted to standard, mainstream syntactic

7.5 Conclusions 283

models and which is just explicit enough to allow us to express the relationships between form and meaning that we are interested in. We sketched a mechanism for combining the model of lexical and morphological representation and relatedness of Spencer (2013) with the model of attributive modification developed in Ackerman and Nikolaeva (2013), and motivated a special Semantic Function role, A*, for representing attributive modifiers (of whatever lexical/phrasal class). With these descriptive and implementational preliminaries we are now in a position to illustrate the way that our system works over the various types of noun–adjective hybrids we have described earlier. This will be the topic of Chapter 8, where the machinery developed in this chapter will be deployed to investigate the principal empirical phenomenon of interest to us: syntagmatic category mixing in modification-by-nominal-concept constructions.

8 Noun–Adjective Hybrids

8.1 Introduction

Basing our analysis of lexical structure and morphological relatedness on previously introduced representations and the syntactic mechanism sketched in the previous chapter, we are now in a position to capture the properties of the key types of noun–adjective hybrids. In the framework of Spencer (2013) such hybrids may be either true transpositions and hence in an important sense a 'form' of the base noun lexeme, or they can be distinct autonomous lexemes in their own right. We begin in Section 8.2 by focussing on one specific property which serves to define intermediate types of denominal adjectival forms, namely the possibility of modifying the base noun (stem) with an attributive modifier. We will then illustrate our approach by means of a number of 'case studies'. Section 8.3 provides lexical representations of two minimally contrastive types of hybrid denominal adjectives. In Section 8.4 we will consider how lexical representations are integrated into the syntactic representations we have argued for in Chapter 7.

8.2 Syntagmatic Mixing in Noun–Adjective Hybrids

Recall from Chapter 1 that syntagmatic category mixing is found when a word form appears to belong to one morphosyntactic class with respect to one set of words or phrases with which it is in construction, but to another morphosyntactic class with respect to other words/phrases with which it is in construction (the 'internal' vs. 'external' syntax of Haspelmath (1996)). This section shows that one particular type of syntagmatic mixing, the Base Noun Modifiability Property (BNMP), is the salient feature of noun–adjective hybrids and must be reflected in their lexical representations.

8.2.1 The Principle of Lexemic Transparency

Syntagmatic mixing is particularly common with true transpositions. In Chapter 5, Section 5.4 we pointed out that, potentially, all three major lexical

8.2 Syntagmatic Mixing in Noun–Adjective Hybrids   285

categories can undergo transposition (Spencer, 1999, 2005b, 2013). However, as far as syntagmatic mixing is concerned, the literature focusses almost exclusively on the kind illustrated by the English POSS-ACC nominalization in which an action nominal takes noun specifiers but takes complements and modifiers as a verb: *the children's singing the song so sweetly*. What is much less frequently observed is the fact that exactly the same syntagmatic mixing is found with deverbal participles (the 'adjectival representation of the verb'), as in the Russian example shown in (1).

(1)   Russian attributive participle

devuška   tixo   pojuščaja   pesnju
girl[F].NOM.SG quietly singing.F.NOM.SG song

'a/the girl quietly singing a/the song'

Moreover, we would expect to find eight other types of syntagmatic mixing. For instance, in languages in which the noun or adjective has predicative-inflected forms, the verb representation might permit modification that is typical of the base noun/adjective. Schematically, in addition to *Tom man-is* we might have *Tom* [[*tall man*]-*is*], and in addition to *Harriet* [*tall-is*] we might have *Harriet* [[*very tall*]-*is*] or *Harriet than Dick* [[*tall-er*]-*is*]. Similarly, the nominal representation of an adjective might permit specification of that adjective, schematically [[*very happy*]-*ness*].

Spencer (2013) does not address syntagmatic mixing in any detail, but the analysis (tentatively) proposed in that work for property nominals and relational adjectives is to link syntagmatic category mixing to the lexemic status of the derived word. Following this line of reasoning, we will for the most part concentrate on syntagmatic category mixing arising from the operation of the GPF which defines lexical relatedness in a given language.

The crucial question to ask about the GPF is whether it introduces a change in the LI. Our working assumption will be the Strong Derived Category Membership Hypothesis proposed in Spencer (2013, 358). In a nutshell, this hypothesis states that syntagmatic category mixing is found when a derived lexical entry is still regarded by the syntax, so to speak, as an exemplar of the base lexical entry. In other words, we tie the possibility of syntagmatic mixing to the notion of 'lexeme': syntagmatic mixing indicates that the morphological process which defines the denominal adjective does not define a new lexeme as such, but rather defines a new form of the base lexeme, as is the case with all true transpositions. For instance, English -*ing* nominals and regular participles will actually be forms of the base verb lexeme. We can code this intuition in the

286 *Noun–Adjective Hybrids*

GPFM model by saying that syntagmatic mixing is found when output of the GPF fails to induce a change in the LI. If a derived word shows syntagmatic mixing, then this can be taken as a symptom that the LI has not been changed and that we are dealing with intra- or within-lexemic relatedness.

A major criterion for deciding that a transposition is really a distinct lexeme is lexemic lexical opacity: unlike a genuine transposition, a transpositional lexeme fails to permit any rule of syntax to treat it as though it were still a member of its base lexeme's category. This can be taken as an indication that we are seeing a change of the LI and new lexeme formation. We can summarize these claims by proposing the principle in (3), in accordance with the definition of syntagmatic category mixing given in (2).

(2) Syntagmatic category mixing
Assume a lexeme, L, with SYN attributes $\alpha = \{a, b, c, ...\}$. Suppose L appears in a syntactic environment E such that L in E exhibits at least one syntactic dependency determined by some subset of α and at least one syntactic dependency determined by some $d \notin \alpha$. Then we say that L (in E) exhibits syntagmatic category mixing and L (in E) is a syntagmatically mixed category.

(3) Principle of Lexemic Transparency
Assume a lexeme L, LI = L_1, related to a base B, LI=L_2 by some GPF φ. Then L can exhibit syntagmatic category mixing only if L_1=L_2.

The Principle of Lexemic Transparency can be factorized into two potentially distinct claims:

(4) Principle of Lexemic Transparency factored
Assume a lexeme L, LI = L_1, related to a base B, LI=L_2 by some GPF φ, and given some morphosyntactic dependency $\Delta(L,B)$:

(i) If Δ is determined by the syntactic category of B, then L_1=L_2
(ii) If L_1=L_2, then Δ is determined by the syntactic category of B

(Clause (i) of (4) is related to locality conditions such as the Lexical Integrity Condition of Lapointe (1980), the Atom Condition of Williams (1981) or the Adjacency Condition of Allen (1978), but it is independent of the phrase structure assumptions under which those conditions are stated.)

Note that we would clearly not expect to see syntagmatic mixing if the GPF fails to alter specifically the syntactic component of the lexical representation in any significant way. This does not actually follow from the architecture we are

8.2 Syntagmatic Mixing in Noun–Adjective Hybrids 287

assuming, it must be stressed. The noun MEAL in English in one of its meanings denotes an *Event* (*The meal lasted three hours*). In principle, we could imagine a language which treated a lexeme like MEAL in part as a verb by virtue of the ontological category of *Event* that it denotes. In such a language we might see the translation equivalent of, say, *John's meal ham and eggs* with the meaning 'The meal during which John ate ham and eggs'. We believe that such instances are likely to be rare, and certainly rarer than the instances of syntagmatic mixing induced by the application of the GPF which changes the SYN value of a representation. So the strongest statement we could make is that syntagmatic category mixing is found if and only if we have an application of the GPF that preserves the LI. Such a principle would rule out mixing with representations such as MEAL.[1]

As it stands, the Principle of Lexemic Transparency is simply a principle, that is, an observation. We can imagine implementing this principle formally in a number of ways. One approach would be to simply write the principle into rules of syntactic combination. On this account the Head-Modifier construction, for example, would be made sensitive to the LI of the derived word. However, this seems to violate the very principle of Lexical Integrity that it is designed to enshrine: how would the Head-Modifier construction have access to the derivational history of such an adjective? For this reason we will propose that the difference between a category that permits mixing and a syntactically opaque derived category that does not permit mixing is encoded in the representations themselves. We will do this by enriching the notion of argument structure representation in lexical representations. In the case of (canonical) derivation, in which all of the components of the lexical entry including the LI are redefined, the SYN attribute is defined by two

---

[1] However, this is probably too strong. For one thing, it would seem that there do exist instances of syntagmatic mixing with underived lexical entries that show morpholexical incoherence of certain types. In particular, we might encounter syntagmatic mixing where we have a lexical representation whose SYN attribute itself induces incoherence in the entry. For instance, we have defined a relatedness type which we called the *Angestellte(r)*-noun, the result of regular grammatical processes in German. But there exists one noun in German in this class which no longer has a derivational base and which thus has to be treated as an independent lexical entry and not the result of application of the GPF: *Beamte(r)* 'civil servant'. This noun shows the same mixing as other *Angestellte(r)*-nouns, in that is takes the 'weak' adjectival declension in definite NPs and the 'strong' declension elsewhere – a type of syntagmatic mixing. One might argue that Russian *stolovaja* 'canteen' nouns exhibit mild syntagmatic mixing too. Nouns in Russian take the genitive singular form after numerals whose final component is two to four (paucal) and the genitive plural after numerals whose final component is five upwards. But feminine gender nouns tend to take nominative plural agreement forms after the paucal numerals, and feminine gender *stolovaja* nouns follow them: *dve stolovye/*stolovoj* 'two canteens'.

288 *Noun–Adjective Hybrids*

principles: the Derived Lexical Entry Principle and the Default Cascade. In all other (non-canonical) cases of relatedness the SYN value has to be specified as part of the GPF. When the GPF defines an instance of inter-lexemic relatedness, the LI of the base is preserved, the Default Cascade cannot come into play, and so the SYN function of the GPF, f_{syn}, has to specify the syntactic category of the output. In practice, this principally means specifying the SF role of the output.

8.2.2 *The Base Noun Modifiability Property*

Let us now focus on one specific instance of syntagmatically mixed attributive modifier constructions, namely those showing the BNMP.

In (5) we define mixing with respect to attributive modification by restricting our definitions to attributive modifier constructions.

(5)   Mixed Modifier Corollary

Assume a modifier M modifying a head H of lexeme index L_1. Let H be systematically derived from a lexeme B of lexemic index L_2. Then, if $L_1=L_2$, the morphosyntactic type of modification of H by M can be determined by the syntactic category of the base lexeme, B (that is, the modification can show syntagmatic category mixing by treating the modified element as though it were still of category B).

For instance, suppose we have a noun lexeme B and the modifier M is an adjective, such that it can modify B, then that adjective can modify H as though it were the original noun, B, provided that H and B share the same Lexemic Index (and vice versa). This is illustrated schematically in (6).

(6)   [HP [MP M_i] [H [B B_i]-aff]]

The corollary in (5) is essentially a paraphrase of the Strong Derived Category Membership Hypothesis.

In Spencer (2013) it is argued that the transparency effect with inflected forms is the automatic consequence of the fact that attributive modification is defined over the entire lexical representation of the head noun, independently of its inflectional realization, so that the attributive modification process is, so to speak, blind to the inflectional form of the noun lexeme being modified. For example, in English the expression *black cats* has to be thought of as a construction in which the lexeme BLACK modifies the lexeme CAT. It is not the case that (any specific form of) the adjective modifies, say, the plural form of the noun. Inflection for plural number is, in principle, independent of the influence of modifiers or determiners (though some modifiers/determiners may

8.2 Syntagmatic Mixing in Noun–Adjective Hybrids 289

impose a specific choice of inflected form: *a/one/this cats*, *many/these/fewer than two cat*).

This also applies to denominal adjectives which show the BNMP. In simple terms, an attributive adjective may modify a certain type of denominal adjective because the grammar treats that denominal adjective as a form of the base noun, for instance as the adjectival representation of that noun and not as an autonomous adjectival lexeme. This implies that the syntagmatically mixed denominal adjective behaves as though it were still a noun for essentially the same reasons that a case-marked noun behaves like a noun with respect to modification. Following the Principle of Lexemic Transparency, there is no change in the LI.

Such lexical transparency effects can be seen in those languages in which the noun base of a denominal adjective can be modified. Consider again the Tundra Nenets example cited in Chapter 3, (21), repeated here as (7):

(7) pər'id'en'a-q sarm'ik°-rəxa-x°h wen'ako-x°h
 black-PL   wolf-SIM.A-DU   dog-DU
 '(two) dogs (looking) like black wolves'

In the case of Tundra Nenets we cannot demonstrate conclusively that the similitudinal adjective is an inflected form of the noun lexeme, as we will do for Selkup in later sections, because Tundra Nenets similitudinal adjectives cannot be formed from possessor-inflected noun forms. Nonetheless, there seems to be no reason, given the typology of lexical relatedness presented in Spencer (2013), why we should not say that similitudinal adjectives in Tundra Nenets preserve the LI of the base noun. So, following the Principle of Lexemic Transparency, the adjective lexeme BLACK in (7) modifies the lexeme WOLF. The lexeme WOLF has to appear in the similitudinal adjective form in order to modify the lexeme DOG, and in order to convey the similitudinal semantics. This conclusion is supported by the observation that the formation of similitudinal adjectives of this kind is fully productive (Nikolaeva, 2014b, 32ff). If we were to claim instead that the similitudinal adjective is a distinct lexeme from the base noun, then we would have an instance of a Lexical Integrity violation and a violation of clause (i) of the Principle of Lexemic Transparency in (4). Similarly, if we encountered a language in which adjectives could be derived from noun forms inflected for case, number, or possession, but in which the base nouns could no longer be modified attributively, we would have a counter-example to clause (ii) of (4).

Note that it only makes sense to equate the BNMP with Lexical Integrity violations where we are talking about two distinct lexemes. For instance, if a

290 *Noun–Adjective Hybrids*

language has a word formation process that derives a proprietive or ornative adjective lexeme from a (distinct) noun lexeme, then we expect the derived word to be syntactically opaque in the sense that the syntactic and semantic process should not have access to properties of the base noun lexeme. Thus, let us take MILKY to be, on one reading, a proprietive adjective derived from MILK, and having the interpretation 'possessing milk'. The 'derivational history' of the derived word could thus be represented as [$_A$[$_N$ milk]y]. Following the principle of Lexical Integrity, we would not expect a modifier to be able to modify the 'constituent' milk: *a goat's/skimmed/pasteurized milky drink* (cf. *a drink made from goat's/skimmed/pasteurized milk*). However, suppose we consider a language in which nouns inflect for a comitative/proprietive case with the meaning 'with N, having N', and suppose that in those circumstances a noun can serve as a modifier to another noun (like a prepositional phrase in the English *a drink with milk*). In such an instance, we would fully expect the case-marked form of the noun to be 'transparent', so that we would expect to be able to say *a [pasteurized milk-WITH] drink* (just like the English *a drink with pasteurized milk*).

By contrast, where the derivation gives rise to a completely opaque category, we can take this to be an indication that we are seeing new lexeme formation, as defined by change in the LI. This new lexeme formation does not give rise to syntagmatic mixing, and this is exactly what we saw in noun-to-adjective transpositional lexemes. We will return to them in Section 8.3.1.

8.3   Syntax of Denominal Modifiers

This section provides a syntactic analysis of the two types of relational adjectives we have already seen. The first type of relational adjective is a transpositional lexeme. It is derived from a noun without any additional semantic predicate, but the resulting adjective respects Lexical Integrity in the sense that the base noun is entirely opaque to syntactic and semantic processes that target nouns. The second type of relational adjective is the type which typically gives rise to hybrid behaviour. In this type the derived adjective exhibits the BNMP.

8.3.1   *Relational Adjectives as Transpositional Lexemes*

As we mentioned in Chapter 3, English, like other Indo-European languages, has denominal adjectives which effectively serve as the adjectival form of a noun. Thus, adjectives such as *tidal, prepositional, tabular, lunar, marine, lateral* in their basic meanings are identical semantically to (certain readings of) the nouns *tide, preposition, table, moon, sea, side*. For instance, the word *prepositional* is effectively no more than the adjectival form of the noun *preposition*, serving, therefore, as an attributive modifier and hence no different in meaning from the noun itself, as we can see from the fully synonymous compounds. All prepositional phrases are also preposition phrases and vice versa. Tidal fluctuations are no more than fluctuations in the tide, the first lunar landing was the same event as the first moon landing/landing on the moon, and so on.

So the combination of relational adjective and head noun normally has the same meaning as the compound (where it is licensed by usage). For this reason it is tempting to treat such words as transpositions from noun to adjective, or the adjectival representation of the base noun (the denominal equivalent of a participle). This would mean that denominal adjectives would bear the same LI as the base noun, being exponents of the transpositional feature [REPR:$\langle$N,A$\rangle$].

However, treating such words as true transpositions would not accord with traditional lexicographic practice. Dictionaries do not list (regular) past or present participles of verbs in English or corresponding forms in other languages such as Russian, but English relational adjectives are normally listed as distinct lexical entries. Nor would such a treatment be entirely compatible with our Principle of Lexemic Transparency and its Mixed Modifier Corollary introduced in Section 8.2.1. This is because English derived adjectives fail to show the BNMP. Thus, *high tidal fluctuations* cannot be fluctuations in/at high tide (*[*high tid*]al fluctuations*), but only high fluctuations in the tide (*high [tidal fluctuations]*), and *monosyllabic prepositional phrase* can only refer to a phrase which consists entirely of just one syllable (*monosyllabic [prepositional phrase]*), not a phrase headed by a monosyllabic preposition (*[*monosyllabic preposition*]al phrase*). Spencer (2013, 359) therefore proposed that such denominal adjectives in English (and by parity of reasoning in Romance, Balto- Slavic, Greek and other European languages) are not transpositions at all, but are autonomous lexemes in their own right, which, however, have a semantic content identical to that of their noun base. In other words, these are 'transpositional lexemes' (see Chapter 5).

Such transpositional lexemes are adjectives precisely so that they can function as attributive modifiers to nouns. This is particularly so in languages such as Romance or Slavic which generally lack a productive endocentric, Germanic-style, N-N compounding strategy and we often find relational adjectives fulfilling the primary function of modification-by-noun.

292   Noun–Adjective Hybrids

In Slavic languages adjectives have a rich inflectional paradigm. In such languages the default situation is one in which the Property specification of the SEM attribute automatically defines the A* SF role in the SYN|ARG-STR attribute. This in turn automatically defines the inflectional class to be that of the default adjectival class.

For instance, consider Russian relational adjectives derived with the suffix *-n-*, briefly introduced in Chapter 3, Section 3.3.2. Like canonical qualitative adjectives, they normally precede the head and agree with it in case, number, and gender (although their syntactic behaviour does differ in part from the behaviour of qualitative adjectives as they do not normally occur as predicates and lack so-called 'short forms').[2] It is not normally possible to discern any fixed conceptual content in such relational adjectives. Each particular interpretation depends on the lexical semantics of the relevant nouns and the general knowledge of the world. For instance, while the adjective *zvëzd-n-yj* usually has the proprietive meaning of 'with/having stars' as in *zvëzd-n-oe nebo* 'starry sky', with other head nouns it can have other meanings, e.g. *zvëzd-n-ye vojny* 'star wars', *zvëzd-n-yj god* 'sidereal year', *zvëzd-n-aja karta* 'star chart' (see also other examples cited in Mezhevich, 2002). The adjective *moloč-n-yj* derived from *moloko* 'milk' usually means 'made of milk' but can also occur in the following expressions:

(8)   moloč-n-yj kombinat   'milk factory, dairy factory'
      moloč-n-yj produkt   'dairy produce, milk product'
      moloč-n-aja produkcija   'milk production'
      moloč-n-aja dieta   'milk diet (dairy foods diet)'
      moloč-n-yj brat   'son of one's wetnurse' (literally 'milk brother')
      moloč-n-yj saxar   'lactose' (literally 'milk sugar')'

Exactly the same variability is found with English 'milk' compounds: *milk pudding* (with so-called 'phrasal stress') means 'pudding made out of/with milk', but other translations from (8) (with 'compound stress') show the same variation (*milk factory/product/production/diet*), and *milk sugar* is a perfectly comprehensible nonce formation meaning 'sugar which has some connection with milk (e.g. derived from milk, added to milk in a particular recipe, forming a solution in water with the colour of milk, etc.). Overall, then, the meaning of Russian relational adjectives in *-n-* is as general as in English N-N compounds. The range of functions and uses of relational adjectives

---

[2]   Polish has a very similar, but if anything more extensive system of relational adjectives (Szymanek, 2010; Cetnarowska, 2015).

corresponds very closely to the range of functions and uses of modifying nouns in N-N compounds, which are effectively absent in Russian. However, like English compounds, Russian relational adjectives do tend to have fixed functions, making them look like true derived adjectives.[3]

In Russian relational adjectives, as in their English counterparts, the base noun does not retain any nominal morphosyntax: we do not find inbound attributive modification of the base. If modification is required, the 'relational adjective + noun' construction will usually be paraphrased by means of the construction in which the adjective is replaced by the genitive form of the base noun, or by a prepositional phrase headed by that noun. Thus, the expression, *moloč-n-yj puding* 'milk pudding' means essentially *puding iz moloka* 'pudding (made) from milk'. The postmodifier constructions have to be used whenever the modifying noun is itself modified. So the example in (9a) can only have the meaning 'milk pudding which is fresh', not 'pudding made from fresh milk', as shown in (9b).

(9) a. svež-ij   moloč-n-yj   puding
         fresh-M.NOM milk.REL.A-M.NOM pudding[M].NOM
         'fresh milk-pudding'

         = svežij [moloč-n-yj puding]

         ≠ [svežij moloč]-n-yj puding

     b. puding iz   svež-ego molok-a
         pudding from fresh-GEN milk-GEN
         'fresh-milk pudding'

In other words, Russian relational adjectives fail to exhibit the BNMP.

In Chapter 2 we sketched the widely accepted analysis of the modification-by-noun semantics of N-N compounding in which the compounding construction introduces a pragmatically/contextually determined interpreted relation ℜ between the attribute noun and its head. We modified this analysis in Chapter 7, Section 7.3.3 to account for relational adjectives (both as transpositional lexemes and as true transpositions). The relational adjective lexicalizes the ℜ relation by incorporating it into its semantic representation. This was illustrated for the English suppletive transpositional lexeme MARINE from SEA. The derived

---

[3] They may also acquire a metaphorical qualitative meaning, similar to English, e.g. *serdeč-n-aja bolezn'* 'heart disease' and *serdeč-n-yj čelovek* 'warm-hearted person' (literally 'heart person'). The former is interpreted as involving a relation between the notions 'disease' and 'heart', and the latter expresses a quality of the modified noun and does not contain a direct reference to the concept 'heart'. This is because, as in English, the distinction between relational and qualitative adjectives is primarily semantic and the boundary between them may be vague.

294 Noun–Adjective Hybrids

	base noun	derived relational adjective lexeme
FORM	MORCLASS N NOUN FEATURES NUM sg,pl	MORCLASS u (= A by Default Cascade) ADJ FEATURES GRADE positive
SYN	$\langle R \rangle$ Spec[]	u (= $\langle A\langle x\rangle\rangle$ by Default Cascade)
SEM	$[_{Thing}\ \lambda y.\mathbf{noun}(y)]$	$[_{Property}\ \lambda x\lambda y\lambda P\exists\Re[[_{Thing}P(x)]\ \wedge$ $[_{Thing}\ \lambda y.\mathbf{noun}(y)]\ \wedge\ \Re(x,y)]]$
LI	L_1	L_2

Figure 8.1 *Derivation of a relational adjective lexeme from a base noun lexeme in languages such as Russian*

relational adjective lexeme now denotes the contextually determined relation, $\Re$, applied to the semantics of the base noun and that of the head noun which the relational adjective modifies. The SEM representation is therefore subtly different from that of the base noun, though not by virtue of enrichment with an interpretable semantic predicate. Thus, the meaning of the adjective will be effectively the same as that of the noun in all *de re* contexts of interpretation (that is, the noun and adjective will have the same extension).

The relational adjective lexeme relatedness function is shown in Figure 8.1 for Russian, in which canonical adjectives are morphologically differentiated from all other parts of speech. In Figure 8.2 we see the structure for the Russian transpositional lexeme LYŽNYJ 'pertaining to skis'. Notice that *lyž-n-yj* is treated as a distinct lexeme with a distinct LI here. That LI is treated as regularly derived from that of the noun, SKIS, by application of a function, f_{reladj}, applied to the LI of the noun, SKIS. Moreover, although there is reference to the nominal origin of the adjective in the SEM representation, this aspect of the representation is not accessible to any process other than at a very general conceptual level at which we can say that LYŽNYJ means 'pertaining to skis'. This is because the ARG-ST representation unequivocally defines the derived adjective as an adjective, effectively obscuring its nominal origin.

The default specification of MORSIG in both FORM and SYN attributes will specify LYŽNYJ as an adjective, as shown in (10), which specifies that the word bears concordial or agreement features. Thus, it can modify a noun such as MAZ' 'grease', shown in (11).

8.3 *Syntax of Denominal Modifiers* 295

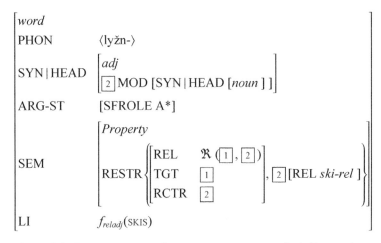

Figure 8.2 *Representation of* LYŽNYJ *'pertaining to skis' (Russian)*

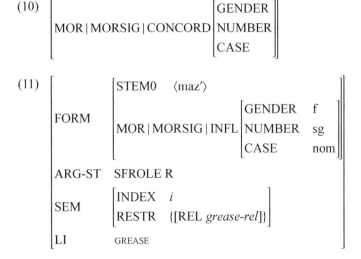

Note that the semantic representation is still that of the base noun, and the only semantic contribution of the relational adjective is the introduction of the $\mathcal{R}$ relation. That relation relates the meaning of the head noun (TARGET, where $\boxed{1}$ is the tag of the head noun of the NP) to that of the base noun lexeme (RESTRICTOR). Note, too, that the relational adjective, while retaining just the semantics of the base noun, lacks the attributes that would make that noun referential, i.e. the attributes INDEX and INSTANCE. In Figure 8.3 we see the relational adjective LYŽNYJ modifying the noun *maz'* 'grease'.

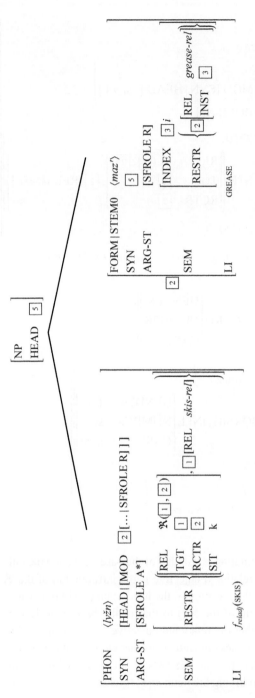

Figure 8.3 *Structure for Russian lyžnaja mazʼ 'ski grease'*

8.3 *Syntax of Denominal Modifiers* 297

In this section we have applied the analysis of English transpositional lexemes sketched in Chapter 7 to the very similar, but more frequent and systematic, Russian relational adjective transpositional lexemes. The relational adjective is a distinct lexeme from its noun base, but its conceptual content is the same. As an adjective, however, it introduces the contextually defined relation $\mathcal{R}$ into its SEM attribute. As a consequence, the semantic interpretation of the relational adjective-modified noun head construction is identical to that of the typical Germanic endocentric N-N compound.

Because Russian relational adjectives are transpositional lexemes, they are opaque to inbound modification; that is, they fail to exhibit the BNMP.

In the next section we contrast this type of relational adjective with a genuine noun-to-adjective transposition from Chukchi.

8.3.2 *Chukchi Relational Adjectives*

In Section 3.3.2 we noted that true transpositional relational and possessive adjectives are found in the Chukotko-Kamchatkan language Chukchi. As far as we can tell, the grammatical system of relational and possessive adjectives is essentially the same in the whole language group (including Koryak and Alutor, together with the recently extinct Kerek, though some relevant details are lacking in our sources for these other languages).[4] Here we discuss mainly the situation in Chukchi following Dunn (1999) and Skorik (1961).[5]

Chukchi relational adjectives are formed with the suffix *-kin(e)/ken(a)*. This can be added to nouns, including proper nouns, as well as to other parts of speech (Dunn, 1999, 148, 151). The meaning of the derived adjective is essentially that of the base lexeme together with the entailment that the denotation of the modified head noun bears the $\mathcal{R}$ relation to the base lexeme of the relational adjective. The possessive adjective is formed with the suffix *-in(e)/en(a)*.

Skorik (1961, 286) explicitly compares Chukchi relational and possessive adjective forms with Russian possessive constructions (and he explicitly states

---

4   Kurebito (2002) observes that the distribution of relational adjective allomorphs in Chukchi follows the Animacy Hierarchy in a manner that parallels the suppletive allomorphy of the ergative case. Intriguing though this observation is, it is not sufficient evidence to treat either relational adjectives or possessive adjectives as some kind of genitive case.

5   Chukchi and Koryak exhibit dominant-regressive vowel harmony, under which the regressive vowels {e, i, u} alternate with their dominant correlates {a, e, o} in words containing a dominant vowel or some other trigger of vowel harmony. The domain of harmony is the morphological word, including compound words such as those involving incorporation. Vowel harmony is a reasonably robust indicator of wordhood, therefore. For convenience, we will cite individual regressive roots and affixes in both regressive and dominant harmonic forms.

298   *Noun–Adjective Hybrids*

(1961, 286–287, fn. 214), that they are "grammatical forms" of the noun, i.e. transpositions). Thus, he gives the glosses shown in (12) for various forms of the root *utt/ott* 'tree, wood' modifying the noun *wətwət* 'leaf' (Skorik, 1961, 286, fn. 213) (*drevesnyj* = relational adjective from *derevo* 'tree').

(12)   Glosses for three types of modification by nominal

	Chukchi	Russian gloss	
incorporated modifier:			
	ottə-wətwət	*drevesnyj list*	[lit.] 'arboreal leaf'
possessive adjective:			
	utt-in wətwət	*list dereva, iz dereva*	'leaf of tree, from tree'
relational adjective:			
	uttə-kin wətwət	*list, kotoryj na dereve*	'leaf which is on a tree'

From these glosses it is clear that the relational adjective expresses a temporary, stage-level property, while the possessive adjective expresses a more permanent, individual-level property.

Perhaps the clearest indication that we are dealing with true transpositions is the fact that both relational adjectives and possessive adjectives can be derived not just from common nouns (and from proper names and kin terms in the case of possessive adjectives), but also from a variety of function words, such as demonstratives, pronominals, and quantifiers. For instance, Skorik (1961, 272–273, Paradigm 23) presents the full declension for the relational adjectives derived from the interrogative determiners *rʔe* 'which? what?', *miŋke* 'from where? whence?' and *tite* 'when?' (see also Skorik, 1961, 277).

A further indication that we are dealing with true transpositions comes from the morphology. The human class ('second declension') of nouns has a full set of distinct number forms in all cases. Possessive adjective forms can be derived from both singular and non-singular (plural for Chukchi (Dunn, 1999, 151), dual or plural for Koryak/Alutor (Kibrik et al., 2004, 287)) forms.

The strongest evidence that relational adjectives or possessive adjectives in a given language are true transpositions, given our framework of assumptions, is the BNMP. Unfortunately, it is difficult to find instances of the base noun being modified by an attributive adjective or a specifier in the texts because the construction itself is rather infrequent and it rarely seems to be the target of elicitation by fieldworkers. Nonetheless, as we pointed out in Chapter 3.3.2, given the right context, illustrations of the BNMP can be found in Chukchi.

In Chukotko-Kamchatkan languages unfocussed attributive modifiers (adjectives or nouns) will typically be incorporated into the head noun (see Spencer (1995) for Chukchi, Kibrik et al. (2004, 288–289) for Alutor). This

8.3 Syntax of Denominal Modifiers   299

means that we can expect to see relatively few instances of inbound attributive modification with relational adjectives and possessive adjectives. However, what we do expect to see is cases in which such a modifier has been incorporated by the base noun before that noun itself gets marked for the relational adjective/possessive adjective category.

In fact, the literature contains isolated instances of this happening. In (13) we see the possessive adjective *gənnik-in* from *gənnik* 'animal' modified with the incorporated interrogative specifier *rʔe-/rʔa-* (Skorik, 1961, 243–246) .

(13)   rʔe-gənnik-in   nalgepə getekəlin kʔeli?
       WH-animal-POSS.A skin.ABL made   hat
       'From the skin of which animal is the hat made?'

       qapar-ena-jpə
       wolverine-POSS.A-ABL
       'From a wolverine's'

In example (17), Chapter 3, Section 3.3.2 we saw cases in which numerals were incorporated into a possessive adjective. In (14) (Skorik, 1961, 274) we see a further example, in which the noun *kiw* 'day' is modified by a numeral before assuming the possessive adjective form.

(14)   ŋiren-kiw-kin   taqʔat
       two-day-POSS.A supplies
       'two days of supplies'

In (15) and (16) (Skorik, 1961, 274) we see cases in which the modifier of the base noun lexeme, *ʔаttʔət* 'dog', *pojg* 'spear', is a noun.

(15)   ŋinqeje ətləg-ʔаttʔ-ine-t   rʔarqa-t   nenajaaqenat
       boys   father-dog-POSS.A-PL harness-PL used
       'The boys used the harnesses from father's dogs'

(16)   pəlwəntə-pojgə-ken ŋilgən təlpʔigʔi
       metal-spear-POSS.A strap   broke
       'The strap from the metal spear broke'

In (17) (Skorik, 1961, 285) we see an example in which an unincorporated possessive pronoun modifies the noun base of the possessive adjective *moogərəken* 'pertaining to a beginning'.

(17)   turg-in   moogərə-ken   keliwətgər jep amcoka
       you[PL]-POSS.A beginning-POSS.A time   yet not.arrived
       'The time of your beginning has not yet come'

300　*Noun–Adjective Hybrids*

Finally, we can ask how Chukchi expresses recursion in the possessive construction corresponding to *my brother's friend's uncle's ... neighbour*. In his survey of possessive forms, Dunn (1999, 149–151) remarks: "Recursive possessors do not occur very often. Example 033 [reproduced in (18) below] is a rare example."

> (18)　Jare-n　　　　　　uweqəc-in　　　　　　　ətləgə-n
> 　　　　Jare-POSS.A.3SG.ABS husband-POSS.A.3SG.ABS father-3SG.ABS
> 　　　　'[He was] Jare's husband's father'

The evidence points to an analysis of Chukchi relational/possessive adjectives as true transpositions or adjectival representations of nouns. This means that nouns in Chukchi bear [REPR:⟨N,A⟩] in their MORSIG. Like participles in many languages, there is more than one kind of DNA, in Chukchi, so the REPR feature has to distinguish two subtypes: [REPR:⟨⟨N,A⟩, {RelA, PossA}⟩]. A noun bearing either feature specification will therefore be furnished with the *-(k)in(e)/(k)en(a)* suffix and, crucially, will have its SFROLE attribute enriched to ⟨A*⟨R⟩⟩. By virtue of the Default Cascade, it will therefore acquire the agreement features associated with adjectives (in both attributive and predicative use), and the SYN attribute will also be enriched to permit the DNAs to modify a noun head.

The lexical content of the noun lexeme will not be altered, but the RESTRICTION of the SEM attribute will be enriched to include the $\mathfrak{R}$ relation. A complete analysis would also specify the subtle semantic differences between the relational adjective and the possessive adjective categories, but we have insufficient information to be able to specify precisely what those differences are or how they relate to the semantics of possession more generally. We have noted that the relational adjective formation process can apply to words of other categories in Chukchi. We lack sufficient information to be able to make definitive claims about this, but it is worth noting that there are other instances of attributive modifiers being formed from more than one category. The Turkish *-ki* formative mentioned in Section 3.4.1 is one example, as is the *-t:u* attributivizer of the Nakh-Daghestanian language Archi (Bond and Chumakina, ms.), which attaches to words and phrases of pretty well any category. Such instances of pancategorial transposition to adjective can be studied only against the background of a proper typological survey of transpositions to adjective, specifically of deverbal participles, which is currently lacking.

To summarize, Chukchi relational adjectives contrast with their Russian counterparts in two main ways. One is their productivity: while Russian relational adjectives are, perhaps, more common than, say, their English counterparts, this category does not seem to be productive in the way that Chukchi relational adjectives seem to be (recall that Skorik explicitly describes them as 'grammatical forms of the noun'). Moreover, we have seen limited, but telling, evidence that relational (and possessive) adjectives in Chukchi exhibit the BNMP, and are thus better considered as forms of the base noun lexeme than as autonomous lexemes; that is, Chukchi DNAs are true transpositions, not transpositional lexemes.

The status of Russian possessive adjectives remains slightly less clear, however. Given their rather restricted applicability, one could argue that they are very productive: they are found with all personal names (given names) of the appropriate morphophonological form, especially in their hypocoristic or diminutive forms. However, unlike the possessive adjectives of Upper Sorbian, they fail to exhibit the BNMP, and in that respect behave like Russian relational adjectives, namely as autonomous transpositional lexemes.

8.4 Representations of Noun-to-Adjective Derivations

We conclude our survey with a discussion of six cases of syntagmatically mixed denominal forms. The first four cases we consider are those of relational and possessive adjectives in which the morphology defines adjectival representations of nouns in a similar manner to the way in which derived denominal adjective lexemes are defined. We begin with the Samoyedic language Selkup, discussed in Nikolaeva (2008) and extensively in Spencer (2013, Ch 10). There are three regular and productive noun-to-adjective transpositions. One of them is a standard instance of a relational adjective, but the other two introduce an additional semantic predicate while still remaining demonstrably forms of (adjectival representations of) the base noun lexeme. What is particularly striking about all three DNAs is that they can be formed from nouns which are inflected for possessor agreement, guaranteeing that they are adjectival representations of nouns and not autonomous lexemes.

We then turn our attention to Evenki proprietives. These are, in a sense, the complement to the Selkup denominal adjectives, in that the base noun lexeme can inflect for number but not for possessor agreement. Evenki adjectives can show concord with their head noun, and so we discuss the way that this is implemented in our model. We then consider the possessive adjective in Upper Sorbian, discussed in some detail in Chapters 3 and 4. We briefly sketch the way that the Upper Sorbian case might be handled on the basis of our analyses of Selkup and Evenki.

302   *Noun–Adjective Hybrids*

The fifth and sixth cases we consider are constructions in which a nominal word form takes on adjectival properties without apparently undergoing any special transpositional morphology to turn the noun into an adjective. The first of these is the agreeing genitive construction in the Central Cushitic language Awngi. Here, we have a genitive case-marked possessive construction, as in many languages, but the genitive case-marked noun agrees with its head as though it were an adjective – a typical case of Suffixaufnahme. Finally, we consider the case of compounding in another Samoyedic language, Tundra Nenets. This language has juxtapositional N-N compounding, but the dependent noun shows optional adjectival agreement with the head noun, in spite of the absence of any denominal adjectival morphology.

8.4.1   *Selkup Relational Adjectives*

We now turn to the Samoyedic (Uralic) language Selkup (Northern, Taz, dialect), based on the data from Kuznecova et al. (1980) (Spencer, 2013, Ch 10).[6] Selkup has a great variety of morphological devices for creating transpositions from one lexical category to another, to the extent that Kuznecova et al. explicitly demarcate this aspect of the grammar in their description under the heading of *representacija* ('representation'), following Smirnickij (1959). Here we concentrate on some of their examples of adjectival representation of nouns, that is denominal forms of various types derived by suffixation. What we will see is that the adjectival representations of nouns, while fulfilling the canonical syntactic function of adjectives, namely attributive modification, retain significant traces of their nominal past and behave in many respects like inflected forms of nouns. They are thus syntagmatically mixed, the nominal equivalent of the deverbal participles discussed in Chapter 6.

Before we discuss denominal adjectives, we provide a brief overview of Selkup nominal inflection. Selkup nouns share the general structure of Uralic nouns in having three suffix position slots for number, possessor agreement, and case. Number/possessor and possessor/case are often cumulated, but this fact will not play any role in our discussion. Selkup has singular, dual, and plural number forms for nouns and for possessor agreement, and in addition has distinct collective forms for nouns. It distinguishes the following case

---

[6]   We use the transcriptional conventions used by Helimski (1998), except that we represent palatalization of consonants with the prime symbol, as in /l'/ and we write /č/ as /c/. We use schwa, ə, for Helimski's ë. Approximate phonetic values are those of the IPA except: c = ʧ, n'=nʲlʲ = lʲ, š = ʃ; ä = æ, ü = y, ö = ø, ï = i, å= ɔ.

8.4 Representations of Noun-to-Adjective Derivations   303

forms (the names reflect the canonical uses of each case, of course): nominative, accusative, genitive, instrumental, caritive, translative, coordinative, dative-allative, illative, locative, elative, prolative, and vocative. The number forms for the unpossessed nominative form of the noun QOQ 'leader' are shown in (19) after (Kuznecova et al., 1980, 197).

(19)   Number marking on /qoq/ 'leader'

dual	qoqqɪ
plural	qoot
collective	qool'mï

A typical example of a fully inflected noun is shown in (20) (constructed following Kuznecova et al., 1980, 201).

(20)   qoo-iint-ït-kåålïk
       leader-PL-2PL.POSS-CARITIVE
       'without your (2+) leaders (2+)'

Adjectives fall into two morphological classes, l'-adjectives and non-l'-adjectives, depending on whether they end in the formative -l' or not. Neither type inflects except (marginally) for comparative degree. Some adjectives are derived from nouns by means of various suffixes, usually ending in -l'. A simple denominal adjective is illustrated by the Selkup proprietive construction, formed by suffixing -sïmïl' to a noun base. This has essentially the same properties as the Tungusic proprietives already discussed. The proprietive suffix can attach to a noun which is itself modified by an adjective, as shown in (21a). However, it cannot attach to a noun which bears possessor agreement: see (21b).

(21)   a. ontï mååt-sïmïl'   qum
           own house-PROPR.A man
           'man with (his) own house'

       b. (*təpïn) *mååt-tï-sïmïl'   qum
           (3SG.GEN) house-3SG-PROPR.A man
           'man with his (own) house'

The example in (21b) is ungrammatical whether or not possessor agreement is doubled by an overt genitive case.

Importantly, Kuznecova et al. make a clear formal distinction between simple denominal adjectives and the adjectival representations of nouns. Both function as modifiers, but adjectival representations are analysed as part of the

304   *Noun–Adjective Hybrids*

nominal paradigm and they are explicitly excluded from the class of adjectives proper (Kuznecova et al., 1980, 265).

There are three synthetic adjectival representations of nouns, which Kuznecova et al. refer to as 'relational' (*otnositel'naja forma*), 'co-ordinative' (*koordinativnaja forma*), and locative (*lokativnaja forma*).[7] The relational representation is formed by suffixing *-l'* to the second stem of the noun, while the similitudinal and locative representations are formed by means of a suffix which contains the *-l'* formative (though it cannot easily be separated as a distinct affix). The glosses provided for the relational type make it clear that the semantic relationship between the relational form and the base noun is very general, as in English N-N compounding. The meaning of the 'co-ordinative' type is "corresponding to something/someone, identical to something/someone in size or some other property" (Kuznecova et al., 1980, 193). We take this formation to be a kind of (perhaps semantically restricted) similitudinal adjective. The locative form is semantically self-explanatory. Typical examples are shown in (22).

(22)   Adjectival representations of Selkup nouns
relational representation	kana-l'	'dog's, related to dogs'
similitudinal representation	alako-ššal'	'similar to a boat'
locative representation	mååt-qïl'	'located in the/a house'

The crucial difference between denominal adjectives and adjectival representations of nouns is that, unlike true adjectives, adjectival representations of nouns take nominal possessive inflections. Thus, in addition to the relational form of the unpossessed noun QAQLÏ 'sledge', *qaqlïl'* 'pertaining to a sledge', we have forms such as *qaqlïnul'* 'pertaining to our.DU sledge' and *qaqlïntïtïl'* 'pertaining to their.PL sledge'. Similarly, in addition to the form *qaqlooqïl'* 'located in the sledge', we have *qaqlooqïnïtïl'* 'located in our.PL sledge'. In (23a) we see the similitudinal suffix attached to a noun which is modified by an adjective, and in (23b) we see it attached to a noun bearing possessor agreement morphology doubled by a genitive pronominal, therefore contrasting with (21) (Kuznecova et al., 1980, 193, 194):

(23)   a.   wərkï alako-ššal' antï
large boat-SIM.A canoe
'canoe similar to a large boat'

---

[7]   In addition, there are a number of periphrastic attributive forms made up of a combination of the oblique case of the base noun with the present participle of the verb 'to be', similar to what we saw earlier in Hungarian and Tundra Nenets. They appear to have been undergoing various degrees of agglutination in Selkup.

8.4 Representations of Noun-to-Adjective Derivations   305

b. mat   pååra-nï-šal'   qum
   1SG.GEN size-1SG-SIM.A man

   'man of my size (lit. man similar to my size)'

A further intriguing observation is that the suffixes of three adjectival representations are incompatible with case markers. In relation to locative representation, this is not surprising, given the meaning. It is worth observing that the locative representation suffix *-qïl'* is effectively the locative case *-qin* further suffixed by the adjectival *-l'* element. However, it remains puzzling why relational and similitudinal suffixes are not compatible with at least the meaningful case markers, given that they combine with possessor inflection. In other words, it is not difficult to conjure up meanings for relational adjectives which would include cases. For instance, Kuznecova et al. (1980, 191) cite the example *kïïmïl' kïr* 'bloody wound' from *kəm/kïïmï-* 'blood'. There is no obvious reason why we should not see an example derived from the caritive case (in *-kåålïk*) of this noun to give something such as **kïïmï-kåålïk-ïl' kïr* 'bloodless wound', but such constructions seem to be unattested. In the same way it is unclear why we cannot have forms translatable as 'similar to with a knife (instrumental)' or 'similar to at the river (locative)', yet they are impossible. In other words, the relational/similitudinal adjective suffix is not only compatible with inflected (possessive) forms of lexemes, it also occurs in the same slot where a case suffix would be expected.

What this shows is that Selkup has a standard noun-to-adjective non-meaning-bearing transposition (relational adjective), but additionally has two transpositions that introduce extra predicates: SIMILAR_TO (SIMIL) and LOCATED_AT (LOC). These are meaning-bearing transpositions, that is transpositions which are accompanied by a semantic enrichment of the lexical representation. In this respect they are the transpositional correspondents of meaningful (inherent) inflection.

The three suffixes of the adjectival representations of nouns are thus in complementary distribution with the case markers. Moreover, semantic case marking, for example local cases with meanings such as 'at X', 'in X', 'from the surface of X', and so on, is a typical example of meaningful inflection. Given this, the most economical way of describing the Selkup nominal system is to say that relational adjective suffixes are actually in paradigmatic opposition to the case markers. In effect, this is to define them as a kind of case inflection (cf. what we say about the Tungusic proprietive, for instance in Evenki, later in

306   *Noun–Adjective Hybrids*

this section).[8] Since the locative and similitudinal representations involve the addition of a semantic predicate, they are closer to being an instance of Booij's inherent inflection than contextual inflection.

This 'inflectional' interpretation of the relational adjective forms also follows from the fact that the three types of adjectival representation can apply to nouns inflected for possessor agreement (a form of contextual inflection in Booij's terms). It is, admittedly, unusual for affixes with such different morphosyntactic functions to be allotted to the same position class slot in nominal inflection, but comparable phenomena are fairly common in verb morphology, where we may find a pronominal agreement marker in a position normally occupied by aspect markers, or a polarity marker in a position normally occupied by subject markers. The point is that such constructions in Selkup behave morphologically as though they were part of the inflectional system, and not as a kind of derivation such as that exemplified by proprietive adjectives in Selkup, which create a new lexeme in its own right.

The task is now to ensure that the grammar defines the morphology of the Selkup transpositions without treating them as a bona fide new lexeme, that is without treating them as a form of derivation. We will present an analysis of the relational noun–adjective hybrids in the spirit of Spencer's (2017b) analysis of participles (see also Chapter 6). We will then consider how this framework might handle the similitudinal representation of nouns.

As we have stressed, the analysis takes as its point of departure the claim that these three types of DNA are all representations of the noun lexeme. This means that, as with the Chukchi DNAs, we assume that the MORSIG of Selkup nouns includes the feature [REPR:$\langle\langle$N,A$\rangle$,$\{\sigma\}\rangle$], where σ ranges over three features: RA, SIMIL, LOC, specifying plain relational adjectives, similitudinal relational adjectives and locational relational adjectives.[9]

We begin with an informal summary of our analysis. We start with the lexemic entry of the noun itself, the maximally underspecified representation. The Default Cascade (Chapter 6, Section 6.3.4) is applied to this representation to specify all the default properties of that noun. These include the MORSIG attribute, which specifies the properties for which the noun inflects, namely number, possessor agreement, and case, together with the three types of

---

[8]   Interestingly, Kiefer (1987), discussing the complex question of how many case forms there are in Hungarian, adopts the criterion that a suffix is a case suffix if and only if it can attach to an inflected form of the noun, which in Hungarian includes, of course, a noun inflected for possessor agreement, similar to Selkup.

[9]   In the interests of trying to keep our exposition uncluttered we leave implicit some of the technical details of implementation. However, some of these will be introduced in our discussion of Tungusic proprietives later in this section.

8.4 Representations of Noun-to-Adjective Derivations   307

relational adjective, as defined by the REPR feature. Since Selkup relational adjectives can take possessor agreement, we need to provide for inflecting the noun for both possessor agreement and REPR. However, relational adjectives do not inflect for number or case, so Selkup grammar has to include an appropriate Feature Cooccurrence Restriction, that is, a stipulation excluding the combination of REPR with {NUMBER, CASE}. This stipulation cannot, it seems, be derived from more general principles. As we will see, Evenki nouns inflect for the same features as Selkup nouns, but Evenki relational adjectives permit the base noun to inflect for number but not for possessor agreement.

As an implementation measure we assume that the number, possessor agreement, and case properties are realized in three blocks of realization rules, though the form of those rules will be somewhat complex due to various patterns of multiple exponence and fusion found in the system. Those details are immaterial to our analysis, however, so we do not provide an explicit statement of them here. The crucial point is that standard noun inflection feeds a fourth block of realization rules defining the form of relational adjectives.

The REPR feature is more complex than standard Head inflectional features. As we detailed in Chapter 6, any application of the GPF which realizes forms of a lexeme marked by the REPR feature will include an f_{syn} function altering the ARG-ST value of the SYN attribute of the lexical representation, by laying the SF A* role over the noun's R SF role and introducing a thematic argument, ARG1, corresponding to the head noun which the adjective modifies. This change means that the representation is now subject to the Default Cascade clause which defines the default properties of adjectives, or more accurately, which spells out default properties of lexical representations bearing the outer SF role [SFROLE$_e$ A*]. Recall that we are dealing with mixed categories which cannot, strictly speaking, be described as either 'noun' or 'adjective'. The Default Cascade will also enrich the SYN attribute by a HEAD|MOD specification constraining the (adjectival representation of the) lexeme to modify a noun head (in its default syntactic use, that is, when used as an attributive modifier), just as in the case of a simplex adjective.

In Selkup no more needs to be said about the three adjectival representations of nouns. However, there are many languages in which the simplex adjective category has more complex morphosyntactic properties, specifically in which the adjective can show some sort of agreement or concord with the head noun. For such languages, the GPF realizing the REPR feature will include a statement in the f_{syn} function which modifies the MORSIG attribute by adding a CONCORD feature (which will be copied, by default, onto the

308   *Noun–Adjective Hybrids*

[FORM MORSIG] attribute). We return to this point when we discuss Evenki proprietive adjectives in Section 8.4.3.

As with relational adjectives in other languages, the Selkup relational adjective has essentially the same kinds of functions as the genitive case; that is, it expresses the general $\Re$ relation between two entities. Thus, the relational adjective formation process has no effect on the semantic interpretation of the base noun, and, indeed, in this respect it could be said to contrast sharply with case forms such as the spatial cases, which have clearly defined default interpretations. Relational adjective morphology is integrated, in effect, into case-marking morphology. Moreover, to a certain extent we can say that the relational adjective form is even integrated into the inflectionally defined morphosyntax. Kuznecova et al. (1980, 192) note that there are certain verbs which select that form of the noun as their subcategorizing complement, e.g. *peerïqo* 'look for' (*qomtä-l' peerusa* 'he was looking for (the) money') and *miršïttïqo* 'work (piece of wood) with an axe' (*narapo-l' miršïttak* 'I am making a pole'). So, if meaning-bearing adjectival representations of nouns are mixed inherent inflection, this type rather represents mixed contextual inflection.

In Figure 8.4 we see the structure for the Selkup equivalent of the expression 'ski grease' (Kuznecova et al., 1980, 191), as shown in the example in (24). The relational adjective *tol'cïl'* is formed regularly from the noun TOL'CÏ 'skis'.

(24)   tol'cï-l'   mïtïn
       skis-REL.A grease
       'ski grease'

Let us assume the representation of a basic noun such as SKIS, including its FORM and SYN values for the MORSIG declaration. In the case of a relational adjective transposition, the feature [REPR:⟨⟨N,A⟩,σ⟩] will trigger transposition of a base noun lexeme to the corresponding relational adjective. The GPF applied to a pairing of ⟨*N*,[REPR:⟨N,A⟩]⟩ (where '*N*' is the LI of some noun) is defined so as to apply to an entry whose SF role is R. The pairing ⟨SKIS,[REPR:⟨N,A⟩]⟩ therefore actually applies to the representation in (25), in which we show the REPR attribute in the MORSIG declaration of the base noun's lexical representation.

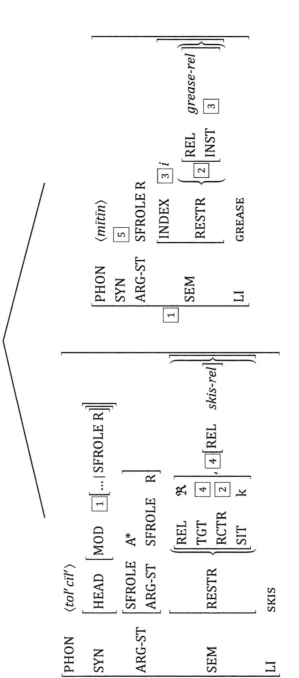

Figure 8.4 *Structure for Selkup* tol'cil' mïtïn *'ski grease'*

(25) Partial lexical representation for Selkup TOL'CÏ 'skis'

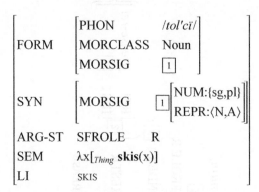

Notice that the relational adjective itself bears a SEM attribute which includes the general ℜ relation linking the meaning of 'skis' and the meaning of 'grease'. That relation is not introduced constructionally by the concatenation process as it is in the case of English-type N-N compounds. The GPF defined over the feature pairing ⟨*N*, {[REPR:⟨N,A⟩],σ}⟩, for noun lexeme *N* and where σ may include possessor agreement features, defines an adjective with the same LI, *N*, possibly inflected for possessor agreement but having the form of an adjective. The SEM attribute is modified minimally by the addition of the ℜ relation.

We assume that there is a realization rule, which defines the derived compound SF role for the relational adjective, as shown in (26).

(26) $f_{syn}(\langle \text{SKIS},[\text{REPR}:\langle N,A \rangle] \rangle) \Rightarrow \text{ARG-ST}|\text{SF A*}\langle x \langle R \rangle \rangle$

The rule in (26) provides part of the definition of the SYN attribute of the derived word's lexical representation. It effectively shifts the morpholexical category of the base noun to that of adjective. Finally, the Attributive Modifier Rule ((26), Chapter 7) defines the relational adjective as an attributive modifier, specifying the SYN attribute with a MOD attribute, as shown in (27).

(27) $\begin{bmatrix} \text{VAL}|\text{MOD} & \boxed{1}[\text{ARG-ST}|\text{SFROLE R}] \\ \text{ARG-ST} & \begin{bmatrix} \text{ARG1} & \boxed{1} \\ \ldots \end{bmatrix} \end{bmatrix}$

The noun component *tol'cï* 'skis' is still available for modification by an adjective such as *pool'* 'wooden' (itself a relational adjective from the noun POO 'wood, tree'), as shown in (28).

(28) poo-l'   tol'cï-l'   mïtïn
      wood-REL.A skis-REL.A grease
      'grease for wooden skis'

8.4 Representations of Noun-to-Adjective Derivations   311

Kuznecova et al. explicitly analyse this expression as [[[*pool' tol'cï*]*l'*] *mïtïn*]. In Figure 8.5 we see a partial diagram for (28), omitting the head noun *mïtïn*. In both Figure 8.4 and Figure 8.5 the relational adjective is able to modify the following noun because its HEAD attribute includes a MOD attribute which seeks a word/phrase of the category ARG-ST|SFROLE R. The fact that this [SFROLE R] attribute is 'embedded', so to speak, inside the target expression's ARG-ST attribute is immaterial (note that the rule does not specify an outer SF role [SFROLE$_e$ R]). The relational adjectives of English, Russian, and other languages, which exhibit lexical opacity to such modification as we saw in the previous section, entirely lack the [SFROLE R] specification in their ARG-ST attribute and hence are treated solely as adjectives. In effect, the compound ARG-ST representation is the syntactic reflex of the morphological REPR.

Recall that the type labels *noun, adjective, verb* are not actually necessary and, as we have argued extensively, they get in our way in relation to mixed categories. We can therefore replace reference to such types by reference to SFROLE values, as shown in Figure 8.6. This representation will apply both to ordinary morphologically simple nouns as well as to nouns which have been transposed into adjectives.

The word formation rule (GPF) defining such relational adjectives needs to include a statement as shown in (29).

(29)   Consider a lexeme with ARG-ST

$$
\left[
\text{ARG-ST}
\begin{bmatrix}
\text{ARG1} \\
\text{ARG2} \\
\dots \\
\text{SFROLE } \alpha
\end{bmatrix}
\right]
$$

Let GPF($£,\delta$) be a LI-preserving function defining SFROLE $\beta \neq \alpha$. Then GPF($£,\delta$) delivers an ARG-ST attribute of the form

$$
\left[
\text{ARG-ST}
\begin{bmatrix}
\text{ARGm} \\
\text{ARGn} \\
\dots \\
\text{SFROLE } \beta \\
\text{ARG-ST [SFROLE } \alpha \text{]}
\end{bmatrix}
\right]
$$

where ARG1, ARG2, ARGm, ARGn, ..., are (possibly null) thematic arguments of the lexeme.

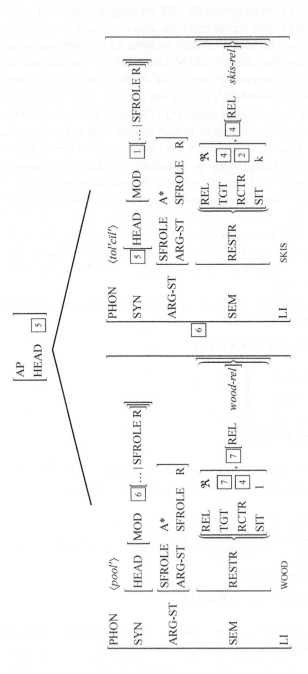

Figure 8.5 *Structure for Selkup* pool' tol'cil' *'pertaining to wooden (skis)'*

8.4 Representations of Noun-to-Adjective Derivations

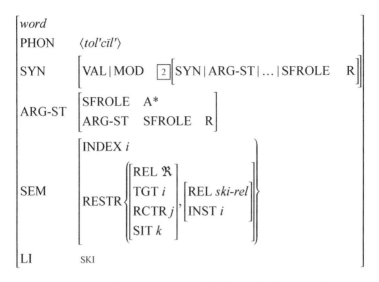

Figure 8.6 *Lexical representation of Selkup* tol'cïl' *'pertaining to skis'*

In other words, we 'embed' the base noun lexeme's ARG-ST|SFROLE inside the derived ARG-ST. This is an implementation of the notation ⟨A*⟨x, ⟨R⟩⟩⟩, as in Spencer (1999, 2013). The representation is that of an attributive modifier which can modify an appropriate noun in the standard way.

In these representations we are treating the nominal base of the relational adjective as non-referential, in keeping with the assumed meaning of these expressions. They are fully equivalent, in that respect, to recursively constructed N-N compounds in English of the type *metal ski grease* (i.e. grease for metal skis). However, there are other constructions in which the base noun retains its referentiality. This is particularly clear when we consider relational adjectives derived from the possessor-inflected form of the noun. Kuznecova et al. (1980, 192) cite a number of cases in which a possessed noun appears in the adjectival representation modifying a head noun, for instance those shown in (30).

314 Noun–Adjective Hybrids

(30) äsä-nï-l'   mååt-tï   nïïnï   ašša
      father[GEN.SG]-1SG.POSS-REL.A house-ILL.SG from.there NEG
      pååraltɛntak
      will.return.1SG
      'I will not return from there to my father's house'

The stem form *äsä-nï-* is the suppletive genitive singular of the noun əsï 'father'. The relational adjective formative *-l'* is added to the genitive singular form of a possessed noun (with unpossessed nouns the formative is added directly to the base form, identical to the nominative singular). We will ignore this detail since it concerns only the workings of the morphology. The form *mååttï* is in the illative case, indicating motion towards.

We represent possession as an instantiation of the $\mathcal{R}$ relation (Chapter 7, Section 7.4). Selkup nouns agree in person and number with their possessors, and exhibit a form of 'pro-drop' in possessive constructions in the sense that an overt pronominal possessor is not normally expressed; the possessor agreement morphology is sufficient. The representation for the nominative singular 1SG possessed form of the lexeme QOK 'leader', namely, *qoŋmi* 'my leader', will be identical to that of Tundra Nenets *tem'i* 'my reindeer', mutatis mutandis. The representation for *äsä-nï-l'* 'pertaining to my father' is shown in Figure 8.7. The representation for the complete phrase *äsä-nï-l' mååt-tï* is shown in Figure 8.8.

In Selkup denominal adjectives the POSSAGR property, but not the NUM property, of the base noun is preserved in the transposition. This fact does not (necessarily) follow from anything else in the grammar, and it certainly does not follow from the architecture of inflectional morphology generally. It therefore needs to be stipulated as part of the language's GPF. There are two ways to achieve this. First, we can state the restriction directly, as shown in (31).

(31) $f_{syn}(\langle \mathcal{N}, \{[REPR:\langle N,A\rangle]\}\rangle) \Rightarrow$ MORSIG $\supset$ POSSAGR

This statement would need to be supplemented with a default statement that all other nominal properties are excluded, however. That type of exclusion would seem natural for languages in which relational adjectives inherit few or no truly nominal inflectional properties (for instance, Chukchi). The alternative is to assume by default that the relational adjective inherits nominal properties except where these are explicitly excluded. Thus, we would set up the Feature Cooccurrence Restriction shown in (32) as a constraint on representations.

8.4 Representations of Noun-to-Adjective Derivations

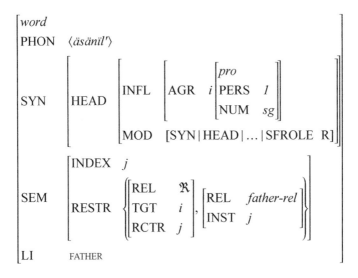

Figure 8.7 Structure for Selkup possessed noun relational adjective äsänïl' 'pertaining to my father'

(32) Selkup: Feature Cooccurrence Restriction on REPR
Given GPF(⟨£,{σ}⟩). Where [REPR:⟨yes,⟨N,A⟩, {τ}⟩] ⊂ σ, then where Φ is an attribute name and φ a set of values of Φ, ∀Φ,φ [Φ:φ] ∈ σ implies Φ = [POSSAGR].

By virtue of (32) the denominal adjective is free to inflect for possessor agreement (but for no other nominal properties). This also means that the base noun is able to combine syntactically with a possessor NP. We now have a representation which shows (partial) paradigmatic mixing: the derived word agrees with the base noun lexeme's possessor as though it were still a noun, but it agrees with the head noun it modifies as though it were an adjective, so the lexical representation of the derived adjective must also reflect the fact that it selects a noun to modify in the syntax.

There remains the question of how the morphological FORM attribute is specified in the relational adjective. We are assuming a maximally simple system in which much of the lexical specification is provided by default. In that case the expectation will be that the FORM|MORSIG attribute will be copied without change from the SYN|MORSIG attribute (so that the **Corr** function will be the identity function). However, we must be very explicit at this point. We therefore follow with appropriate modifications the treatment of Russian participles given in Spencer (2017b).

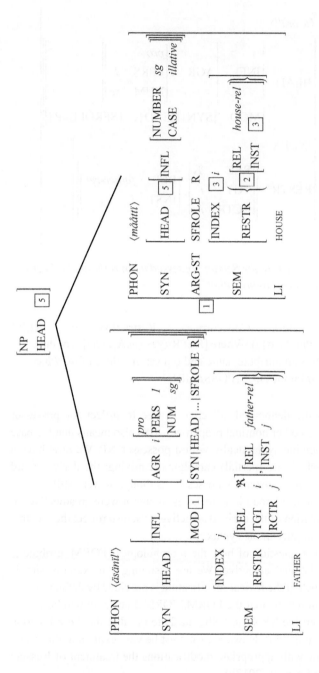

Figure 8.8 *Structure for Selkup äsänïl' määttï 'to my father's house'*

8.4 Representations of Noun-to-Adjective Derivations   317

The GPF ($\langle$SKIS,$\{[$REPR:$\langle$N,A$\rangle]\})$) takes as its input the lexemic entry of a noun, namely that shown in (25). This includes a MORSIG value, shared between FORM and SYN attributes. However, because the relational adjective acquires some of the properties of an adjective, we must enrich its CONTENT paradigm so as to permit this. That means that we have to redefine the SYN|MORSIG declaration to include the relevant adjectival properties. We also want those adjectival properties to be reflected in the FORM attribute of the derived word. Other things being equal, the relational adjective will simply inherit all of the base noun's inflectional properties without acquiring any adjectival properties.

What this means is that the GPF defining the relational adjective trans-position has to define any parochial s-MORSIG and m-MORSIG values by stipulating those nominal properties which are preserved and those adjectival properties that are acquired. In general, the function will have to specify s-MORSIG features that map by default to m-MORSIG features, such as adjectival agreement features, as well as morphomic m-MORSIG features such as adjectival inflectional class.

Finally, we must be completely explicit about the kind of lexical representation that serves as the input to the transpositional GPF. If we were dealing with a genuinely derivational process, we could assume that the input was close to the traditional lexicographer's lemma and hence highly underspecified. In (near-)canonical cases of derivation, the SYN attribute of the input lexeme could be left completely unspecified, for instance.[10] However, the transpositional GPF is triggered by the feature [REPR], which has to be specified in the MORSIG of lexemic entries. That is, in order to code the fact that a language has a (productive) transpositional relational adjective formation process, we need to specify the value SYN|MORSIG|REPR:$\langle$N,A$\rangle$ for noun lexemes. But this means that the SYN attribute must specify at least the MORSIG attribute, which in turn means that we need to know what the lexical class of the lexeme is. Under our assumptions, that means that we need to define the SYN|ARG-ST|SFROLE. This is illustrated in (33).

---

[10] Where we have a 'morpholexically incoherent' input lexeme, such as a noun which denotes an *Event*, then such underspecification is not possible, of course.

318 *Noun–Adjective Hybrids*

(33) Shared MORSIG for hypothetical noun lexemes

$$\begin{bmatrix} \text{FORM} & \begin{bmatrix} \text{STEM0} & |\text{noun}| \\ \text{MORCLASS:} & \{\text{Noun, declension, \ldots}\} \\ \text{MORSIG} & \boxed{1} \end{bmatrix} \\ \text{SYN} & \begin{bmatrix} \text{MORSIG} & \boxed{1} \begin{bmatrix} \text{NUM:} & \{\text{sg,pl}\} \\ \text{POSSAGR:} & \{\ldots\} \\ \text{REPR:} & \langle N, A \rangle \end{bmatrix} \end{bmatrix} \\ \text{ARG-ST} & \text{SFROLE} \quad R \\ \text{SEM} & \ldots \\ \text{LI} & \ldots \end{bmatrix}$$

Application of the GPF as currently formulated will then give us the representation in (34) (where 'AdjDecl' represents whatever adjectival inflection class our hypothetical relational adjective falls into, 'f_{RA}' represents whatever morphophonological function delivers the relational adjective form from the noun stem, and STEM$_{rel}$ represents the base form of the relational adjective (which will possibly serve as input to further inflection – for instance, agreement).

(34) Shared MORSIG for hypothetical relational adjective

$$\begin{bmatrix} \text{FORM} & \begin{bmatrix} \text{STEM}_{rel} & f_{RA}(\text{noun}) \\ \text{MORCLASS:} & \{\text{AdjDecl, \ldots}\} \\ \text{MORSIG} & \boxed{1} \end{bmatrix} \\ \text{SYN} & \begin{bmatrix} \text{MORSIG} & \boxed{1}[\text{POSSAGR: }\{\ldots\}] \end{bmatrix} \\ \text{ARG-ST} & \text{SFROLE} \quad \langle A\langle x \langle R \rangle\rangle\rangle \\ \text{SEM} & \ldots \\ \text{LI} & \ldots \end{bmatrix}$$

The GPF has defined an enriched SYN|ARG-ST|SF attribute which now corresponds to that of a (morphological) adjective. The representation shown in (34) will now be subject to the Default Cascade, which will specify more of its properties, ensuring that it behaves syntactically as an attributive adjective. All adjectives, we can assume, are subject to the syntactic default shown in (35), which defines any lexical representation with the ('external') SFROLE A* to bear the MOD attribute as one of its HEADs.

8.4 Representations of Noun-to-Adjective Derivations

(35) If $\begin{bmatrix} \text{ARG-ST} \begin{bmatrix} \text{ARG1} \\ \ldots \\ \text{SFROLE A*} \end{bmatrix} \end{bmatrix}$

then SYN|HEAD ⇒ [MOD [SYN|ARG-ST|…|SFROLE R]]

Given these rules and representations, application of the relational adjective GPF (that is, GPF(⟨N,{[REPR:⟨⟨N,A⟩],φ⟩,σ}⟩)) to a noun such as 'skis' will deliver the lexical representation shown in (36). This representation is almost complete except that it is not specified for the possessor agreement properties of the noun. It thus represents an instance of a 'paradigm-within-a-paradigm', though not for the same reasons that we usually find with transpositions. Here, the underspecification arises from underspecification in the representation of the base noun lexeme, not underspecification for purely adjectival properties (such as CONCORD).

(36) (Almost) fully specified lexical representation of Selkup *tol'cïl'* 'pertaining to skis'

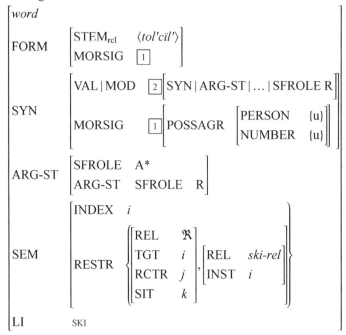

320 *Noun–Adjective Hybrids*

8.4.2   Meaning-Bearing Transpositions: Selkup

We now turn to the two meaning-bearing adjectival representations of Selkup nouns, the similitudinal and locative adjectival representations, focussing for concreteness on similitudinal adjectives.

Similitudinal adjectives are paradigmatically as well as syntagmatically mixed, just like relational adjectives: from the noun base the similitudinal adjective inherits the possibility of co-occurring with and showing agreement with possessors. From the adjective class it inherits the attributive modifier grammatical function. Semantically, too, the construction is mixed. By inheritance from the adjective it has the ontological category of *Property*, but the construction is so defined that the specific property in question incorporates the semantics of the base noun. Similitudinal adjectivization adds semantic content to the noun representation, creating a representation of the form SIMIL(N) 'some object similar (along some dimension) to N'. This semantic difference means that such a word clearly denotes a property as well as denoting an object (and in this respect can be said to differ from the pure relational adjectives we have just seen, such as *tol'cïl'*). For this reason it will contract a particular set of relations to other property-denoting words (i.e. adjectives) in the Selkup lexicon (see the discussion of Tungusic proprietives in Nikolaeva (2008).

Similitudinal adjective transposition is delivered by the GPF applied to a lexical representation of a noun specified for the properties $\{[REPR:\langle\langle N,A\rangle,\{SIMIL\}\rangle],\sigma\}$. This GPF is identical to that which delivers the vanilla relational adjective illustrated above by *tol'cïl'*, except that the f_{sem} component of the GPF will enrich the semantic representation of the base noun lexeme with the SIMIL predicate, as illustrated in Figure 8.9. Thus, the similitudinal adjective derived from BOAT will give rise to forms we can translate as 'similar to a boat, similar to my boat, similar to their boat, etc.', where the base noun can be either uninflected or can inflect for possessor agreement. However, that base noun cannot take any other inflections, specifically NUMBER:{sg, du, pl, collective} marking, so the GPF will not deliver forms corresponding to 'similar to boats, similar to my boats, similar to their boats, etc.'.

The GPF for similitudinal adjective formation is shown schematically in (37).

8.4 Representations of Noun-to-Adjective Derivations 321

(37) Simplified lexical representation of schematic *alakoššal'*, 'boat-like'

	base noun	adjective
FORM:	X	-(š)šal'
	N features	A features
	[Number]	
	[Case]	
	[PossAgr]	N features: [PossAgr]
SYN:	Spec[], ...	
ARG-ST:	$\langle R \rangle$	$\langle A^*_r \langle SYN \langle L1, u \rangle \rangle \rangle = \langle A^*_r \langle R \rangle \rangle$
SEM:	$SEM(L_1)$	$[_{Property}\ \lambda P \lambda x[P(x) \wedge SIMIL(x,SEM(L_1))]$
LI:	L_1	GDP $(= L_1)$

Figure 8.9 *GPF for Selkup similitudinal adjective representation*

$$
\begin{bmatrix}
\text{FORM} & \text{STEM}_{sim} & |\,\text{alako-ššal'}\,| \\
\text{ARG-ST} & \text{SFROLE} & \langle A^*\langle R \rangle \rangle \\
\text{SEM} & \lambda x \lambda \delta[_{Property}\ SIMIL(\text{BOAT})(x,\delta)] \\
\text{LI} & \text{BOAT} &
\end{bmatrix}
$$

This application preserves the LI value of the base noun, but creates the compound SF role headed by A*, and adds the SIMIL predicate to the noun's semantic representation. The SEM representation here is meant to be interpreted as 'similar to a boat along some contextually determined dimension, δ'.[11] For the locative adjectival representation of nouns it will be roughly as follows: $[_{Property}\ \lambda x \exists y[\text{Place}(y) \wedge \textbf{noun}(y) \wedge \textbf{noun}(x) \wedge \text{LOC}(x,y)]]$.

As with the plain relational adjective, the representation in (37) is highly underspecified: there is no specification, in particular, of the syntactic and morphological category of the adjective. The SYN value is projected by default from the ontological category of the SEM value by virtue of the Default Cascade: since BOAT-LIKE is a *Property*, the ARG-ST attribute bears the compound SF role enriched with the A* role. From that specification the Default Cascade will specify the morphological category of the word: [MOR-CLASS: AdjDecl], and, in fact, will assign it to the default inflectional class

---

[11] In the interests of readability we have given only a very crude characterization of the similitudinal predicate. A slightly more sophisticated version of '(property of being) a boat similar to a canoe (along some dimension, Δ)' would be $\lambda x[\textbf{boat}(x) \wedge \exists y \exists \Delta[\textbf{simil}(x,y,\Delta) \wedge \textbf{canoe}(y)]]$. Thus, the representation of the similitudinal form of the noun CANOE will be $\lambda x \lambda P[P(x) \wedge \exists y \exists \Delta[\textbf{simil}(x,y,\Delta) \wedge \textbf{canoe}(y)]]$, and the similitudinal predicate itself, as applied to a noun such as CANOE, $\lambda z.\textbf{canoe}(z)$, will be $\lambda N[\lambda x \lambda P[P(x) \wedge \exists y \exists \Delta[\textbf{simil}(x,y,\Delta) \wedge N(y)]]]$.

322   *Noun–Adjective Hybrids*

for adjectives. The Default Cascade is governed in part by the values of the MORSIG attribute that all lexemes bear. Once the Default Cascade specifies the A* SF role for the lexeme, then it also specifies that the lexeme bears a MORSIG feature which defines those properties for which the lexeme inflects. The Default Cascade will also specify that the Attributive Modifier Rule comes into play, guaranteeing that the derived adjective can serve in the syntax as an attributive modifier. The output of the GPF and the Attributive Modifier Rule is now that shown in (38).

(38)   Lexical representation of schematic *alako-ššal'*, 'boat-like' with MORSIG

$$
\begin{bmatrix}
\text{FORM} & \begin{bmatrix} \text{STEM}_{\text{sim}} & \text{/alako-ššal'/} \\ \text{MORCLASS:} & \{\text{AdjDecl}, \ldots\} \\ \text{MORSIG} & \text{AGR [NUM:}\{\text{sg,du,pl}\}] \end{bmatrix} \\[4ex]
\text{SYN} & \begin{bmatrix} \text{VAL|MOD} & \boxed{1}[\text{ARG-ST SFROLE R}] \\ \text{MORSIG} & \text{AGR [NUM:} \{\text{sg,du,pl}\}] \end{bmatrix} \\[4ex]
\text{ARG-ST} & \begin{bmatrix} \text{ARG1} & \boxed{1} \\ \ldots \\ \text{SFROLE} & \langle \text{A*}_{\text{r}}\langle\text{R}\rangle\rangle \end{bmatrix} \\[3ex]
\text{SEM} & \lambda\text{x}[_{\text{Property}} \text{ SIMIL}(\text{BOAT})(\text{x})] \\[1ex]
\text{LI} & \text{SIM}(\text{BOAT})
\end{bmatrix}
$$

8.4.3   *Tungusic (and Nenets) Derived Adjectives – with Agreement*

In Chapter 3, Section 3.3.2 we introduced a number of phenomena from Uralic and Tungusic languages, including syntagmatic mixing in proprietive adjectives. Nikolaeva (2008) provides a wealth of data from Tungusic proprietive DNAs showing that they exhibit the BNMP as well as other morphosyntactic properties, indicating that the base noun of the proprietive is syntactically active. We provide an updated version of her analysis, translated into the notational and descriptive conventions we have outlined above.

Nikolaeva provides examples from both Southern (Nanai, Oroch, Udihe) and Northern (Even, Evenki) Tungusic languages of Siberia. We will eventually focus on the Northern Tungusic languages, which show (optional) attributive modifier concord. In (39) (Nikolaeva, 2008, 974) we see the basic construction

8.4 *Representations of Noun-to-Adjective Derivations* 323

in Evenki, in which the proprietive, marked by the suffix -*či*, agrees in number and case with its head noun.

(39) a. ŋinaki-či-l-va   beje-l-ve
          dog-PROPR-PL-ACC man-PL-ACC
          'men (ACC) with a dog'

      b. oro-či-l-du   asa-l-du
          reindeer-PROPR-PL-DAT woman-PL-DAT
          'to the women with a reindeer'

In (40) (Nikolaeva, 2008, 976) we see that the base noun of the proprietive, marked with -*ku* (Nanai), -*či* (Evenki), and -*r* (Even), can inflect for nominal number, in both Northern Tungusic (40b, 40c) and in Nanai (40a).

(40) a. daŋsa-sal-ku   tetredi-sal-ku   nučikend'uen
          book-PL-PROPR notebook-PL-PROP children
          'children with books and notebooks'   [Nanai]

      b. oro-l-či-du
          reindeer-PL-PROPR-DAT
          'with reindeer(PL)'   [Evenki]

      c. hamu-r-alkar
          flag-PL-PROPR
          'with flags'   [Even]

The base noun of the proprietive exhibits the BNMP and can take the following phrasal modifiers: an adjective (41), a quantifier (42), an oblique NP (43), or an appositional phrase (44) (Nikolaeva, 2008, 997).

(41) a. ic'a sita-xi   a:nta
          small child-PROPR woman
          'woman with a small child'   [Udihe]

      b. ajakta mamača-ŋi-ki
          evil   old.woman-POSS-PROPR
          'with an evil old woman'   [Oroch]

      c. ńamapču a:w-la:n
          warm   hat-PROPR
          'with a warm hat'   [Evenki]

(42) a. zube sita-xi   a:nta
          two child-PROPR woman
          'woman with two children'   [Udihe]

324   *Noun–Adjective Hybrids*

    b. xai-daxem xad'on-ko
       what-ever equipment-PROPR
       'with all sorts of equipment'   [Nanai]

(43) ŋala-gdo-i   gida-ko
      hand-DAT-REFL spear-PROPR
      'with a spear in his hands'   [Nanai]

(44) Tokko gerbi-či   bira
      Tokko name-PROPR river
      'the river with the name Tokko'   [Evenki]

The modifiers of the sort cited here are inseparable from the proprietive and form a syntactic constituent with it. In Northern Tungusic, we see optional number agreement in an adjective which modifies the base noun of the proprietive, as shown in (45) for the modifiers *aja* 'good' (45a) and *xulańa* 'red' (45b) (Nikolaeva, 2008, 997).

(45) a. aja-l   oro-l-či-du   asi:-du
         good-PL reindeer-PL-PROPR-DAT woman-DAT
         'to the woman with good reindeer (PL)'   [Evenki]

      b. xulańa-l hamu-r-alkar
         red-PL   flag-PL-PROPR
         'with red flags'   [Even]

Finally, we add one intriguing observation about the morphosyntax of the proprietive in Evenki. In (46) we see two Evenki examples in which the proprietives *ugu-či* 'having a bank/banks' and *pektire:wu-či* 'having a gun', marked by the suffix *-či*, are modified by adjectives which also have the *-či* suffix, *gugda-či* 'high' and *menŋi-či* 'own' (Nikolaeva, 2008, 981). The suffix on the adjectives is difficult to understand except as an instance of case concord. This suggests that the proprietive form/representation of the noun (in Evenki, at least) is a kind of case.

(46) a. gugda-či   ugu-či   bira
         high-PROPR bank-PROPR river
         'river with high banks'

      b. menŋi-či   pektire:wu-či
         own-PROPR gun-PROPR
         'with his own gun'

8.4 Representations of Noun-to-Adjective Derivations   325

We now present an analysis of Evenki (45a) updating the analysis presented in Nikolaeva (2008, 983–986). The analysis proceeds in essentially the same way as our analysis of Selkup denominal adjectives. We will therefore take this opportunity to spell out more explicitly some of the implementational points that we left implicit in our earlier discussion.[12] We start with the maximally underspecified representation of the noun *reindeer*, LI, REINDEER, shown in (47).

(47)   Maximally underspecified lexical representation of REINDEER

$$
\begin{bmatrix}
\text{LI} & \text{REINDEER} \\
\text{SEM} & [_{\text{Thing}}\ \lambda x.\textbf{reindeer}(x)] \\
\text{SYN} & \ldots \\
\text{FORM} & \text{STEM0 /oro/}
\end{bmatrix}
$$

The SYN|ARG-ST attribute specification is projected from the SEM attribute's ontological class specification by the Default Cascade, which will also specify the basic syntactic properties of lexical items, including the MORSIG attribute. The MORSIG of the Evenki noun specifies the potential values of the properties of number, case, and possessor agreement. For clarity we provide the REPR attribute with the 'proprietive' property, here represented as a value of an attribute REPR-SEM, indicating the meaning of a meaning-bearing transposition. These properties are summarized in (48).

(48)

$$
\text{MORSIG}\begin{bmatrix}
\text{NUM} & \{\text{sg,pl}\} \\
\text{CASE} & \{\text{nom,acc},\ldots,\text{propr}\} \\
\text{POSSAGR} & \begin{bmatrix}\text{NUM} & \{\ldots\} \\ \text{PER} & \{\ldots\}\end{bmatrix} \\
\text{REPR} & \begin{bmatrix}\langle\text{N,A}\rangle \\ \text{REPR-SEM} & \text{propr}\end{bmatrix}
\end{bmatrix}
$$

The partially specified lexemic entry for REINDEER shown in (49) is compatible with the Default Cascade in combination with specifications particular to Evenki (for the reader's convenience we indicate some of the feature values which would be underspecified in the actual lexemic entry).

---

[12] Since much of the analysis presupposes 'information flow' from semantic to morphosyntactic representations, we present the lexical representations in the reverse order from that customary in the literature, that is with the LI and the semantic representation at the top of the AVM.

(49) (Partially specified) lexemic entry for REINDEER

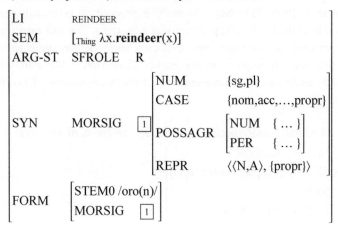

We now turn to the proprietive representation of the noun. We have argued (Chapter 3) that the proprietive is an example of a meaning-neutral transposition (effectively a relational adjective). The proprietive f_{sem} component of the GPF is therefore identical to that of the base noun save for the $\Re$ relation, which we therefore introduce into the RESTRICTION attribute of the SEM value of the derived adjective, as seen in (50). Note that here the TARGET argument is the modified head noun and the RESTRICTOR is the 'possessed' noun, the inverse of the usual possessive construction.

(50) Semantically specified partial lexical representation of Evenki *oro-či* 'having (a) reindeer'

$$\begin{bmatrix} word \\ \text{LI} \quad \text{REINDEER} \\ \text{SEM} \quad \text{RESTR} \left\{ \begin{bmatrix} \text{REL} & \Re(\boxed{1},\boxed{2}) \\ \text{TGT} & \boxed{1} \\ \text{RCTR} & \boxed{2} \end{bmatrix}, \boxed{2}[\text{REL} \quad \textit{reindeer-rel}] \right\} \\ \text{FORM} \quad \langle oroči \rangle \end{bmatrix}$$

The f_{syn} component of the proprietive GPF has the effect of realizing the ARG-ST clause determined by the [REPR:⟨⟨N,A⟩, {proprietive}⟩], specifying the now-familiar compound SF role. Thus, we assume in (51) essentially the same realization rule as proposed for Selkup denominal adjectives.

8.4 Representations of Noun-to-Adjective Derivations   327

(51) $f_{syn}(\langle\text{REINDEER}, \{[\text{REPR}:\langle\langle N,A\rangle, \{\text{proprietive}\}\rangle)]\}\rangle)$ $\Rightarrow$ ARG-ST|SF
       $A^*\langle x\langle R\rangle\rangle$

The $f_{syn}(\langle\text{REINDEER}, \{[\text{REPR}:\langle\langle N,A\rangle, \{\text{proprietive}\}\rangle)]\}\rangle)$ function therefore delivers the ARG-ST shown in (52).

(52)
$$\left[\text{ARG-ST}\begin{bmatrix}\text{ARG1} \\ \text{SFROLE A}^* \\ \text{ARG-ST [SFROLE R]}\end{bmatrix}\right]$$

The application of this clause in the GPF again creates a structure which is defined by the Default Cascade as that of an attributive adjective, with the appropriate additional VAL|MOD attribute as defined by constraint, already demonstrated in (27). In addition, the derived adjective's MORSIG acquires by default the CONCORD attribute of adjectives.

Recall that Evenki nouns inflect for number, case, and possessor agreement,[13] but unlike Selkup denominal adjectives, Evenki proprietives can inflect for nominal number but not for possessor agreement. This means that we must declare a restriction on the compatibility of the [REPR:$\langle$yes,$\langle N,A\rangle\rangle$] feature with other features. This is shown in (53).

(53)   Evenki: Feature   Cooccurrence   Restriction   on   REPR
       Given GPF($\langle£, \{\sigma\}\rangle$). Where [REPR:$\langle$yes,$\langle N,A\rangle, \{\tau\}\rangle$] $\subset \sigma$, then
       where Φ is an attribute name and φ a set of values of Φ, $\forall\Phi,\varphi$
       [Φ:φ] $\in \sigma$ implies $\Phi \neq$ [CASE], $\Phi \neq$ [POSSAGR].

To summarize, the application of the proprietive GPF to the noun lexemic entry will give rise to a representation defining the basic semantic and syntactic properties shown in (54).

---

[13]   As we noted in Chapter 4, Section 4.2, Evenki proprietive adjectives can also take an outer layer of evaluative suffixes (diminutives, augmentatives) which apply to the base noun, apparently. This means that we must assume a further, final block of nominal realization rules to introduce those affixes. The fact that the proprietive adjectives are further inflected for evaluative properties just emphasises the fact that we are dealing with the adjectival representation of a noun lexeme, and not a derived adjective lexeme, of course. However, since we have not investigated evaluative morphology in detail, and since evaluative morphology brings its own set of descriptive and analytical problems, we do not discuss those forms further.

(54) Partial lexical representation of Evenki *oro-či* 'having (a) reindeer' with ARG-ST specification

$$\begin{bmatrix} word \\ \text{LI} \quad \text{REINDEER} \\ \text{SEM} \quad \text{RESTR} \left\{ \begin{bmatrix} \text{REL} & \mathfrak{R}(\boxed{1},\boxed{2}) \\ \text{TGT} & \boxed{1} \\ \text{RCTR} & \boxed{2} \end{bmatrix}, \boxed{2}[\text{REL} \quad \textit{reindeer-rel}] \right\} \\ \text{ARG-ST} \begin{bmatrix} \text{ARG1} \; \boxed{1} \\ \text{SFROLE A*} \\ \text{ARG-ST} \quad \text{SFROLE R} \end{bmatrix} \\ \text{FORM} \quad \langle oroči \rangle \end{bmatrix}$$

(We assume that general principles governing ARG-ST representations will guarantee that the first argument of the POSS predicate in the SEM attribute is identified with the (sole) thematic argument of the derived adjective's ARG-ST.) The Default Cascade will recognize the representation in (54) as conforming to that of an attributive adjective and will therefore specify the SYN attribute as that of an attributive modifier, as seen in (55).

(55) Partial lexical representation of Evenki *oro-či* 'having (a) reindeer' with VAL specification

$$\begin{bmatrix} word \\ \text{LI} \quad \text{REINDEER} \\ \text{SEM} \quad \text{RESTR} \left\{ \begin{bmatrix} \text{REL} & \mathfrak{R}(\boxed{1},\boxed{2}) \\ \text{TGT} & \boxed{1} \\ \text{RCTR} & \boxed{2} \end{bmatrix}, \boxed{2}[\text{REL} \quad \textit{reindeer-rel}] \right\} \\ \text{ARG-ST} \begin{bmatrix} \text{ARG1} \; \boxed{1} \\ \text{SFROLE A*} \\ \text{ARG-ST} \quad \text{SFROLE R} \end{bmatrix} \\ \text{SYN} \quad \begin{bmatrix} \text{VAL} | \text{MOD} \quad \boxed{1}[\text{ARG-ST} | \text{SFROLE R}] \end{bmatrix} \\ \text{FORM} \quad \langle oroči \rangle \end{bmatrix}$$

The proprietive GPF specifies a number of inflectional properties specific to this type of derived adjective. In particular, the f_{syn} function specifies that the

8.4 Representations of Noun-to-Adjective Derivations   329

number but not the possessor agreement inflectional properties of the noun are preserved in the transposition. At the same time, we have seen evidence that the proprietive morphology itself is akin to a case ending. We therefore assume that Evenki nouns inflect for a special proprietive case but that this case is only realized as part of the proprietive transposition. This means that the GPF will define a MORSIG attribute for the proprietive adjective that includes an underspecified NUM attribute and the [CASE:proprietive] attribute, as seen in (56). For convenience of exposition we record the inflectional properties of an inflected noun with an attribute HEAD|INFL, so that the representation in (56) is effectively pre-specified for the exceptional 'proprietive case'.

(56)   Partial lexical representation of Evenki *oro-či* 'having (a) reindeer' with MORSIG specification

$$
\begin{bmatrix}
\textit{word} \\
\text{LI} \quad \text{REINDEER} \\
\text{SEM} \quad \text{RESTR} \left\{ \begin{bmatrix} \text{REL} & \mathfrak{R}(\boxed{1},\boxed{2}) \\ \text{TGT} & \boxed{1} \\ \text{RCTR} & \boxed{2} \end{bmatrix}, \boxed{2}[\text{REL} \quad \textit{reindeer-rel}] \right\} \\
\text{ARG-ST} \begin{bmatrix} \text{ARG1} \boxed{1} \\ \text{SFROLE A*} \\ \text{ARG-ST} \quad \text{SFROLE} \quad \text{R} \end{bmatrix} \\
\text{SYN} \begin{bmatrix} \text{VAL}\,|\,\text{MOD} & \boxed{1}[\text{ARG-ST}\,|\,\text{SFROLE R}] \\ \text{HEAD} & \text{INFL} \boxed{p} \\ \text{MORSIG} & \begin{bmatrix} \text{NUM u} \\ \boxed{p}\,\text{CASE:proprietive} \end{bmatrix} \end{bmatrix} \\
\text{FORM} \quad \langle\textit{oroči}\rangle
\end{bmatrix}
$$

Finally, the Default Cascade will enrich the MORSIG attribute of the derived adjective so as to permit it to show concord with its head noun. The SYN|MORSIG attribute itself defines properties which are reflected in the morphological form of the adjective, of course. This means that the MORSIG value of the FORM attribute can be taken to be isomorphic with the SYN|MORSIG attribute. However, it is noticeable that the [CASE:proprietive] marking is actually realized by the affix, which serves as the exponent of the proprietive adjective itself. There is a sense, then, in which the FORM attribute does not express the [CASE:proprietive] property in any direct way at all. This is a mild SYN~FORM mismatch, in other words. For that reason it would be more accurate to say that all the features of the SYN|MORSIG are 'copied' to the FORM|MORSIG attribute with the exception of the [CASE:proprietive] marking. Since this is a minor implementational point, we will not explore it further and for expositional simplicity just assume that the FORM|MORSIG attribute is re-entrant with the SYN|MORSIG attribute, as shown in (57).

(57) Final lexical representation of Evenki *oro-či* 'having (a) reindeer'

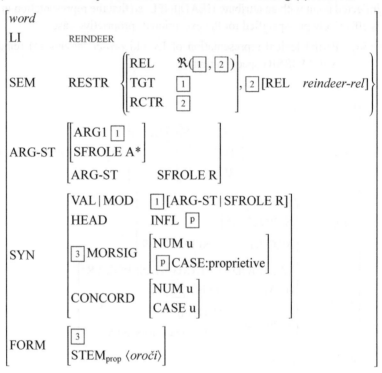

The resulting lexical entry is underspecified in two senses. First, it permits the base noun to appear in singular or plural form, and second it is underspecified for the CONCORD properties it acquires as the result of syntactic agreement.

The two manifestations of underspecification are subtly different, however. The nominal marking which we see in the word *oro-l-či* 'having (several) reindeer' is defined by realization rules operating over the bare noun root *oro(n)*. We can assume that the noun inflectional morphology is arranged in three blocks, I, II, III, realizing (principally) number, case, and possessor agreement. Attributively used adjectives (that is, adjectives that have not been

8.4 Representations of Noun-to-Adjective Derivations   331

converted into nouns) agree in number and case (but not possessor agreement) with essentially the same suffixal morphology as nouns. We can therefore assume that an adjective is subject to Blocks I and II of the nominal inflection realization rules. For the derivation of proprietives it is simplest to assume that the suffix is introduced in a fourth block, IV, but that the application of realization rules in Blocks II and III is pre-empted by the feature co-occurrence restriction on proprietives banning the proprietive from being formed on a noun marked for case or possessor agreement.

Because the proprietive morphology defines an adjectival set of forms with adjectival CONCORD features in its MORSIG, it is subject to the same set of realization rules that define number/case on the simplex noun. However, the GPF defines the stem of the proprietive on the singular or plural inflectional stem of the noun, so that we can have what appears to be double marking of plural number: *oro-l-či-l-du:* 'to(DAT) the ones having (several) reindeer'. In this respect the Evenki proprietive and Selkup denominal adjectives are slightly different because the Evenki proprietive looks more like the result of derivational morphology: the Evenki GPF defines a derived adjective stem which then itself undergoes inflection as an adjective. It thus illustrates rather clearly the 'lexeme-within-a-lexeme' property which is characteristic of true transpositions.

8.4.4   *Possessive Adjectives in Upper Sorbian*

Before we leave the topic of DNA transpositions, we return briefly to the intriguing case of the Upper Sorbian possessive adjective. In some ways this construction has become the poster child of such noun-to-adjective mixed categories because of the detailed studies of Corbett (1987) and Sadock (1991). However, in many respects this is a somewhat aberrant construction when viewed from a wider cross-linguistic perspective, and it is not entirely clear what the construction tells us about category mixing generally.

Recall that the possessive adjective in Upper Sorbian, as in other Slavic languages, is an adjective derived from a base noun denoting a person (often, though not exclusively, a kin term or a proper name). It expresses essentially the same content as a genitive case-marked noun phrase such as is found elsewhere in Upper Sorbian and in most of the Slavic languages. We repeat here the examples in (3) from Chapter 4, Section 4.2.2 as (58).

(58)   star-eje   žon-in-a   drasta
       old-F.GEN.SG woman[F]-POSS.A-F.NOM.SG dress[F].NOM.SG
       'the old woman's dress'

332 Noun–Adjective Hybrids

Here the adjective *stareje* 'old' modifies the noun root *žon-* 'woman' in the possessive adjective *žonina*.

The base noun itself fails to inflect, unlike the denominal adjectives of Selkup and Evenki just described. It is therefore not possible to say just from the inflectional paradigm of the possessive adjective that it is definitely a form of adjectival representation of the base lexeme, rather than a distinct autonomous lexeme in its own right. In fact, the only real evidence we have for treating the Upper Sorbian possessive adjective as an instance of a noun-to-adjective transposition is the fact that it exhibits the BNMP. Thus, if our treatment of syntagmatic category mixing with respect to attributive modification of the base noun rested solely on the behaviour of the Upper Sorbian possessive adjective, we would rightly be accused of proposing a circular analysis. On the other hand, given the data from Uralic and Tungusic, it is reasonable to suppose that the Upper Sorbian possessive adjective is also one of the types of DNA that preserves the base noun's LI.

The analysis of the Upper Sorbian possessive adjective, then, would proceed essentially as that of the Evenki proprietive, except that the possessive adjective's base noun is defined as the possessor N of the modified head noun, exactly as in the case of possessive pronouns.[14] The GPF defining the possessive adjective provides an adjectival complex SFROLE $\langle A^*\langle x\langle R\rangle\rangle\rangle$ which then triggers the specification of the adjectival external syntax we have seen with Evenki proprietives. There remains one idiosyncrasy, however, not seen in the examples considered so far. Adjectives in Slavic agree in number, gender, and case with their heads. Since number and gender are fused with each other and with case marking, it is impossible for an adjective to show agreement in only a subset of these properties. The gender of the possessive adjective's base noun poses no problem for an agreeing adjectival, since that specification is an inherent lexical property in the first place. Thus, *stareje* 'old' is marked for feminine gender. The adjective *stareje* seems to take singular as its default number agreement marking. Recall that the base noun of the Upper Sorbian possessive adjective fails to show a number contrast, so that strictly speaking that base noun is marked neither as singular nor as plural. Therefore, ordinary agreement-by-feature-copying cannot apply here. The problem comes with case agreement. Rather than assuming, say, the default nominative form,

---

[14] This raises the interesting question of what syntactic position is occupied by the possessive adjective, or indeed by adjectival possessive pronouns, the specifier (SPR) position of possessive and other determiners, or the modifier position of qualitative adjectives. We leave that question open. See Despić (2013) for the claim that the structurally similar Serbian-Croatian possessive adjectives are adjuncts to the NP, and not specifiers.

8.4 Representations of Noun-to-Adjective Derivations   333

stareje appears in the genitive. This makes intuitive sense if the genitive case and the possessive adjective have the same function, but it does not emerge from the grammar itself, it seems, without stipulation.

In the light of Nikolaeva's (2008) observations about proprietive case concord in Evenki which we summarized in Section 8.4.3, we could, perhaps, propose the following solution. The f_{syn} function of the possessive adjective GPF specifies a sole fixed value of [CASE: genitive] in the SYN|MORSIG attribute of the possessive adjective. However, the SYN $\Rightarrow$ FORM mapping fails to copy that specification in the FORM|MORSIG, so that the base noun exhibits no case marking at all. Thus, syntactic agreement processes have access to the [CASE: genitive] specification, but purely morphological rules do not.

This is at present, however, no more than a tentative suggestion as to how one might ultimately develop an analysis of this rather peculiar construction. In particular, we would have to ensure that other syntactic processes that target genitive case-marked nouns do *not* have access to the SYN|CASE: genitive marking. For instance, a number of adpositionals in Upper Sorbian select complements marked in the genitive case, but those adpositionals are not able to select a possessive adjective complement. Perhaps we would need to say that selection and other processes by default only have access to the external SF role, and that access to the embedded SF role has to be stipulated. That, however, would seem to run counter to our explanation of the BNMP effects and hence our defence of Lexical Integrity, since we have been assuming that modification targets any occurrence of the [SF R] role wherever it is found in the ARG-ST attribute. Given that the Upper Sorbian construction is perhaps typologically rather unrepresentative, we will leave the question of how to account for the genitive case concord unresolved.

8.4.5   Awngi Agreeing Genitives

In this section we consider the phenomenon of agreeing genitives, briefly exemplified in Chapter 3 and often discussed under Frans Plank's designation of Suffixaufnahme. As we demonstrated in Chapter 3, there are languages in which a noun marked by the genitive case shares agreement properties with other attributes. This instantiates the phenomenon of Suffixaufnahme. We can argue that Suffixaufnahme is best generalized to situations in which a genitive-marked noun is treated morphosyntactically as an adjectival modifier. In those constructions the noun is inflected for case, but that case form then behaves like an attributive adjective and thus appears to shift its syntactic category. Here we would normally expect such a genitive attributive form to

334 *Noun–Adjective Hybrids*

be modified in the manner of the base noun, not in the manner of an adjective. Yet when this occurs, inflectional morphology shows paradigmatic category mixing and we obtain a kind of syntagmatic category mixing too: 'to the left' the word behaves like a noun, while 'to the right' it behaves like an adjective.

The main problem posed by agreeing genitives and especially the agreeing compound nouns in Nenets, which will be analysed in the next section, is what perspective we should adopt when analysing their categorial status. We can treat agreeing genitives as:

(i) a genitive case form of the noun that unexpectedly takes adjective-like agreement morphology
(ii) a possessive adjective form whose stem is syncretic with the genitive case form
(iii) something else

Agreeing genitives occur in a number of language groups, including the Daghestanian and Australian languages, and also in Central Cushitic. Hetzron (1995, 326) describes an agreeing genitive construction in the Ethiopian Cushitic language Awngi (see also Spencer, 2013, 355–356). Awngi nouns inflect for number and a variety of cases and have masculine or feminine gender (distinguished in the singular only), whereas attributive adjectives agree in number, gender, and case. The genitive inflection exists in masculine, feminine, and plural forms, agreeing with the possessum, as shown in the examples in (59).

(59) a. murí-w   aqí
          village-GEN[M] man[M]
          'the man of the village'

      b. murí-t   ɣuna
          village-GEN[F] woman[F]
          'the woman of the village'

      c. murí-kw   aq(ká)/ɣunaɣúná
          village-GEN[PL] men[PL]/women[PL]
          'the men/women of the village'

This agreeing genitive form then takes on the case endings of a case-marked possessed noun, as shown in (60). As can be seen here, the genitive can combine with the other case suffixes, in this instance the ablative (but also the accusative, dative, directive 'towards', adverbial 'in the manner of', and invocative 'for the sake of').

8.4 Representations of Noun-to-Adjective Derivations   335

(60) wolijí-w-des   aqí-w-des   ŋə́n-des
      old-GEN[M]-ABL man-GEN[M]-ABL house[M]-ABL
      'from the old man's house'

At first glance it might seem that the genitive was really an adjectivizing element rather than a noun suffix, but Hetzron (1995, 327–329) shows that it is essentially a noun, not an adjective. For instance, the construction is recursive and when a genitive modifies a noun which itself is in the genitive, the first noun agrees with the second in case, as shown in (61).

(61) gud-a-w-skʷ-da   ɣuna-w-skʷ-da
      good-F-GEN[PL]-GEN[PL]-LOC woman[F]-GEN[M]-GEN[PL]-LOC

      cənkút-əkʷ-da   ŋə́n-əkʷ-da
      nice-GEN[PL]-LOC house[M]-GEN[PL]-LOC

      wodel-ká-da ábjél-ká-da
      large-PL-LOC doorway-PL-LOC
      'in the large doorways of the nice house of the good woman'

In the Awngi examples we see particularly clear instances in which a genitive case-marked noun is effectively treated morphosyntactically as though it were an adjective. The fact that the Awngi construction is being used essentially to permit a noun to attributively modify another noun means that we have category mixing of the kind seen in other types of denominal modifier. However, in this instance the category mixing is precisely what we would expect, since the agreeing modifiers are themselves nothing but inflected forms of the noun and not in any obvious sense derived adjectives. Perhaps most compellingly, the genitive marker triggers the same sort of agreement as on other nouns in number, gender, and case, as seen in (61). In Figure 8.10 we reproduce Hetzron's (1995, 327) illustration of the pattern of agreement dependencies.

In Table 8.1 we provide the GPF which defines the agreeing genitive forms. The label '-affix' denotes appropriate genitive case morphology. According to the General Default Principle we would expect the genitive case-marked form to inherit the SYN value of the base form (that is, the uninflected noun lexeme), but this expectation is overridden by the agreeing genitive function, which specifies the semantic function role as that of an adjective, in much the same way as we see with transpositions proper. However, unlike more standard instances of transposition, this type is based on an already inflected form of the lexeme rather than on some uninflected stem. In this respect it is similar to deverbal nominalizations based on the infinitive form of a verb. Since there is no special morphology which creates a specifically adjectival

336 *Noun–Adjective Hybrids*

Table 8.1 *GPF for Awngi agreeing genitives*

	base noun	agreeing genitive
FORM	X	X–affix
ARG-ST	N features [Number:{sg,pl}] [Case:genitive] ⟨R⟩	GDP A features: [Agr] ⟨A*$_r$⟨SYN⟨L1, u⟩⟩⟩ = ⟨A*$_r$⟨R⟩⟩
SYN	Spec[], …	GDP [$_{NP}$ …]
SEM		
LI	L1	GDP (= L1)

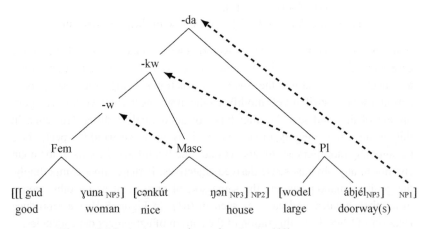

Figure 8.10 *Agreement dependencies in (61)*

form of the genitive-marked noun we can think of this as an instance of m-inert transposition in the typology of Spencer (2013).

We have followed Hetzron in taking the agreeing genitives to be nouns with unusual morphosyntax. However, there is an important sense in which it is inappropriate to ask whether the agreeing genitive is 'really' a noun or 'really' an adjective. As with mixed categories generally, the question is ill-formed: the word inherits certain noun properties, not least its meaning and the fact that it takes attributive modifiers and specifiers like a noun, but it inherits (some of) the 'external morphosyntax' of an adjective. Once we have

8.4 Representations of Noun-to-Adjective Derivations   337

identified the crucial properties of the word type, the question of the form's 'real' category becomes at best irrelevant and at worst incoherent. Notice that the compound SF role does much of the analytical work here. The agreeing genitive is an adjective by virtue of its A* role, which allows it to enter agreement morphosyntax constructions, but its visible R role permits modifiers to treat it as still a noun, together with the fact that it shares the Lexemic Index of the base noun, just like any true transposition.

8.4.6   Tundra Nenets Compounds

In Tundra Nenets modification-by-noun is expressed by prenominal juxtaposition, in which the attributive nominal is used non-referentially, as shown in (62). Such compounds contrast with the genitive case-marked possessive construction, in which the possessor phrase is referential (Nikolaeva, 2014b, 165–167).

(62)　　a.　ti　　　　ya
　　　　　　　reindeer soup
　　　　　　　'reindeer soup' (soup made of reindeer meat)

　　　　　b.　sax°r xīd'a
　　　　　　　sugar cup
　　　　　　　'sugar cup, cup used for sugar'

　　　　　c.　m'erc'a p'i
　　　　　　　wind　night
　　　　　　　'windy night'

The reason why these compounds are of interest to us is that the dependent nominative, that is the modifying noun, shows optional number agreement with the head, as seen in (63a). In this it does not differ from qualitative adjectives, as shown in (63b).

(63)　　a.　n'arawa-q loŋkey°-q
　　　　　　　copper-PL button-PL
　　　　　　　'copper buttons'

　　　　　b.　serako-q loŋkey°-q
　　　　　　　white-PL button-PL
　　　　　　　'white buttons'

Although there are cases of lexicalized compounds in which the modifying noun is entirely inert to morphosyntax, in the case of transparent,

338   *Noun–Adjective Hybrids*

non-lexicalized compounds we can find modification of the dependent noun by an adjective (as in English), shown in (64 and 65).

(64)   a.   səwa [l'id'aŋk° pəni]
             good beaver   coat
             'good coat made of beaver (skin)'

         b.   [səwa l'id'aŋk°] pəni
             good beaver   coat
             'coat made of good beaver (skin)'

(65)   a.   səwa [s'ay° xɪd'a]
             good tea   cup
             'good cup of tea'

         b.   [səwa s'ay°] xɪd'a
             good tea   cup
             'cup of good tea'

The attributive noun agrees only for plural number. Singular is unmarked, and dual number agreement is rejected by some speakers (Nikolaeva, 2014b, 167), but it is generally rather infrequent on attributive modifiers. There is no case concord in compounds. In addition, just as in many languages with N-N compounding, the dependent noun does not itself inflect for inherent properties of number, case, or possessor inflection. Thus, the compounding construction must be so analysed that it neutralizes possessor and case agreement, which is otherwise found with attributive adjectives, though adjectival concord for any features is optional and is "unique and quite complex" (Nikolaeva, 2014b, 151).[15]

Morphosyntactically, then, one way of thinking of the agreeing attributive noun in (63a) is to treat it as effectively a denominal adjective (though a featurally defective one) which is the output of morphologically inert derivation. In other words, the agreeing Nenets compounds are entirely parallel to the Awngi agreeing genitives. This is illustrated in Figure 8.11.

Recall from Chapter 7, Section 7.4 that the semantics of the relational adjective is given by the expression in (66).

---

[15]   Unlike the Awngi inflecting genitives and the Selkup relational adjectives discussed earlier in the chapter, the compound noun cannot take possessors or possessive inflections. Thus, the examples in (i), with the intended meaning 'soups made of my reindeer', are ungrammatical:

(i)   a. *tí-n°   ya-q   b. *mən'° tí-n°   ya-q
         reindeer-1SG-PL soup-PL   1SG   reindeer-1SG-PL soup-PL

8.4 Representations of Noun-to-Adjective Derivations   339

	base noun	agreeing dependent (nominative)
FORM:	X	GDP
	N features	none
		A features: ([Agr:[Number:{sg, pl}]])
ARG-ST:⟨R⟩		ARG-STR: ⟨A*$_r$⟨SYN⟨L1, u⟩⟩⟩
		= ⟨A*$_r$⟨R⟩⟩ (from SEM)
SYN:	Spec[] , ...	GDP
		[$_{NP}$ ...]
SEM:	[$_{Thing}$ λz.**noun**(z)][$_{Property}$ λP[λxλy∃ℛ[P(x) ∧ NOUN(y) ∧ ℛ(x,y)]]]	
LI:	L1	GDP (= L1)

Figure 8.11 *GPF for agreeing modifier nouns in Tundra Nenets compounds*

(66)   [$_{Property}$ λ𝒩[λP[λxλy∃ℛ[P(x) ∧ 𝒩(y) ∧ ℛ(x,y)]]]]

This means that the attributive form of 'copper' in (63a) is given by applying the function in (66) to the representation for 'copper', λz.**copper**(z), to give the expression in (67).

(67)   [$_{Property}$ λ𝒩[λP[λxλy∃ℛ[P(x) ∧ 𝒩(y) ∧ ℛ(x,y)]]]]([λz.**copper**(z)])

The expression in (67) reduces to the formula in (68), corresponding to the SEM representation for the agreeing nominative given in Figure 8.11.

(68)   [$_{Property}$ λ𝒩[λP[λxλy∃ℛ[P(x) ∧ **copper**(y) ∧ ℛ(x,y)]]]]

The alternative would be to treat the compounds as ordinary compounds, which on our account would mean deriving their meaning constructionally, locating the ℛ relation on the compound's mother node, not on the modifying noun. In that case the lexemic entry for the attributive noun would not change, but all of the property differences between the base lexemic entry and dependent noun illustrated in Figure 8.11 would then have to be introduced somehow by the construction. The failure of modifying nouns to take nominal inherent inflections could, no doubt, be derived from the fact that the noun is non-referential, though arguably we would want to derive the non-referentiality from the fact that the noun now lacks the properties it needs to be able to refer.

340 *Noun–Adjective Hybrids*

For that reason, we prefer the noun-to-adjective conversion analysis shown in Figure 8.11.

8.5 Conclusions

We conclude by briefly, in schematic form, summarizing the analyses presented in the chapter. We use obvious abbreviatory devices to make the representations easier to read. We begin with the Chukchi relational adjective, then follow with the Selkup similitudinal adjective and the Evenki proprietive. We next summarize the analysis of the agreeing genitives of Awngi and the agreeing compounds in Tundra Nenets. Finally, we briefly discuss the possessive adjective constructions.

For any given language the default morphosyntactic properties of a word class are given by the specific formulation of the Default Cascade. In the case of the adjective class this always means specification of the syntactic VALENCE attribute as attributive modifier (excluding, for instance, lexical exceptions such as adjectives which are only used predicatively): SYN|VAL|MOD $\boxed{\text{h}}$. It will also often involve specification of CONCORD properties: [SYN|MORSIG|CONCORD]. In languages with noun-to-adjective transpositions (pure relational adjectives, meaning-bearing noun-to-adjective transpositions, possessive adjectives) the MORSIG attribute of a noun will include the transpositional feature [REPR:$\langle\{no,yes\}\langle\langle N,A\rangle,\sigma\rangle\rangle$]. The GPF which defines the relational adjective/possessive adjective for a given noun lexeme (the external [SFROLE$_e$ R]) performs a number of functions. First and foremost it defines the transpositional compound [SFROLE $\langle A^*\langle x\langle R\rangle\rangle\rangle$]. At the level of the SEM attribute it adds the $\mathfrak{R}$ relation. The representation is thus subject to the Default Cascade, which specifies adjectival morphosyntactic properties associated with [SFROLE$_e$ A*] representations, VALENCE, CONCORD, and so on. However, being a true transposition, with 'embedded' [SFROLE R], the base noun of the relational adjective/possessive adjective is to a greater or lesser degree morphosyntactically 'visible'. This is reflected morphologically in Selkup (adjectival representations of nouns take noun possessor agreement morphology) and Evenki (proprietive adjectives take noun plural morphology).

The resulting adjectival representation of the noun lexeme is part of the ('inflectional'?) paradigm of the base noun. This is reflected formally in our model by the fact that a true transposition preserves the Lexemic Index of the base noun. However, in some respects the transposition behaves like a separate lexeme, for instance in its syntax as an attributive modifier. This is particularly clear when the language shows adjective-noun agreement (concord). The GPF which realizes the REPR feature thus defines not a single inflected word form but rather a subparadigm of word forms. The realized subparadigm is then independently defined by a distinct application of the GPF realizing those concord properties, a 'lexeme-within-a-lexeme'. It is in this way that the model captures the (wholly misleading!) intuition that transpositions are 'derivational'.

The pure relational adjective combines with a head noun in the syntax and semantically 'modifies' that head noun through the ℜ relation, defining the head as TARGET and the modifying noun as RESTRICTOR. In respect of the meaning-bearing transpositional adjectives of Selkup (and perhaps the Evenki proprietives) the semantic modification is more conventional, being mediated through the (*Property*) predicates of similarity, location, and so on.

8.5.1   The Chukchi Relational Adjective

The Chukchi relational adjective in *-kin* was exemplified by *uttə-kin* 'pertaining to a tree/trees', as in *uttə-kin (wətwət)* '(leaf) which is on a tree' from /utt/ 'tree, wood'. We begin with the maximally underspecified lexemic representation for UTT 'tree', as shown in (69).

(69) $\begin{bmatrix} \text{FORM} & [\text{STEM0/utt/}] \\ \text{SEM} & [_{\text{Thing}} \text{TREE}(x)] \end{bmatrix}$

This undergoes specification (as a typical noun) by the Default Cascade to give the basic lexical representation/lexical entry shown in (70).

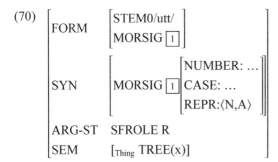

342 *Noun–Adjective Hybrids*

In respect of relational adjective formation, the GPF realizes the REPR feature, enriching the SFROLE attribute to give a compound SF, but neutralizing the number/case contrast on the noun, as shown in (71).

(71)
$$\begin{bmatrix} \text{FORM} & \begin{bmatrix} \text{STEM}_{rel} \text{ /uttə-kin/} \\ \text{MORSIG } \boxed{1} \end{bmatrix} \\ \text{SYN} & \begin{bmatrix} \text{MORSIG } \boxed{1} \text{[CONCORD: ...]} \end{bmatrix} \\ \text{ARG-ST} & \text{SFROLE } \langle A^* \langle x \langle R \rangle \rangle \rangle \\ \text{SEM} & [_{\text{Thing}} \text{ TREE(x)}] \end{bmatrix}$$

The GPF also specifies the relational adjective as a syntactic attributive modifier, so that it has the same external syntax as a simplex adjective, as shown in (72). (In Chukchi, this includes the possibility of being incorporated into the head noun.)

(72)
$$\begin{bmatrix} \text{FORM} & \begin{bmatrix} \text{STEM}_{rel} \text{ /uttə-kin/} \\ \text{MORSIG } \boxed{1} \end{bmatrix} \\ \text{SYN} & \begin{bmatrix} \text{MORSIG } \boxed{1} \text{[CONCORD: ...]} \\ \text{VAL | MOD} \end{bmatrix} \\ \text{ARG-ST} & \text{SFROLE } \langle A^* \langle x \langle R \rangle \rangle \rangle \\ \text{SEM} & [_{\text{Thing}} \text{ TREE(x)}] \end{bmatrix}$$

Finally, the GPF also enriches the SEM attribute by introducing the $\mathfrak{R}$ relation. This is now a representation of the base noun lexeme, but with the syntactic combinatorics of an attributive adjective, as shown in (73).

(73)
$$\begin{bmatrix} \text{FORM} & \begin{bmatrix} \text{STEM}_{rel} \text{ /uttə-kin/} \\ \text{MORSIG } \boxed{1} \end{bmatrix} \\ \text{SYN} & \begin{bmatrix} \text{MORSIG } \boxed{1} \text{[CONCORD: ...]} \\ \text{VAL | MOD} \end{bmatrix} \\ \text{ARG-ST} & \text{SFROLE } \langle A^* \langle x \langle R \rangle \rangle \rangle \\ \text{SEM} & [_{\text{Thing}} \text{ TREE(x)} \wedge \mathfrak{R}] \end{bmatrix}$$

8.5.2 The Selkup Similitudinal Adjective

The Selkup similitudinal adjective is illustrated by the word *alako-ššal'* 'similar to a boat', from *alako* 'boat'. These adjectives are defined in a very similar way to the relational adjectives of Chukchi. The main differences are (i) the SEM attribute is enriched by an additional predicate, SIM; (ii) Selkup nouns exhibit possessor agreement and this morphology is preserved by the transposition. We start with the lexical representation of the base noun lexeme shown in (74), which we assume is already specified for redundant properties.

(74)
$$\begin{bmatrix} \text{FORM} & \begin{bmatrix} \text{STEM0/alako/} \\ \text{MORSIG } \boxed{1} \end{bmatrix} \\ \text{SYN} & \begin{bmatrix} \text{MORSIG } \boxed{1} \begin{bmatrix} \text{NUMBER: } \ldots \\ \text{CASE: } \ldots \\ \text{POSSAGR: } \ldots \text{ REPR:} \langle \langle N,A \rangle, \\ \{\text{RA,SIMIL, LOC}\}\rangle \end{bmatrix} \end{bmatrix} \\ \text{ARG-ST} & \text{SFROLE R} \\ \text{SEM} & [_{\text{Thing}} \text{BOAT}(x)] \end{bmatrix}$$

In respect of similitudinal adjective formation, the GPF realizes the REPR:⟨⟨N,A⟩, {SIMIL}⟩ feature, which defines a relational adjective transposition but with the additional 'similar to' meaning. The GPF defines a compound SFROLE attribute, but neutralizes the number/case contrast on the noun, retaining just the POSSAGR attribute, as shown in (75).

(75)
$$\begin{bmatrix} \text{FORM} & \begin{bmatrix} \text{STEM}_{\text{sim}} \text{ /alako-ššal'/} \\ \text{MORSIG } \boxed{1} \end{bmatrix} \\ \text{SYN} & \begin{bmatrix} \text{MORSIG } \boxed{1} [\text{POSSAGR: } \ldots] \end{bmatrix} \\ \text{ARG-ST} & \text{SFROLE } \langle A*\langle x\langle R\rangle\rangle\rangle \\ \text{SEM} & [_{\text{Thing}} \text{BOAT}(x)] \end{bmatrix}$$

The GPF also specifies the similitudinal adjective as a syntactic attributive modifier, so that it has the same external syntax as a simplex adjective, as shown in (76).

344 *Noun–Adjective Hybrids*

(76)
$$\begin{bmatrix} \text{FORM} & \begin{bmatrix} \text{PHON /alako-ššal'/} \\ \text{MORSIG } \boxed{1} \end{bmatrix} \\ \text{SYN} & \begin{bmatrix} \text{MORSIG } \boxed{1}\,[\text{POSSAGR: ...}] \\ \text{VAL}\,|\,\text{MOD} \end{bmatrix} \\ \text{ARG-ST} & \text{SFROLE } \langle \text{A}^*\langle x \langle R \rangle \rangle \rangle \\ \text{SEM} & [_{\text{Thing}} \text{BOAT(x)}] \end{bmatrix}$$

In addition, the GPF respecifies the SEM attribute by adding the similitudinal predicate. This defines a property concept-denoting term, so the ontological category of the SEM value is changed to *Property*, just as would be the case with a genuinely derivational process which defines a distinct, autonomous lexeme: see (77).

(77)
$$\begin{bmatrix} \text{FORM} & \begin{bmatrix} \text{PHON /alako-ššal'/} \\ \text{MORSIG } \boxed{1} \end{bmatrix} \\ \text{SYN} & \begin{bmatrix} \text{MORSIG } \boxed{1}\,[\text{POSSAGR: ...}] \\ \text{VAL}\,|\,\text{MOD} \end{bmatrix} \\ \text{ARG-ST} & \text{SFROLE } \langle \text{A}^*\langle x \langle R \rangle \rangle \rangle \\ \text{SEM} & [_{\text{Property}} \text{SIMIL(BOAT(x))}] \end{bmatrix}$$

Selkup lacks adjective-noun agreement (or any other adjectival inflection) so that no further features are added to the adjectival MORSIG. However, the resulting representation is reminiscent of that of a partially underspecified adjective lexeme because it is underspecified for the (purely nominal) features of possessor agreement.

8.5.3   *The Evenki Proprietive*

The Evenki proprietive is formed in almost the same way as the Selkup relational adjective, with the added subtlety that the $\mathfrak{R}$ relation defines a kind of inverse genitive/possessive relationship between the head and the proprietive adjective. In the text we saw the derivation of the form *oroči* 'having a reindeer' from the singular form *oro(n)* '(a) reindeer'. Here we will consider the proprietive based on the plural form *orolči* 'having (several) reindeer'. We again begin with the lexemic representation of the noun with redundant features specified, as shown in (78).

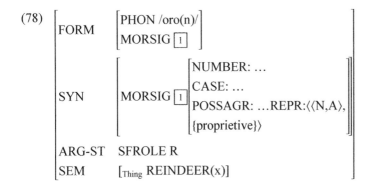

The GPF for the form *orolči* is defined over the feature set {[REPR:⟨⟨N,A⟩, {proprietive}⟩],[NUMBER:plural]}, which specifies the proprietive of the plural noun. The Feature Cooccurrence Restriction defined over the proprietive transposition neutralizes (eliminates) possessor agreement features in the noun's MORSIG by not copying them to the MORSIG of the transposed adjectival representation. On the other hand, it pre-specifies the CASE attribute as [CASE:proprietive]. The noun plural morphology is introduced by a realization rule in Block I. The plural form then serves as the input to the proprietive morphology which is introduced in Block IV (by-passing Blocks II and III). The GPF also specifies the compound SF ROLE of the relational adjective, and adds the (proprietive version of the) ℜ relation to the SEM representation, as shown in (79).

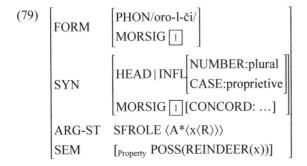

The compound SFROLE defines the representation as that of an adjective and hence the Default Cascade now specifies default adjectival properties, namely, the attributive modifier VALENCE attribute and the CONCORD attribute: see (80).

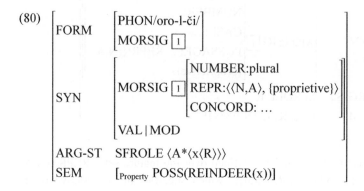

(80)

$$\begin{bmatrix} \text{FORM} & \begin{bmatrix} \text{PHON/oro-l-či/} \\ \text{MORSIG } \boxed{1} \end{bmatrix} \\ \text{SYN} & \begin{bmatrix} \text{MORSIG } \boxed{1} \begin{bmatrix} \text{NUMBER:plural} \\ \text{REPR:}\langle\langle N,A\rangle, \{\text{proprietive}\}\rangle \\ \text{CONCORD: ...} \end{bmatrix} \\ \text{VAL} \mid \text{MOD} \end{bmatrix} \\ \text{ARG-ST} & \text{SFROLE } \langle A^*\langle x\langle R\rangle\rangle\rangle \\ \text{SEM} & [_{\text{Property}} \text{POSS(REINDEER}(x))] \end{bmatrix}$$

This is now the representation for the proprietive adjective, underspecified for CONCORD properties.

8.5.4 The Awngi and Tundra Nenets Agreeing Noun Forms

For Awngi agreeing genitives, the derivation proceeds exactly as for the semantically neutral relational adjectives of Chukchi or Selkup, except that the GPF defines the adjectival representation over the genitive singular inflected form rather than an uninflected root/stem form. For the agreeing compounds of Tundra Nenets, we assume exactly the same derivations as for the Awngi agreeing genitives except that the GPF is defined over the base form. In both cases we can assume that the ℜ relation between head and modifier is introduced in whatever way such that a relation is introduced in languages or constructions which lack CONCORD. For instance, in Chapter 7, following Spencer (1999), we speculated that in endocentric N-N compounds the ℜ relation is introduced at the level of the construction as a whole and that it is not part of the lexical representation of the modifying noun as such. This type of analysis would presumably work equally well for the semantics of agreeing genitives and compounds.

8.5.5 Excursus on Possessive Adjectives

Our analysis also touched on the derivation and morphosyntactic properties of possessive adjectives. We have been careful to remain relatively non-specific about the possessive adjective category. The possessor relation is one between a head noun and a modifying NP/DP, not a common noun. The basic semantic relation in the case of alienable possession is the $\mathfrak{R}$ relation, but in the case of inalienable possession the $\mathfrak{R}$ relation has to be reinterpreted so that the RESTRICTOR role of $\mathfrak{R}$ expresses the possessor function and the TARGET role expresses the possessed (possessum) function. Syntactically, however, the possessor function is also realized by the specifier (SPR) of the possessed noun. Thus, we have argued, in any syntactic framework it will be necessary to develop a rigorous treatment of possessive constructions which takes into account the role played by adjectival attributive constructions.

In the absence of a sufficiently explicit model of possession we leave open the details of the morphosyntax of the Chukchi possessive adjective in -*in* or the Upper Sorbian possessive adjective.[16] We would argue that these are no different from relational adjectives. The GPF defines an adjectival representation, possibly including specification for CONCORD, and the SEM attribute of the noun lexeme is expanded to include the $\mathfrak{R}$ relation. The f_{syn} component of the GPF will additionally specify an appropriate version of the VAL attribute, permitting it to modify the head N while also defining the phrase it heads as the specifier.

The problem of possessors which are realized by (denominal) adjectives thus brings into sharp relief some of the problems posed by possessor constructions in general, but it also provides some pointers as to the best way of accounting for possessive constructions more generally.

---

[16] For the same reason we remain uncommitted about exactly how the possessed forms of Selkup denominal adjectives are to be represented in the syntax, since, strictly speaking, these are now noun–adjective hybrid *phrases*, and not just hybrid words.

9　*Conclusions and Prospects*

This study has been an exploration of one, very specific, type of category denominal attributive modifiers that retain some properties of the nouns from which they are derived. Although descriptive and theoretical work contains numerous examples of such categories, there have been very few detailed investigations and no cross-linguistic study has been carried out to date. Our book has surveyed attributive modifiers with nominal properties in a number of related and unrelated languages and has discussed parameters of their variation. We have therefore presented an empirical base from which possible analyses of such noun–adjective hybrids can be outlined by offering a larger typological picture.

During the course of our investigations, we have provided arguments in favour of a general approach to the problem of lexical and syntactic categories within a formal and explicit model, which departs radically from traditional assumptions about lexical categories. It is an approach which brings formal grammar in some ways closer to the position advocated by proponents of Cognitive Linguistics and by certain typologists, but which differs from those approaches in that it still relies crucially on discrete sets of categories which can be manipulated by formal devices and which can therefore in principle be interfaced with formal models of morphology, syntax, and semantics. Our model thus illustrates the Principle of Representational Independence of Spencer (2013), which is itself a partial statement of the crucial architectural assumption running through our approach. This is the principle that lexical representations are factorized into more or less fine-grained (but discrete) properties that can be combined in a variety of ways to give a large number of classes and subclasses of words, often cross-cutting traditional distinctions (and often lacking established names even in the theoretical literature).

Many of these additional categories are those that have come to be known as mixed categories. While the great majority of the literature on mixed categories focusses on deverbal nominalizations, we have focussed almost

Conclusions and Prospects 349

exclusively on a subset of denominal adjectives. The discussion has centred around two related but distinct aspects of mixing: paradigmatic mixing, in which a word's form shows some of the morphological properties of one category and some properties of another category, and syntagmatic mixing, in which a word form contracts some syntactic relations with some parts of the phrase as though it belonged to one category and some relations as though it belong to a different category.

The particular instantiation of syntagmatic mixing exhibited by denominal adjectives is the Base Noun Modifiability Property. In a number of languages we encounter structures like that of the Evenki proprietive, discussed in detail in Chapter 8, where it is possible for an adjective to modify, and even agree with, the noun from which the proprietive adjective is derived: [good-PLURAL reindeer-PLURAL]-PROPRIETIVE-F.DATIVE woman[F]-DATIVE 'to the woman who has good reindeer'. In English, Russian, and other familiar (European) languages such a construction is not possible. A denominal adjective such as English *tidal* or Russian *knižnyj* 'pertaining to a book/books' does not exhibit the Base Noun Modifiability Property: *[*high tid*]*al* (*currents*).

On the face of it, any adjective in any language which systematically exhibits the Base Noun Modifiability Property is *ipso facto* violating (one interpretation of) Lexical Integrity. Such violations would seriously call into question lexicalist models of morphosyntax, which crucially rely on a distinction between morphology and syntax and hence a word–phrase distinction. However, we argue that the Base Noun Modifiability Property (and by extension a number of other cases of syntagmatic category mixing) does not count as evidence against Lexical Integrity. We provide a simple solution to this problem by demonstrating that denominal adjectives which exhibit the Base Noun Modifiability Property have the hallmarks of (true) transpositions. A transpositional denominal adjective is simply an adjectival representation of the base noun lexeme and not an autonomous lexeme in its own right, with its own, distinct Lexemic Index (LI). Thus, the Evenki proprietive adjective is actually a member of the inflectional paradigm of the noun REINDEER. But this means that the adjective GOOD is modifying a word form which, at some level of representation, is realizing a form of a noun lexeme in that phrase. Ultimately, cases like the Evenki proprietive no more constitute a violation of Lexical Integrity than do inflectional noun forms modified by an adjective, as in the Hungarian *jó háza-i-k-ban*, good house-PLURAL-3PLURAL.POSSESSOR-INESSIVE, 'in their good houses' in this language and many others.

The intuition that an Evenki proprietive adjective is actually just a noun in disguise is one that is commonly expressed, but for it to be plausible,

350   *Conclusions and Prospects*

it is necessary to provide an explicit model of morphosyntax which can implement it. We have argued for a particular version of the Paradigm Function Morphology (PFM) class of models (Stump (2001) for PFM1 and Stump (2016) for PFM2), the Generalized Paradigm Function Morphology (GPFM) model of Spencer (2013). In Stump's original PFM class of models a Paradigm Function (PF) defines the inflectional paradigm of a lexeme. In the GPFM model the PF is generalized to a Generalized Paradigm Function (GPF) which defines all types of systematic lexical relatedness, including systematic derivational morphology (to the extent that this exists). The GPFM model is designed to provide an account of precisely the kinds of transposition we are dealing with here. The PFM class of models, including Network Morphology (Brown and Hippisley, 2012), are based on default inheritance logic, which raises interesting technical problems when we come to interface the morphology with an explicit account of syntax. We have selected an HPSG framework, that of Ackerman and Nikolaeva (2013), which has the advantage of having been developed specifically for attributive modification (involving mixed categories), a rare thing in the syntactic research literature. However, we should point out that, in principle, it ought to be possible to interface our model of lexical representation with any model of syntax that recognizes a word/phrase, morphology/syntax distinction.

Traditionally, all forms of transposition (action nominalizations, participles, relational adjectives, and others) have been considered to be 'derivational' because they change the word's lexical category. Spencer (2013) argues that this definition rests on too naive a set of assumptions about the concept of lexical category itself, and that it fails to recognize the implications of the full panoply of category mixing that we can observe cross-linguistically. However, it must be admitted that in the great majority of those languages with transpositions there is a descriptive problem: a denominal adjective typically has an inflectional paradigm which is (almost) entirely that of an adjective, not (necessarily) that of a noun. An explicit account of transpositions must therefore explain how this can come about, without falling into contradiction. This is what Spencer (2017b) calls the 'paradigm-within-a-paradigm' problem, and which we have relabelled (more pointedly) the 'lexeme-within-a-lexeme' problem. The solution we have proposed requires us to build up an explicit, but somewhat non-standard, model of lexical representation and lexical relatedness.

The first assumption we make is that we can state all the redundant properties of a lexical representation, including the grossest ones such as lexical

Conclusions and Prospects 351

category membership, as defaults. This is one of the principal architectural proposals of the PFM/Network Morphology class of models, including GPFM.

The second assumption we make is that we can deploy a notion of 'Semantic Function Role', SFROLE, as part of the ARG-ST attribute of lexical representation. The SF roles for the canonical exemplars of the N, V, A categories are labelled R, E, A*. Being part of the ARG-ST of a word means that they serve to mediate the interface between the semantic representation and the morphosyntactic representation. In the case of SFROLEs the interface is between the ontological category of the word in its Lexical Conceptual Structure and the morphosyntactic category. The SFROLE is what mediates morphosyntactic properties such as its valence and complementation properties, and other properties that determine the word's syntactic distribution, as well as its morphological form. To represent a word whose morphosyntax reflects that of more than one category, i.e. a mixed category, we have adopted the device of the compound SFROLE. A denominal adjective mixed category, while remaining in the default case a *Thing*-denoting word, can have the compound SFROLE $\langle A*\langle R\rangle\rangle$, in which both A* and R roles play a part in determining the word's morphosyntax.

The compound SFROLE labels are 'layered' in the sense that the outermost role (A* for denominal adjectives) governs external syntax while the innermost role (R) governs internal syntax. In the case of a representation with ARG-ST|SFROLE $\langle R\langle A*\rangle\rangle$ we have a property nominalization of the kind illustrated by Japanese *-sa* nouns, a word which is essentially an adjective with the distribution of a noun. (A consequence of this organization for phrase structure configurations is that we will typically observe Phrasal Coherence, though as we noted in Chapter 4 this, too, is defeasible in some languages.)

Finally, we assume a strict (i.e. non-defeasible, definitional) link between the compound SFROLE and lexemic status. Lexemic individuation is the problem of deciding when two word forms are members of the same lexeme or members of distinct lexemes. It is a difficult and poorly explored topic in theoretical models of morphosyntax (Spencer, 2015a). However, we assume that we can in principle distinguish lexemes from each other, and we grant that certain sets of word forms enjoy a privileged type of lexical relatedness, namely being forms of one and the same lexeme. In the simplest cases these are the uncontroversial inflected forms of that lexeme, but there are intermediate cases such as diminutives/augmentatives, argument structure alternants, and, of course, transpositions about which there is no agreement in the literature. All word forms are furnished with an LI, an independent attribute of all lexical representations which establishes their lexemic affiliation. The key assumption

352 *Conclusions and Prospects*

we are making is that the true transpositions are special: having a compound SFROLE entails sharing the LI of the base lexeme from which the transposition is 'derived' (better, of which the transposition is a 'representation'). Thus, a denominal adjective, even if it shows a full inflectional paradigm proper to an adjective of the language, is a member of the paradigm of the base lexeme, just as though it were a garden-variety inflected form.

As pointed out by Malchukov (2004) for action nominalizations, among others, languages differ in the way they permit transpositions to retain the base lexeme's morphosyntactic properties, as well as the extent to which derived morphosyntactic properties are acquired. Therefore, the model of morphosyntax has to provide a mechanism for defining which base properties are retained/lost and which derived category properties are acquired. In our model this is achieved through a combination of defaults and overrides in the GPF. These constraints are governed by a special morphosyntactic feature, whose function is precisely to define the form of transpositions: REPR(ESENTATION).

Any lexicalist model of morphology has to include a declaration of those properties which a given class of word can or must express. In our model this declaration takes the form of an attribute MORSIG ('morphosyntactic signature'), which specifies those s-features ('CONTENT paradigm properties') with which a word is associated, as well as the word's m-features ('FORM paradigm properties'). The justification for making the MORSIG a lexical attribute is precisely its role in the definition of mixed categories (Spencer, 2017b). One of the effects of the GPF when it realizes the REPR attribute is to respecify the word's MORSIG. It therefore redefines the word's morphosyntax by specifying which base properties are retained and which derived properties are acquired, as well as any constructional properties that are not represented in the base lexeme or among the properties of the derived category. The default situation is defined by the Default Cascade: a derived representation with an 'external' SFROLE$_e$ A* will be defined as an adjective, while retaining some of those properties it would have had as a simplex noun. The resulting representation then has precisely those properties that make it mixed and no others.

To summarize, the SFROLEs serve as elaborated proxies for traditional category labels. The A* role defines crucial properties of typical properties such as CONCORD, and especially the VALENCE|MOD property of syntactic attributive modifiers. The R role determines reference-related properties such as determination, but also defines the word as a potential value of the MOD attribute, i.e. as an attributively modifiable category. Thus, while the

Conclusions and Prospects   353

function of the SFROLEs overlaps with those of familiar lexical category (c-structure) labels, they are neither intensionally nor extensionally equivalent (Spencer, 1998, 1999, 2013). They are not intensionally equivalent to the traditional labels because the latter are designed to define solely distributional properties. The SFROLE by contrast defines distribution only indirectly, through selectional and other properties defined at ARG-ST and elsewhere. The conception of the SFROLE developed in the GPFM model is distinct extensionally from the traditional labels precisely because of the existence of the articulated compound SFROLEs. It is these compound SFROLEs which permit us to define precisely those kinds of syntagmatic mixing found with true transpositions, and which permit us to ascribe the occurrence of syntagmatic mixing to the fact that a transposition is part of the paradigm of the base lexeme and not a distinct lexeme in its own right. It is these distinctions that, by definition, the traditional labels cannot capture. In fact, it is hard to see what function the traditional labels would play in our model, other than as (sometimes misleading and inconvenient) mnemonics for more articulated, factorized definitions of lexical properties (Spencer, 1998).

This machinery then provides us with an account of how the Base Noun Modifiability Property can emerge. The transpositional denominal adjective is the adjectival representation of a noun lexeme, and being a noun it can in principle be modified, specified, and so on. Moreover, it can still denote a referring expression, and hence permit anaphoric cross-reference. The nounhood of some denominal adjectives, e.g. Selkup relational, similitudinal, and locational adjectives, and the Evenki proprietive adjectives, is also evident from their morphology, since they inflect for possessor agreement (Selkup denominal adjectives) and plural number (Evenki proprietives). Indeed, in some languages the attributive modifier form of the noun does not even need to receive special morphological marking to make it look like an adjective in that language. The agreeing genitives of Awngi and a variety of other languages, and the agreeing compound nouns of Tundra Nenets, are pure noun forms which take concordial morphology.

One of the lexical attributes that can be factorized is semantic representation. The semantics of a word, in the sense of its conceptual content, is generally taken to be an immutable property of that word, at least in the PFM models, and indeed, in most cases inflectional morphology does not introduce any change in the conceptual content of a lexeme. In this, inflection is traditionally held to differ from derivational morphology, whose canonical function is precisely to enrich the base word's meaning so as to create a new lexeme. But there seem to be cases where we have to say that inflection does add conceptual content

354 *Conclusions and Prospects*

(one of the types of 'inherent inflection' in Booij's (1996) terms). Similarly, while a true transposition is generally meaning-neutral, there are two senses in which a denominal adjective will have a distinct SEM value from its noun base. First, in the case of pure relational adjectives we have assumed that the SEM attribute is enriched by the pragmatically/contextually determined $\mathfrak{R}$ relation, the weakest kind of semantic enrichment. But in addition, we have seen cases such as the similitudinal and locative denominal adjectives of Selkup and similar types of derived adjectives in other languages which are just like relational adjectives except that they introduce a *Property*-denoting semantic predicate.

Conversely, just because two derivationally related words have the same conceptual content this does not necessarily mean that they share a Lexemic Index (*pace* Sag (2012) and other authors). There are words with the appearance of noun-to-adjective, verb-to-adjective, verb-to-noun, etc. transpositions that in fact represent distinct lexemes, the 'transpositional lexemes' of Spencer (2013, 2016). The (so-called) relational adjectives of English, French, Russian, and other European languages are examples of this. Since they are distinct lexemes from the nouns they are derived from, they have the simple SFROLE A*, just like underived adjectives. Thus, they cannot be 'recognized' as nouns in the syntax. Specifically, they respect Lexical Integrity by not exhibiting the Base Noun Modifiability Property.

Our study leaves open a number of questions and raises others. The first question is how widespread the Base Noun Modifiability Property is cross-linguistically. A detailed targeted study of languages with systematic noun-to-adjective morphology would be a prerequisite to answering this question. By 'targeted', we mean a study which focusses on only those languages that have that construction and for which reliable descriptions are available, as opposed to a typological survey based on a (randomly selected) 'balanced sample'.

Second, we have in various places compared denominal adjectives with endocentric N-N compounds, modification by oblique phrases, and possessive constructions, and we have offered a preliminary account of the relation between these constructional types. However, our selection of languages is rather modest and a more detailed, targeted, cross-linguistic survey comparing all the ways in which 'modification-by-nominal-concept' is achieved would be valuable here.

Third, our study can be extended to an exploration of the other logically possible types of transposition between N, V, and A. For instance, although there has been a fair deal of work on the typology of action nominals in various frameworks, virtually no typological or cross-linguistic work has been conducted on the at least equally frequent phenomenon of deverbal participles (Shagal, 2017, being a notable exception). There is virtually no discussion in the literature of adjective-to-noun transpositions (property nominalizations), and what there is (e.g. Spencer, 2013) fails to recognize that in European languages, again, we are dealing with transpositional lexemes, not true transpositions (see Spencer, 2016). Finally, one of the least well understood types of transposition is the verbal representation of N, A, that is predicative nouns and adjectives. Careful consideration of noun-to-verb transpositions, in particular, should throw light on the problem of 'flexible word classes' and the debate as to whether all languages have a 'noun-verb' distinction.[1]

Finally, we have compared relational adjective-type transpositions with possessive adjectives at various points. An adjective which realizes the grammatical function normally realized by an NP/DP in the specifier position of the head noun is difficult to accommodate to any explicit model of morphosyntax. We have suggested tentatively that it is (sometimes, at least) wrong to analyse possessive constructions as the result of coercing the argument structure of the head noun to include a possessor argument. Rather, the possessive semantic relation is introduced by enriching or specifying the SEM attribute of the possessor head with the $\mathfrak{R}$ relation, in much the same way that the $\mathfrak{R}$ relation is added to the SEM attribute of a noun in the formation of a relational adjective. For cases of juxtaposition and modification-by-noun, however, where neither element of the construction is morphologically marked, we have tentatively offered a genuinely constructional analysis in which the $\mathfrak{R}$ relation resides at the level of the construction itself. Needless to say, such an analysis would require more detailed justification, especially from N-N compounding cross-linguistically, before it can be accepted. It appears to us, however, to represent a promising avenue to explore.

A poorly studied construction type, particularly one which is all but absent in the more familiar languages of the world, is, on the face of it, an unpromising candidate for far-reaching conclusions about fundamental notions such as the word–phrase divide, Lexical Integrity, and even the very notion of lexico-syntactic categories themselves. However, we believe that noun–adjective hybrids have much to tell us about just those questions, and others, and that these and similar phenomena can provide a rich source of insight into foundational issues in linguistic theory.

---

[1] Our own view is that if, as we and many others claim, the traditional word class labels are too gross and need to be factorized into finer-grained distinctions, much of the discussion in the typological literature arguing for languages with 'no word classes' is rendered incoherent.

Bibliography

Aarts, Bas. 2006. Conceptions of categorization in the history of linguistics. *Language Sciences*, **28**, 361–385.

Aarts, Bas, and Haegeman, Liliane. 2006. English word-classes and phrases. Pages 117–145 of: Aarts, Bas, and McMahon, April (eds), *The Handbook of English Linguistics*. Oxford: Blackwell Publishers.

Ackema, Peter, and Neeleman, Ad. 2004. *Beyond Morphology: Interface Conditions on Word Formation*. Oxford: Oxford University Press.

Ackerman, Farrell, and Nikolaeva, Irina 2013. *Descriptive Typology and Linguistic Theory: A Study in the Morphosyntax of Relative Clauses*. Stanford, CA: CSLI Publications.

Ackerman, Farrell, and Webelhuth, Gert. 1998. *A Theory of Predicates*. Stanford, CA: CSLI Publications.

Alexiadou, Artemis. 2003. Some notes on the structure of alienable and inalienable possessors. Pages 167–188 of: Coene, Martine, and D'hulst, Yves (eds), *From NP to DP*. Amsterdam: John Benjamins Publishing Co.

   2010a. Nominalizations: a probe into the architecture of grammar. Part I: the nominalization puzzle. *Language and Linguistics Compass*, **4**, 496–511.

   2010b. Nominalizations: a probe into the architecture of grammar. Part II: the aspectual properties of nominalizations, and the lexicon vs. syntax debate. *Language and Linguistics Compass*, **4**, 512–523.

Alexiadou, Artemis, and Stavrou, Melita. 2011. Ethnic adjectives as pseudo-adjectives: a case study on syntax–morphology interaction and the structure of DP. *Studia Linguistica*, **65**, 117–146.

Alexiadou, Artemis, and Wilder, Christopher. 1998. Adjectival modification and multiple determiners. Pages 305–332 of: Alexiadou, Artemis, and Wilder, Christopher (eds), *Possessors, Predicates and Movement in the Determiner Phrase*. Amsterdam: John Benjamins Publishing Co.

Alexiadou, Artemis, Haegeman, Liliane, and Stavrou, Melita (eds). 2007. *Noun Phrase in the Generative Perspective*. Berlin: Mouton de Gruyter.

Allen, Margaret. 1978. *Morphological Investigations*. Ph.D. thesis, Cornell University, New York.

Amritavalli, R., and Jayaseelan, K. A. 2003. The genesis of syntactic categories and parametric variation. Pages 19–41 of: Yoon, Hang-Jin (ed.), *Generative Grammar in a Broader Perspective: Proceedings of the 4th GLOW in Asia 2003*. Seoul: Hankook, for Generative Linguists of the Old World.

Bibliography   357

Anderson, John M. 1997. *A Notional Theory of Syntactic Categories*. Cambridge: Cambridge University Press.

2007. *The Grammar of Names*. Oxford: Oxford University Press.

Anderson, Stephen R. 1992. *A-Morphous Morphology*. Cambridge: Cambridge University Press.

Aoun, Yosef. 1981. Parts of speech: a case of redistribution. Pages 3–24 of: Belletti, Adriana, Brandi, Luciana, and Rizzi, Luigi (eds), *Theory of Markedness in Generative Grammar: Proceedings of the 1979 GLOW Conference*. Pisa: Scuola Normale Superiore di Pisa.

Apresjan, Jurij Derenikovič. 1974. Regular polysemy. *Linguistics*, **12**, 5–32.

Arad, Maya. 2005. *Roots and Patterns: Hebrew Morpho-syntax*. Dordrecht: Springer Verlag.

Arnold, Douglas, and Spencer, Andrew. 2015. A constructional analysis for the skeptical. Pages 41–60 of: Müller, Stefan (ed.), *Proceedings of the HPSG22 Conference*. Stanford, CA: CSLI Publications.

Aronoff, Mark. 1976. *Word Formation in Generative Grammar*. Cambridge, MA: The MIT Press.

1994. *Morphology by Itself: Stems and Inflectional Classes*. Cambridge, MA: The MIT Press.

Arsenijevic, Boban, Boleda, Gemma, Gehrke, Berit, and McNally, Louise. 2014. Ethnic adjectives are proper adjectives. Pages 17–30 of: Baglini, Rebekah, Grinsell, Timothy, Keane, Jonathan, Roth Singerman, Adam, and Thomas, Julia (eds), *Proceedings of the 46th Annual Meeting of the Chicago Linguistic Society*, vol. 46. Chicago: Chicago Linguistic Society.

Backhouse, Anthony E. 2004. Inflected and uninflected adjectives in Japanese. Pages 50–73 of: Dixon, R. M. W., and Aikhenvald, Alexandra (eds), *Adjective Classes: A Cross-Linguistic Typology*. Oxford: Oxford University Press.

Baker, Mark, C. 1985. Syntactic affixation and English gerunds. Pages 1–11 of: *Proceedings of the West Coast Conference on Formal Linguistics*, vol. 4.

1988a. *Incorporation: A Theory of Grammatical Function Changing*. Chicago: University of Chicago Press.

1988b. Morphology and syntax: an interlocking dependence. Pages 9–32 of: Everaert, Martin, Evers, Arnold, Huybrechts, Riny, and Trommelen, Mieke (eds), *Morphology and Modularity: In Honour of Henk Schultink*. Dordrecht: Foris Publications.

2003. *Lexical Categories: Verbs, Nouns and Adjectives*. Cambridge: Cambridge University Press.

Baker, Mark C., and Croft, William A. 2017. Lexical categories: legacy, lacuna, and opportunity for functionalists and formalists. *Annual Review of Linguistics*, **3**, 179–197.

Bally, Charles. 1944. *Linguistique generale et linguistique française*. Berne: Francke.

Barker, Christopher. 1997. *Possessive Descriptions*. Stanford, CA: CSLI Publications.

2011. Possessives and relational nouns. Pages 1109–1130 of: Maienborn, Claudia, von Heusinger, Klaus, and Portner, Paul (eds), *Semantics: An International Handbook of Natural Language Meaning*, vol. 2. Berlin: De Gruyter Mouton.

358 Bibliography

Bauer, Laurie, Lieber, Rochelle, and Plag, Ingo. 2013. *The Oxford Reference Guide to English Morphology.* Oxford: Oxford University Press.

Bauer, Winifred. 1997. *The Reed Reference Grammar of Maori (with William Parker, Te Kareongawai Evans, and Te Aroha Noti Teepa).* Auckland: Reed Books.

Beard, Robert. 1995. *Lexeme-Morpheme Base Morphology.* Stony Brook, NY: SUNY Press.

Beck, David. 2002. *The Typology of Parts of Speech Systems: The Markedness of Adjectives.* London: Routledge.

Bell, Melanie J., and Plag, Ingo. 2012. Informativeness is a determinant of compound stress in English. *Journal of Linguistics,* **48,** 485–520.

Bergsland, Knut. 1997. *Aleut Grammar.* Fairbanks, Alaska: Alaska Native Center.

Besnier, Niko. 2000. *Tuvaluan: a Polynesian Language of the Central Pacific.* London: Routledge.

Bhat, D. N. S. 1994. *The Adjective Category: Criteria for Differentiation and Identification.* Amsterdam: John Benjamins Publishing Co.

2000. Word classes and sentential functions. Pages 47–63 of: Vogel, Petra M., and Comrie, Bernard (eds), *Approaches to the Typology of Word Classes.* Berlin: Mouton de Gruyter.

Bhatia, Tej K. 1993. *Punjabi.* London: Routledge.

Bierwisch, Manfred. 1989. Event nominalization: proposals and problems. Pages 1–73 of: Motsch, Wolfgang (ed.), *Wortstruktur und Satzstruktur.* Berlin: Akademie der Wissenschaften der DDR.

Bierwisch, Manfred. 2007. Semantic form as interface. Pages 1–32 of: Späth, Andreas (ed.), *Interfaces and Interface Conditions.* Berlin: De Gruyter.

Bisang, Walter. 2011. Word classes. Pages 280–302 of: Song, Jae Jung (ed.), *The Oxford Handbook of Linguistic Typology.* Oxford: Oxford University Press.

Bisetto, Antonietta. 2010. Relational adjectives crosslinguistically. *Lingue e Linguaggio,* **9,** 65–85.

Bochnak, Ryan M. 2013. The non-universal status of degrees: evidence from Washo. Pages 79–92 of: Keine, Stefan, and Slogget, Shayne (eds), *Proceedings of the North East Linguistic Society, 42.* Amherst: GLSA Publications.

Boeder, Winfried. 2005. The South Caucasian languages. *Lingua* (Helga van den Berg, ed., Caucasian, special issue), **115**(1–2), 5–89.

Boeder, Winfried, and Schroeder, Christoph. 2000. Relational coding in Georgian and Turkish noun phrases: syntax, derivational morphology, and 'linking' by means of participles. *Turkic Languages,* **4,** 153–204.

Bögel, Tina, Butt, Miriam, and Sulger, Sebastian. 2008. Urdu ezafe and the morphology-syntax interface. Pages 129–149 of: Butt, Miriam, and King, Tracy Holloway (eds), *Proceedings of the LFG08 Conference.* Stanford, CA: CSLI Publications.

Bogoraz, Vladimir G. 1900. *Materialy po izučeniju čukotskogo jazyka i fol'klora, sobrannye v Kolymskom okruge* [Materials for the Study of the Chukchi Language and Folklore, Collected in the Kolyma District]. St Petersburg: Publishing House of the Russian Academy of Sciences.

Bibliography 359

Boguslavskaja, Ol'ga Ju. 1989. *Struktura imennoj gruppy: Opredelitel'nye konstrukcii v dagenstanskix jazykax* [The Structure of the Noun Phrase: Attributive Constructions in the Dhagestanian Languages]. Ph.D. thesis, Moscow State University, Moscow.
 1995. Genitives and adjectives as attributes in Daghestanian. Pages 230–239 of: Frans Plank (ed.), *Double Case: Agreement by Suffixaufnahme*. Oxford: Oxford University Press.

Bonami, Olivier, and Crysmann, Berthold. 2016. The role of morphology in constraint-based lexicalist grammars. Pages 449–481 of: Hippisley, Andrew, and Stump, Gregory T. (eds), *The Cambridge Handbook of Morphology*. Cambridge: Cambridge University Press.

Bonami, Olivier, and Stump, Gregory. 2016. Paradigm function morphology. Pages 449–481 of: Hippisley, Andrew, and Stump, Gregory T. (eds), *The Cambridge Handbook of Morphology*. Cambridge: Cambridge University Press.

Bond, Oliver. 2019. Canonical typology. Pages 409–434 of: Audring, Jenny, and Masini, Francesca (eds), *Oxford Handbook of Morphological Theory*. Oxford: Oxford University Press.

Bond, Oliver, and Chumakina, Marina. n.d. *Attributives in Archi: a Mixed Category with Multiple Bases*. Unpublished manscript, University of Surrey.

Booij, Geert. 1988. The relation between inheritance and argument linking: deverbal nouns in Dutch. Pages 57–74 of: Everaert, Martin, Evers, Arnold, Huybrechts, Riny, and Trommelen, Mieke (eds), *Morphology and Modularity: In Honour of Henk Schultink*. Dordrecht: Foris Publications.
 1996. Inherent versus contextual inflection and the split morphology hypothesis. Pages 1–16 of: Booij, Geert, and van Marle, Jaap (eds), *Yearbook of Morphology 1995*. Dordrecht: Kluwer Academic Publishers.

Booij, Geert, and van Haften, Ton. 1988. On the external syntax of derived words: evidence from Dutch. Pages 29–44 of: Booij, Geert, and van Marle, Jaap (eds), *Yearbook of Morphology 1*. Dordrecht: Kluwer Academic Publishers.

Borer, Hagit. 2013. *Structuring Sense: Taking Form*. Oxford: Oxford University Press.

Borsley, Robert D. 1995. On some similarities and differences between Welsh and Syrian Arabic. *Linguistics*, **33**, 99–122.

Bošković, Željko. 2008. What will you have, DP or NP? Pages 101–114 of: Elfner, Emily, and Walkow, Martin (eds), *Proceedings of the 37th Meeting of the North East Linguistics Society*. Amherst: Graduate Linguistic Student Association, University of Massachusetts.

Bosque, Ignacio, and Picallo, Carme. 1996. Postnominal adjectives in Spanish DPs. *Journal of Linguistics*, **32**, 349–385.

Bouillon, Pierrette. 1996. Mental state adjectives: the perspective of Generative Lexicon. Pages 143–148 of: *COLING '96 Proceedings of the 16th International Conference on Computational Linguistics*. Association for Computational Linguistics, Copenhagen.
 1999. The adjective 'vieux': the point of view of 'Generative Lexicon'. Pages 147–166 of: Viegas, Evelyne (ed.), *Breadth and Depth of Semantic Lexicons*. Dordrecht: Kluwer.

360   *Bibliography*

Bouillon, Pierrette, and Busa, Federica. 2001. Introduction. Pages 3– 4 of: Bouillon, Pierrette, and Busa, Federica (eds), *The Language of Word Meaning*. Cambridge: Cambridge University Press.

Breban, Tine. 2017. Proper names used as modifiers: a comprehensive functional analysis. *English Language and Linguistics*, 1–21.

Bresnan, Joan. 1997. Mixed categories as head sharing constructions. In: Butt, Miriam, and King, Tracy Holloway (eds), *The Proceedings of the LFG '97 Conference*. Stanford, CA: CSLI Publications.

2001. *Lexical-Functional Syntax*. Oxford: Blackwell Publishers.

Bresnan, Joan, and Mugane, John. 2006. Agentive nominalizations in Gĩkũyũ and the theory of mixed categories. Pages 201–234 of: Butt, Miriam, Dalrymple, Mary, and King, Tracy Holloway (eds), *Intelligent Linguistic Architectures: Variations on Themes by Ronald M. Kaplan*. Stanford, CA: CSLI Publications.

Bresnan, Joan, Asudeh, Ash, Toivonen, Ida, and Wechsler, Stephen. 2016. *Lexical-Functional Syntax*. 2nd edn. Oxford: Wiley-Blackwell.

Broschart, Jürgen. 1997. Why Tongan does it differently: categorial distinctions in a language without nouns and verbs. *Linguistic Typology*, **1**, 123–165.

Brown, Dunstan P., and Hippisley, Andrew. 2012. *Network Morphology: A Defaults-based Theory of Word Structure*. Cambridge: Cambridge University Press.

Brown, Dunstan P., Chumakina, Marina, and Corbett, Greville G. (eds). 2012a. *Canonical Morphology and Syntax*. Oxford: Oxford University Press.

Brown, Dunstan P., Chumakina, Marina, Corbett, Greville G., Popova, Gergana D., and Spencer, Andrew. 2012b. Defining 'periphrasis': key notions. *Morphology*, **22**, 233–275.

Bybee, Joan. 1985. *Morphology: A Study of the Relation between Meaning and Form*. Amsterdam: John Benjamins Publishing Co.

Cabredo Hofherr, Patricia, and Matushansky, Ora (eds). 2010. *Adjectives: Formal Analyses in Syntax and Semantics*. Amsterdam: John Benjamins Publishing Co.

Carleton, Troi, and Waksler, Rachelle. 2000. Pronominal markers in Zenzontepec Chatino. *International Journal of American Linguistics*, **66**(3), 381–395.

Carlson, Gregory N. 1977. *Reference to Kinds in English*. Ph.D. thesis, University of Massachusetts at Amherst, Amherst, MA.

Cetnarowska, Bożena. 2015. Categorial ambiguities with the noun phrase: relational adjectives in Polish. Pages 115–153 of: Błaszczak, Joanna, Klimek-Jankowska, Dorota, and Migdalski, Krzysztof (eds), *How Categorial Are Categories? New Approaches to the Old Questions of Noun, Verb, and Adjective*. Berlin: Mouton de Gruyter.

Cetnarowska, Bożena, Pysz, Agnieszka, and Trugman, Helen. 2011. Distribution of classificatory adjectives and genitives in Polish NPs. Pages 273–303 of: Dębowska-Kozłowska, Kamila, and Dziubalska-Kołaczyk, Katarzyna (eds), *On Words and Sounds: A Selection of Papers from the 40th PLM, 2009*. Newcastle upon Tyne: Cambridge Scholars Publishing.

Chappell, Hilary, and McGregor, William. 1989. Alienability, inalienability and nominal classification. Pages 24–36 of: *Proceedings of the Fifteenth Annual Meeting of the Berkeley Linguistics Society*, vol. 15. Berkeley Linguistics Society.

1996. Prolegomena to a theory of inalienability. Pages 3–30 of: Chappell, Hilary, and McGregor, William (eds), *The Grammar of Inalienability: A Typological Perspective on Body Part Terms and the Part-Whole Relation*. Berlin: Mouton de Gruyter.

Chaves, Rui P. 2014. Grammatical alignments and the gradience of lexical categories. Pages 167–220 of: Hoffmeister, Philip, and Norcliffe, Elisabeth (eds), *The Core and the Periphery: Data-Driven Perspectives on Syntax Inspired by Ivan A. Sag*. Stanford, CA: CSLI Publications.

Chisarik, Erika, and Payne, John. 2001. Modelling possessor constructions in LFG: English and Hungarian. Pages 33–46 of: Butt, Miriam, and King, Tracy Holloway (eds), *The Proceedings of the LFG '01 Conference, University of Hong Kong, Hong Kong*. Stanford, CA: CSLI Publications.

Chomsky, Noam. 1970. Remarks on nominalization. Pages 184–221 of: Jacobs, R., and Rosenbaum, P. (eds), *Readings in English Transformational Grammar*. Waltham, MA: Blaisdell.

1981. *Lectures on Government and Binding*. Dordrecht: Foris.

1986. *Barriers*. Cambridge, MA: The MIT Press.

Christen, Simon. 2001. Genitive positions in Baltic and Finnic languages. Pages 499–520 of: Dahl, Östen, and Koptjevskaja-Tamm, Maria (eds), *Circum-Baltic Languages: Their Typology and Contacts*. Amsterdam: John Benjamins Publishing Co.

Cinque, Guglielmo. 1994. On the evidence for partial N movement in the Romance DP. Pages 85–110 of: Cinque, Guglielmo, Koster, Jan, Pollock, Jean-Yves, Rizzi, Luigi, and Zanuttini, Raffaella (eds), *Paths Towards Universal Grammar*. Washington, DC: Georgetown University Press.

1999. *Adverbs and Functional Heads: A Cross-Linguistic Perspective*. Oxford: Oxford University Press.

2010. *The Syntax of Adjectives: A Comparative Study*. Cambridge, MA: The MIT Press.

Cole, D. T. 1979. *An Introduction to Tswana Grammar*. Johannesburg: Longman.

Copestake, Ann, Flickinger, Dan, Pollard, Carl, and Sag, Ivan A. 2005. Minimal recursion semantics: an introduction. *Research on Language and Computation*, **3**, 281–332.

Corbett, Greville G. 1987. The morphology-syntax interface. *Language*, **63**, 299–345.

1995. Slavonic's closest approach to suffix copying: the possessive adjective. Pages 265–282 of: Frans Plank (ed.), *Double Case: Agreement by Suffixaufnahme*. Oxford: Oxford University Press.

2006. *Agreement*. Cambridge: Cambridge University Press.

2007. Canonical typology, suppletion, and possible words. *Language*, **83**, 8–42.

2010. Canonical derivational morphology. *Word Structure*, **2**, 141–155.

2012. *Features*. Cambridge: Cambridge University Press.

362 Bibliography

Creissels, Denis. 2000. Typology. Pages 231–258 of: Heine, Bernd, and Nurse, Derek (eds), *African Linguistics: An Introduction*. Cambridge: Cambridge University Press.

2006. Suffixes casuels et postpositions en hongrois. *Bulletin de la Société de Linguistique de Paris*, **101**, 225–272.

Cristofaro, Sonia. 2009. Grammatical categories and relations: universality vs. language specificity and construction-specificity. *Language and Linguistics Compass*, **3**, 441–479.

Croft, William A. 1990. *Typology and Universals*. Cambridge: Cambridge University Press.

1991. *Syntactic Categories and Grammatical Relations: The Cognitive Organization of Information*. Chicago: Chicago University Press.

2000. Parts of speech as language universals and as language-particular categories. Pages 65–102 of: Vogel, Petra M., and Comrie, Bernard (eds), *Approaches to the Typology of Word Classes*. Berlin: Mouton de Gruyter.

2001. *Radical Construction Grammar*. Oxford: Oxford University Press.

2003. *Typology and Universals*. 2nd edn. Cambridge: Cambridge University Press.

Croft, William A., and van Lier, Eva. 2012. Language universals without universal categories (commentary on Sandra Chung, "Are lexical categories universal? The view from Chamorro"). *Theoretical Linguistics*, **38**, 57–72.

Cruse, Alan D. 1986. *Lexical Semantics*. Cambridge: Cambridge University Press.

Crystal, David. 1967. English word classes. *Lingua*, **17**, 24–56.

Culicover, Peter, and Jackendoff, Ray S. 2005. *Simpler Syntax*. Oxford: Blackwell Publishers.

Dalrymple, Mary. 2001. *Lexical Functional Grammar*. San Diego, CA: Academic Press.

2015. Morphology in LFG. Pages 43–62 of: Butt, Miriam, and King, Tracy Holloway (eds), *Proceedings of the LFG15 Conference*. Stanford, CA: CSLI Publications.

Davis, Henry, Gillon, Carrie, and Matthewson, Lisa. 2014. How to investigate linguistic diversity: lessons from the Pacific Northwest. *Language*, **90**, e180–e226.

Davis, Karen. 2003. *A Grammar of the Hoava Language, Western Solomons*. Canberra: Pacific Linguistics, Research School of Pacific and Asian Studies, Australian National University.

Dayley, Jon P. 1989. *Tümpisa (Panamint) Shoshone Grammar*. Berkeley, CA: University of California Press.

Delfitto, Denis, and Melloni, Chiara. 2009. Compounds don't come easy. *Lingue e Linguaggio*, **8**, 75–104.

Demonte, Violeta. 2008. Meaning-form correlations and adjective position in Spanish. Pages 71–100 of: Kennedy, Christopher, and McNally, Louise (eds), *The Semantics of Adjectives and Adverbs*. Oxford: Oxford University Press.

Despić, Miloje. 2013. Binding and the structure of NP in Serbo-Croatian. *Linguistic Inquiry*, **44**, 239–270.

Dixon, R. M. W. 1982. Where have all the adjectives gone? Pages 1–62 of: *Where Have All the Adjectives Gone? and Other Essays in Semantics and Syntax*. Amsterdam: Mouton.

1991. *A New Approach to English Grammar, on Semantic Principles*. Oxford: The Clarendon Press.

Bibliography 363

2000. Categories of the noun phrase in Jarawara. *Journal of Linguistics*, **36**, 487–510.

2004. Adjective classes in typological perspective. Pages 1–49 of: Dixon, R. M. W., and Aikhenvald, Alexandra (eds), *'Adjective Classes: A Cross-Linguistic Typology'*. Oxford: Oxford University Press.

Downing, Pamela. 1977. On the creation and use of English nominal compounds. *Language*, **55**, 810–842.

Dryer, Matthew S. 2007. Noun phrase structure. Pages 151–205 of: Shopen, Timothy (ed.), *Language Typology and Syntactic Description*, Vol. 2, Complex Constructions. Cambridge: Cambridge University Press.

Dunn, Michael J. 1999. *A Grammar of Chukchi*. Ph.D. thesis, Australian National University, Canberra.

Enfield, Nicholas J. 2004. Adjectives in Lao. Pages 323–347 of: Dixon, R. M. W., and Aikhenvald, Alexandra (eds), *Adjective Classes; A Cross-Linguistic Typology*. Oxford: Oxford University Press.

Erschen-Rasch, Margarete I. 2007. *Türkisch: Lehrbuch für Anfänger und Fortgeschrittene*. Wiesbaden: Harrassowitz Verlag.

Evans, Nicholas. 1995. *A Grammar of Kayardild: With Historical-Comparative Notes on Tangkic*. Berlin: Mouton de Gruyter.

Evans, Nicholas, and Osada, Toshiki. 2005. Mundari: the myth of a language without word classes. *Linguistic Typology*, **9**, 351–390.

Evgen'eva, A. P. (ed.). 1985. *Slovar' russkogo jazyka v četyrëx tomax* [A Dictionary of Russian in Four Volumes]. Moscow: Russkij jazyk.

Fabb, Nigel. 1984. *Syntactic Affixation*. Ph.D. thesis, Massachusetts Institute of Technology, Cambridge, MA.

Fábregas, Antonio. 2007. The internal syntactic structure of relational adjectives. *Probus*, **19**, 1–36.

2011. Rising possessors in Spanish. *Iberia*, **3**(1), 1–34.

Fábregas, Antonio, and Marín, Rafael. 2017. Problems and questions in derived adjectives. *Word Structure*, **10**, 1–26.

Farrell, Patrick. 2001. Functional shift as category underspecification. *English Language and Linguistics*, **5**, 109–130.

Fassi Fehri, Abdelkabir. 1993. *Issues in the Structure of Arabic Clauses and Words*. Dordrecht: Kluwer Academic Publishers.

Fradin, Bernard. 2008. On the semantics of denominal adjectives. Pages 84–97 of: Ralli, Angela, Booij, Geert, Scalise, Sergio, and Karasimos, Athanasios (eds), *On-line Proceedings of the Sixth Mediterranean Morphology Meeting (MMM6)*. Università degli Studi di Bologna, Bologna.

2017. The multifaceted nature of denominal adjectives. *Word Structure*, **10**, 27–53.

Fraurud, Kari. 1990. Definiteness and the processing of noun phrases in natural discourse. *Journal of Semantics*, **7**(4), 395–433.

Friedman, Victor A. 1993. Macedonian. Pages 249–305 of: Comrie, Bernard, and Corbett, Greville G. (eds), *The Slavonic Languages*. London: Routledge.

Geoghegan, Richard H. 1944. *The Aleut Language, the Elements of Aleut Grammar with a Dictionary in Two Parts Containing Basic Vocabularies of Aleut and English*. Washington, DC: United States Department of the Interior.

364 Bibliography

Ghomeshi, Jila. 1997. Non-projecting nouns and the ezafe construction in Persian. *Natural Language and Linguistic Theory*, **15**, 729–788.

Giegerich, Heinz J. 2005. Associative adjectives in English and the lexicon-syntax interface. *Journal of Linguistics*, **41**, 571–579.

2015. *Lexical Structures. Compounding and the Modules of Grammar*. Edinburgh: Edinburgh University Press.

Gil, David. 1994. The structure of Riau Indonesian. *Nordic Journal of Linguistics*, **17**, 179–200.

2005. Genitives, adjectives, and relative clauses. Article 60. Pages 246–249 of: Haspelmath, Martin, Dryer, Matthew S., Gil, David, and Comrie, Bernard (eds), *World Atlas of Linguistic Structures*. Oxford: Oxford University Press; available at http://wals.info/.

Giorgi, Alessandra, and Longobardi, Giuseppe. 1991. *The Syntax of Noun Phrases*. Cambridge: Cambridge University Press.

Giusti, Giuliana. 2008. Agreement and concord in nominal expressions. Pages 201–237 of: de Cat, Ceclie, and Demuth, Katherine (eds), *The Bantu-Romance Connection: A Comparative Investigation of Verbal Agreement, DPs, and Information Structure*. Linguistik Aktuell/Linguistics Today 131. Amsterdam: John Benjamins Publishing Co.

Givón, Talmy. 1984. *Syntax: A Functional-Typological Introduction*. Amsterdam: John Benjamins Publishing Co.

Göksel, Aslı, and Kerslake, Celia. 2005. *Turkish: A Comprehensive Grammar*. London: Routledge.

Golovko, E. V. 1997. Aleutskij jazyk [Aleut]. Pages 101–116 of: Volodin, A. P., Vaxtin, N. B., and Kibrik, A. A. (eds), *Jazyki Mira: Paleoaziatskie jazyki* [Languages of the World. Paleosiberian Languages]. Moscow: Publishing House Indrik.

Grimshaw, Jane. 1991. *Extended Projection*. Unpublished manuscript, Rutgers University.

Haegeman, Liliane. 2010. Spurious *een* and the syntax of interrogative *wek* ('which') and demonstrative *zuk* ('such') in West Flemish. *Lingua*, **120**, 850–863.

Haiman, John. 1983. Iconic and economic motivation. *Language*, **59**, 781–819.

1985. *Natural Syntax: Iconicity and Erosion*. Cambridge: Cambridge University Press.

Hale, Kenneth, and Keyser, Jay. 2002. *Prolegomenon to a Theory of Argument Structure*. Cambridge, MA: The MIT Press.

Halle, Morris, and Marantz, Alex. 1993. Distributed morphology and the pieces of inflection. Pages 111–176 of: Hale, Kenneth, and Keyser, Samuel J. (eds), *The View from Building 20: Essays in Honor of Sylvain Bromberger*. Cambridge, MA: The MIT Press.

Harley, Heidi. 2009. Compounding and distributed morphology. Pages 129–144 of: Lieber, Rochelle, and Štekauer, Pavol (eds), *The Oxford Handbook of Compounding*. Oxford: Oxford University Press.

Haspelmath, Martin. 1996. Word-class-changing inflection and morphological theory. Pages 43–66 of: Booij, Geert, and van Marle, Jaap (eds), *Yearbook of Morphology 1995*. Dordrecht: Kluwer Academic Publishers.

2003. The geometry of grammatical meaning: semantic maps and crosslinguistic comparison. Pages 211–242 of: Tomasello, Michael (ed.), *The New Psychology of Language*, vol. 2. Mahwah, NJ: Lawrence Erlbaum Associates.

2007. Pre-established categories don't exist: consequences for language description and typology. *Linguistic Typology*, **11**, 119–132.

2008. Frequency vs. iconicity in explaining grammatical asymmetries. *Cognitive Linguistics*, **19**, 1–33.

Hawkins, Roger. 1981. Towards an account of the possessive constructions: NPs and the N of NP. *Journal of Linguistics*, **17**, 247–269.

Hegedűs, Veronika. 2016. *Changing Copulas and the Case of Hungarian Prenominal PPs*. Talk delivered to the 18th Diachronic Generative Syntax Conference, Ghent University.

Heim, Irene, and Kratzer, Angelika. 1998. *Semantics in Generative Grammar*. Oxford: Blackwell Publishers.

Heine, Bernd. 1997. *Possession. Cognitive Sources, Forces, and Grammaticalization*. Cambridge: Cambridge University Press.

2001. Ways of explaining possession. Pages 311–328 of: Baron, Irène, Herslund, Michael, and Sorensen, Finn (eds), *Dimensions of Possession*. Typological Studies in Language 47. Amsterdam: John Benjamins Publishing Co.

Helimski, Eugene. 1998. Selkup. Pages 548–579 of: Abondolo, Daniel (ed.), *The Uralic Languages*. London: Routledge.

Hengeveld, Kees. 1992. *Non-verbal Predication: Theory, Typology, Diachrony*. Berlin: Mouton de Gruyter.

Hengeveld, Kees, and Rijkhoff, Jan N. M. 2005. Mundari as a flexible language. *Linguistic Typology*, **9**, 406–431.

Hetzron, Robert. 1995. Genitival agreement in Awngi: variation on an Afroasiatic theme. Pages 325–335 of: Frans Plank (ed.), *Double Case. Agreement by Suffixaufnahme*. Oxford: Oxford University Press.

Higginbotham, James. 1985. On semantics. *Linguistic Inquiry*, **16**(4), 547–593.

1993. Grammatical form and logical form. Pages 173–196 of: Tomberlin, James (ed.), *Philosophy of Language and Logic: Philosophical Perspectives*, vol. 8. Altascadero, CA: Ridgeview Publishing Company.

Hopper, Paul J., and Thompson, Sandra A. 1984. The discourse basis for lexical categories in universal grammar. *Language*, **60**, 703–752.

1985. The iconicity of the universal categories 'noun' and 'verb'. Pages 151–183 of: Haiman, John (ed.), *Iconicity in Syntax*. Amsterdam: John Benjamins Publishing Co.

Huddleston, Rodney, and Pullum, Geoffrey K. 2002. *The Cambridge Grammar of the English Language*. Cambridge: Cambridge University Press.

Hudson, Richard A. 2003. Gerunds without phrase structure. *Natural Language and Linguistic Theory*, **21**, 579–615.

Jackendoff, Ray S. 1977. *X̄ Syntax: A Study of Phrase Structure*. Cambridge, MA: The MIT Press.

1990. *Semantic Structures*. Cambridge, MA: The MIT Press.

366   *Bibliography*

2009. Compounding in the parallel architecture and conceptual semantics. Pages 105–128 of: Lieber, Rochelle, and Štekauer, Pavol (eds), *The Oxford Handbook of Compounding*. Oxford: Oxford University Press.

Jackson, Geoff, and Jackson, Jenny. 1999. *An Introduction to Tuvaluan*. Suva: Oceania Printers.

Jauncey, Dorothy G. 2011. *Tamambo, the Language of West Malo, Vanuatu*. Canberra: The Australian National University.

Jokinen, Kristiina. 1991. *On the Two Genitives in Finnish*. EUROTYPE, Theme 7: Noun Phrase Structure. Working Paper 14, Strasbourg.

Kachru, Yamuna. 2006. *Hindi*. Amsterdam: John Benjamins Publishing Co.

Kageyama, Taroo. 2001. Word plus: The intersection of words and phrases. Pages 245–276 of: van der Weijer, Jeroen, and Nishihara, Tetsuo (eds), *Issues in Japanese Phonology and Morphology*. Berlin: Mouton de Gruyter.

Kathol, Andreas. 2002. Nominal head-marking constructions: two case studies from Luiseño. Pages 189–201 of: Eynde, Frank Van, Hellan, Lars, and Beermann, Dorothee (eds), *The Proceedings of the 8th International Conference on Head-Driven Phrase Structure Grammar*. Stanford, CA: CSLI Publications.

Keenan, Edward L., and Polinsky, Maria. 1998. Malagasy (Austronesian). Pages 563–623 of: Spencer, Andrew, and Zwicky, Arnold (eds), *The Handbook of Morphology*. Oxford: Blackwell Publishers.

Kenesei, István. 2018. On the definition of word classes. www.researchgate.net/publicatio n/323425374_On_the_definition_of_word_classes.

Kenesei, István, Vágo, Robert M., and Fenyvesi, Anna. 1998. *Hungarian*. London: Routledge.

Kennedy, Christopher. 1999. *Projecting the Adjective. The Syntax and Semantics of Gradability and Comparison*. New York: Garland Publishing Inc.

2007a. Modes of comparison. Pages 141–165 of: Elliott, Malcolm, Kirby, James, Sawada, Osamu, Staraki, Eleni, and Yoon, Suwon (eds), *Proceedings of the Forty-Third Annual Regional Meeting of the Chicago Linguistic Society*. Chicago: University of Chicago, for Chicago Linguistic Society.

2007b. Vagueness and grammar: the semantics of relative and absolute gradable adjectives. *Linguistics and Philosophy*, **30**, 1–45.

Kennedy, Christopher, and McNally, Louise. 2005. Scale structure, degree modification, and the semantics of gradable predicates. *Language*, **81**, 345–381.

2010. Color, context, and compositionality. *Synthese*, **174**, 79–98.

Kibort, Anna, and Corbett, Greville G. 2010. Introduction. Pages 1–13 of: Kibort, Anna, and Corbett, Greville G. (eds), *Features: Perspectives on a Key Notion in Linguistics*. Oxford: Oxford University Press.

Kibrik, Aleksandr. 1995. Direct-oblique agreement of attributes in Daghestanian. Pages 216–229 of: Frans Plank (ed.), *Double Case: Agreement by Suffixaufnahme*. Oxford: Oxford University Press.

Kibrik, Aleksandr E., Kodzasov, Sandro V., and Muravyova, Irina A. 2004. *Language and Folklore of the Alutor People*. Suita, Japan: ELPR Publications.

Kiefer, Ferenc. 1987. The cases of Hungarian nouns. *Acta Linguistica Academiae Scientarum Hungaricae*, **37**, 93–101.

Bibliography 367

Kinkade, M. Dale. 1983. Salish evidence against the universality of 'noun' and 'verb'. *Lingua*, **60**, 25–40.

Koenig, Jean-Pierre. 1999. *Lexical Relations*. Stanford, CA: CSLI Publications.

Kolliakou, Dimitra. 1999. De-phrase extractability and individual/property denotation. *Natural Language and Linguistic Theory*, **17**, 713–781.

Koopman, Hilda. 1984. *The Syntax of Verbs: From Verb Movement Rules in the Kru Languages to Universal Grammar*. Dordrecht: Foris Publications.

Koptjevskaja-Tamm, Maria. 1995. Possessive and relational forms in Chukchi. Pages 301–321 of: Frans Plank (ed.), *Double Case. Agreement by Suffixaufnahme*. Oxford University Press.

1997. Possessive NPs in Maltese: alienability, iconicity and grammaticalization. *The Maltese NP Meets Typology* (Special issue of Rivista di Linguistica, edited by A. Borg and Frans Plank), **8**(1), 245–274.

2000. Romani genitives in cross-linguistic perspective. Pages 123–149 of: Elšík, Viktor, and Matras, Yaron (eds), *Grammatical Relations in Romani: The Noun Phrase*. Amsterdam: John Benjamins Publishing Co.

2001a. Adnominal possession. Pages 960–970 of: Haspelmath, Martin, König, Ekkehard, Oesterreicher, Wulf, and Raible, Wolfgang (eds), *Language Typology and Language Universals*, vol. 2. Berlin: Walter de Gruyter.

2001b. 'A piece of the cake' and 'a cup of tea': partitive and pseudo-partitive nominal constructions in the Circum-Baltic languages. Pages 523–568 of: Dahl, Östen, and Koptjevskaja-Tamm, Maria (eds), *The Circum-Baltic Languages: Their Typology and Contacts*. Vol 2. Amsterdam: John Benjamins Publishing Co.

2002. Adnominal possession in the European languages: form and function. *Sprachtypologie und Universalienforschung*, **55**, 141–171.

2003a. Possessive noun phrases in the languages of Europe. Pages 621–722 of: Frans Plank (ed.), *Noun Phrase Structure in the Languages of Europe*. Berlin: Mouton de Gruyter.

2003b. A woman of sin, a man of duty, and a hell of a mess: non-determiner genitives in Swedish. Pages 515–558 of: Frans Plank (ed.), *Noun Phrase Structure in the Languages of Europe*. Berlin: Mouton de Gruyter.

2004. 'Maria's ring of gold': adnominal possession and non-anchoring relations in the European languages. Pages 155–181 of: Kim, Ji-Yung, Lander, Yuri, and Partee, Barbara H. (eds), *Possessives and Beyond: Semantics and Syntax*. Amherst, MA: GLSA Publications.

2013. A *Mozart sonata* and the *Palme murder*: the structure and uses of proper-name compounds in Swedish. Pages 253–290 of: Börjars, Kersti, Denison, David, and Scott, Alan (eds), *Morphosyntactic Categories and the Expression of Possession*. Amsterdam: John Benjamins Publishing Co.

Koptjevskaja-Tamm, Maria, and Šmelev, Aleksej. 1994. Alešina s Mašej stat'ja (o nekotoryx svojstvax russkix "pritjažatel'nyx prilagatel'nyx") [Alyoša and Maša's paper: on some properties of Russian possessive adjectives]. *Scando-Slavica*, **40**, 209–228.

Kornfilt, Jaklin, and Whitman, John. 2011. Afterword: nominalizations in syntactic theory. *Lingua*, **121**, 1297–1313.

368　*Bibliography*

Koshiishi, Tetsuya. 2011. *Collateral Adjectives and Related Issues*. Bern: Peter Lang Verlag.

Kraft, Charles H., and Kirk-Greene, A. M. H. 1973. *Teach Yourself Hausa*. Sevenoaks: Hodder and Stoughton.

Kroeger, Paul. 1993. *Phrase Structure and Grammatical Relations in Tagalog*. Dissertations in Linguistics. Revised and corrected version of 1991 Stanford University dissertation.

Kurdoev, Kanat Kalashevich. 1978. *Grammatika kurdskogo jazyka. Na materialie dialektov kurmandži i sorani* [A Grammar of Kurdish: the Dialects of Kurmanji and Sorani]. Moscow: Nauka.

Kurebito, Megumi. 2002. 'Possessive' and 'relational' in Koryak viewed from the Animacy Hierarchy. Pages 35–45 of: Miyaoka, Osahito, and Endo, Fubito (eds), *Languages of the North Pacific Rim*, vol. 9. Osaka: ELPR Publications.

Kuznecova, Ariadna Ivanovna, Xelimskij, Evgenij Arnol'dovič, and Gruškina, Elena Vladislavovna. 1980. *Očerki po sel'kupskomu jazyku* [Studies in Selkup]. Moscow: Moscow State University Publishing House.

Laczkó, Tibor. 1995. *The Syntax of Hungarian Noun Phrases – A Lexical-Functional Approach*. Frankfurt am Main: Peter Lang Verlag.

    1997. Action nominalization and the possessor function within Hungarian and English noun phrases. *Acta Linguistica Hungarica*, **44**, 413–475.

Lander, Yury. 2009. Varieties of genitive. Pages 581–92 of: Malchukov, Andrej, and Spencer, Andrew (eds), *The Oxford Handbook of Case*. Oxford: Oxford University Press.

Langacker, Ronald W. 1987. *Foundations of Cognitive Grammar, Vol. 1: Theoretical Prerequisites*. Stanford, CA: Stanford University Press.

    1991. *Foundations of Cognitive Grammar, Vol. 2: Descriptive Applications*. Stanford, CA: Stanford University Press.

    1993. Reference-point constructions. *Cognitive Linguistics*, **4**, 1–38.

    1995. Possession and possessive constructions. Pages 51–79 of: Taylor, John R., and MacLayry, Robert E. (eds), *Language and the Cognitive Construal of the World*. Trends in Linguistics, Studies and Monographs 82. Berlin: Mouton de Gruyter.

Lapointe, Steven. 1980. *A Theory of Grammatical Agreement*. Ph.D. thesis, University of Massachusetts at Amherst.

Larson, Richard, and Segal, Gabriel. 1995. *Knowledge of Meaning. An Introduction to Semantic Theory*. Cambridge, MA: The MIT Press.

Larson, Richard K., and Takahashi, Naoko. 2007. Order and interpretation in prenominal relative clauses. In: *Proceedings of the Workshop on Altaic Formal Linguistics II*. Cambridge: MA: MIT Working Papers in Linguistics 54. MWPL54? web.mit.edu

Lascarides, Alex, and Copestake, Ann. 1999. Default representation in constraint-based frameworks. *Computational Linguistics*, **25**(1), 55–105.

Lazard, Gilbert. 2005. What are we typologists doing? Pages 1–23 of: Frajzyngier, Zygmunt, Hodges, Adam, and Rood, David S. (eds), *Linguistic Diversity and Language Theories*. Amsterdam: John Benjamins Publishing Co.

Le Bruyn, Bert S. W., and Schoorlemmer, Erik. 2016. Editorial: Possession: puzzles in meaning and form. *Lingua*, **182**, 1–11.

Lecarme, Jacqueline. 2008. Tense and modality in nominals. Pages 195–225 of: Guéron, Jacqueline, and Lecarme, Jacqueline (eds), *Time and Modality*. Dordrecht: Springer Verlag.

Lees, R. B. 1960. *The Grammar of English Nominalizations*. The Hague: Mouton.

Lefebvre, Claire, and Muysken, Pieter. 1988. *Mixed Categories: Nominalizations in Quechua*. Dordrecht: Kluwer Academic Publishers.

Levi, Judith N. 1978. *The Syntax and Semantics of Complex Nominals*. New York: Academic Press.

Levin, Beth, and Rappaport Hovav, Malka. 1994. A preliminary analysis of causative verbs in English. *Lingua*, **92**, 35–77.

  1995. *Unaccusativity: At the Syntax-Lexical Semantics Interface*. Cambridge, MA: The MIT Press.

  2005. *Argument Realization*. Cambridge: Cambridge University Press.

Lewis, G. L. 1967. *Turkish Grammar*. Oxford: The Clarendon Press.

Li, Charles N., and Thompson, Sandra A. 1981. *Mandarin Chinese: A Functional Reference Grammar*. Berkeley, CA: University of California Press.

Lieber, Rochelle. 1980. *On the Organization of the Lexicon*. Ph.D. thesis, Massachusetts Institute of Technology, Cambridge, MA.

  1992. *Deconstructing Morphology*. Chicago: University of Chicago Press.

Lin, Chien-Jer Charles. 2011. Processing (in)alienable possessions at the syntax-semantics interface. Pages 351–367 of: Folli, Raffaella, and Ulbrich, Christiane (eds), *Interfaces in Linguistics: New Research Perspectives*. Oxford: Oxford University Press.

Lin, J.-W. 2008. The order of stage-level and individual-level relatives and superiority effects. *Language and Linguistics*, **9**, 839–864.

Liu, Hsin-Yun. 2003. *A Profile of the Mandarin Noun Phrase: Possessive Phrases and Classifier Phrases in Spoken Discourse*. Munich: LINCOM Europa.

Lowe, John. 2015. *Participles in Rigvedic Sanskrit. The Syntax and Semantics of Adjectival Verb Forms*. Oxford: Oxford University Press.

  2016. Participles, gerunds and syntactic categories. Pages 401–421 of: Arnold, Doug, Butt, Miriam, Crysmann, Berthold, King, Tracy Holloway, and Müller, Stefan (eds), *Proceedings of the Joint 2016 Conference on Head-Driven Phrase Structure Grammar and Lexical Functional Grammar*. Stanford, CA: CSLI Publications.

Lytkin, V. I. (ed.). 1955. *Sovremennyj komi jazyk: učebnik dlja vysšix učebnyx zavedenij* [The Modern Komi Language: A Textbook for Universities]. Syktyvkar: Komi Publishing House.

Mahieu, Marc-Antoine. 2013. The genitive case and the possessive construction in Finnish. Pages 19–54 of: Carlier, Anne, and Verstraete, Jean-Christophe (eds), *The Genitive*. Amsterdam: John Benjamins Publishing Co.

Mahootian, Shahrzad. 1997. *Persian*. London: Routledge.

Maiden, Martin. 1992. Irregularity as a determinant of morphological change. *Journal of Linguistics*, **28**, 285–312.

  2005. Morphological autonomy and diachrony. Pages 137–175 of: Booij, Geert, and van Marle, Jaap (eds), *Yearbook of Morphology 2004*. Dordrecht: Springer Verlag.

370   *Bibliography*

2011. Allomorphy, autonomous morphology and phonological conditioning in the history of the Daco-Romance present and subjunctive. *Transactions of the Philological Society*, **109**, 59–91.

Malchukov, Andrej L. 2000. *Dependency Reversals in Noun-Attributive Constructions*. Munich: LINCOM EUROPA.

2004. *Nominalization/Verbalizations: Constraining a Typology of Transcategorial Operations*. Munich: LINCOM EUROPA.

2006. Constraining nominalization: function-form competition. *Linguistics*, **44**, 973–1008.

Malouf, Robert. 1999. West Greenlandic noun incorporation in a monohierarchical theory of grammar. Pages 47–62 of: Webelhuth, Gert, Koenig, Jean-Pierre, and Kathol, Andreas (eds), *Lexical and Constructional Aspects of Linguistic Explanation*. Stanford, CA: CSLI Publications.

2000a. *Mixed Categories in the Hierarchical Lexicon*. Stanford, CA: CSLI Publications.

2000b. Verbal gerunds as mixed categories in HPSG. Pages 133–166 of: Borsley, R. (ed.), *The Nature and Function of Syntactic Categories*. Syntax and Semantics, no. 32. New York: Academic Press.

Marchand, Hans. 1969. *The Categories and Types of Present-Day English Word-Formation: A Synchronic Diachronic Approach*. 2nd edn. Munich: C. H. Beck'sche Verlagsbuchhandlung.

Martin, Samuel E. 2004. *A Reference Grammar of Japanese*. Honolulu: University of Hawaii Press.

Maslova, Elena S. 2003. *A Grammar of Kolyma Yukaghir*. Berlin: Mouton de Gruyter.

Massam, Diane. 2001. Pseudo noun incorporation in Niuean. *Natural Language & Linguistic Theory*, **19**(1), 153–197.

Mathiassen, Terje. 1996. *A Short Grammar of Lithuanian*. Columbus, OH: Slavica Publishers, Inc.

1997. *A Short Grammar of Latvian*. Columbus, OH: Slavica Publishers, Inc.

Matisoff, James A. 1973. *The Grammar of Lahu*. Berkeley, CA: University of California Press.

Matthews, Peter H. 1993. *Grammatical Theory in the United States from Bloomfield to Chomsky*. Cambridge: Cambridge University Press.

McGregor, R. S. 1995. *Outline of Hindi Grammar*. 3rd edn. Oxford/Delhi: Oxford University Press.

McNally, Louise. 2016. Modification. Pages 442–464 of: Aloni, Maria, and Dekker, Paul (eds), *The Cambridge Handbook of Formal Semantics*. Cambridge: Cambridge University Press.

McNally, Louise, and Boleda, Gemma. 2004. Relational adjectives as properties of kinds. Pages 179–196 of: Bonami, Olivier, and Cabredo Hofherr, Patricia (eds), *Empirical Issues in Formal Syntax and Semantics*, vol. 5. Paris: CNRS, for Colloque de Syntaxe et Sémantique à Paris.

Megerdoomian, Karine. 2012. The status of the nominal in Persian complex predicates. *Natural Language & Linguistic Theory*, **30**, 179–216.

Mel'čuk, Igor A. 1982. *Towards a Language of Linguistics: A System of Formal Notions for Theoretical Morphology*. Munich: W. Fink.

2006. *Aspects of the Theory of Morphology* (edited by David Beck). Berlin: Mouton de Gruyter.

Mezhevich, Ilana. 2002. English compounds and Russian relational adjectives. Pages 95–114 of: *Proceedings of the North Western Linguistics Conference 2002* Burnaby, British Columbia: Simon Fraser University Linguistics Graduate Student Association.

Miner, Kenneth. 1986. Noun stripping and loose incorporation in Zuni. *International Journal of American Linguistics*, **2**, 242–254.

Mithun, Marianne. 2000. Noun and verb in Iroquoian languages: multicategorisation from multiple criteria. Pages 397–420 of: Vogel, Petra M., and Comrie, Bernard (eds), *Approaches to the Typology of Word Classes*. Berlin: Mouton de Gruyter.

Morzycki, Marcin. 2016. *Modification*. Cambridge: Cambridge University Press.

Mosel, Ulrike, and Hovdhaugen, Even. 1992. *Samoan Reference Grammar*. Oslo: Scandinavian University Press.

Moser, Rosemarie. 2004. *Kabba. A Nilo-Saharan Language of the Central African Republic*. Munich: LINCOM EUROPA.

Mugane, John. 1996. *Bantu Nominalization Structures*. Ph.D. thesis, University of Arizona.

Müller, Stefan. 2007. *Head-Driven Phrase Structure Grammar: Eine Einführung*. Stauffenburg Einführungen, no. 17. Tübingen: Stauffenburg Verlag.

Nagano, Akiko, and Shimada, Masaharu. 2015. Relational adjectives in English and Japanese and the RA vs. PP debate. Pages 105–133 of: Audring, Jenny, Koutsoukos, Nikos, Masini, Francesca, and Raffaelli, Ida (eds), *MMM9 Online Proceedings*. Mediterranean Morphology Meeting, Patras.

Nedjalkov, Igor. 1994. Evenki. Pages 1–34 of: Kahrel, Peter, and van den Berg, René (eds), *Typological Studies in Negation*. Amsterdam: John Benjamins Publishing Co.

1997. *Evenki*. London: Routledge.

Newman, Paul. 2000. *The Hausa Language: An Encyclopedic Reference Grammar*. New Haven: Yale University Press.

Newmark, Leonard. 1957. *Structural Grammar of Albanian*. Bloomington: Indiana University Publications.

Newmeyer, Frederick J. 1979. Review of Judith N. Levi 'The Syntax and Semantics of Complex Nominals'. *Language*, **55**, 396–407.

Nichols, Johanna. 1986. Head-marking and dependent-marking grammar. *Language*, **62**, 56–119.

1992. *Linguistic Diversity in Space and Time*. Chicago: University of Chicago Press.

Nichols, Johanna, and Bickel, Balthasar. 2013. Locus of marking in possessive noun phrases. In: Dryer, Matthew S., and Haspelmath, Martin (eds), *The World Atlas of Language Structures Online*. Leipzig: Max Planck Institute for Evolutionary Anthropology.

Nikitina, Tatiana V., and Haug, Dag Trygve Truslew. 2016. Syntactic nominalization in Latin: a case of non-canonical subject agreement. *Transactions of the Philological Society*, **114**, 25–50.

Nikolaeva, Irina. 1999. *Ostyak*. Munich: LINCOM Europa.

372 Bibliography

2002. Possession vs. nominal attribution in Uralic. Pages 239–250 of: Helimski, Eugen, and Widmer, Anna (eds), *Wŭśa wŭśa – Sei gegrüsst! Beiträge zur Finnougristik zu Ehren von Gert Sauer dargebracht zu seinem siebzigsten Geburtstag.* Veröffentlichungen der Societas Uralo-Altaica 57. Wiesbaden: Otto Harrassowitz.

2003. The structure of the Tundra Nenets noun phrase. In: Bakró-Nagy, M., and Rédei, K. (eds), *Ünnepi kötet Honti László tiszteletére* [A Festschrift for László Honti]. Budapest: Hungarian Academy of Sciences Publishing.

2005. Review article on E. Maslova 'A Grammar of Kolyma Yukaghir'. *Linguistic Typology*, **9**, 299–325.

2008. Between nouns and adjectives: a constructional view. *Lingua*, **118**, 969–996.

2012. Nominal modification in Udihe and beyond. Pages 183–212 of: Malchukov, Andrei, and Whaley, Lindsay J. (eds), *Recent Advances in Tungusic Linguistics.* Wiesbaden: Harrassowitz Verlag.

2014a. Altaic. Pages 493–508 of: Lieber, Rochelle, and Štekauer, Pavol (eds), *The Oxford Handbook of Derivational Morphology.* Oxford: Oxford University Press.

2014b. *A Grammar of Tundra Nenets.* Berlin: Mouton de Gruyter.

Nikolaeva, Irina, and Spencer, Andrew. 2012. Possession and modification – a perspective from Canonical Typology. Pages 207–238 of: Brown, Dunstan P., Chumakina, Marina, and Corbett, Greville G. (eds), *Canonical Morphology and Syntax.* Oxford: Oxford University Press.

Nikolaeva, Irina, and Tolskaya, Maria S. 2001. *A Grammar of Udihe.* Berlin: Mouton de Gruyter.

Noonan, Michael. 1992. *A Grammar of Lango.* Berlin: Mouton de Gruyter.

Otoguro, Ryo. 2006. *Morphosyntax of Case: A Theoretical Investigation of the Concept.* Ph.D. thesis, University of Essex.

Öztürk, Balkız, and Taylan, Eser Erguvanlı. 2016. Possessive constructions in Turkish. *Lingua*, **182**, 88–108.

Panagiotidis, Phoevos. 2011. Categorial features and categorizers. *The Linguistic Review*, **28**, 325–346.

2014. Indices, domains and homophonous forms. *Theoretical Linguistics*, **40**, 415–427.

Partee, Barbara H. 1983–1997. Uniformity vs. versatility: the genitive, a case study. Appendix to Theo Janssen (1997), Compositionality. Pages 464–70 of: van Benthem, Johan, and ter Meulen, Alice (eds), *The Handbook of Logic and Language.* Dordrecht: Elsevier Publishers.

2010. Privative adjectives: subsective plus coercion. Pages 273–285 of: Bauerle, Rainer, Reyle, Uwe, and Zimmermann, Thomas E. (eds), *Presuppositions and Discourse.* Amsterdam: Elsevier Publishers.

Partee, Barbara H., and Borschëv, Vladimir. 1998. Integrating lexical and formal semantics. Pages 229–241 of: *Proceedings of the 2nd Tbilisi Symposium on Language, Logic and Computation.* Tbilisi State University.

2003. Genitives, relational nouns, and argument-modifier ambiguity. Pages 67–112 of: E. Lang, C. Maienborn, and Fabricius-Hansen, C. (eds), *Modifying Adjuncts.* Berlin: Mouton de Gruyter.

Bibliography 373

Paton, William Frederick. 1971. *Ambrym (Lonwolwol) Grammar*. Canberra: The Australian National University, Pacific Linguistics.

Payne, John. 1995. Inflecting postpositions in Indic and Kashmiri. Pages 283–298 of: Plank, Frans (ed.), *Double Case: Agreement by Suffixaufnahme*. Oxford: Oxford University Press.

Pereltsvaig, Asya. 2007. *Copular Sentences in Russian. A Theory of Intra-Clausal Relations*. Dordrecht: Springer Verlag.

Perlmutter, David. 1988. The split-morphology hypothesis: evidence from Yiddish. Pages 79–101 of: Hammond, Michael, and Noonan, Michael (eds), *Theoretical Morphology*. San Diego, CA: Academic Press.

Perry, John R. 2005. *A Tajik Persian Reference Grammar*. Leiden: E. J. Brill.

Plank, Frans (ed.). 1995a. *Double Case: Agreement by Suffixaufnahme*. Oxford: Oxford University Press.

Plank, Frans. 1995b. (Re-)introducing Suffixaufnahme. Pages 283–298 of: Plank, Frans (ed.), *Double Case. Agreement by Suffixaufnahme*. Oxford: Oxford University Press.

Plungian, Vladimir Aleksandrovič. 1995. *Dogon*. Munich: LINCOM Europa.

Pollard, Carl J., and Sag, Ivan A. 1994. *Head-Driven Phrase Structure Grammar*. Chicago: University of Chicago Press.

Poulos, G., and Msimang, C. T. 1998. *A Linguistic Analysis of Zulu*. Cape Town: Via Afrika Limited.

Progovac, Ljiljana. 1998. Determiner phrase in a language without determiners. *Journal of Linguistics*, **34**, 165–179.

Pustejovsky, James. 1991. The Generative Lexicon. *Computational Linguistics*, **17**(4), 409–441.

1993. Type coercion and lexical selection. Pages 73–96 of: Pustejovsky, James (ed.), *Semantics and the Lexicon*. Dordrecht: Reidel.

1995. *The Generative Lexicon*. Cambridge, MA: The MIT Press.

2016. Lexical semantics. Pages 33–64 of: Aloni, Maria, and Dekker, Paul (eds), *The Cambridge Handbook of Formal Semantics*. Cambridge: Cambridge University Press.

Rainer, Franz. 2013. Can relational adjectives really express any relation? An onomasiological perspective. *SKASE*, **10**, 12–40.

Rappaport Hovav, Malka, and Levin, Beth. 1998. Building verb meanings. Pages 97–134 of: Butt, Miriam, and Geuder, Wilhelm (eds), *The Projection of Arguments*. Stanford, CA: CSLI Publications.

Rauh, Gisa. 2010. *Syntactic Categories: Their Identification and Description in Linguistic Theories*. Oxford: Oxford University Press.

Richards, Norvin. 2013. Lardil 'case stacking' and the timing of case assignment. *Syntax*, **16**, 42–76.

Rießler, Michael. 2016. *Adjective Attribution*. Berlin: Language Science Press.

Rijkhoff, Jan, and van Lier, Eva (eds). 2013. *Flexible Word Classes. Typological Studies of Underspecified Parts of Speech*. Oxford: Oxford University Press.

374   *Bibliography*

Rizzi, Luigi. 1997. The fine structure of the left periphery. Pages 281–337 of: Haegeman, Liliane (ed.), *Elements of Grammar: Handbook in Generative Syntax.* Dordrecht: Springer Netherlands.

Ross, John R. 1973. A fake NP squish. Pages 96–140 of: Bailey, Charles-James N., and Shuy, Roger W. (eds), *New Ways of Analyzing Variation in English.* Washington, DC: Georgetown University Press.

Round, Erich. 2015. Rhizomorphomes, meromorphomes and metamorphomes. Pages 29–52 of: Baerman, Matthew, Brown, Dunstan, and Corbett, Greville G. (eds), *Understanding and Measuring Morphological Complexity.* Oxford: Oxford University Press.

Sadler, Louisa, and Arnold, Doug. 1994. Prenominal adjectives and the phrasal/lexical distinction. *Journal of Linguistics,* **30**, 187–226.

Sadler, Louisa, and Spencer, Andrew. 2001. Syntax as an exponent of morphological features. Pages 71–96 of: Booij, Geert, and van Marle, Jaap (eds), *Yearbook of Morphology 2000.* Dordrecht: Kluwer.

Sadock, Jerrold M. 1980. Noun incorporation in Greenlandic. *Language,* **56**, 300–319.

1991. *Autolexical Syntax: A Theory of Parallel Grammatical Representations.* Chicago: The University of Chicago Press.

Sag, Ivan A. 2012. Sign-based construction grammar: an informal synopsis. Pages 69–202 of: Boas, Hans C., and Sag, Ivan A. (eds), *Sign-Based Construction Grammar.* Stanford, CA: CSLI Publications.

Sag, Ivan, Wasow, Thomas, and Bender, Emily. 2003. *Syntactic Theory: A Formal Introduction.* Stanford, CA: CSLI Publications.

Samvelian, Pollet. 2007. A (phrasal) affix analysis of the Persian ezafe. *Journal of Linguistics,* **43**, 605–645.

Sasse, Hans-Jakob. 1988. Der irokesische Sprachtyp. *Zeitschrift für Sprachwisenschaft,* **7**, 173–213.

1993. Syntactic categories and subcategories. Pages 646–686 of: Jacobs, Joachim, von Stechow, Arnim, Sternefeld, Wolfgang, and Vennemann, Theo (eds), *Syntax: Ein Internationales Handbuch Zeitgenossischer Forschung.* Berlin: de Gruyter.

2001. Scales between nouniness and verbiness. Pages 495–509 of: Haspelmath, Martin, König, Ekkehard, Oesterreicher, Wulf, and Raible, Wolfgang (eds), *Language Typology and Language Universals,* Vol. 1. Berlin: Mouton de Gruyter.

Scalise, Sergio, and Bisetto, Antonietta. 2009. The classification of compounds. Pages 34–53 of: Lieber, Rochelle, and Štekauer, Pavol (eds), *The Oxford Handbook of Compounding.* Oxford: Oxford University Press.

Schachter, Paul, and Otanes, Fe T. 1972. *Tagalog Reference Grammar.* Berkeley, CA: University of California Press.

Schroeder, Christoph. 2000. Attribution in Turkish and the function of *-ki.* Pages 205–214 of: Göksel, Aslı, and Kerslake, Celia (eds), *Proceedings of the Ninth International Conference on Turkish Linguistics.* Wiesbaden: Harrossowitz.

Schultze-Berndt, Eva. 2000. *Simple and Complex Verbs in Jaminjung. A Study of Event Categorisation in an Australian Language.* Nijmegen: University of Nijmegen.

Selkirk, Elisabeth O. 1977. Some remarks on noun phrase structure. Pages 285–316 of: Culicover, Peter, Wasow, Thomas, and Akmajian, Adrian (eds), *Formal Syntax.* New York: Academic Press.

1982. *The Syntax of Words*. Cambridge, MA: The MIT Press.

Shagal, Ksenia. 2017. Towards a typology of participles. Unpublished PhD thesis, Department of Modern Languages, University of Helsinki, Helsinki.

Shimoyama, Junko. 2011. Degree quantification and the size of noun modifiers. Pages 356–367 of: McClure, William, and den Dikken, Marcel (eds), *Japanese/Korean Linguistics*, vol. 18. Stanford, CA: CSLI Publications.

Siegel, Muffy E. A. 1980. *Capturing the Adjective*. New York: Garland Publications.

Skorik, Petr Ja. 1961. *Grammatika chukotskogo jazyka* [A Grammar of Chukchi], vol. 1. Leningrad: Nauka.

Smirnickij, Aleksandr I. 1959. *Morfologija anglijskogo jazyka* [English Morphology]. Moscow: Nauka.

Smirnov, Jurij A. 1976. *Grammatika jazyka pandžabi.* [A Grammar of Punjabi] Moscow: Nauka.

Sneddon, James Neil. 1996. *Indonesian: A Comprehensive Grammar*. London: Routledge.

Spencer, Andrew. 1995. Incorporation in Chukchi. *Language*, **71**, 439–489.

1998. Relational adjectives and the redundancy of lexical categories. Pages 19–29 of: Booij, Geert, Ralli, Angela, and Scalise, Sergio (eds), *Proceedings of the First Mediterranean Conference of Morphology*. Patras: University of Patras.

1999. Transpositions and argument structure. Pages 73–102 of: Booij, Geert, and van Marle, Jaap (eds), *Yearbook of Morphology 1998*. Dordrecht: Kluwer Academic Publishers.

2002. Gender as an inflectional category. *Journal of Linguistics*, **38**, 279–312.

2003. Does English have productive compounding? Pages 329–341 of: Booij, Geert, DeCesaris, Janet, Ralli, Angela, and Scalise, Sergio (eds), *Topics in Morphology. Selected Papers from the Third Mediterranean Morphology Meeting, Barcelona, September 20–22, 2001*. Institut Universitari de Lingüística Applicada, Universtitat Pompeu Fabra, Barcelona.

2005a. Case in Hindi. Pages 429–446 of: Butt, Miriam, and King, Tracy Holloway (eds), *The Proceedings of the LFG '05 Conference*. Stanford, CA: CSLI Publications.

2005b. Towards a typology of 'mixed categories'. Pages 95–138 of: Orgun, C. Orhan, and Sells, Peter (eds), *Morphology and the Web of Grammar: Essays in Memory of Steven G. Lapointe*. Stanford, CA: CSLI Publications.

2007. Extending deponency: implications for morphological mismatches. Pages 45–70 of: Baerman, Matthew, Corbett, Greville G., Brown, Dunstan, and Hippisley, Andrew (eds), *Deponency and Morphological Mismatches*. Proceedings of the British Academy, no. 145. Oxford: The British Academy and Oxford University Press.

2008. Review of R. M. W. Dixon and A. Y. Aikhenvald (2004). Adjective classes. A cross-linguistic typology. *Language*, **84**, 407–410.

2010a. Factorizing lexical relatedness. Pages 133–171 of: Olsen, Susan (ed.), *New Impulses in Word-Formation*. Hamburg: Helmut Buske Verlag.

376 *Bibliography*

2010b. Lexical relatedness and the lexical entry – a formal unification. Pages 322–340 of: Müller, Stefan (ed.), *Proceedings of the HPSG10 Conference*. Stanford, CA: CSLI Publications.

2011. What's in a compound? Review article on Lieber and Štekauer (eds) 2009. 'The Oxford Handbook of Compounding'. *Journal of Linguistics*, **47**, 481–507.

2013. *Lexical Relatedness: A Paradigm-Based Model*. Oxford: Oxford University Press.

2015a. Individuating lexemes. Pages 357–377 of: Butt, Miriam, and King, Tracy Holloway (eds), *Proceedings of LFG15*. Stanford, CA: CSLI Publications.

2015b. Participial relatives in LFG. Pages 378–398 of: Butt, Miriam, and King, Tracy Holloway (eds), *Proceedings of LFG15*. Stanford, CA: CSLI Publications.

2016. How are words related? Pages 1–26 of: Siddiqi, Daniel, and Harley, Heidi (eds), *Morphological Metatheory*. Amsterdam: John Benjamins Publishing Co.

2017a. On lexical entries and lexical representations. Pages 321–350 of: Bonami, Olivier, Boyé, Gilles, Dal, Georgette, Giraudo, Hélène, and Namer, Fiammetta (eds), *The lexeme in Descriptive and Theoretical Morphology*. Berlin: Language Science Press.

2017b. Split-morphology and lexicalist morphosyntax: the case of transpositions. Pages 385–420 of: Bowern, Claire, Horn, Laurence, and Zanuttini, Raffaella (eds), *On Looking into Words (and Beyond)*. Berlin: Language Science Press.

2019. Canonical compounds. Pages 31–64 of: Baerman, Matthew, Bond, Oliver, and Hippisley, Andrew (eds), *Perspectives on Morphology: Papers in Honour of Greville G. Corbett*. Edinburgh: Edinburgh University Press.

Spencer, Andrew, and Luís, Ana Ribeiro. 2012. *Clitics: An Introduction*. Cambridge: Cambridge University Press.

Spencer, Andrew, and Nikolaeva, Irina. 2017. Denominal adjectives as mixed categories. *Word Structure*, **10**, 79–99.

Spencer, Andrew, and Otoguro, Ryo. 2005. Limits to case – a critical survey of the notion. Pages 119–145 of: Amberber, Mengistu, and de Hoop, Helen (eds), *Competition and Variation in Natural Languages: The Case for Case*. Oxford: Elsevier.

Spencer, Andrew, and Stump, Gregory. 2013. Hungarian pronominal case and the dichotomy of content and form in inflectional morphology. *Natural Language and Linguistic Theory*, **31**, 1207–1248.

Sperber, Dan, and Wilson, Deirdre. 1986. *Relevance: Communication and Cognition*. Oxford: Blackwell Publishers.

Sproat, Richard, and Shih, Chilin. 1988. Prenominal adjectival ordering in English and Mandarin. Pages 465–489 of: Blevins, James, and Carter, Juli (eds), *Proceedings of the 18th Meeting of the North East Linguistics Society*. Amherst: Graduate Linguistic Student Association, for University of Massachusetts.

Stassen, Leon. 1997. *Intransitive Predication*. Oxford: Oxford University Press.

Storto, Gianluca. 2004. Possessives in context. Pages 59–86 of: Kim, Ji-Yung, Lander, Yuri, and Partee, Barbara H. (eds), *Possessives and Beyond: Semantics and Syntax*. Amherst, MA: GLSA Publications.

Bibliography 377

Stump, Gregory. 2001. *Inflectional Morphology: A Theory of Paradigm Structure*. Cambridge: Cambridge University Press.

2002. Morphological and syntactic paradigms: arguments for a theory of paradigm linkage. Pages 147–180 of: Booij, Geert, and van Marle, Jaap (eds), *Yearbook of Morphology 2001*. Dordrecht: Kluwer Academic.

2006. A theory of heteroclite inflectional paradigms. *Language*, **82**, 279–322.

2016. *Inflectional Paradigms. Content and Form at the Syntax-Morphology Interface*. Cambridge: Cambridge University Press.

Sugioka, Yoko. 2011. Nominalization affixes and multi-modularity of word formation. Pages 143–162 of: Yuasa, Etsuyo, Bagchi, Tista, and Beals, Katharine (eds), *Pragmatics and Autolexical Grammar. In Honor of Jerry Sadock*. Amsterdam: John Benjamins Publishing Co.

Sugioka, Yoko, and Ito, Takane. 2016. Derivational affixation in the lexicon and syntax. Pages 347–386 of: Kageyama, Taro, and Kishimoto, Hideki (eds), *Handbook of Japanese Lexicon and Word Formation*. Boston, MA: de Gruyter.

Szabolcsi, Anna. 1987. Functional categories in the noun phrase. Pages 167–190 of: Kenesei, István (ed.), *Approaches to Hungarian*, vol. 2. Szeged: JATE.

1994. The noun phrase. Pages 179–274 of: Kiefer, Ferenc, and Kiss, Katalín É. (eds), *The Syntactic Structure of Hungarian*. San Diego, CA: Academic Press.

Szeverényi, Sandor. 2014. Derivational suffixes as/or classifiers? – The word formation of the Nganasan adjectives. *Tomskij zhurnal LING i ANTHRO* [Tomsk Journal of Linguistics and Anthropology], **4**, 49–58.

Szymanek, Bogdan. 2010. *A Panorama of Polish Word-Formation*. Lublin: Wydawnictwo KUL.

Taylor, John R. 1989. Possessive genitives in English. *Linguistics*, **27**, 663–686.

1995. *Linguistic Categorization: Prototypes in Linguistic Theory*. Oxford: Oxford University Press.

1996. *Possessives in English. An Exploration in Cognitive Grammar*. Oxford: Oxford University Press.

ten Hacken, Pius. 2013. Compounds in English, in French, in Polish, and in general. *SKASE*, **10**, 97–113.

Timberlake, Alan. 2004. *A Reference Grammar of Russian*. Cambridge: Cambridge University Press.

Tröbs, Holger. 1998. *Funktionale Sprachbeschreibung des Jeli (West-Mande)*. Cologne: Köppe Verlag.

Trugman, Helen. 2004. *Syntax of Russian DPs, and DP-Internal Agreement Phenomena*. Ph.D. thesis, Tel Aviv University.

Truswell, Robert. 2004. *Attributive Adjectives and the Nominals They Modify*. Ph.D. thesis, University of Oxford, Oxford.

Usačeva, Marina N. 2012. Lokativnye padeži v sostave grupp s prostranstvennym značeniem v permskix jazykax [Grammatical cases in Permic locational noun phrases]. Pages 141–217 of: Kuznecova, Ariadna I. (ed.), *Finno-ugorskie jazyki: fragmenty grammatičeskogo opisanija. Formal'nye i funkcional'nye podxody* [Finno-Ugric Languages: Topics in Grammatical Description (Formal and Functional Approaches)]. Moscow: Russkie slovari.

378 Bibliography

van den Berg, René. 1989. *A Grammar of the Muna Language*. Dordrecht: Foris Publications. Reprinted: SIL e-Books, 52, SIL International 2013.

van der Auwera, Johann, and Gast, Volker. 2011. Categories and prototypes. Pages 166–188 of: Song, Jae Jung (ed.), *The Oxford Handbook of Linguistic Typology*. Oxford: Oxford University Press.

van Hout, Angeliek, and Roeper, Thomas. 1988. Events and aspectual structure in derivational morphology. Pages 175–200 of: Harley, Heidi (ed.), *Papers from the UPenn/MIT Roundtable on Argument Structure and Aspect, MIT Working Papers in Linguistics*, vol. 32. Cambridge, MA: Department of Linguistics, MIT.

van Riemsdijk, Henk. 1983. The case of German adjectives. Pages 223–252 of: Heny, Frank, and Richards, Barry (eds), *Linguistic Categories: Auxiliaries and Related Puzzles*, vol. 1. Dordrecht: D. Reidel.

Van Valin, J., Robert D. 2008. RPs and the nature of lexical and syntactic categories in role and reference grammar. Pages 161–178 of: Van Valin, Jr., Robert D. (ed.), *Investigations of the Syntax-Semantics-Pragmatics Interface*. Amsterdam: John Benjamins Publishing Co.

vander Klok, Jozina. 2009. Direct adjectival modification in Javanese. Pages 211–225 of: Chung, Sandra (ed.), *Proceedings of the 16th Meeting of the Austronesian Formal Linguistics Association*. Santa Cruz, CA: University of California.

Vergnaud, Jean-Roger, and Zubizarreta, Maria Luisa. 1992. The definite determiner and the inalienable construction in French. *Linguistic Inquiry*, **23**, 595–652.

Vikner, Carl, and Jensen, Per Anker. 2002. A semantic analysis of the English genitive: interaction of lexical and formal semantics. *Studia Linguistica*, **56**, 191–226.

Vogel, Petra M., and Comrie, Bernard (eds). 2000. *Approaches to the Typology of Word Classes*. Berlin: Mouton de Gruyter.

von Prince, Kilu. 2016. Alienability as control: the case of Daakaka. *Lingua*, **182**, 69–87.

Wade, Terence. 1992. *A Comprehensive Russian Grammar*. Oxford: Blackwell Publishers.

Ward, Gregory L., Sproat, Richard, and McKoon, Gail. 1991. A pragmatic analysis of so-called anaphoric islands. *Language*, **67**, 439–474.

Wescoat, Michael T. 2002. *On Lexical Sharing*. Ph.D. thesis, Stanford University.

Westermann, Diedrich. 1930. *A Study of the Ewe Language*. London: Oxford University Press.

Wetzer, Harrie. 1996. *The Typology of Adjectival Predication*. Empirical approaches to language typology, no. 17. Berlin: Mouton de Gruyter.

Wierzbicka, Anna. 2000. Lexical prototypes as a universal basis for cross-linguistic indentification of 'parts of speech'. Pages 285–317 of: Vogel, Petra M., and Comrie, Bernard (eds), *Approaches to the Typology of Word Classes*. Berlin: Mouton de Gruyter.

Williams, Edwin. 1981. On the notions 'lexically related' and 'head of word'. *Linguistic Inquiry*, **12**, 254–74.

  1982. The NP Cycle. *Linguistic Inquiry*, **13**(2), 277–295.

Wunderlich, Dieter. 1996. Minimalist morphology: the role of paradigms. Pages 93–114 of: Booij, Geert, and van Marle, Jaap (eds), *Yearbook of Morphology 1995*. Dordrecht: Kluwer Academic Publishers.

Bibliography 379

Wurzel, Petra. 1997. *Rojbas. Einführung in die kurdische Sprache*. Wiesbaden: Dr. Ludwig Reichert Verlag.

Zaliznjak, Andrej Anatol'evič. 2003. *Grammatičeskij slovar' russkogo jazyka: Slovoizmenenie* [A Grammatical Dictionary of Russian]. 4th edn. Moscow: Russkie slovari.

Zimmermann, Ilse. 1993. The syntax of 'Possessor' phrases. Pages 201–225 of: Fanselow, Gisbert (ed.), *The Parametrization of Universal Grammar*. Amsterdam: John Benjamins Publishing Co.

Žukova, A. N. 1972. *Grammatika korjakskogo jazyka* [Koryak grammar]. Leningrad: Nauka.

Language Index

Achagua, 83
Akhvakh, 109–110
Albanian, 77, 113, 121, 123
Aleut, 74
Altaic, 102, 104, 167
Alutor, 231, 297, 298
Arabic, 157–163
   Maltese Arabic, 71–72, 118
   Modern Standard Arabic, 157
Aramaic, 118
Arawá, 82
Armenian, 116
Austronesian, 61, 63, 66, 68, 69, 76
Awngi, 114, 302, 333–337, 346–347

Balto-Slavic, 291
Bantu, 121, 123, 153
Besyermyan Udmurt, 106
Bulgarian, 130, 218, 276

Celtic, 118
Chagatay, 88
Chamalal, 110
Chatino, 82
Chinese, 7, 43–45, 81, 82
Chukchi, 77, 99–101, 149, 231, 249, 263,
   297–301, 306, 314, 340–343, 346, 347
Chukotko-Kamchatkan, 298, *see* Alutor;
   Chukchi; Koryak
Cushitic, 114, 302, 334

Daakaka, 48
Daghestanian, 109, 110, 112, 114, 116, 300,
   334
Danish, 118
Dizi, 83–84
Dogon, 82, 83

English, 6–8, 13, 15, 21, 22, 24, 25, 27–29,
   33–35, 38, 43, 44, 48, 50, 53, 55–57, 60,
   61, 63, 66, 85–90, 92–96, 101, 102, 105,
   108, 111, 116, 119–120, 127, 128, 132,
   134, 143, 144, 146, 148, 153, 162, 168,
   174, 176, 179, 182, 183, 193, 197–199,
   201, 202, 205–207, 211, 218, 228, 229,
   232, 237, 243–245, 285, 290–293, 297,
   304, 310, 311, 313, 349, 354
   Middle, 208
   Old, 208
Even, 322–324
Evenki, 102–104, 139, 301, 305, 307, 308,
   322–333, 340, 341, 344–346, 349, 353
Ewe, 79–80

Fijian, 157
Finnish, 31, 116–118
French, 38, 55, 60, 92, 94, 129, 218, 354

Gaelic, *see* Scottish Gaelic
Georgian, 88, 91, 95, 107, 108, 114, 116,
   138–139, 254
   Old, 114
German, 26, 28, 88, 96, 129, 167, 193, 199,
   202, 245, 272, 287
Germanic, 53, 56, 85, 86, 116–118, 120, 196,
   291, 297
Greek, 93, 94, 96, 108, 116, 291
Gĩkũyũ, 153–156, 160, 162

Hausa, 7, 43, 122–124
Hebrew, 116, 158
Hindi-Urdu, 113, 121, 123, 136–138, 142
Hoava, 61, 63–64, 69
Hokkien, 74
Hua, 43

380

Language Index 381

Hungarian, 31, 66, 105–107, 111–112, 242, 273, 304, 306

Icelandic, 118
Indo-Aryan, 121
Indonesian, 76, 82, 273, 275, *see also* Riau Indonesian
Iranian, 66, 73, 74
Iroquoian, 8
Italian, 31, 55, 56, 96, 118

Jaminjung, 5
Japanese, 7, 27, 45, 61, 77, 118, 196, 351
Jarawara, 82
Jeli, 80

Kabba, 80
Kannada, 6
Kartvelian, 114, 138
Kayardild, 82
Kazakh, 88
Khanty, *see* Northern Khanty
Khinalug, 48
Kikuyu, *see* Gĩkũyũ
Kolyma Yukaghir, 6, 64–66, 75, 231
Komi Permyak, 106
Komi Zyrian, 101
Korean, 7
Koryak, 231, 297, 298
Koyukon, 83
Kurmanji Kurdish, 74, 113, 123

Lahu, 82
Lai, 6
Lango, 80–81
Lardil, 113
Latin, 94, 108, 208, 217, 233, 272, 276
Latvian, 31, 117
Lele, 61
Lithuanian, 116, 117
Lonwolwol, 50

Macedonian, 179, 218, 276
Malagasy, 66
Malayalam, 6, 43
Mandarin, *see* Chinese
Mande, 80
Maori, 68–69

Minangkabau, 76
Miya, 71, 79
Mohawk, 13
Mongolic, 102
Muna, 6
Mundari, 9

Nanai, 322–324
Navajo, 227, 228
Nenets, *see* Tundra Nenets
Nepalese, 121
Nganasan, 88
Niger-Congo, 43, 82
Niuean, 61
Northern Khanty, 74–76
Numic, 66

Oroch, 322, 323
Ostyak, *see* Northern Khanty

Persian, 61, 73–74
Polish, 92, 93, 116, 292
Puluwat, 83
Punjabi, 121, 199

Quechua, 7, 144

Riau Indonesian, 8
Romance, 55, 56, 94, 118, 129, 155, 196, 199, 217, 243, 272, 276, 291
Romani, 98, 114–115
Rumanian, 276
Russian, 21, 23–24, 38, 61, 92, 93, 96–97, 99, 107, 108, 116–117, 136–137, 164–165, 167, 168, 179, 188, 193, 194, 197–199, 202, 208–210, 213–221, 227, 228, 230, 234–238, 250–253, 264, 272, 276–278, 285, 287, 291–297, 300, 301, 311, 315, 349, 354

Salishan, 8
Samoan, 69
Samoyedic, 167, 231, 301, 302
Sanskrit, 31, 163–165, 217
Scottish Gaelic, 116
Selkup, 31, 32, 35, 95, 110, 149, 199, 238, 289, 301–322, 325–327, 331, 332, 338, 340, 341, 343–344, 346, 347, 353, 354

382 *Language Index*

Serbian-Croatian, 218, 332
Sino-Tibetan, 74, 81, 82
Slavic, 36, 96–99, 107, 116–118, 126, 179,
    196, 218, 276, 291, 292, 331, 332
    West, 218
Slovene, 218
Sorbian, *see* Upper Sorbian
Spanish, 93
Svan, 138–139
Swahili, 121
Swedish, 116–118

Tagalog, 66–68
Tajik, 74
Takelma, 43
Taleshi, 66
Tamambo, 69
Tangic, 82
Tibeto-Burman, 71
Tinrin, 43
Tongan, 8
Tsakhur, 110
Tswana, 121–122
Tundra Nenets, 66, 87, 88, 90–91, 95,
    103–104, 107, 111–112, 137, 231,
    254–255, 258–259, 267, 270–273,
    337–340, 346–347, 353
Tundra Yukaghir, 64
Tungusic, 21, 102, 103, 139, 140, 273, 303,
    305, 306, 320, 322–332
    Northern, 103, 322–324, *see also* Even;
        Evenki
    Southern, 322, 323, *see also* Nanai; Oroch;
        Udihe

Turkic, 102
Turkish, 65, 66, 71, 108–111, 179, 300
Tuscarora, 8
Tuvaluan, 61–63
Tümpisa (Panamint) Shoshone, 66

Udihe, 70–71, 94–95, 102, 116, 140–142, 322,
    323
Udmurt, *see* Besyermyan Udmurt
Upper Sorbian, 97–98, 132–135, 137–139,
    143, 146, 151, 301, 331–333, 347
Uralic, 31, 66, 74, 101, 103, 104, 106, 110,
    302, 322, 332
Uralo-Yukaghir, *see* Kolyma Yukaghir
Urdu, *see* Hindi-Urdu
Uyghur, 88

Vata, 43

Welsh, 152–153, 155
West Greenlandic, 134–135, 141, 150, 151
Western Nilotic, 80

Yakut, 88
Yamphu, 71
Yoruba, 43
Yukaghir, *see* Kolyma Yukaghir, Tundra
    Yukaghir

Zapotecan, 82
Zulu, 122

Author Index

Aarts, Bas, 10, 16
Ackema, Peter, 57
Ackerman, Farrell, 3, 32, 38, 49, 52, 175, 243, 249, 253, 255–259, 264, 270–273, 283, 350
Alexiadou, Artemis, 51, 82, 86, 92, 93, 96, 127
Allen, Margaret, 286
Amritavalli, R., 6
Anderson, John M., 7, 8
Anderson, Stephen R., 186
Aoun, Yosef, 146
Apresjan, Jurij Derenikovič 197, 200
Arad, Maya, 9
Arnold, Douglas, 202
Aronoff, Mark, 180, 217
Arsenijevic, Boban, 92, 96

Backhouse, Anthony E., 7
Baker, Mark C., 4, 6, 8, 11, 13–16, 19, 45, 127, 242, 280
Bally, Charles, 92
Barker, Christopher, 46, 49–52
Bauer, Laurie, 90
Bauer, Winifred, 68
Beard, Robert, 8, 26, 196
Beck, David, 78
Bell, Melanie J., 87
Bergsland, Knut, 74
Besnier, Niko, 61
Bhat, D. N. S., 6, 14, 43, 59
Bhatia, Tej K., 199
Bierwisch, Manfred, 190, 224
Bisang, Walter, 4, 6
Bisetto, Antonietta, 93
Bochnak, M. Ryan, 43
Boeder, Winfried, 66, 91, 138
Bögel, Tina, 74
Bogoraz, Vladimir G., 100

Boguslavskaja, Ol'ga Ju., 109, 110, 114
Bonami, Olivier, 22, 163
Bond, Oliver, 229, 300
Booij, Geert, 29, 145, 153, 197, 353
Borer, Hagit, 158
Borsley, Robert D., 157
Bošković, Željko, 242
Bosque, Ignacio, 92, 94
Bouillon, Pierrette, 54
Breban, Tine, 86
Bresnan, Joan, 11, 25, 32, 37, 51, 126, 127, 144, 151–157, 160, 162, 187, 270
Broschart, Jürgen, 8
Brown, Dunstan P., 186, 234, 235, 237, 350
Bybee, Joan, 23, 230

Carleton, Troi, 82
Carlson, Gregory N., 92
Cetnarowska, Bożena, 93, 116, 292
Chappell, Hilary, 47, 48, 59, 82
Chaves, Rui P., 168, 250
Chisarik, Erika, 116
Chomsky, Noam, 11, 47, 240, 242
Christen, Simon, 117
Cinque, Guglielmo, 45, 92, 244
Cole, D. T., 121, 122
Copestake, Ann, 261
Corbett, Greville G., 19, 32, 36, 97, 98, 132, 135, 213, 331
Creissels, Denis, 79, 106
Cristofaro, Sonia, 6
Croft, William A., 4, 6, 13, 16, 17, 42, 43, 82, 147, 168, 281
Cruse, Alan D., 53
Crystal, David, 13
Culicover, Peter, 10

384   *Author Index*

Dalrymple, Mary, 44, 152, 164, 165, 167
Davis, Henry, 8
Davis, Karen, 61, 63
Dayley, Jon P., 66
Delfitto, Denis, 55
Demonte, Violeta, 92
Despić, Miloje, 242, 332
Dixon, R. M. W., 14, 42–44, 82
Downing, Pamela, 56
Dryer, Matthew S., 2
Dunn, Michael J., 100, 231, 297, 298, 300

Enfield, Nicholas J., 6, 15
Erschen-Rasch, Margarete I., 108
Evans, Nicholas, 8, 9, 82

Fabb, Nigel, 127
Fábregas, Antonio, 14, 82, 93, 94, 96
Farrell, Patrick, 9
Fassi Fehri, Abdelkabir, 157
Fradin, Bernard, 92, 93
Fraurud, Kari, 51
Friedman, Victor A., 179

Geoghegan, Richard H., 74
Ghomeshi, Jila, 73
Giegerich, Heinz J., 92, 93
Gil, David, 8, 44, 76
Giorgi, Alessandra, 92
Giusti, Giuliana, 242
Givón, Talmy, 5
Göksel, Aslı, 66, 110
Golovko, E. V., 74
Grimshaw, Jane, 146

Haegeman, Liliane, 242
Haiman, John, 82
Hale, Kenneth, 14
Halle, Morris, 127
Harley, Heidi, 128
Haspelmath, Martin, 6, 26, 82, 83, 187, 231, 233, 281, 284
Hawkins, Roger, 49, 51
Hegedűs, Veronika, 111
Heim, Irene, 40
Heine, Bernd, 47, 48, 50, 53, 57, 82
Helimski, Eugene, 302
Hengeveld, Kees, 4, 6, 8, 9

Hetzron, Robert, 114, 334, 335
Higginbotham, James, 40, 52, 224
Hopper, Paul J., 6
Huddleston, Rodney, 24, 87, 106, 243, 244
Hudson, Richard A., 146

Jackendoff, Ray S., 4, 11, 16, 42, 47, 55, 190, 241
Jackson, Geoff, 62
Jauncey, Dorothy G., 69
Jokinen, Kristiina, 118

Kachru, Yamuna, 121
Kageyama, Taroo, 61
Kathol, Andreas, 52
Kayne, Richard S.
Keenan, Edward L., 66
Kenesei, István, 106, 111, 250
Kennedy, Christopher, 41–44
Kibort, Anna, 32
Kibrik, Aleksandr E., 231, 298
Kiefer, Ferenc, 306
Kinkade, M. Dale, 8
Koenig, Jean-Pierre, 194, 265
Kolliakou, Dimitra, 116
Koopman, Hilda, 43
Koptjevskaja-Tamm, Maria, 3, 46, 48, 51, 53, 57, 59, 70, 71, 74, 82, 85, 100, 114, 116–118, 121, 136, 156
Kornfilt, Jaklin, 127
Koshiishi, Tetsuya, 96, 264
Kraft, Charles H., 123
Kroeger, Paul, 152
Kurdoev, Kanat Kalashevich, 74
Kurebito, Megumi, 297
Kuznecova, Ariadna Ivanovna, 302

Laczkó, Tibor, 51, 111
Lander, Yury, 116
Langacker, Ronald W., 5, 46, 51
Lapointe, Steven, 144, 286
Larson, Richard, 40
Lascarides, Alex, 147
Lazard, Gilbert, 82
Le Bruyn, Bert S. W., 50
Lecarme, Jacqueline, 242
Lees, R. B., 53
Lefebvre, Claire, 15, 144
Levi, Judith N., 53, 55, 92

Author Index 385

Levin, Beth, 190
Lewis, G. L., 109
Li, Charles N., 82
Lieber, Rochelle, 128, 145
Lin, Chien-Jer Charles, 82
Lin, J.-W, 92
Liu, Hsin-Yun, 82
Lowe, John, 163, 165

Mahieu, Marc-Antoine, 117
Mahootian, Shahrzad, 73
Maiden, Martin, 217
Malchukov, Andrej L., 23, 230, 352
Malouf, Robert, 19, 21, 138, 146–148, 150, 156–160, 162, 182
Marchand, Hans, 90
Martin, Samuel E., 27
Maslova, Elena S., 6, 64, 65, 231
Massam, Diane, 61
Mathiassen, Terje, 117
Matisoff, James A., 82
Matthews, Peter H., 10
McGregor, R. S., 121
McNally, Louise, 59, 92
Megerdoomian, Karine, 61
Mel'čuk, Igor A., 20
Mezhevich, Ilana, 93, 292
Miner, Kenneth, 61
Mithun, Marianne, 8
Morzycki, Marcin, 40–42
Mosel, Ulrike, 69
Moser, Rosemarie, 80
Mugane, John, 153
Müller, Stefan, 245, 246

Nagano, Akiko, 45, 93, 118, 120
Nedjalkov, Igor, 104
Newman, Paul, 123
Newmark, Leonard, 121
Newmeyer, Frederick J., 56
Nichols, Johanna, 48, 59, 82, 83, 273
Nikitina, Tatiana V., 151
Nikolaeva, Irina A., 2, 3, 21, 33, 40, 45, 48, 50, 52, 53, 58, 60, 61, 64, 66, 70, 71, 73, 74, 77, 78, 90, 94, 102–104, 111, 121, 139, 141, 230, 261, 273, 278, 279, 282, 289, 301, 320, 322, 325, 333, 337, 338
Noonan, Michael, 80, 81

Otoguro, Ryo, 121
Öztürk, Balkız, 66

Panagiotidis, Phoevos, 14
Partee, Barbara H., 42, 46, 47, 49, 51, 52
Paton, William Frederick, 50
Payne, John, 121
Pereltsvaig, Asya, 242
Perlmutter, David, 186
Perry, John R., 74
Plank, Frans, 1, 113, 125
Plungian, Vladimir Aleksandrovič, 82
Pollard, Carl J., 244, 245
Poulos, G., 122
Progovac, Ljiljana, 242
Pustejovsky, James, 53, 54, 197

Rainer, Franz, 93, 120
Rappaport Hovav, Malka, 190
Rauh, Gisa, 4, 6, 10, 11, 14, 16
Richards, Norvin, 113
Rießler, Michael, 59
Rizzi, Luigi, 242
Ross, John R., 250
Round, Erich, 217

Sadler, Louisa, 61, 86, 165, 215, 222
Sadock, Jerrold M., 126, 130–132, 134, 331
Sag, Ivan, 44, 176, 177, 180–182, 224, 245, 246
Samvelian, Pollet, 73
Sasse, Hans-Jakob, 4, 6, 8, 16, 17
Scalise, Sergio, 55
Schachter, Paul, 67, 68
Schroeder, Christoph, 108, 110
Schultze-Berndt, Eva, 5
Selkirk, Elisabeth O., 116, 132
Shagal, Ksenia, 355
Shimoyama, Junko, 45
Siegel, Muffy E. A., 40
Skorik, Petr Ja., 100, 297–299
Smirnickij, Aleksandr I., 302
Smirnov, Jurij A., 199
Sneddon, James Neil, 76, 273
Spencer, Andrew, 1–3, 15, 16, 19–23, 27–29, 31, 32, 35, 38, 43, 52, 53, 55–57, 84, 87, 93, 106, 114, 121, 128, 129, 144, 148, 149, 156, 163, 164, 166, 168, 171–175, 184, 186–191, 195, 196, 198, 199,

386 Author Index

Spencer, Andrew (*cont.*)
  202–206, 209, 211, 212, 215, 218, 221,
  222, 225–227, 229–231, 233, 234,
  236–239, 247, 250, 251, 253–255, 261,
  264, 265, 270, 279, 283–285, 288, 289,
  291, 298, 301, 302, 306, 313, 315, 334,
  336, 346, 348, 350–355
Sperber, Dan, 49
Sproat, Richard, 44
Stassen, Leon, 7, 15
Storto, Gianluca, 49
Stump, Gregory, 163–165, 186, 189, 191, 204,
  205, 207, 213, 214, 217, 222, 234, 236,
  238, 250, 350
Sugioka, Yoko, 27
Szabolcsi, Anna, 51, 242
Szeverényi, Sandor, 88
Szymanek, Bogdan, 292

Taylor, John R., 47, 49, 50
ten Hacken, Pius, 93
Timberlake, Alan, 199
Tröbs, Holger, 80
Trugman, Helen, 116
Truswell, Robert, 41

Usačeva, Marina N., 106

van den Berg, René, 6
van der Auwera, Johann, 16
van Hout, Angeliek, 128
van Riemsdijk, Henk, 146
Van Valin, Robert D., Jr, 168
vander Klok, Jozina, 45
Vergnaud, Jean-Roger, 82
Vikner, Carl, 51
von Prince, Kilu, 48

Wade, Terence, 198
Ward, Gregory L., 36
Wescoat, Michael T., 129, 155
Westermann, Diedrich, 80
Wetzer, Harrie, 59
Wierzbicka, Anna, 4
Williams, Edwin, 49, 111, 286
Wunderlich, Dieter, 11, 224
Wurzel, Petra, 74

Zaliznjak, Andrej Anatol'evič 198
Zimmermann, Ilse, 242
Žukova, A. N., 231

Subject Index

A* Semantic Function Role, 247–249
a-of-association, 121–123
a-structure, 232, *see also* argument structure, ARG-ST
ACC-ING, 25, 26
adjectival representation, 32, 149, 175, 223, 276, 280, 285, 289, 291, 300–308, 313, 320–322, 327, 332, 340, 345–347, 349, 353, *see also* transposition, noun-to-adjective
adjective, 1–3
  associative, 92, 93, *see also* adjective, relational
  attributive, 2, 44–46, 57, 60, 66, 67, 74–77, 81, 90, 103, 104, 107, 114, 124, 163, 230, 232, 248, 249, 254, 256, 260, 272, 289, 298, 318, 327, 328, 333, 334, 338, 342
  canonical, 1, 142, 230, 247, 248, 255, 260, 292, 294, 302, *see also* modification, attributive
  caritive, 105, 305
  classificatory, 57, 92, *see also* adjective, relational
  colour, 43, 44, 77, 229
  comitative, 101, *see also* adjective, proprietive
  compound, 27, 90
  denominal, 1, 3, 29–31, 35, 37–39, 87–105, 107, 137, 138, 140, 142, 155, 171, 254, 261, 262, 284, 285, 289–291, 300–304, 306, 314, 315, 322, 325–327, 331, 332, 338, 347, 349–354
  ethnic, 86, 96, 99
  gradable, 3, 15, 21, 42–44, 46, 62, 78, 174, 231, *see also* gradable property, concept
  intersective, 41, 43, 45, 92, 105, 260
  locative, 199, 304–306, 320, 321, 354
  modal, 42
  ornative, 290
  possessive, 34, 35, 61, 95–102, 115, 126, 130, 132–137, 143, 261, 263, 267, 276–279, 297–301, 331–334, 340, 347, 355
  predicative, 167, 168, 196, 199, 231, 251, 256, 285, 300, 340, 355
  privative, 42, 93, 101–105
  proprietive, 101–105, 117, 138–142, 273, 290, 292, 301, 303, 305, 306, 308, 320, 322–332, 340, 341, 344–346, 349, 353
  pseudo-adjective, 92, *see also* adjective, relational
  qualitative, 174, *see also* adjective, gradable
  relational, 24, 34, 35, 38, 39, 53, 56, 70, 87, 91–96, 98–102, 107, 118, 120, 149, 163, 182, 196, 221, 223, 231, 237, 238, 258, 261, 263–265, 267, 277, 285, 290–297, 301, 301–320, 326, 338, 340–347, 350, 353–355
  restrictive, 109–110
  similitudinal, 88–90, 304–306, 320–322, 340, 343–344, 353, 354
  subsective, 41, 42, 92
  temporal, 108
  transitive, 224–226
  zooic, 99
ADJUNCT, 155, 164, 244
adjunct, 44, 46, 119, 153–155, 162, 332, *see also* Head-Adjunct Rule
adjunction, 44, 49, 100
adposition, 29, 106, 107, 270, 279, *see also* phrase, adpositional; preposition; postposition
adverb, 5, 8, 10, 89, 110, 119, 141, 148, 179

388 Subject Index

adverbial, 2, 26, 111, 158, 232, *see also* case, adverbial
affix(ation), 37–38, 88, 97, 120, 121, 125, 127, 132, 134, 136, 139–141, 180, 217, 235, 306, 327
  lexical, 143, 155
  phrasal, 67, 73, 108, 111, 120–124, 131, 134, 136, 137, 142
  prefix, 193–194, 209, 210
  semi-affix, 90
  syntactic, 127–129, 134–143, 155, 169
  wide scope, 135, 136, 138
agreeing genitive, 113–115, 118, 302, 333–338, 340, 346, 353
agreement, 4, 8, 20, 21, 23–25, *see also* concord
  possessor, 29, 32, 39, 63, 75, 107
Aktionsart, 23, 173, 201
alienability split, 70, 71, 79, 80, 83
anaphora, 91
  outbound, 36, 104
anaphoric island, 36
Animacy Hierarchy, 297
ARG-ST, 150, 178, 181, 184, 189, 190, 204, 224, 225, 231, 245, 249, 253–256, 262, 264, 265, 267, 273, 292, 294–296, 307, 309–313, 316–319, 321, 322, 325–330, 333, 339, 341–346, 351, 353, *see also* a-structure, argument structure
argument
  highest, 206, 225, 232, 248, 253
  object, 25, 26, 145, 158, 232
  subject, 25, 26, 148, 157, 180, 232
argument structure, 21, 25, 47, 51, 62, 69, 119, 127, 144–146, 148, 150, 151, 153–155, 160, 161, 165, 169, 173, 181, 190, 193, 197, 204, 206, 224, 225, 229, 234, 240, 249, 250, 253, 267, 278, 287, 351, 355, *see also* a-structure, ARG-ST
articulated (feature), 12
ascriptive function (of compound), *see* compound, ascriptive function
aspect, 8, 13, 23, 166, 173, 195, 215–218, 220, 232, 234, 238, 242, 306
  imperfective, 111, 112, 194, 215, 216, 220
  perfective, 209, 215–217, 221, 223
associative marker, 121, *see also* a-of-association
associative relation, 49, 50

attribute
  ADJUNCT, *see* ADJUNCT
  ARG-ST, *see* ARG-ST
  CONCORD, *see* CONCORD
  CONT, 147
  F-STR, *see* F-STR
  FORM, *see* FORM
  GAP, 245
  lexical, 25, 195, 198, 205, 209, 352, 353
  LI, *see* LI
  MOD, *see* MOD
  MORSIG, *see* MORSIG
  SEM, *see* SEM
  SYN, *see* SYN
  VAL, *see* VAL(ENCE)
Attributive Modifier Rule, 255–258, 263, 265, 310, 322
attributive transparency, 35, 132
augmentative, 139, 197, 198, 327, 351, *see also* evaluative morphology
Autolexical Syntax, 126, 130–136, 139, 151
auxiliary, 7, 132, 176, 179, 216, 218

base lexeme, 26, 29, 33–36, 89, 99, 153, 168, 173–175, 180, 183, 195, 196, 200, 201, 204, 206, 209, 226, 233, 235–238, 254, 285, 286, 297, 332, 352, 353
Base Noun Modifiability Property, 35, 39, 90, 129, 284, 288–290

c-structure, 151–155, 157, 159, 161–163, 165–169, 172, 224, 353
canonical, 1, 225, 237, 247, 276, 279, 282
  adjective, *see* adjective, canonical
  approach, 19, 43, 78, 79, 225, 230, *see also* Canonical Typology
  derivation, *see* derivation, canonical
  function, 14, 15, 34, 116, 247, 280, 353
  property, 19, 34, 86, 230
  relatedness, 238
  relation, 213
Canonical Typology, 22, 278, 279
case
  absolutive, 100
  accusative, 23, 32, 104, 112, 157, 158, 161, 303, 334
  adverbial, 334
  caritive, 303

comitative, 104, 290, *see also* case,
proprietive
coordinative, 303
dative, 103, 276, 334
dative-allative, 303
directive, 334
elative, 303
ergative, 100, 150, 297
genitive, 1, 29, 31, 39, 59–61, 66, 70, 71,
77, 79, 86, 91, 94, 96, 98, 100, 104,
112, 113, 115–118, 120, 121, 123, 124,
132, 139, 142, 148, 158, 161, 270, 273,
276, 279, 280, 282, 287, 293, 297,
302–304, 308, 314, 331, 333, 337, 338,
344, 346, *see also* possessive genitive;
agreeing genitive
property denoting, 116
Saxon, 34
illative, 303, 314, 316
instrumental, 111, 135, 137, 141, 303, 305
invocative, 334
locative, 32, 106, 108, 109, 112, 303, 305
nominative, 23, 65, 70, 97, 107, 114, 287,
303, 314, 332, 337
oblique, 2, 65, 91, 104–106, 110–112, 114,
121, 304
partitive, 116
prolative, 112, 303
proprietive, 104, 290
translative, 303
vocative, 121, 303
category, *see also* class
functional, 13, 51, 96, 247
lexical, 1, 8, 84, 154, 155, 172, 223, 224,
226, 249, 302, 350, 352
mixed, 1–4, 22–38, 84–87, 112, 124,
126–172, 175, 178, 182, 187, 188, 203,
213, 223, 226, 230–233, 237, 239, 247,
249, 250, 253, 254, 307, 311, 331, 335,
336, 348, 350–352
paradigmatically, 22–25, 29, 85, 89, 95,
103, 114, 125, 126, 230, 315, 320,
334, 349
syntagmatically, 22, 24–30, 33–35, 38,
51, 85, 86, 89, 91, 95, 102, 103, 105,
114, 125, 126, 133, 137, 138, 140,
142, 143, 150, 151, 153, 174, 230,
231, 237, 283–290, 301, 302, 320,
322, 332, 334, 349, 353
morphomic, 218, 219

ontological, 191, 204, 213, 225, 227–229,
287, 320, 321, 344, 351
causative, 26, 173, 197, 207
class, *see also* category
word, 1, 3–22, 26, 30, 84, 147, 175, 178,
189, 190, 196, 204, 225, 230, 250, 253,
317, 340, 355, *see also* part of speech
flexible, *see* flexible (word class)
classifier, 63
clitic, 59, 61, 67, 73, 77, 120, 121, 123, 124,
130–132, 134, 217, 276, *see also* edge
inflection; phrasal affix
Cliticization Principle, 131
Cognitive Grammar, 5, 8
composite node approach, 144, 148
compositionality, 9
compound, 3
appositional, 56
ascriptive function, 41, 93
endocentric, 56, 87, 93, 120, 151, 265, 291,
297, 346, 354
morphological, 87
noun-noun, 29, 31, 33, 37, 53–57, 66,
85–87, 90–93, 100, 102, 117–120, 129,
145, 263, 265, 270, 272, 291–293, 297,
302, 304, 310, 313, 338, 346, 354, 355
compound adjective, *see* adjective, compound
compound preposition, 106
compound Semantic Function Role, *see*
Semantic Function Role, compound
compounding, 29, 33, 34, 55–57, 66, 80, 81,
85–87, 91, 94, 116, 128, 134, 187, 249,
260, 265, 267, 270, 275, 291, 293, 302,
304, 338, 355
conceptual structure, 6, *see also* Lexical
Conceptual Structure
CONCORD, 230, 234, 252, 253, 258, 259,
307, 319, 327, 330, 331, 340, 342,
345–347, 352
concord, 31, 32, 71, 103, 104, 110, 113, 114,
122, 164, 167, 234, 258, 301, 307, 322,
324, 329, 333, 338, 340, 341, 353, *see*
also agreement
constituent structure, 12, 59, 60, 73, 130–132,
134, 143, 145, 162, 163, *see also*
c-structure
construct state, 29, 71–72, *see also* ezafe,
izafet

390 Subject Index

construction, *see also* constructional marker;
Modifier-Head Construction, small
construction
associative, 81
comitative, 136–137
comparative, 41, 62
possessive, 48–51, 61, 63, 66, 67, 69–71,
78, 82–84, 102, 118, 121, 124, 157,
162, 244, 258, 260, 267–278, 280, 297,
300, 302, 314, 326, 337, 347, 354, 355
Construction Grammar, 168, 239, 244, 273
Constructional Integrity Constraint, 131, 132,
135, 139
Strong, 131
Weak, 131
constructional marker, 59, 60, 63, 74, 80, 83,
107, 120, 123
CONTENT paradigm, 165, 190, 204,
213–223, 250, 317, 352
conversion, 9, 24, 201, 228, 236, 340
m-inert, 199, 201
coordination, 38, 56, 104, 136–138, 142, 250
Correspondence function, 214

DATR, 234, 238
declension, 23, 24, 96, 98, 99, 122, 189, 202,
233, 251, 287, 298
default, 14, 21, 38, 43, 49, 52, 61, 69, 159,
167, 185, 186, 205, 210, 222, 225–228,
234, 238, 294, 306–308, 318, 327, 340,
346, 351, 352, *see also* inheritance,
default; Default Cascade; General Default
Principle; Identity Function Default
Default Cascade, 204, 213, 226–230, 234, 288,
294, 300, 306, 307, 318, 321, 322, 325,
327–329, 340, 341, 346, 352
default unification, 147
defectiveness, 187, 190
definiteness, 20, 30, 31, 72, 77, 99, 179, 242
Degree, 247
denotation, 3, 7, 17, 18, 21, 23, 33, 34, 37, 40,
41, 47, 50, 57, 58, 68, 76, 93, 96, 99, 101,
120, 188, 196, 227, 249, 260, 263, 278,
280, 297
property, 93, 116
dependency grammar, 146, 156
dependent marking, 59, 66, 121
deponency, 190, 221
derivation, 36, 183, 186, *see* derivational
morphology

canonical, 29, 36, 87, 188, 191, 203, 205,
207, 226, 227, 235, 287, 317
m-inert, 200–202, 338
syntactically inert, 201
derivational morphology, 26, 34, 36, 89, 98,
99, 153, 161, 180, 187, 196, 198, 206,
210, 226, 228, 276, 331, 350, 353, *see*
derivation
Derived Lexical Entry Principle, 212, 227, 288
determiner, 2, 25, 30, 31, 49, 60, 99, 103, 104,
116, 121, 129, 131, 132, 176, 239, 244,
249, 276, 288, 298, 332
diminutive, 139, 197, 198, 236, 301, *see also*
evaluative morphology
discourse, 6, 14, 18, 20, 36, 65, 75, 91, 197,
242
function, 6, 9
Distributed Morphology, 14, 96, 127, 128, 130
distributional approach (to word classes),
10–13, 18, 24, 353
double marking, 65, 70, 74, 331
Downing's solution, 56
dual projection approach, 16, 37, 126–130,
142, 143, 146, 151, 155, 169

economy, 83
edge inflection, *see also* clitic; phrasal affix
encoding strategy, 58–61, 71, 73, 78, 100, 122,
278, 280–282
entailment, 41, 42, 93, 209
evaluative morphology, 197–198, 201, 236,
237, 327
Eventuality, 16, 190, 191, 224, 225, 228, 229,
287, 317
external syntax, 26, 91, 98, 100, 102, 113, 143,
149, 231, 254, 263, 284, 332, 342, 343,
351
ezafe, 29, 67, 73–74, 113, 123, *see also*
construct state, izafet

F-STR, 249, 253, 256, 258, 259, 271, 272
f-structure, 151–155, 161, 164, 165, 169, 256
factorization, 2, 170, 186–192, 213
feature
[±N], 11, 14, 146, 237
[±V], 11, 14, 146, 237
binary, 7, 11, 13–15, 48, 245
categorial, 14, 143, 146
CONTENT, *see* CONTENT paradigm

FORM, *see* FORM paradigm
HEAD, 135, 147, 179, 183, 206, 210, 233, 256, 307, 318
   Head Feature Principle, 245
   inflectional, 135, 179, 183, 206, 210, 233, 307
   m-feature, 165–167, 180, 190, 213, 215–217, 220–223, 250–252, 317, 352
   MOD, *see* attribute, MOD
   morphomic, 165, 221, 223, 317
   REPRESENTATION, 38, 204, 205, 230–234, 238
   s-feature, 165, 180, 190, 213, 215, 216, 219–223, 250, 317, 352
feature structure, 44, 147, 180, 181, 185, 191, 258
flexible (language), 9
flexible (word class), 9, 355
FORM, 173, 184, 188, 189, 191–195, 197, 200–203, 205, 206, 210, 211, 213, 221–223, 227, 235, 238, 250–252, 264, 267, 294, 308, 310, 315, 317–319, 321, 322, 325, 326, 328–330, 333, 336, 339, 341–346
FORM paradigm, 165, 190, 204, 213–223, 250
free reading, 49, 50
functional structure, 12, 51, 59, 118, *see also* f-structure

General Default, 205, 211, 335
General Default Principle (GDP), 205
Generalized Paradigm Function (GPF), 205, 350
Generalized Paradigm Function Morphology (GPFM), 38, 350
Generative Lexicon, 53, 54, 119, 197
gerund, 21, 25, 47, 109, 127, 143, 144, 147, 148, 150, 162, 198, *see also* ACC-ING
government, 20, 35, 190, 195
gradable property, 17, 20, 37, 43, 64, 280
   concept, 21, 42, 43, 46, 62, 231, *see also* adjective, gradable
grammatical function, 1, 118, 151, 153, 160–161, 225, 243, 256
grammaticalization, 7, 79, 106, 107, 111, 124, 218, 281

Haspelmath's Generalization, 187

head, 1–3, 16, 20, 25, 29, 35, 37, 39–41, 45–48, 53, 55, 57–61, 63, 64, 67, 68, 72–74, 79, 80, 82, 85, 89, 98–102, 104, 105, 113, 118, 120, 124, 127, 131, 133–136, 139, 144, 146, 151–153, 155–157, 224, 244, 245, 250, 260, 262, 264, 280, 282, 288, 293, 298, 341, 342, 346, 347, *see also* Head Application Principle; Head-Modifier Rule; Modifier-Head Construction
   extended, 151–153, 155, 157, 160–162, 169
   functional, 10, 44, 60, 241–242, *see also* category, functional
   lexical, 2, 46, 60, 119, 155, 168, 244
Head Application Principle, 210
head marking, 31, 59, 65, 66, 70, 83, 112, 116, 123, 130, 131, 201
head movement, 129, 130, 134, 152, 157
head raising, 127, *see also* head movement
Head-Adjunct Structure, 246
Head-Driven Phrase Structure Grammar, 3, *see also* HPSG
Head-Modifier Rule, 245
hierarchy
   inflectional, 235
   inheritance, 21, 22, 146, 176, 181–185, 253
   lexeme, 176–178, 183, 235, 236
   LFT, 235
   part of speech, 176, 177, 179, 249
   sign, 176–178, 183
   type, 148–150
   word structure, 234
hierarchy, Animacy, *see* Animacy Hierarchy
hierarchy, Relevance, *see* Relevance Hierarchy
homonymy, 68, 72, 116, 192–193, 202, 207–209, 281
homophony, *see* homonymy
HPSG, 3, 11, 19, 38, 44, 73, 146, 150, 168, 171–173, 175, 177, 179–186, 191, 225, 239, 240, 244–247, 249, 250, 253, 255, 256, 261, 270, 350

iconicity, 82, 83
Identity Function Default, 205
incorporation, 61, 127–129, 297
   noun, 13, 61, 130, 132, 134, 150
   pronominal, 32, 83
indeterminate category projection theory, *see* composite node approach

392 Subject Index

inferential-realization morphology, 167, 169, 186, 191, 204
infinitive, 26, 167, 335
  substantivized, 28
inflection, 8, 10–12, 20, 21, 26, 33, 35, 36, 89, 97, 98, 114, 131–134, 167, 173, 180, 183, 185–189, 192, 193, 195–198, 201, 202, 205, 206, 210–212, 215, 217, 221, 223, 226, 230, 231, 233, 235–237, 252, 256, 288, 305, 306, 308, 314, 328–331, 334, 353, *see also* uninflectability
  canonical, 29, 188, 203, 213
  class, 23, 35, 132, 189, 198, 227, 252, 292, 317, 318, 322, *see also* declension
  contextual, 29–32, 35, 113, 187, 195, 205, 242, 306, 308
  edge, 74
  inherent, 29–32, 113, 173, 187, 195, 197, 198, 201, 305, 306, 308, 339, 353
  meaning-bearing, 305, *see also* inflectional, inherent
inflectional class, *see* inflection, class
ingressive, 208, 209
inheritance, 22, 146, 147, 151, 320
  default, 21, 38, 147, 167, 169, 203, 234, 235, 350
  multiple, 168, 181, 182
  orthogonal, 235, 236
inheritance hierarchy, *see* hierarchy, inheritance
interface, 36
  morphology-semantics, 351
  morphology-syntax, 164, 165
  semantics-syntax, 190, 204, 225
intermorpheme, 86
internal syntax, 26, 27, 35, 143, 145, 187, 231, 284, 351
izafet, 65, *see also* construct state, ezafe

juxtaposition, 8, 60–61, 63, 65, 66, 74, 75, 79–84, 273, 275, 279, 282, 302, 355

kin(ship) term, 46, 47, 72, 96, 99, 101, 267, 276, 298, 331

Lees' solution, 53, 55
lexeme, *see also* transpositional lexeme
Lexeme Individuation, 38, 171–175, 191
lexeme-formation template, 235

Lexemic Index, 24, 164, 191, 237, 238, 288, 337, 340, 349, 354
lexical class, *see* class, word
Lexical Coherence, 159
Lexical Conceptual Structure, 16, 190, 250, 351
lexical entry, 20, 22, 35, 89, 147, 154, 165, 188, 191, 204, 210–212, 221, 222, 224, 227, 234, 235, 237, 246, 250–252, 285, 287, 330, 341
Lexical Functional Grammar, 11, *see also* LFG
Lexical Identifier, 173, 184, 191, 258, *see also* LI
Lexical Index, 191
Lexical Integrity, 38, 182, 286, 349, 354, 355
lexical opacity, 39, 174, 175, 182, 286, 311, *see also* lexical integrity
lexical representation, 2, 20, 22, 25, 28, 29, 35, 38, 87, 145, 150, 151, 156, 157, 159, 160, 162, 164, 169, 171–192, 195, 202, 203, 205, 213, 221, 223, 225–227, 230, 234, 237–239, 249, 255, 256, 258, 263–265, 284, 286–288, 305, 307, 308, 310, 315, 317–320, 325, 326, 328–330, 341, 343, 346, 348, 350, 351
lexical semantics, 32, 34, 42, 48, 50, 88, 94, 209, 292
lexical sharing, 129, 155
lexicon, 9, 14, 165, 169, 171, 182, 184, 185, 199, 202, 203
LFG, 11, 32, 38, 44, 51, 126, 151–169, 191, 225, 239, 244, 247, 253, 256, 270
LI, 24, 164–167, 188, 189, 191–192, 195–201, 203, 205, 206, 209–212, 227, *see also* Lexical Identifier, 250–356
LID, *see* Lexical identifier
Linearity Constraint, 131, 132, 135, 139
  Strong, 135
  Weak, 131
linker, 66–68, 113, 123, 124
listeme, 182, 183, 185
loose compounding, *see* incorporation

m-inert, *see* conversion, m-inert;derivation, m-inert; inflection, m-inert
Mainstream Generative Grammar, 10, 82, 127, 242, 244, 247
markedness, 83
marking, *see* dependent marking; double marking; head marking; juxtaposition

masdar, 160–162
Minimalist Program, 11
MOD, 44, 190, 244–246, 252, 254–256, 264,
   267, 307, 310, 311, 318, 319, 322,
   327–330, 340, 342, 344, 346, 352
modification, *see also* Attributive Modifier
   Rule; Head-Modifier Rule,
   Modifier-Head Construction
   attributive, 2, 15, 30, 34–38, 40–46, 59, 64,
      68, 70–72, 74, 79–81, 85, 89, 90, 92,
      100, 105, 110, 111, 115, 116, 121, 124,
      129, 190, 238–240, 244–258, 282, 283,
      288, 293, 299, 302, 332, 350
      canonical, 3, 40, 42–46, 58, 62, 69, 78,
         84, 121, 278, 280
      inbound, 34, 90, 293, 297, 299
   direct, 44–45
   indirect, 44–45, 110
   intersective, 41, 42, 46, 78
   modification-by-adjective, 40, 84, 248, 249
   modification-by-nominal-concept, 3, 70–72,
      78, 84, 239, 258, 275, 276, 279, 283,
      354
   modification-by-noun, 33, 37, 40, 43,
      52–53, 56–60, 62–64, 66–72, 74, 75,
      77–81, 83–85, 87, 91–93, 99, 100, 113,
      115–118, 120–124, 258–267, 278–280,
      291, 293, 337, 355
   modification-by-oblique, *see* modifier,
      oblique
Modification-by-Noun Rule, 265, 267,
   270–272
modifier, 2, 17, 25, 31, 35–37, 40, 44, 46, 49,
   53, 55, 58, 59, 62, 64, 66, 69, 71, 73–75,
   78, 80, 81, 85–91, 94, 98, 102, 103, 105,
   107, 109–111, 113–115, 117–119, 129,
   134, 135, 138, 140, 141, 150, 153, 158,
   164, 178, 227, 239, 245–247, 260, 262,
   264, 273, 275, 279, 280, 282, 285, 288,
   290, 299, 303, 323, 324, 332, 333, 335,
   346, *see also* Attributive Modifier Rule;
   Head-Modifier Rule, Modifier-Head
   Construction
   attributive, 1–3, 8, 15, 20, 29, 35–37, 40–46,
      49, 76, 82, 83, 85–87, 91, 97, 100, 102,
      103, 108–110, 113, 120, 124, 136, 149,
      196, 225, 232, 244–247, 253, 255, 258,
      260, 263, 280, 283, 284, 288, 291, 298,
      300, 307, 310, 313, 320, 322, 328, 336,
      338, 340, 342, 343, 346, 348, 352, 353

degree, 89, 174, 231
denominal, 33, 290
direct, 45, 118
indirect, 45, 105, 112
intersective, *see* adjective, intersective
oblique, 105–112, 354
Modifier-Head Construction, 255, 256, 259
mood, 195, 218, 232, 242
   conditional, 218, 219
Morpholexical Signature, *see* MORSIG
Morpholexically Coherent, 21
morphologically inert, *see* conversion,
   m-inert;derivation, m-inert; inflection,
   m-inert
morphome, 215, 217, 219, *see also* category,
   morphomic; feature, morphomic
morphotactics, 138–140
MORSIG, 221–223, 233, 234, 294, 295, 300,
   306–308, 310, 314, 315, 317–319, 322,
   325–327, 329–331, 333, 340–346, 352
multiple exponence, 307

Network Morphology, 204, 234–238, 350, 351
nominal
   action, 127, 144, 146, 149, 156, 159, 161,
      174, 196, 231, 285, 350, 352, 354
   agent, 128, 145
   event, 196
   subject, 127, 191, 205
nominalization
   POSS-ACC, 26–28, 128, 143, 144, 150, 285
   POSS-ING, 25, 26, 148
   property, *see* transposition,
      adjective-to-noun
non-anchoring relation, 53, 57, 64, 115–118
non-compositionality, 57
non-configurational, 40
notional approach (to word classes), 4, 5, 7, 8,
   16, 21, 146, 213, 225
noun
   abstract, 75
   base, 1, 29, 31, 33–35, 88–91, 93–105, 108,
      109, 114, 115, 137, 139, 141, 142, 171,
      173, 223, 237, 254, 263, 267, 277, 284,
      285, 289–291, 293–295, 298, 299, 301,
      304, 307, 308, 310, 313–315, 317,
      319–324, 326, 327, 330–334, 336, 337,
      339, 340, 342, 343, 349
   canonical, 28, 34, 49, 142, 230, 247

394   *Subject Index*

noun (*cont.*)
   common, 41, 51, 66, 101, 147, 148, 280, 298, 347
   count, 103, 192, 193
   proper, 25, 66, 148, 297
   relational, 5, 47, 48, 50, 83, 106, 107, 119, 240, 277, 278
   sortal, 14, 50, 51
noun incorporation, *see* incorporation, noun
Noun Licensing Condition, 15
noun–adjective hybrid, 1, 2, 4, 25, 28–32, 35–39, 129, 136, 149, 151, 171, 172, 186, 200, 203, 223, 230, 238, 244, 254, 267, 278, 283–348, 355
novel node approach, 146, 148, 149
numeral, 2, 100, 102, 141, 287, 299

oblique complement, *see* oblique phrase
oblique phrase, 2, 102, 107, 108, 110, 112, 150, 154, 323, 354, *see also* case, oblique
ontological category, *see also* Property; Thing; Event
ontological class, *see* ontological category
opacity, *see* lexical opacity
ownership, 46, 47, 49, 52, 72, 101, 280

Pāṇinian Determinism, 167
paradigm, 10, 115, 167, 173, 189, 202, 211
   CONTENT, *see* CONTENT paradigm
   FORM, *see* FORM paradigm
   linkage, 190
   realized, 186, 190, 214
Paradigm Function, 214
Paradigm Function (PF), 189, 205–207, 350
Paradigm Function Morphology (PFM), 350
   PFM2, 163, 186, 190, 214, 222, 350
paradigm linkage, 214
paradigm-within-a-paradigm, 38, 204, 234, 238, 319, 350
parameterized-state-of-affairs, 147
part of speech, 4, 8, 10, 146, 172, 173, 175, 182, 202, 213, 225, 226, 233, 246, 250, 254, 294, 297, *see also* class, word; part of speech hierarchy
   HPSG, 175–180, 256
participle, 3, 23, 26, 64, 80, 88, 111, 112, 149, 163–169, 174, 175, 182, 193, 196, 198, 205, 206, 218, 221, 230–234, 238, 285, 291, 300, 302, 304, 306, 315, 350, 355

l-participle, 209, 218, 219
   passive, 198, 199, 201, 209, 232, 233
particle, 5, 74, 81, 111, 118, 179, 218, 219
passive, *see* voice, passive
percolation, 145
periphrasis, 186, 190, 196, 215, 218, 220, 231, 256, 304
Persistence of L-indexing, 207
phrasal affix, *see also* clitic; edge inflection
Phrasal Coherence, 156–163, 351
phrase
   adpositional, 2, 15, 78, 105–107, 110, 123, 129, 155, 179, 225, 246, 253, 333
   postpositional, 105, 107
   prepositional, 33, 67, 73, 105, 106, 118–120, 145, 293
polyfunctionality, 37, 52, 58, 77, 281
polysemy, 202, 207–209, 281
   systematic, 53, 197, 207
possessed, *see* possessee
possessee, 46–52, 57, 59, 62, 63, 65, 68, 70, 71, 73, 74, 78, 80, 82, 83, 91, 100, 102, 114, 115, 121, 123, 157, 224, 226, 248, 258, 267, 270, 272, 273, 275, 277, 279, 313–315, 326, 334, 347
possession
   alienable, 40, 46–52, 57, 58, 62, 63, 65, 66, 69–72, 74, 78–84, 116, 117, 267, 270, 273, 275–280, 347
   extrinsic, 46, 49, 50, *see also* possession, alienable
   inalienable, 37, 40, 46–50, 52, 58, 63, 65, 69–72, 74, 78–84, 101, 117, 267, 270, 273, 275–279, 282, 347
   intrinsic, 46
Possession-Modification Scale, 37, 77, 79, 84, 278, 281, 282
possessive class, 48, 69
possessive genitive, 83, 91, 117
possessive host, 50
possessive relation, 37, 46, 47, 69, 78, 83, 96, 114–116, 270, 344
possessor, 32, 40, 47–53, 57, 59, 60, 62, 65, 66, 68, 70–73, 75, 77, 78, 81–83, 90, 91, 98–100, 102–104, 109, 115, 119, 121, 122, 136, 139, 150, 157, 158, 160–162, 221, 242, 248, 267, 270, 272, 273, 276–280, 289, 300–302, 305, 313–315, 319, 320, 332, 337, 338, 347, 355
   pronominal, 59, 83, 96, 272, 276, 314

Subject Index 395

possessum, *see* possessee
postposition, 64, 77, 80, 106–107, 110–112,
  121, 136, 142, *see also* phrase,
  postpositional; adposition; preposition
pseudo-postposition, 106
predicate
  complex, 82
  semantic, 26, 33–36, 50, 56, 85, 88–113,
    121, 125, 173, 174, 180, 188, 196, 198,
    199, 213, 235–237, 254, 267, 278, 290,
    294, 301, 306, 354
predicate calculus, 224
predication, 5, 9, 14, 17, 43, 51, 147, 196
preposition, 8, 25, 63, 71, 105, 120, 124, 190,
  225, *see also* phrase, prepositional;
  adposition; postposition
preterite, *see* tense, past
Principle of Representational Independence,
  195
Principles and Parameters, 11, 129
pronominal incorporation, *see* incorporation,
  pronominal
proper name, 31, 85, 86, 98, 101, 276, 298,
  331
Property, 294, 295, 320, 321, 341, 344, 354
propositional act function, 16, 17
prototype, 16–22, 43, 47, 225, 229
psoa, 147

quale, 54, 55, 119, 120
qualia structure, 54, 119, 120

ℜ-relation, 3, 52, 57, 85, 96, 98, 102, 116,
  239, 255, 256, 258–267, 271, 273, 275,
  277–280, 282, 293–297, 300, 308–310,
  312, 314–316, 319, 326, 328–330,
  340–342, 344–347, 354, 355
realization relation, 164
reduplication, 64, 69
reference, 9, 17, 225, 280, 352
referential index, 14, 15, 19, 280
referential point, 51, 279
referential(ity), 7, 9, 20, 29, 31, 32, 91, 99,
  103, 115, 116, 258, 279, 313
referentially dependent (feature), 11, 12
relatedness, 207
  dynamic, 192–202, 204, 205, 213
  lexical, 2, 22, 25–29, 31, 38, 168, 171–172,
    174, 180, 186–188, 191–205, 226, 227,

  230, 234, 236–238, 247, 249, 283–289,
    294, 350, 351
  morphological, 180, 186, 204, 283, 284
  paradigmatic, 205, 213, 236
  semantic, 208, 281
  static, 192–194, 199, 200, 212
relative clause, 2, 3, 29, 45, 64, 77, 78, 82, 89,
  110–113, 245, 273
  participial, 3, 26, 196
  possessive, 255
Relevance Hierarchy, 23, 230
REPRESENTATION, *see* feature,
  REPRESENTATION
representation, *see* adjectival representation;
  lexical representation
role
  RESTRICTOR, 260, 273, 278–280, 295,
    326, 341, 347
  TARGET, 255, 260, 273, 277, 278, 280,
    295, 326, 341, 347
Role and Reference Grammar, 168

SBCG, 171–173, 175, 177, 180–186, 191,
  239, 246, 247, 249, 250, 261
scope
  semantic, 41, 138, 142, 243
  wide, 37, 38, 97, 125, 134, 136, 137, 139,
    141, 142, *see also* affix(ation), wide
    scope
selectional properties, 24, 34, 148, 149, 190,
  234, 250, 333, 353
SEM, 178, 180, 181, 184, 188–192, 195–198,
  200, 201, 203, 205, 206, 212, 213, 225,
  227, 228, 235, 237, 250–252, 256,
  258–265, 267, 268, 292, 294–297, 300,
  309, 310, 312, 313, 315, 316, 318, 319,
  321, 322, 325, 326, 328–330, 336,
  339–347, 354, 355
Semantic Function Role, 204, 223–226, 253,
  333, 351
  A*, 226, 232, 247, 253–255, 264, 295, 296,
    307, 309, 312, 313, 318, 319, 322, 329,
    332, 340
  compound, 226, 231, 234, 254, 310, 319,
    321, 322, 326–328, 330, 337, 342, 343,
    345, 346, 351–353
  E, 226, 232
  R, 226, 248, 253–255, 262, 264, 267, 296,
    309–313, 315, 316, 319, 326, 329, 333,
    340

396　*Subject Index*

Semantic Function Role (*cont.*)
　Rel(ation), 225, 226
semantic map, 281
semantic representation, 4, 16, 36, 50, 52, 58,
　88, 89, 92, 111, 134, 150, 173, 175, 188,
　190, 193, 195, 200, 207, 209, 224, 225,
　227, 239, 248, 250, 260, 262, 293, 295,
　320, 321, 325, 351, 353, *see also* Lexical
　Conceptual Structure; SEM
set intersection, 41, 57, 280
sign, 180–182, *see also* hierarchy, sign
Sign-Based Construction Grammar, 38, 168,
　see also SBCG
single projection approach, 16, 37, 126,
　143–146, 151, 155, 156, 169, 223
small construction, 61, 86, 275
specifier, 1, 14, 25, 30, 31, 44, 46, 49, 51, 85,
　89–91, 145, 150, 151, 157, 244, 247, 270,
　273, 275, 276, 278, 279, 285, 298, 299,
　332, 336, 347, 355
split morphology, 186
stem, 132, 175, 189, 193, 194, 210, 214, 217,
　251, 252, 260, 331, 334, 335
　oblique, 114
Subject Nominal, 206, 207, 235, 236
Subject Nominalization, 180, 211, 224
substantivierter Infinitiv, *see* infinitive,
　substantivized
Suffixaufnahme, 1, 31, 97, 100, 104, 113–115,
　302, 333
suppletion, 213
SYN, 178, 181, 184, 188–193, 195, 197,
　200–203, 205, 206, 212, 213, 221–223,
　226, 227, 235, 245, 250–253, 256, 258,
　259, 261–265, 267, 268, 271–273,
　286–288, 292, 294–296, 300, 307–310,
　312, 313, 315–319, 321, 322, 325, 326,
　328–330, 333, 335, 336, 339–346
syncretism, 186, 190, 214, 221
synonymy, 173, 193, 200, 202

tense
　future, 215, 217, 220
　past, 21, 168, 180, 183, 218, 219, 221
theta-role, 15, 51
Thing, 16, 43, 190, 191, 211, 224, 225,
　227–229, 264, 294, 310, 325, 326,
　339, 351

time stability, 5
transposition, 26, 27, 34, 38, 103, 128, 148,
　149, 156, 167, 174, 182, 187–189, 192,
　196, 198–200, 203–205, 207, 209, 223,
　227, 230–234, 236–238, 254, 256, 280,
　284–286, 291, 293, 298, 300–302, 306,
　317, 319, 335–337, 340, 341, 345,
　349–355, *see also* transpositional lexeme
　adjective-to-noun, 231, 355
　m-inert, 196, 265, 336
　meaning-bearing, 32, 39, 198, 200, 254,
　　305, 308, 320–322, 340, 341
　noun-to-adjective, 32, 91–105, 231, 265,
　　297, 301, 305, 332, 340, 354, *see also*
　　adjective, relational
　verb-to-adjective, 26, 163, 205, 232, 354
　verb-to-noun, 174, 354
transpositional lexeme, 27, 34, 173–175, 192,
　200, 201, 237, 263, 264, 280, 286,
　290–297, 354, 355
type genitive, *see* case, genitive, property
　denoting
type-shifting, 51, 66, 258, 270, 273, 280
typology, 2, 8, 22, 27, 31, 36, 52, 55, 58–84,
　103, 135, 174, 202, 217, 278, 281, 289,
　336, 354, *see also* Canonical Typology

underspecification, 185, 317, 319, 330
uninflectability, 167, 179
universals, 6, 14, 23, 230

VAL(ENCE), 150, 160, 178, 181, 184,
　244–246, 249, 253, 255, 256, 259, 264,
　267, 271–273, 310, 313, 319, 322,
　327–330, 340, 342, 344, 346, 347, 352
verb
　canonical, 230
　stative, 69, 229
voice, 23, 195, 232, 234
　passive, 199

word class, *see* class, word
word formation, *see* derivational morphology
Word Grammar, 146, 156
word order, 30, 32, 59, 67, 68, 76, 80, 90,
　157, 282

Other books in the series (continued from page ii)

153. MATTHEW BAERMAN, DUNSTAN BROWN and GREVILLE G. CORBETT: *Morphological Complexity*
154. MARCEL DEN DIKKEN: *Dependency and Directionality*
155. LAURIE BAUER: *Compounds and Compounding*
156. KLAUS J. KOHLER: *Communicative Functions and Linguistic Forms in Speech Interaction*
157. KURT GOBLIRSCH: *Gemination, Lenition, and Vowel Lengthening: On the History of Quantity in Germanic*
158. ANDREW RADFORD: *Colloquial English: Structure and Variation*
159. MARIA POLINSKY: *Heritage Languages and Their Speakers*
160. EGBERT FORTUIN and GETTY GEERDINK-VERKOREN: *Universal Semantic Syntax: A Semiotactic Approach*
161. ANDREW RADFORD: Relative Clauses: *Structure and Variation in Everyday English*
162. JOHN H. ESLING, SCOTT R. MOISIK, ALISON BENNER and LISE CREVIER-BUCHMAN: *Voice Quality: The Laryngeal Articulator Model*
163. JASON ROTHMAN, JORGE GONZÁLEZ ALONSO and ELOI PUIG-MAYENCO: *Third Language Acquisition and Linguistic Transfer*
164. IRINA NIKOLAEVA and ANDREW SPENCER: *Mixed Categories: The Morphosyntax of Noun Modification*

Earlier issues not listed are also available